Political Realignment

Other Books with Oxford University Press

The Participation Gap
Social Status and Political Inequality
(Oxford, 2017)

Political Parties and Democratic Linkage
How Parties Organize Democracy
With David Farrell and Ian McAllister (Oxford, 2011)

Citizens, Context, and Choice
How Context Shapes Citizens' Electoral Choices
With Christopher Anderson (Oxford, 2011)

Oxford Handbook of Political Behavior
With Hans-Dieter Klingemann (Oxford, 2007)

Citizens, Democracy, and Markets around the Pacific Rim
Congruence Theory and Political Culture
With Doh Chull Shin (Oxford, 2006)

Democratic Challenges, Democratic Choices
The Erosion in Political Support in Advanced Industrial Democracies (Oxford, 2004)

Democracy Transformed?: Expanding Citizen Access in Advanced Industrial Democracies
With Bruce Cain and Susan Scarrow (Oxford, 2003)

Parties without Partisans
Political Change in Advanced Industrial Democracies
With Martin Wattenberg (Oxford, 2000)

Challenging the Political Order
New Social and Political Movements in Western Democracies
With Manfred Kuechler (Oxford, 1990)

Political Realignment

Economics, Culture, and Electoral Change

Russell J. Dalton

Realignment
↓
new allegiances & loyalties
↓

OXFORD
UNIVERSITY PRESS

Great Clarendon Street, Oxford, OX2 6DP,
United Kingdom

Oxford University Press is a department of the University of Oxford.
It furthers the University's objective of excellence in research, scholarship,
and education by publishing worldwide. Oxford is a registered trade mark of
Oxford University Press in the UK and in certain other countries

© Russell J. Dalton 2018

The moral rights of the author have been asserted

First Edition published in 2018

Impression: 1

All rights reserved. No part of this publication may be reproduced, stored in
a retrieval system, or transmitted, in any form or by any means, without the
prior permission in writing of Oxford University Press, or as expressly permitted
by law, by licence or under terms agreed with the appropriate reprographics
rights organization. Enquiries concerning reproduction outside the scope of the
above should be sent to the Rights Department, Oxford University Press, at the
address above

You must not circulate this work in any other form
and you must impose this same condition on any acquirer

Published in the United States of America by Oxford University Press
198 Madison Avenue, New York, NY 10016, United States of America

British Library Cataloguing in Publication Data
Data available

Library of Congress Control Number: 2018939447

ISBN 978–0–19–883098–6

Printed and bound in Great Britain by
Clays Ltd, Elcograf S.p.A.

Links to third party websites are provided by Oxford in good faith and
for information only. Oxford disclaims any responsibility for the materials
contained in any third party website referenced in this work.

To the memory of my parents

Robert W. Dalton, 1918–1994
Alfreda E. Dalton, 1918–2018

To the memory of my parents

Robert W. Dalton, 1918–1996
Vincent T. Dalton, 1928–2018

Preface

I view social modernization as the process by which human civilization broadly develops and improves. This has been a central theme of my career research interests. But modernization also involves disruption that affects people in unintended or undesired ways. Some people are winners and some are losers in the race to modernize. Some people embrace change and want society to move faster; some long for an earlier time when society was more familiar to them and their situation was more secure. This book steps back from current events and surveys the broad horizon of how social modernization has changed the framework of political competition for citizens and political parties. I discuss the electoral and political implications of these trends.

This has been a difficult book to write—not in terms of data analysis or the writing itself. The difficulty is the topic. Contemporary democracies have become highly polarized on sensitive issues. The 2016 US presidential elections brought these feelings to a head among Americans (and judging by their comments, for many of my European colleagues on Facebook). Some of my conservative FB friends in red states celebrated the same events. Brexit and other political events seemingly have similar effects on many Europeans. Feelings have been inflamed along the political divides in these democracies.

As I discussed this research project with academic colleagues, the most common response was that one side of the political divide (their side) was right, and the other was wrong. When I talked to non-academic friends for a counterview, since almost all social scientists are liberals, they agreed but placed right and wrong on the opposite sides. And it goes beyond right and wrong—too often people on both sides view this as a struggle between good versus evil, or the light side versus the dark side. At times I felt as if I were watching David Berry's earlier summary of political divisions in the United States:[1]

> Do we truly believe that ALL red-state residents are ignorant, racist, fascist, knuckle-dragging, NASCAR-obsessed, cousin-marrying, roadkill-eating, tobacco-juice-dribbling, gun-fondling, religious fanatic, rednecks; or that ALL blue-state residents are godless, unpatriotic, pierced-nose, Volvo-driving, France-loving,

Preface

left-wing communist, latte-sucking, tofu-chomping, holistic-wacko, neurotic, vegan, weenie, perverts?

Such invective is neither illuminating nor accurate, in most instances. But insert different descriptive adjectives, and the same stereotypes might apply to discussions of voters in the Brexit referendum, or polarized citizens in other established democracies.

These conversations made me think more about this topic and, I hope, express ideas and evidence in less accusatory ways. I want to avoid the good versus evil labeling in this book because research is different from proselytizing. Some people are too extreme, and go beyond the boundaries of democratic tolerance and respect for human rights—and these excesses should be identified and criticized. But many on the 'other side' are friends or relatives, who have different value orientations but good intentions.

My goal is to illuminate the political changes occurring in affluent democracies and discuss their implications. As a young professor at Florida State University, I co-edited a book on public opinion and voting in the early 1980s (*Electoral Change in Advanced Industrial Societies*).[2] One of the main findings was the emergence of a new cultural cleavage in democratic party systems from Europe to North America to Japan. Now, many of the observations in those chapters seem prescient on the nature of contemporary politics. The old conflicts over economic conditions and the role of the state are still with us, albeit in different forms. What is new (or really not so new) is the stark conflict over cultural issues that were just beginning to affect democratic party systems in the 1970s.

Even if Hillary Clinton had won the 2016 U.S. elections, the needs of those displaced by economic change or suffering from limited opportunities would have still existed. Even if the British had voted to remain in Europe, the frustrations of the exit voters would remain. The dissatisfaction that motivated some Germans to vote for the AfD in 2017 goes beyond ethnocentrism to the social and economic grievances of these citizens. Democracy exists to resolve such conflicts.

Any book is not just a single person's efforts, and I owe a great deal to friends and colleagues who helped in this research. First, I would like to thank the many scholars who participated in the European Election Studies that are the primary basis of the research presented here. This is a rich and unparalleled source for studying the evolution of public opinion and partisanship in Europe, pairing both citizen and elite surveys. I am indebted to those who collected these data and who have shared them with the international research community.

I owe special appreciation to Carl Berning, Diego Garzia, and Oddbjörn Knutsen who read portions of this manuscript and offered valuable suggestions for improvement. In addition, many individuals helped with advice of many sorts along the way. This book is an extension of prior work with David Farrell and Ian McAlister, and I am in their debt. Michael Migalski thankfully retrieved lost data from the 1979 EP Candidates study that was an invaluable aid to this research. I greatly appreciate Dominic Byatt and Olivia Wells at Oxford University Press for their support on this and prior Oxford books; Doreen Kruger kindly and effectively polished the prose. I also want to thank Trevor Allen, Maneesh Arora, Ryan Bakker, Elizabeth Cohen, Peter Ditto, Ami Glazer, Lisbet Hooghe, Ronald Inglehart, Hanspeter Kriesi, Beth Loftus, Gary Marks, Robert Rohrschneider, Anthony Smith, Jacques Thomassen, Martin Wattenberg, and Christian Welzel. Hanspeter Kriesi deserves special acknowledgment because his long-term study of these issues; his multiple books from the project provided a roadmap when I started this research journey. The Center for the Study of Democracy provided an academic home during this project, and Shani Brasier was, as always, supportive in innumerable ways. Thanks to all of you.

Russell J. Dalton
Hollywood, California

Notes

1. Dave Barry, An off-color rift: Whether we vote red or blue, we all put our boxers on one leg at a time, *Washington Post*, December 19, 2004; p. W32.
2. Russell Dalton, Scott Flanagan, and Paul Beck, eds. *Electoral Change in Advanced Industrial Democracies*. Princeton: Princeton University Press, 1984.

Contents

List of Figures	xiii
List of Tables	xv
1. The Evolution of Political Competition	1

Part I. Social Structure and Political Cleavages

2. Citizens, Issues, and Political Cleavages	27
3. The Social Distribution of Cleavage Positions	50
4. Political Cleavages across Nations	72
5. Elites, Issues, and Political Cleavages	87

Part II. Political Cleavages and Party Alignments

6. Political Cleavages and Political Parties	109
7. Electoral Choice—Voter Demand and Party Supply	133
8. Congruence and Representation	153
9. The American Experience	181

Part III. Conclusion

10. Realignment and Beyond	215

Appendices
    A. Issue Questions from the European Election Studies   237
    B. Citizen Issue Structures by Nation   240
    C. Identifying Party Positions   244
    D. Party Cleavage Positions   248
    E. Party Cleavage Polarization Indices   252
    F. The Complexity of Measurement   255
    G. Construction of Economic and Cultural Indices in the United States   259

Index   265

List of Figures

1.1.	A Stylized Representation of the Political Space	6
1.2.	Social Interests to Political Cleavages to Party Alignments	9
2.1.	National Positions on Economic and Cultural Cleavages, 1979	40
2.2.	National Positions on Economic and Cultural Cleavages, 2009	41
2.3.	National Positions on Economic and Cultural Cleavages, 2014	42
3.1.	Occupation and Cleavage Positions, 1979 and 2014	57
3.2.	Detailed Occupation and Cultural Cleavage Position, 2014	58
3.3.	Location of Social Groups in the Cleavage Space, 1979 and 2014	59
5.1.	Elite Occupation and Cleavage Positions, 1979 and 2009	94
5.2.	National Differences in CEP Cleavage Positions, 2009	98
5.3.	National Differences in CEP Cleavage Positions, 1994	99
5.4.	National Differences in CEP Cleavage Positions, 1979	100
6.1.	Party Locations on the Economic and Cultural Cleavages, 1979	115
6.2.	Party Locations on the Economic and Cultural Cleavages, 1994	117
6.3.	Party Locations on the Economic and Cultural Cleavages, 2009	119
6.4.	Year Party Formed and Cultural Cleavage Position	123
6.5.	Continuity in Party Cleavage Positions, 1994–2009	128
7.1.	Location of Party Families in the Political Space	135
7.2.	Party System Polarization and Strength of Cleavage Voting	142
8.1.	Party Voters and Party Elites on the Economic Cleavage, 2009	158
8.2.	Party Voters and Party Elites on the Cultural Cleavage, 2009	159
8.3.	Party Voters and Party Elites on the Economic and Cultural Cleavages, 1979	161
8.4.	Voter-Party Representation Gap by Party Cleavage Position	166
8.5.	The Representation Gaps for Party Families	167
9.1.	Positions of Citizens and Presidential Candidates on Liberal–Conservative Scale	186
9.2.	Public's Positioning of Presidential Candidates on Economic Issues	188

List of Figures

9.3.	Public's Positioning of Presidential Candidates on Cultural Issues	190
9.4.	Education and Age Correlation with Cultural Cleavage	194
9.5.	Economic and Cultural Correlates of Candidate Preferences	196
9.6.	Candidate Supply in the 2016 Primaries	199
10.1.	Attitudes toward Social Change over Time	222
10.2.	Attitudes toward Social Change, Cultural Cleavage Positions, and Vote	223
E.1.	Comparing Party Locations on the Cultural Cleavage	254
F.1.	Merged Comparison of Voters and Parties on the Economic Cleavage	256
F.2.	Merged Comparison of Voters and Parties on the Cultural Cleavage	257

List of Tables

1.1.	The European Election Studies	15
2.1.	Citizen Issue Structures, 1979	33
2.2.	Citizen Issue Structures, 2009	37
2.3.	Citizen Issue Structures, 2014	39
3.1.	Social Status Correlates of the Economic and Cultural Cleavages	55
3.2.	Attitudinal Correlates of the Economic and Cultural Cleavages	61
3.3.	Multivariate Models Predicting the Economic and Cultural Cleavages	64
4.1.	The Primary Issues Defining Political Cleavages Across Nations, 2009	75
4.2.	The Primary Issues Defining Political Cleavages Across Nations, 2014	77
4.3.	Multivariate Models Predicting the Economic Cleavage by Nation	80
4.4.	Multivariate Models Predicting the Cultural Cleavage by Nation	81
4.5.	Predicting Cleavage Positions by National Traits	83
5.1.	Elite and Citizen Issue Structures, 1979	89
5.2.	Elite Issue Structures, 1994	90
5.3.	Elite and Citizen Issue Structures, 2009	91
5.4.	Social Status and Elite Cleavage Positions, 1979	93
5.5.	Social Status and Elite Cleavage Positions, 1994 and 2009	96
6.1.	The Correlates of Parties' Economic and Cultural Positions	122
7.1.	Voter Cleavage Positions and Party Choice	138
7.2.	Voter Cleavage Positions and Party Choice by Nation	141
7.3.	Multivariate Models Predicting Party Preferences	144
7.4.	Issue Salience and Models of Party Choice	146
8.1.	Predictors of Aggregate Voter-Party Congruence	163
8.2.	Predictors of Individual-Level Representation Gap	172
9.1.	The Correlates of Candidate Preferences in the 2016 Primaries	201
9.2.	Modeling Clinton vs. Trump Preferences	202
B.1.	Citizen Issue Structures by Nation, 2009	241
B.2.	Citizen Issue Structures by Nation, 2014	242

List of Tables

C.1.	Party Issue Positions from the Party Expert Surveys	245
C.2.	Relationships between Party Cleavage Positions	246
D.1.	Party Cleavage Scores in 1979	248
D.2.	Party Cleavage Scores in 1994	249
D.3.	Party Cleavage Scores in 2009	250
E.1.	Party Polarization Scores for Economic and Cultural Cleavage	253
F.1.	Cleavage Dimensions for Citizens and Elites, 2009	256
G.1.	Principal Components Analyses of US Cleavages	260

1

The Evolution of Political Competition

The rise of new parties running on alternative election platforms, and recent unpredicted election outcomes from Brexit to Donald Trump's 2016 victory in the United States, heighten the sense that politics is changing in fundamental ways. Indeed, much of the contemporary research on citizens, elections, and parties emphasizes the dramatic changes we are now witnessing. The issues of political debate seem to be rapidly changing, and new issues arise to challenge older, familiar themes. Voters are more fluid in their political choices, rather than following habitual voting loyalties. Election outcomes also appear more volatile, and the number of competing parties is increasing.

At one level, I agree with this description, and I have contributed to research on electoral change.[1] Yet at the same time, there are elements of our political past (and future) that reflect continuity. Many of the issues in contemporary debates are a continuation of long-standing cleavages. The *economic cleavage* is the most notable example; the economic issues of the post–World War II era might have been resolved, but new manifestations of the same underlying values are still at hand. In addition, many of the supposedly new issues of affluent democracies reflect a broad *cultural cleavage* dealing with the tension between the progressive forces of social modernization and advocates for the status quo.

Electoral politics is always complex because of the changing context and content of each election. This applies even when we think of electoral politics as a one-dimensional Downsian competition. But it becomes more complex when we consider a multidimensional space of political competition. Voters—and parties—have to make choices on two (or more) competing political cleavages. For voters, the ideal choice is not as apparent as in a simple Left–Right one-dimensional world. For parties, the appropriate strategy to balance distinct voter bases becomes more complex. And too often, it seems, candidates and parties use the complexity of multiple cleavages to mask their real intentions from the voters. Promise A and deliver B seems more common in contemporary elections. This is one reason why spatial modeling experts say that chaos can occur when politics is structured in multidimensional terms.[2]

Equally important, the underlying social bases of the economic and cultural cleavages are substantially different. The economic cleavage is largely a conflict about competing self-interests and ideologies over the role of the state versus the market in resolving these tensions. Even though electoral alignments are not fixed, I show that there has been a realignment of citizen positions on the economic cleavage. By *realignment* I mean an enduring change in the pattern of social group positions on economic issues.[3]

In addition, the cultural cleavage has prompted a realignment of social groups' positions on these issues. Cultural cleavage positions are often tied to basic social issues and identities (as well as competing self-interests), which are more difficult to compromise and which can evoke intense feelings. The feelings aroused by debates over immigration, gender-related issues, or the European Union (EU) often have a very different tone than debates over unemployment rates or tax rates. Current political controversies can often contain a toxic mix of divergent views, and it is difficult to objectively evaluate competing claims. Some analysts argue that policy tensions have become so severe that they may produce a deconsolidation of contemporary democracies—a claim I think is overstated.

This book marshals unique empirical evidence to understand the evolution of political cleavages in the established democracies from the 1970s to the 2010s. I begin by describing the changing political demands of the citizenry as they respond to societal change and past public policies. Citizens' political opinions have changed substantially over this long time span, which places a different set of demands on the political systems. The analyses then consider how the political parties have responded to these changing demands, and how the supply side of party choices has expanded and diversified over time. The party systems of today look very different from the party systems of the 1970s in their policy and social bases, even if some of the names are the same. This study examines how the demand and supply relationship of democratic representation has adapted to these forces, and the tensions they have produced. The longitudinal analyses show where we have been, and where we are heading in the future. The cross-national comparisons show the variations in this journey. The goal is to identify how social modernization has realigned citizen demands and test whether this has realigned party politics and electoral choices for contemporary democracies.

Social Change and Political Cleavages

Established democracies experienced unprecedented social changes from the mid-twentieth century as the forces of postwar recovery and social modernization transformed these nations and their people. Average income levels grew dramatically, the structure of the labor force changed as service activities and knowledge-based occupations replaced many manufacturing jobs. Technology advanced rapidly, education levels rose, the role of women in society and the economy fundamentally changed, and most recently racial and ethnic diversity increased as a byproduct of globalization.[4]

When we look at contemporary politics, the economic cleavage remains an important basis of political competition.[5] These issues include debates about the state's appropriate role in managing the economy, taxation levels, the provision of basic social welfare benefits, and problems related to income inequality. The specific issues of economic competition may vary from election to election, reflecting social and economic conditions—tax policy, social services, unemployment benefits, or other economic issues—but they are connected to an underlying economic cleavage. On the one side are the advocates of an activist state that promotes the social welfare of the citizenry, regulates the economy, and supports social equality. On the other side are those who favor a limited role for the government, a relatively unfettered market economy, and individualism. Both perspectives reflect legitimate political positions in democratic societies. Democracy provides a means of resolving such differences.

Despite the continuity of the broad economic cleavage, the nature of the cleavage changed in significant ways. For example, the changing composition of the labor force produced new class alignments.[6] Professionals and other members of the new middle class comprise a growing bloc of voters leaning toward conservative economic policies and liberal cultural policies. On the supply side, parties that once focused on the working class became more attuned to these new middle-class voters and their interests. A restructuring of the economy also reversed long-term trends in income growth and income inequality, producing a wider inequality gap in most affluent democracies. In many nations, labor unions shed working-class members and increasingly became advocates for public employees. Working-class interests suffered as a result of these trends.

Social modernization is associated with even more dramatic changes on the cultural cleavage. Modernity is a positive force for social change, making contemporary societies more tolerant, more socially consciously, more enlightened, more peaceful, and more democratic.[7] Contemporary publics are the most educated and most informed in the long history of mass democracies. And yet, these modernizing societies also experience increasing polarization on cultural issues. Americans and Europeans are more liberal on matters of gender equality, minority rights, religious norms, and LBGTQ rights than a generation or two ago, but such cultural issues seem to stimulate more political discourse and controversy.

As societies modernize economically or culturally, this may evoke reactions by those who favor the status quo or question some of the changes occurring around them. Some individuals may lose social-economic status, a feeling of security, or a sense of community they identify with the past.[8] Or phrased in different terms, they prefer a society that emphasizes community, stability, stricter moral standards, and values such as duty and patriotism.[9] Historically, these sentiments have often been tied to religious attachments, but this cultural backlash is broader than just religious morality. Different elements come together as a rebuke of the social changes wrought by modernization, and these views become crystallized and mobilized by the very expansion of the modernization process. If societies stopped changing, people might gradually adjust to a new normal. But social modernization is an ongoing process. So a continuing modernization process can generate counter-reactions in some parts of society. The strength of the counter-reaction can vary across cleavages depending on the resources and interests of the contending groups.

While media headlines and popular debates focus on the novel aspects of these political divisions—whether in the rise of far-right parties, an extreme political event, or the changing issue agenda—we should also recognize that many new controversies represent an ongoing experience of modernization forces struggling against the traditional status quo. New issues are new in a real sense, but they are also understandable as the newest expression of a continuing modernization cleavage.

This broad cleavage was apparent long before the current "New Right" became prominent in media coverage and academic research on electoral politics. It was apparent before the "New Left" came to prominence in the 1970s and 1980s. Writing about politics in the 1960s–1970s, for example, Seymour Martin Lipset described this as a continuing *revolt against modernity*:

> Malaise with the changes which accompany modernization or development has led ... to leftist and rightist politics. The former criticize the existing society from the vantage point of a belief in a future utopia, usually described as more egalitarian, more democratic, or more participatory on the part of the masses .... Rightists, on the other hand, emphasize the prior existence of the good integrated society which once characterized their nation. They argue that the corruption of contemporary society is the result of an abandonment of the values and social relationships which characterized some earlier golden age.[10]

Lipset was following in the steps of Richard Hofstadter and others, who had previously described the periodic rise of conservative movements in the United States that opposed secularism, modernity, racial integration, and elements of an elitist political culture.[11]

Lipset then discussed how advanced industrial societies were undergoing profound social changes regarding the role of women, changes in religious and social morals, and increased racial/ethnic diversity as part of this modernization process—driven by the young, better educated, and more cosmopolitan sectors of society. Such social changes generated what he called *backlash politics*:

Backlash politics may be defined as the efforts of groups who sense a diminishing of their importance, influence, and power, or who feel threatened economically or politically, to reverse or stem the direction of change through political means. Since their political concern has been activated by decline, by repeated defeats and failures, backlash politics is often extreme in its tactics and policies and have frequently incorporated theories of ongoing conspiracies by alien forces to undermine national traditions and strength.[12]

Lipset's choice of terms might be overstated or pejorative. Perhaps a more neutral term is that faced by rapidly changing social conditions; some people may experience *future shock* or *culture shock* and want the world to change more slowly, or not at all.[13] Conversely, those who favor the direction of social change often want the tempo to be even faster. Most of us, I believe, grumble at some changes, applaud others, and are unaware of yet other changes.

Lipset wrote about these political tensions in the 1960s–1970s, yet his views could be talking points for a television interview about the cultural conflicts in contemporary societies, and the movements that stimulate the French National Front, UKIP in Great Britain, or the Tea Party/Trump movement in the United States. Instead, Lipset cited Poujadists in France, George Wallace in the United States, and Christian parties in Scandinavia as examples of the backlash movements of the 1970s. This historical aspect of these tensions is often lacking from current electoral research. In short, the *liberal culturalists* and *conservative culturalists* are not really so new in many features, and I use these terms through this book instead of the more common "New Left" and "New Right."[14]

The cultural cleavage became an important political force in the 1960–1970s. Charles Reich's popular *The Greening of America* claimed that citizen values were changing as younger generations developed a new political consciousness that would produce a liberated life-style.[15] Ronald Inglehart's research on postmaterial value change highlights this development.[16] Postmaterial values are concentrated among the young, more educated and more affluent sectors of Western society. These values emphasize individual freedom, tolerance of diversity, social and gender equality, and concern about the quality of life. Thus, empirical evidence documents a distinct liberal shift in attitudes toward many cultural issues across the affluent democracies.[17]

Environmental groups and other New Social Movements (NSMs) of the period, such as the women's movement, human rights groups, social justice groups, and the peace movement, had a growing impact on public discourse and public policy.[18] These networks encouraged the formation of Green parties that advocated an alternative political agenda reaching beyond just environmental issues. The German Greens, for example, initially campaigned under the banner of green politics, but they also emphasized gender equality, social equality, and peace as core values.

Political Realignment

As these new liberal groups became active in affluent democracies, this produced a backlash or culture shock reaction.[19] Culturally conservative social groups challenged parts of this new political framework. For example, religious interests countered the liberal culturalist advocacy on issues related to women and family, and later opposed gay rights proposals and multiculturalism. Thomas Frank's popular book on political change similarly described a conservative backlash to liberal trends among American Midwesterners.[20] The counter-mobilization of a conservative culturalist perspective helped to crystallize a cultural cleavage.

New far-right parties in Europe further shaped this cultural cleavage by linking together diverse issues and articulating an alternative worldview.[21] Simon Bornschier describes the French National Front as the model case for this new pattern of political competition.[22] The party was an early critic of liberal cultural changes, as well as advocating extreme nationalist and xenophobic policies. Similarly, the Progress parties in Denmark and Norway in the 1980s took conservative positions on the new post-industrial issues as well as the struggles of the working class.[23] Slowly evolving over several decades, a conservative culturalist position rose in opposition to the liberal culturalist agenda.

Figure 1.1 presents a stylized image of this contemporary political space using social and political groups as examples.[24] The horizontal dimension

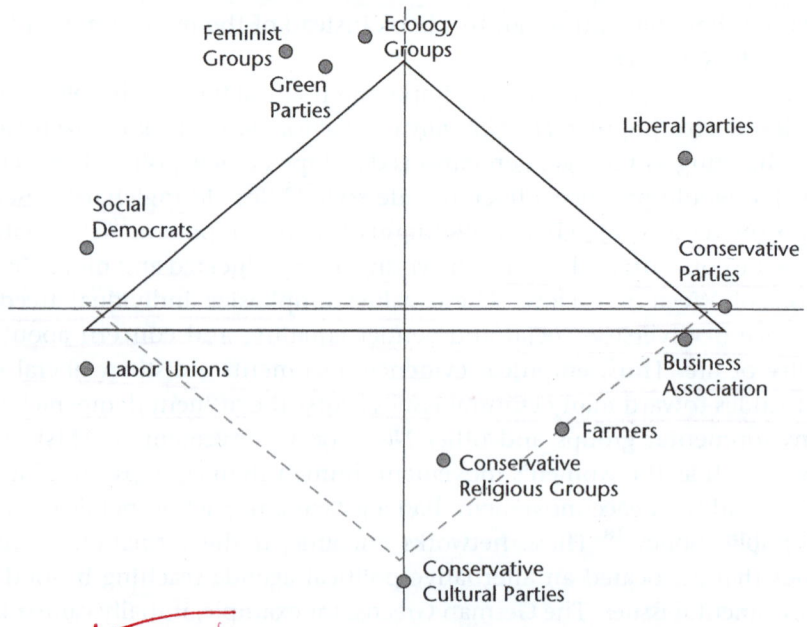

Figure 1.1. A Stylized Representation of the Political Space
Source: The author.

represents the traditional economic cleavage. On the Left are labor unions and other political actors that represent progressive economic programs that benefit working-class interests and others in need of state support. On the right are business associations, corporations, and other economically conservative economic interests. As Martin Lipset and Stein Rokkan argued a half-century ago, this cleavage emerged from the industrial revolution, and still influences contemporary politics.[25]

The vertical dimension depicts the cultural cleavage. At the liberal cultural pole are NSMs (ecology groups, the women's movement, human rights groups, etcetera). They are the active advocates for progressive change on cultural issues. These groups are joined by Green parties in many nations—although Green parties vary significantly in their ideology—along with progressive or Left-libertarian parties.[26] Conservative cultural positions are advocated by religious groups, agrarian interests, far-right parties, and others who hold conservative views.

This is a stylized view of the economic and cultural cleavage. It is worthwhile to point out that this chart largely replicates Ronald Inglehart's description of emerging political cleavages in the mid-1970s. His analysis of cleavage structures in eight Western democracies led him to conclude:

> The two dimensions seem to reflect: (1) the traditional Left-Right socio-economic cleavage, with an infrastructure based on the polarization between labor and management (with religious cleavages also assimilated into this dimension, in some countries), and (2) an establishment-antiestablishment (or New Politics) dimension, based on one's reaction to groups [New Social Movements] that have become politically prominent much more recently than organized labor—and that, we suspect today are more active carriers of support for social change.[27]

In short, a significant cultural cleavage formed long before the 2008 recession, before the EU Maastricht Treaty, and before the recent immigration waves into Western Europe in this millennium. Then, globalization, deindustrialization, and European integration further altered social conditions in Europe, North America, and Pacific Rim democracies. These social changes amplified political divisions among these publics.

Moreover, some of the political actors that once might have addressed these issues, such as social democratic parties, seemed to accept a neo-liberal economic model and cater to their new middle-class voters.[28] In the United States, for example, presidents Clinton and Obama were strong advocates for expanding international trade—even when opposed by their own party in Congress. Similarly, public concerns about the expansion of the EU and its economic and cultural consequences were voiced by the public but often ignored by the established political elites.[29] A rich longitudinal study by Geoffrey Evans and James Tilley shows the Labour Party's movement away from its liberal

7

economic orientation and toward liberal culturalism—distancing the party from its traditional working-class base.[30] The growth of far-right parties occurred at least in part because of their advocacy of cultural positions that the established parties avoided. And in advancing this alternative perspective, these parties further crystallized the cultural cleavage.

The triangles in Figure 1.1 symbolize the evolution of academic research. In the 1980s, scholarship focused on the emergence of New Social Movements and Green parties. Researchers examined the upper triangular relationship between traditional Left parties, traditional Right parties, and the New Left.[31] Since the mid-1990s, attention has shifted to the lower triangular relationship between traditional Left parties, traditional Right parties, and the conservative culturalists.[32] The liberal culturalists and conservative culturalists are opposing ends of a political cleavage and should be examined as such rather than examined at only one pole or the other. By viewing this as a cleavage dimension similar to the economic cleavage with polar opposites, we can better represent and understand contemporary political alignments.

Several empirical studies have examined the emerging cultural cleavage and its relationship to the traditional social democratic/conservative economic cleavage. For example, Inglehart described a two-dimensional cleavage structure in the mid-1970s, along with parallel analyses of West Germany and Japan.[33] Even earlier, Warren Miller and Teresa Levitin wrote about the development of a New Politics cleavage in the United States.[34] Paul Goren has tracked the evolution of the economic and cultural issue cleavages in the United States since the 1980s, and their impact on party choice.[35]

Recent party expert surveys of party issue positions identified two broad political cleavages.[36] One is the traditional economic cleavage and the other is a new GAL/TAN dimension that is very similar to my description of the cultural cleavage. The GAL represents Green, alternative and libertarian values; the TAN represents traditional, nationalist, and authoritarian orientations.[37]

The richest longitudinal evidence comes from a series of studies by Hanspeter Kriesi and his colleagues.[38] This research group focused on globalization's impact in producing the economic and cultural insecurities that coalesced in a conservative counterview. They assembled longitudinal data on citizen issue positions from national election studies in six countries to identify the economic and cultural cleavages, and follow their development.[39] They also coded party campaign statements to follow the changes in party positions over time. However, most of their empirical base is limited to six nations, and the relevant questions in most election studies are relatively few (often a half-dozen items for a two-dimensional analysis) and vary across nations and time. I build upon their important research program in this book.

A Template for Research

This book's basic analytic framework is summarized in Figure 1.2. Social structure and living conditions shape political interests as Lipset and Rokkan first formalized. Specific issue interests can coalesce to form a broad political cleavage. Typically, these interests are articulated and mobilized by social groups. The natural example is social class differences leading to an economic cleavage on the role of the state in the economy and the provision of social security to those in need.

At the next stage, partisan alliances form to represent the underlying political cleavages. The content of party coalitions can vary depending on the strategies that elites pursue. Research often makes a direct link between social characteristics and voting choice, without factoring in the way that groups form party alliances as a key determinant of choice. A person's vote for a party may depend on the available party choices, rather than fully representing the voter's political preferences.

The diversity of group-partisan alliances was central to Lipset and Rokkan's description of the formation of party systems across Western Europe. For instance, in the early twentieth century, rural interests aligned with the Radical Left in some nations, and the Right in other nations. The same pattern can apply to the cultural cleavage. For example, the religious composition of a nation can affect how churches respond to gender and gay rights issues. The strategic choice of how labor unions respond to the environmental movement can also shape alliance patterns on the Left.

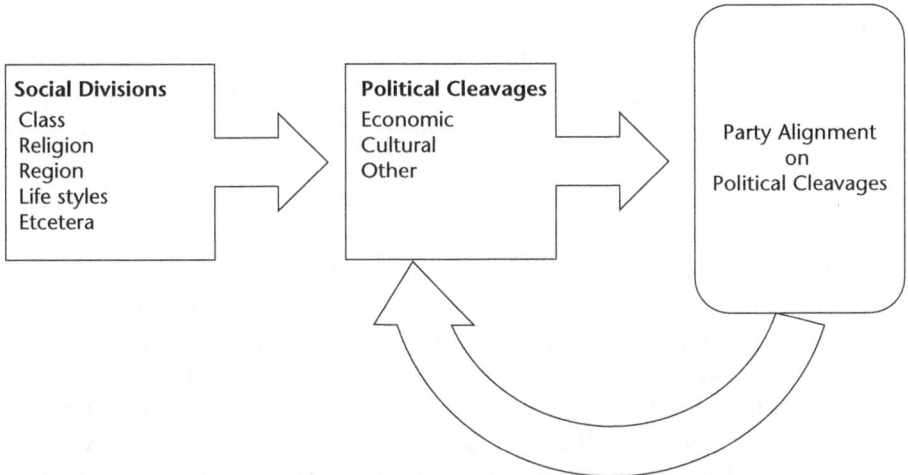

Figure 1.2. Social Interests to Political Cleavages to Party Alignments
Source: The author.

Once these partisan patterns are set, party alignments can then affect citizens' cleavage positions in a partial feedback link. For instance, as parties began to articulate an alternative New Left or Green political agenda, this helped crystallize the cleavage positions of their supporters, identifying which issues went together in which ways. As Social Democratic parties shifted their economic positions, this provided a cue to party supporters to follow them (or seek another party). The same process came into play in recent decades as far-right parties integrated different issue positions to articulate a culturally conservative position. Parties, or other political actors, can give a coherent identity to the policy positions of their supporters.

In short, political cleavages provide a semi-rigid structure for political competition, not a fixed and stationary framework. Political parties have some flexibility in how they position themselves in the cleavage structure, and the choices they offer to voters. We see this flexibility being exercised by parties today, such as Corbyn's newest New Labour Party, Marcon's *En Marche* in France, Trump's transformation of the Republican Party, and the Five Star Movement in Italy.

In some ways, current patterns of political competition represent a new cycle in a continuing process of social modernization in Western democracies—modernization reshapes political demands and party strategies, often with new issue content or new social bases.

Citizens and Political Cleavages

A common research framework in studying electoral politics distinguishes between political supply and demand. In this case, the demand is defined as the policy preferences of the public—what they expect from democracy and elected governments. The supply element is the set of choices that political parties offer for expressing policy preferences. I draw upon this general logic in the chapters that follow.

The empirical analyses begin with a description of *citizen-defined perceptions of the political space*. I use citizens' positions on current political issues to construct a dimensional model of political competition. In this case, the two major dimensions are the economic cleavage and the cultural cleavage.

A prior question, however, concerns the source of these political cleavages and the issue opinions that comprise them. The landmark work by Lipset and Rokkan maintained that the structure of society and the social conditions of individual citizens create the interests that determine political cleavages.[40] Democratic politics is a means to resolve competing social interests, and Lipset and Rokkan tracked these interests back to the social structure. For instance, the shared interests of the working class arose because of their common work

The Evolution of Political Competition

experience and their competition with the interests of the middle class and bourgeoisie. Farmers' interests could be at odds with the interests of urban dwellers. Such group-based interests can provide a framework for political competition, reinforced by interests groups that represent social sectors, such as labor unions, farmer associations, business groups, religious denominations, and others.[41]

However, my use of the term "cleavage" is different from Lipset and Rokkan and some other cleavage scholars. I use the term to identify a set of values or worldview that is expressed in a set of political issues. Contemporary cleavages can develop with less formalized intermediary groups, such as environmental interests or norm-based interests. In fact, I have long argued that political cleavages are increasingly based on common political values rather than formal group alignments, because group alignments have become more fluid and less institutionalized in contemporary society.[42] From this perspective, political competition is based on groups of individuals pursuing their objective self-interest, and resolving this competition through the democratic process.

A more complex basis of political differences derives from conflict over values and norms rather than specific self-interests. Describing the emergence of the cultural cleavage in late 1970s Europe, Ronald Inglehart wrote: "when postmaterialist issues (such as environmentalism, the women's movement, unilateral disarmament, opposition to nuclear power become central, they may stimulate a materialist reaction in which much of the working class sides with the Right to reaffirm the traditional materialist emphasis on economic growth, military security, and domestic law and order."[43] To an extent, these issues involve the self-interest of women who want greater opportunities and rights, minorities who feel discrimination, or other interests. But citizen positions on such issues may also reflect feelings of ethnocentrism, norms about social relations, religious values, and authoritarian/permissive norms. These sentiments reflect the values of individuals and their own identities, which can exist separately from self-interest.

The economic and cultural cleavages thus both reflect a mix of objective self-interests and subjective value judgments. Separating these two aspects is difficult, but it is generally the case that the economic cleavage focuses more on the objective elements, and the cultural cleavage on the value elements. I expect these patterns to shape the correlates of citizen cleavage positions and their importance to the individual and to their electoral choices.

Political Cleavages and Party Alignments

Political parties are the supply side of the cleavage model that links citizens to public policy. While the public is only periodically involved in politics and has less information about public policy, elites typically structure the choices available to voters at election time and represent citizen preferences within the policy process.

Just as for the public, I examine *elite-defined perceptions of the political space* over time. Political elites are more informed about society because of their positions and activities. One might expect them to share the same basic images of political competition as the average person, perhaps in finer detail. And yet, elites are also separated from the average person by being "elite." They might read reports on the social conditions of workers in the *Ruhrgebiet*, but this is different from living those experiences. They might see the statistics on the struggles of immigrants, but this is different than living in the immigrant banlieues around Paris. Indeed, in their own social conditions elites are very different from the average citizen. They may understand the struggles to send children to an elite university but not the difficulty faced by working-class families to ensure their child attends any college. In general, members of national parliaments are better educated, more affluent, older, and will often have professional occupations before entering politics.[44] Elite surveys show that, on the whole, their personal opinions often lean toward the Left, post-material values, and views supportive of modernization.[45]

Consequently, high-level party elites could see different cleavage structures than the citizenry. In addition, elites can either lead or lag public opinion in their perceptions of how the structure of political cleavages is changing. Only by comparing both groups over time can one begin to assess the similarities and differences between citizens' political concerns and those of elites.

Studying party elites is also important because elite discourse can influence mass attitudes since elites provide cues that some citizens follow in forming their own opinions. For example, Edward Carmines and James Stimson demonstrated that changing party positions on racial issues led many Americans to shift their party attachments to conform to the new alignment.[46] Various experiments demonstrate that cuing people with the issue position of the parties produces a shift in responses by partisans on both the Left and the Right.[47] Hypothetically, if prime minister X advocates expanding free trade, and the person likes prime minister X, then they have a positive predisposition to that policy. The greater people's trust in the information source, the greater is the potential persuasive effect.

What sometimes goes unsaid in studies of far-right parties is the question of how other parties have acted.[48] For example, why did the established leftist parties not respond more forcefully and effectively to the economic and social needs of the "losers" of globalization or the increase in income inequality? Representing these individuals could (should) have been a traditional Leftist program, consistent with the historical base of social democratic parties. Labour's Third Way in Britain, the German SPD's *Neue Mitte*, the Left's cohabitation in France, and Bill Clinton's triangulation strategy shifted these parties to the center on economic issues and closer to the growing number of middle-class voters. Similarly, the electoral potential of far-right parties is linked to the strategic choice of other established parties on the Right. The basic lesson is that by focusing on one party and its supporters, such as Greens or far-right parties, one can overlook the true nature of democratic elections as a choice between all of the available options.

Thus, studying party elites provides a comprehensive picture of the parties' positions in the political space. Parties can choose a mix of issues that create different identities, even among parties of the same ideological family. A specific example is the emergence of environmental issues in the 1980s. In some nations (such as Germany), the Social Democratic Party was initially unresponsive to the policy demands of environmental activists—in part because of their commitment to blue-collar labor unions. This pattern encouraged the formation of new Green parties in many instances. In the Netherlands, however, the Labour Party (PvdA) was more responsive to these new interests and attempted to integrate them into the party's constituency. This weakened efforts to establish an independent Green Party from a diverse coalition of minor parties. Since 1989 this small Green Party has won seats but has never risen to the prominence or governing role that the German Greens have wielded.

A more complex example is the List Pim Fortuyn (LPF) in the Netherlands. The party was founded by a charismatic young, gay, liberal professional. The party merged two seemingly contradictory issues as its core. LPF was highly critical of the increased number of Muslims emigrating to the Netherlands. But this was because Fortuyn saw that increased immigration was threatening liberal cultural values, such as accepting gay rights and promoting women's rights.[49] In other words, the LPF staked out two positions at opposite ends of the cultural cleavage. Cultural clashes can produce different ways of thinking.

In short, the significance of an issue and its cleavage alignment can vary over time rather than being constant. The strategic decisions of the parties on what themes and positions to advocate—presumably based on a mix of national interests and party interest—change over time. Political parties face decisions on how to respond to new issues such as gender equality, immigration, climate change, and the other economic and cultural issues. Parties in different nations have chosen different responses depending on their own views, the actions of other parties, and the specific national conditions. Cross-national comparisons provide a means to examine these choices and their consequences of the supply of partisan choices.

A final topic is the agreement between voter demands and party supply on the political cleavages. Has this congruence changed significantly over the past several decades as the processes of social and political change have accumulated? This is a challenging question, and ideal research resources to definitively address this question do not exist. Nevertheless, we can make important progress by focusing the available evidence on how political competition is changing in affluent democracies.

Data Sources

Back to the Future is a popular U.S. film in which the characters move back and forth in time using a DeLorean time machine invented in 1985.[50] The central figure first traveled back to 1955 and met his parents as high school students of his own age. Then he traveled to the future of 2015, which is now our past. Coincidentally, almost all the major characters were the same people at different stages in their lives. In a sense, this is the method of this book, applied to politics.

The theoretical interest in such time travel drove my search for appropriate empirical evidence. I wanted to describe the evolution of political cleavages and their impact on established party systems over the past several decades. Together they shared the modernization changes beginning after World War II. This includes the established democracies of Western Europe, as well as the affluent non-European democracies. Thus, this project requires broad cross-national evidence to compare how cleavages evolved over time—but lacking a time machine.

The research decision to focus on affluent democracies also reflects our theoretical query. Affluent democracies generally experienced the same modernization process that reshaped political cleavages. They share relatively similar socioeconomic conditions, levels of education, and other key social traits. The effects of modernization are less evident outside affluent democracies. The post-communist EU member states in Central/Eastern Europe are still forming, and our theoretical interests are not salient to new democracies in the developing world.

Empirical evidence is quite limited, however. Some scholars have examined national election studies over time.[51] This is a valuable resource, yet the available evidence is limited in several ways. Other studies focus on cross-sectional analyses of recent surveys, such as the European Social Survey.[52] There are obvious limitations to studying a dynamic theoretical model with cross-sectional surveys.

I started in the present and then looked for empirical evidence covering a set of affluent democracies at least 30 years in the past. The European Election Studies (EES) furnish the empirical base for most of this study.[53] Many researchers treat European Parliament (EP) elections as second-order events, where the political stakes are lower and parties highlight EU issues. I see another value for these surveys. The EES simultaneously survey all the member states of the EU during the election season, when citizen opinions are activated by the political discussions of the election. In terms of voting choice, I do not focus on the EP election but on *voting in the last national elections* that is a separate question in these surveys. The EES also ask a common battery of issue questions and other political attitudes in each survey. This contrasts with national election studies occurring in different years when economic or political conditions may vary widely, and ask different questions in each nation.

The real value of the EES lies in two other areas. First, the EES series include three general population surveys that can track the evolution of political cleavages from the late 1970s to 2014. Table 1.1 lists the nations and the sample sizes for each national survey. The 1979 study interviewed citizens in the original nine EU member states. The next appropriate surveys were in 2009 and 2014.[54] These studies included all the members of the enlarged EU at these time points, although I examine only the fifteen established Western democracies. The specific political questions asked in each EES differ, but there is sufficient content to address our research needs.

The ability to track patterns from 1979 to 2009 is our *Back to the Future* experience of moving across three decades in time. How have patterns of political competition been changed by the social and political experiences over this period?

The five years between the 2009 and 2014 surveys are significant because the 2008 recession, and the subsequent financial difficulties and political

Table 1.1. The European Election Studies

Nation	1979 Public	1979 Elite	1994 Elite	2009 Public	2009 Elite	2014 Public
Austria	–	–	–	1000	52	1114
Belgium	982	40	117	1002	75	1084
Denmark	1073	41	105	1000	31	1085
Finland	–	–	–	1000	55	1096
France	1010	128	104	1000	125	1074
Germany	1003	150	393	1004	160	1648
Greece	–	–	–	1000	33	1085
Ireland	997	26	12	1001	8	1081
Italy	1178	158	135	1000	73	1091
Luxembourg	300	12	33	1001	20	538
Netherlands	1023	47	125	1005	78	1101
Portugal	–	–	24	1000	17	1033
Spain	–	–	74	1000	68	1106
Sweden	–	–	514	1002	183	1144
United Kingdom	1318	140	134	1000	258	1421
Total	8884	742	1770	1515	1236	16,701

Note: Table entries are unweighted N in each sample.
Source: 1979, 1994, 2009, and 2014 European Election Studies.

conflict within the EU may have polarized political differences.[55] Compared to 2009, income levels dropped, unemployment rose, credit markets tightened, income inequality increased, and the additional pressures of cumulative immigration accentuated political differences. The Eurozone area experienced an 18-month recession beginning in the fourth quarter of 2011 and ending in the first quarter of 2014. Many analysts attribute the rising support for extreme parties on the Right and Left, and Brexit, to these forces. Thus, the 2014 EES can describe the patterns resulting from Europe's financial crisis.

Second, the 1979, 1994, and 2009 EES interviewed Candidates for the European Parliament (CEP) with questions that parallel the general public surveys.[56] I use the CEPs' issue opinions to measure party positions on the economic and cultural cleavages. Table 1.1 presents the sizes of the elite samples. The 1994 CEP survey lacked a comparable public opinion survey.[57] The data are especially valuable because elites were asked about the same issues as the general public, which allows for a comparison of voter and party elite positions.

To complement the European analyses, I examine the patterns of political change in the United States. The American National Election Studies began asking a series of policy questions in 1972 that partially represent both cleavages; additional issue questions in each election define cleavage positions for the public. Beyond the trend data, there is an in-depth analysis of party support in the 2016 election. The results demonstrate the commonality of cleavage politics across affluent democracies.

Plan of the Book

This study tracks the evolution of political cleavages at the mass and elite levels from the 1970s. Any such mass-elite comparison raises the question of whether to begin with the citizenry or with the elites. The supply–demand framework I have adopted leads to analyses that begin by describing the citizenry in the EU, and how their views have changed over time. This is followed by parallel analyses of party elites. These two research streams then come together to study voting choice and political representation.

Chapter 2 begins these analyses by describing how public opinion on specific issues reflect deeper economic and cultural cleavages, and the evolution of those cleavage from 1979 to 2014. The EES show that a persisting economic cleavage is now joined by a cultural cleavage that has crystallized over time.

Chapter 3 examines how the social characteristics of Europeans influence their positions on the economic and cultural cleavages. In the 1970s, the traditional working-class/middle-class polarization on the economic cleavage was apparent, but these differences have narrowed over time. Social groups have realigned on the cultural cleavage. Higher status occupations and the more educated adopted distinctly liberal positions on the cultural cleavage, with the religious, manual workers, and farmers adopting more conservative positions. In addition, political support suggests how governments have responded to changing citizen demands. For Europe as a whole in the 2009 and 2014 surveys, economic conservatives and cultural liberals are more satisfied with government. Probably not coincidentally, these are positions held by upper social status occupations and the highly educated.

Chapter 4 extends the research to describe the composition of political cleavages for each of the nine early EU member states, and the evolution of these cleavages in 2009 and 2014. The analyses provide a firmer foundation for understanding the cleavage structure in contemporary Europe, and how the social composition of a nation may affect the definition and distribution of cleavage positions.

Chapter 5 identifies the cleavage dimensions for party elites based on CEP surveys. A two-dimensional cleavage structure is visible in 1979, and becomes more clearly crystallized in the 1994 and 2009 surveys. The chapter then examines the distribution of these orientations across European elites and how political realignment among elite social groups has followed the pattern of citizen realignment.

Chapter 6 uses the CEPs' cleavage positions to place political parties in the two-dimensional political space. The evidence shows the persistence of the economic cleavage over time, with modest political adjustments by Leftist and Rightist parties. Party choices have changed more along the cultural cleavage, from the introduction of liberal cultural parties in the 1970s–1980s to the more recent emergence of cultural conservative parties. The supply of party choices available to voters has consequently broadened over time.

Chapter 7 connects the cleavage positions of European citizens to the supply of party choices available from the political parties. The analyses demonstrate the growing importance of the cultural cleavage for party choice, such that it eclipsed the impact of the economic cleavage in most nations in the 2009 survey.

Chapter 8 describes the degree to which parties agree with their supporters in collective and individual terms. The chapter first asks whether voters as a collective find a party that represents their positions well, or if they are satisfied with a party that only partially reflects their views. There is a very close fit between blocs of voters and their chosen parties in this two-dimensional space, but also significant variation. Then the chapter examines the agreement at the individual level—between each voter and their chosen party. While there is strong voter-party congruence at the macro level, this relationship weakens at the micro level.

To broaden the scope of the evidence, Chapter 9 tracks the evolution of political cleavages and party choices for the American electorate.[58] Just as for

Political Realignment

European systems, an economic and cultural dimension frames the party space, although interacting with the United States' racial and ethnic divisions. The cultural dimension emerged earlier in the United States owing to social groups mobilizing against the Vietnam War, and for racial justice, environmental reform, and gender equality. Evidence from the American National Election studies tracks the evolution of these two cleavage dimensions and their impact on presidential candidate choice up to the 2016 presidential election.

Finally, Chapter 10 discusses the realignment of these party systems and the implications for affluent democracies. Cleavages that have persisted for decades, and even strengthened in their political effects, are likely to persist for the foreseeable future. What does this imply for the nature of party competition, democratic discourse, and party systems?

The Past and Future

Nearly fifty years ago, Alvin Toffler wrote the bestseller, *Future Shock*.[59] The futurologist wrote about the rapid pace of social change and what the future would hold. It is thought provoking to reread the predictions of medical miracles, the information revolution, economic transformations, and other technological changes he expected in the near future—and to compare those predictions to the reality today. He was probably right more often than he was wrong.

However, his core argument is not about technological change per se, but about how these dramatic and growing societal changes are affecting people. On the one hand, "the super-industrial revolution can erase hunger, disease, ignorance and brutality... it will radiate new opportunities for personal growth, adventure and delight. It will be vividly colorful and amazingly open to individuality."[60] On the other hand, "Having to live at an accelerating pace... when faced by unfamiliar, strange or unprecedented situations is distinctly another [situation]. By unleashing the forces of novelty, we slam men up against the non-routine, the unpredicted. And, by so doing, we escalate the problems of adaptation to a new and dangerous level. For transience and novelty are an explosive mix."[61]

Toffler noted that some people thrive on these new conditions, and want the future to accelerate and go further. Their personality and social conditions lead in this direction, and they probably benefit from these social trends. Think of the nouveaux riches of Silicon Valley or the elite businesses in London's Canary Wharf. Change and disruption are their mantras.[62] Other people are repelled by these changes and want to halt or reverse the pace of change; they look back to the past as a more idyllic time. Toffler also noted that technological change has unequal effects on the population "For coalminers in Appalachia or textile workers in the French provinces, however, this [social change] proves to be excruciatingly painful."[63]

Toffler was writing about Western societies in the 1960s and the dramatic social changes of the day. Now, some people look back to this period as "the good old days" before the even more dramatic social changes we are now experiencing with the rights revolutions, globalization, and even more rapid technological change. If Toffler's predictions about flying cars and body-less brains were ahead of reality, his predictions of the cultural clash in contemporary democracies seem prescient.

This book shows that one manifestation of future shock is the growing salience of the cultural cleavage among citizens and elites, and increased social polarization on this cleavage. One sees this in election campaigns, political discourse, and at its worst in social media. Too often the cleavage is presented in very stark terms, with pejoratives used to describe people who do not agree with the speaker or the writer of a post on social media. I consciously downplay such rhetoric in this study, not because I am ambivalent about these changes but because research should separate normative preferences from empirical evidence. Moreover, democracy exists to resolve conflicting issue preferences and not to demonize people with whom you disagree.[64]

My goal is simple: to empirically study the realignment of cleavage structures and partisan alignments in contemporary politics so we can better understand where we have been, and the choices available for the future. But getting there is a challenging task.

Notes

1. See, for example, Russell Dalton, Scott Flanagan, and Paul Beck, eds. *Electoral Change in Advanced Industrial Democracies*. Princeton: Princeton University Press, 1984; Russell Dalton and Martin Wattenberg, *Parties without Partisans*. Oxford: Oxford University Press, 1990; Russell Dalton, *Citizen Politics: Public Opinion and Political Parties in Established Democracies*, 7th ed. Washington, DC: CQ Press, 2018.
2. Richard McKelvey, Intransitivities in multidimensional voting models and some implications for agenda control, *Journal of Economic Theory* (1976) 12: 472–82.
3. Angus Campbell, A classification of the presidential elections. In Angus Campbell, Philip Converse, Warren Miller, and Donald Stokes, eds., *Elections and the Political Order*. New York: Wiley, 1966; Dalton, Flanagan, and Beck, *Electoral Change in Advanced Industrial Democracies*, ch. 1.
4. Ronald Inglehart, *Culture Shift in Advanced Industrial Society*. Princeton: Princeton University Press, 1990; Hanspeter Kriesi et al., *West European Politics in the Age of Globalization*. Cambridge: Cambridge University Press, 2008.
5. Oddbjørn Knutsen, *Social Structure, Value Orientations and Party Choice in Western Europe*. London: Palgrave, 2017.

Political Realignment

6. Ronald Inglehart, The changing structure of political cleavages in Western society. In Russell Dalton, Scott Flanagan, and Paul Beck, eds., *Electoral Change in Advanced Industrial Democracies*. Princeton: Princeton University Press, 1984; Herbert Kitschelt, *The Transformation of European Social Democracy*. Cambridge: Cambridge University Press, 1994; Geoffrey Evans and James Tilley, *The New Politics of Class; The Political Exclusion of the British Working Class*. Oxford: Oxford University Press, 2017.

7. Christian Welzel, *Freedom Rising: Human Empowerment and the Quest for Emancipation*. New York: Cambridge University Press, 2013; Steven Pinker, *Enlightenment Now: The Case for Reason, Science, Humanism, and Progress*. New York: Viking, 2017; Ronald Inglehart, *How People's Motivations Are Changing and How This Is Changing the World*. Cambridge: Cambridge University Press, 2017.

8. Jonathan Haidt, *The Righteous Mind: Why Good People Are Divided by Politics and Religion*. New York: Pantheon, 2012; Amitai Etzioni, We must not be enemies. *The American Scholar*, 2017 (https://theamericanscholar.org/we-must-not-be-enemies). A broader literature argues that there is a personality basis to these orientations, linked to traits such as tolerance of uncertainty, openness to new experiences, and feelings of fear and insecurity. John Jost, Jack Glazer, Arie Kruglanski, and Frank Sulloway, Political conservatism as motivated social cognition, *Psychological Bulletin* (2003) 129: 383–93; Dylan Lane and Danielle Sulikowski, Bleeding-heart conservatives and hard-headed liberals: The dual processes of moral judgements, *Personality and Individual Differences* (2017) 115: 30–4; Christopher Johnston, Howard Lavine, and Christopher Federico, *Open versus Closed: Personality, Identity, and the Politics of Redistribution*. New York: Cambridge University Press, 2017.

9. This contrast in citizenship norms is described in: Russell Dalton, *The Good Citizen*, 2nd ed. Washington, DC: CQ Press, 2015; Ronald Inglehart and Pippa Norris, *Rising Tide: Gender Equality and Cultural Change Around the World*. Cambridge: Cambridge University Press, 2003; Pippa Norris and Ronald Inglehart, *Sacred and Secular: Religion and Politics Worldwide*, 2nd ed. New York: Cambridge University Press, 2010.

10. Seymour Martin Lipset, The revolt against modernity. In Per Torsvik, ed., *Mobilization, Center-Periphery Structures and Nation-Building*. Bergen: Universitetsforlaget, 1981, p. 255.

11. Richard Hofstadter, *The Age of Reform*. New York: Vintage, 1955.

12. Lipset, The revolt against modernity, p. 256.

13. Alvin Toffler, *Future Shock*. New York: Random House, 1970.

14. "New" no longer seems to apply for movements and political parties that have existed for several decades. Thus, I chose a terminology focusing on the basis of this cleavage.

15. Charles Reich, *The Greening of America*. New York: Banthan, 1971.

16. Ronald Inglehart, *The Silent Revolution*. Princeton: Princeton University Press, 1977; Inglehart, *Culture Shift in Advanced Industrial Society*. Inglehart, *How People's Motivations are Changing And How this is Changing the World*; Ronald Inglehart and Christian Welzel, *Modernization, Cultural Change, and Democracy*. Cambridge: Cambridge University Press, 2005.

The Evolution of Political Competition

17. Inglehart and Norris, *Rising Tide*; Norris and Inglehart, *Sacred and Secular*; Davin Caughey, Tom O'Grady, and Christopher Warshaw, Policy ideology in European mass publics, 1981–2014, (unpublished manuscript, 2017); Dalton, *Citizen Politics*, chs. 5–6.
18. Hanspeter Kriesi, Ruud Koopmans, Jan Duyvendak, and Marco Giugni, *New Social Movements in Western Europe*. Minneapolis, MN: University of Minnesota Press, 1985; Russell Dalton and Manfred Kuechler, eds., *Challenging the Political Order: New Social and Political Movements in Western Democracies*. New York: Oxford University Press, 1990.
19. Piero Ignazi, The silent counter-revolution, *European Journal of Political Research* (1992) 22: 3–14; Ronald Inglehart and Pippa Norris, Trump and the populist authoritarian parties: The Silent Revolution in reverse, *Perspective on Politics* (2017) 15: 443–5; Cas Mudde, *Populist Radical Right Parties in Europe*. New York: Cambridge University Press, 2007, ch. 5.
20. Thomas Frank, *What's the Matter with Kansas?: How Conservatives Won the Heart of America*. New York: Metropolitan Books, 2004; for an account the the turbulent 1960–70s period in the U.S. see Rick Perlstein, *Nixonland*. New York: Scribner, 2008.
21. Herbert Kitschelt with Anthony McGann, *The Radical Right in Western Europe; A Comparative Analysis*. Ann Arbor: University of Michigan Press, 1995; Piero Ignazi, *Extreme Right Parties in Western Europe*. Oxford: Oxford University Press, 2003; Tim Bale, Cinderella and her ugly sisters: The mainstream and extreme right in Europe's bipolarising party systems, *West European Politics* (2003) 26: 67–90.
22. Simon Bornschier, France: The model case of party system transformation. In Hanspeter Kriesi et al., *West European Politics in the Age of Globalization*. Cambridge: Cambridge University Press, 2008.
23. Jorgen Goul Anderson and Tor Bjorklund, Structural changes and new cleavages: The Progress parties in Denmark and Norway, *Acta Sociologica* (1990) 33: 195–217.
24. Inglehart, The changing structure of political cleavages in Western society.
25. Seymour Martin Lipset and Stein Rokkan, Cleavage structures, party systems, and voter alignments. In Seymour Martin Lipset and Stein Rokkan, eds. *Party Systems and Voter Alignments: Cross-national Perspectives*. New York: Free Press, 1967.
26. Examples of liberal culturalist parties at the time are: D'66 in the Netherlands, Socialist People's Party in Denmark, and the Left Alliance in Finland. Ferdinand Müller-Rommel, *New Politics in Western Europe: The Rise and Success of Green Parties and Alternative Lists*. Boulder, CO: Westview Press, 1989.
27. Inglehart, The changing structure of political cleavages in Western society, p. 60.
28. Kitschelt, *The Transformation of European Social Democracy*.
29. Referendums to endorse the expansion of the EU went down to defeat in Denmark (1992), France (2005), Ireland (2001), the Netherlands (2005), and Norway (1994). The Danes and Swedes both voted to opt out of the common Euro currency. Polls suggested that if Germans had been allowed to vote on accepting the Euro, they would have said *"Nein, Danke"*—but the established parties offered no choice. Most established parties, national governments, and EU elites pressed forward with the European project, even with these contrary signs from the public.

30. Evans and Tilley, *The New Politics of Class*; Thomas Piketty, Brahmin left versus merchant right: Rising inequality and the change structure of political conflict. WID.world working paper series, 2018/7 (www.piketty.pse.ens.fr/conflict).
31. Herbert Kitschelt, Left-Libertarian parties: Explaining innovation in competitive party systems. *World Politics* (1988) 40: 194–234; Müller-Rommel, *New Politics in Western Europe*; Herbert Kitschelt and Staf Hellemans, *Beyond the European Left: Ideology and Political Action in the Belgian Ecology Parties*. Durham, NC: Duke University Press, 1990.
32. Pippa Norris, *Radical Right: Voters and Parties in the Electoral Market*. Cambridge: Cambridge University Press, 2005; Mudde, *Populist Radical Right Parties in Europe*; Kitschelt with McGann, *The Radical Right in Western Europe*.
33. Russell Dalton, The West German party system between two ages. In Russell Dalton, Scott Flanagan, and Paul Beck, eds., *Electoral Change in Advanced Industrial Democracies*. Princeton: Princeton University Press, 1984; Scott Flanagan, Electoral change in Japan. In Russell Dalton, Scott Flanagan, and Paul Beck, eds., *Electoral Change in Advanced Industrial Democracies*. Princeton: Princeton University Press, 1984.
34. Warren Miller and Teresa Levitin, *Leadership and Change: The New Politics and the American Electorate*. Cambridge, MA: Winthrop Publishers, 1976.
35. Paul Goren, *On Voter Competence*. Oxford: Oxford University Press, 2012; Paul Goren and Christopher Chapp, Moral power: How public opinion on culture war issues shapes partisan predispositions and religious orientations, *American Political Science Review* (2018).
36. Lisbeth Hooghe, Gary Marks, and Carol Wilson, Does left/right structure party positions on European integration? In Gary Marks and Marco Steenbergen, eds., *European Integration and Political Conflict*. Cambridge: Cambridge University Press, 2004; Robert Rohrschneider and Stephen Whitefield, *The Strain of Representation: How Parties Represent Diverse Voters in Western and Eastern Europe*. Oxford: Oxford University Press, 2012.
37. Ryan Bakker, Seth Jolly, and Jonathan Polk, Complexity in the European party space: Exploring dimensionality with experts, *European Union Politics* (2012) 13: 219–45; Wouter van der Brug and Joost van Spanje, Immigration, Europe and the "New Socio-cultural Dimension," *European Journal of Political Research* (2009) 48: 309–34.
38. Kriesi et al., *West European Politics in the Age of Globalization*; Bornschier, *Cleavage Politics and the Populist Right. The New Cultural Conflict in Western Europe*. Philadelphia: Temple University Press, 2010; Hanspeter Kriesi et al., *Political Conflict in Western Europe*. Cambridge: Cambridge University Press, 2012; Swen Hutter, Edgar Grande, and Hanspeter Kriesi, *Politcising Europe: Integration and Mass Politics*. Cambridge: Cambridge University Press, 2016.
39. This project has expanded to the full EU membership to study the effects of the Great Recession and the subsequent financial crises in the European Union. See https://www.eui.eu/Projects/POLCON/Documents/POLCONdescriptionwebsite.pdf
40. Lipset and Rokkan, Cleavage structures, party systems, and voter alignments.
41. For a discussion of the traditional interpretation of social cleavages see Lipset and Rokkan, Cleavage structures, party systems, and voter alignments; Stefano

Bartolini and Peter Mair, *Identity, Competition and Electoral Availability: The Stabilization of European Electorates 1885–1985*. Cambridge, Cambridge University Press, 1990, pp. 212–20; Kevin Deegan-Krause, New dimensions of political cleavage. In Russell Dalton and Hans-Dieter Klingemann, eds. *Oxford Handbook of Political Behavior*. Oxford: Oxford University Press, 2011; The Structure of Political Competition in Western European Politics (special issue), *West European Politics* (2010) 33.

42. Dalton, *Citizen Politics*; also see Goren, *On Voter Competence*; Knutsen, *Social Structure, Value Orientations and Party Choice in Western Europe*.
43. Inglehart, The changing structure of political cleavages in Western society, p. 28; also Ronald Inglehart and Pippa Norris, Trump, Brexit, and the rise of populism: Economic have-nots and cultural backlash. HKS Working Paper 16-026, Kennedy School of Government, Harvard University (https://research.hks.harvard.edu/publications/workingpapers/Index.aspx).
44. Mark Bovens and Anchrit Wille. *Diploma Democracy: The Rise of Political Meritocracy*. Oxford: Oxford University Press, 2017; Heinrich Best and Maurizio Cotta, eds. *Parliamentary Representatives in Europe 1848–2000 Legislative Recruitment and Careers in Eleven European Countries*. Oxford: Oxford University Press, 2001. On Britain see Evans and Tilley, *The New Politics of Class*, ch. 6.
45. Inglehart, The changing structure of political cleavages in Western society; Jacques Thomassen and Hermann Schmitt, Policy representation, *European Journal of Political Research* (1997) 32: 165–84; Russell Dalton, Political parties and political representation: Party supporters and party elites in nine nations, *Comparative Political Studies* (1985) 18: 267–99.
46. Edward Carmines and James Stimson, *Issue Evolution: Race and the Transformation of American Politics*. Princeton: Princeton University Press, 1989.
47. Arthur Lupia and Mathew McCubbins, *The Democratic Dilemma: Can Citizens Learn What They Need to Know?* Cambridge: Cambridge University Press, 1998; Peter Ditto et al., At least bias is bipartisan: A meta-analytic comparison of partisan bias in liberals and conservatives, *Perspectives in Psychological Science*, 2018.
48. Timothy Hellwig, *Globalization and Mass Politics: Retaining the Room to Maneuver*. New York: Cambridge University Press, 2015; Jack Vowles and George Xezonakis, eds., *Globalization and Domestic Politics: Parties, Elections, and Public Opinion*. Oxford: Oxford University Press. 2016.
49. Paul Sniderman and Louk Hagendoorn, *When Ways of Life Collide: Multiculturalism and Its Discontents in the Netherlands*. Princeton: Princeton University Press, 2009.
50. The trilogy of movies is describe on the website: http://www.backtothefuture.com/.
51. Kriesi et al., *West European Politics in the Age of Globalization*; Kriesi et al., *Political Conflict in Western Europe*; Hutter, Grande, and Kriesi, *Politicising Europe: Integration and Mass Politics*; Piketty, Brahmin left versus merchant right.
52. Knutsen, *Social Structure, Value Orientations and Party Choice in Western Europe*; Silja Häusermann and Hanspeter Kriesi, What do voters want? Dimensions and configurations in individual-level preferences and party choice. In Pablo Beramendi, Silja Häusermann, Herbert Kitschelt, and Hanspeter Kriesi, eds., *The Politics of Advanced Capitalism*. Cambridge: Cambridge University Press, 2015; Herbert Kitschelt, Social class and the radical right: Conceptualizing political preference

formation and partisan choice. In Jens Rydgren, ed., *Class Politics and the Radical Right*. New York: Routledge, 2013; Inglehart and Norris, Trump, Brexit, and the rise of populism.

53. Further information on the European Election Studies and access to the survey data is available through the project website: http://europeanelectionstudies.net/. I am grateful for the many principal investigators for collecting these surveys and sharing with the international research community.
54. Bernhard Weßels et al., *European Parliament Election Study 2009, Candidate Study*. GESIS Data Archive, Cologne. ZA5048; Marcel Egmond et al., *European Parliament Election Study 2009, Voter Study*. GESIS Data Archive, Cologne. ZA5055; Hermann Schmitt et al., *European Parliament Election Study 2014, Voter Study, First Post-Election Survey*. GESIS Data Archive, Cologne. ZA5160.
55. Simon Bornschier and Hanspeter Kriesi, The populist right, the working class, and the changing face of class politics. In Jens Rydgren, ed., *Class Politics and the Radical Right*. Abingdon and New York: Routledge, 2012; Liesbet Hooghe and Gary Marks, Cleavage theory meets Europe's crises: Lipset, Rokkan, and the transnational cleavage, *Journal of European Public Policy* (2018) 25: 109–35.
56. Additional elite samples were included in the 1989 EES, but the questionnaire did not include a range of non-EU political issues.
57. Lieven de Winter et al., *European Candidates Study 1994*. GESIS Data Archive, Cologne. ZA3077.
58. Also see Goren, *On Voter Competence*.
59. Toffler, *Future Shock*.
60. Toffler, *Future Shock*, p. 187.
61. Toffler, *Future Shock*, p. 187.
62. Greg Ferenstein, *The Age of Optimists* (https://medium.com/the-ferenstein-wire/silicon-valley-s-political-endgame-summarized-1f395785f3c1); David Broockman, Greg F. Ferenstein, and Neil Malhotra The political behavior of wealthy Americans: Evidence from technology entrepreneurs. Stanford Business School Working Paper No. 3581, 2017. https://www.gsb.stanford.edu/faculty-research/working-papers/political-behavior-wealthy-americans-evidence-technology.
63. Toffler, *Future Shock*, p. 87.
64. Adam Przeworski, *Why Bother with Elections?* New York: Polity Press, 2018, ch. 1, 11; Robert Dahl, *On Democracy*. New Haven, Yale University Press, 2000.

Part I
Social Structure and Political Cleavages

Part I

2

Citizens, Issues, and Political Cleavages

Today, it might be difficult to imagine that in the 1950s and early 1960s several distinguished scholars claimed that ideological conflicts were disappearing in established democracies. Daniel Bell provocatively stated that these nations were approaching "The end of ideology": "In the Western world, therefore, there is a rough consensus among intellectuals on political issues: the acceptance of a Welfare State; the desirability of decentralized power; a system of mixed economy and of political pluralism. In that sense, too, the ideological age has ended."[1] The erosion of social class differences in party voting and the developing consensus in support of the welfare state were taken as indicators of the fading of traditional ideological divisions. These scholars argued that instead of such conflict, political parties would develop into broad catch-all parties that campaigned on claims of competence and government performance.[2]

Yet, as older ideological divisions supposedly waned, new political divisions emerged in the affluent democracies. Most notably, Ronald Inglehart and others argued that new postmaterial issues were repolarizing Western publics, stimulating new conflicts over environmental quality, gender equality, social justice, and lifestyle choices.[3] The rise of Green parties and other New Social Movements injected new ideological debates into the politics of affluent democracies. Many researchers, including this author, wrote that new liberal values would expand individual rights, increase political tolerance, address important policy issues, and even expand the democratic process.[4] This process of value change was seen as a boon for Western democracies; the implication was that a better future lay ahead. In large part these predictions were accurate.

However, this is a limited view of the future. Or perhaps researchers simply overlooked Newton's third law: for every action, there is an equal and opposite reaction. As young, better-educated citizens mobilized for new progressive causes, this generated a counter-reaction by other sectors of society that disapproved of this new direction. Conservative religious groups spoke out in opposition to changing gender roles and later gay rights (although other denominations changed their doctrine). The economic and social effects of economic globalization (and European integration) started to reshape the political alignments. The economic losers to globalization grew, but they often seemed invisible to the winners.[5] Increased immigration—especially from outside Western democracies—heightened social tensions and raised new policy challenges.

This chapter uses public opinion on various political issues to map the *citizen-defined political space* produced by the economic and cultural cleavages, and track how this space has changed over time. I use data from three waves of the European Election Studies (EES) in 1979, 2009, and 2014.[6] (Chapter 5 presents comparable analyses for European political elites.) This chapter follows the evolution of the major lines of political competition and then considers the implications of this evolutionary process.

Cleavage Alignments from Issue Opinions

Seymour Lipset and Stein Rokkan's seminal study of electoral politics described the competition in European party systems in terms of longstanding social cleavages: class, religion, region, and urban/rural residence.[7] Social modernization in affluent democracies has eroded some of the social bases of these cleavages as discussed in Chapter 1, but many of their issue expressions still live on.

I use the term *cleavage* to denote long-term ideological or principled positions on enduring political interests. This is different from the Lipset-Rokkan definition of cleavages as emanating from social group competition, such as between labor versus business, or Church–state conflicts.[8] The Lipset-Rokkan framework makes a more direct connection between social interests and political interests, but I argue that the increasing diversity and fluidity of social conditions make such rigid group structures less predictable and less relevant. Moreover, groups were the embodiment of political views, and the political views are what directly shape political behavior. This study therefore focuses on broad issue bases of political competition, and then links these to possible group ties.

Issues are the specific policy controversies facing a nation. A connected set of issues dealing with a general political position defines a cleavage. Government policy actions and election debates normally focus on issues and devote less attention to the broad cleavages underlining the issues. Methodologically, Stephen Ansolabehere and his colleagues demonstrated that these latent issue cleavages provide more reliable and valid measures of citizen orientations and are stronger predictors of voting choices.[9] Similarly, Paul Goren has used the concept of issue cleavages to define the structure of party

Citizens, Issues, and Political Cleavages

competition in the United States.[10] My argument is that these issue cleavages frame democratic political competition over the long run.

The clearest example of a cleavage involves economic issues, where partisan competition defined by social class and labor versus business has morphed into a broader political competition of pro-state versus pro-market orientations, disagreements over appropriate social welfare benefits, and the persisting issues of economic inequality.[11] This broad cleavage is expressed in specific issues that can vary over time. In Britain, for example, it might be parliamentary debates over support for the National Health Service in one election, and tax policies in the next. In Italy, it might be questions about the pension system or programs to reduce unemployment. Or more likely, a nation may face a combination of such issues because they reflect common features of these societies.

The relationship between specific policy issues and an underlying political cleavage becomes more complex when cleavages potentially change. When new issues emerge, several outcomes are possible. One possibility is that the issue is incorporated into (or connected to) an existing long-term cleavage as another expression of the cleavage. For example, when the German Social Democratic Party (SPD) raised the topic of a minimum wage in the early 2000s, it was easily interpretable as an extension of the SPD's past support for the German working class. Other issues might be so specific or transitory that they have limited implications for existing cleavages.[12]

More central to our interests are new issues that reflect emerging societal concerns that may persist over time, and which are relatively independent of existing political cleavages. Such issues have the potential to restructure political competition if the societal implications of these issues are significant. The topic might be truly new, or it might reflect a long-term situation that was recently politicized.[13] A cluster of new issues that reflect common values provides the potential to create a new cleavage of political competition. However, it is difficult to identify a newly emerging cleavage because the long-term aspect of a cleavage and its persistence only becomes apparent with the passage of time.

As discussed in Chapter 1, the rise of a cultural cleavage is at least partially tied to the new social concerns that New Social Movements (NSMs) added to the political agenda beginning in the 1970s.[14] The environmental movement is a prime example. In addition, other NSMs of the period, such as the women's movement, human rights groups, and social justice groups expanded public attention to, and support for, this alternative agenda. As this liberal cultural agenda became more prominent in political debates and often in policy outcomes, other social interests challenged these progressive positions.[15] Some religious denominations countered the liberal culturalist position on issues related to women and family, gay rights proposals, and sexual norms.

Social justice, political correctness, and identity politics generated a push back from other conservative interests. More generally, other researchers maintain that the expansion of European unification and other aspects of globalization created new economic and cultural fears among some citizens, which became common elements of a conservative cultural perspective.[16] Similar cultural tensions are apparent in the United States.[17] The culture clash widened and deepened.

Other recent studies have focused on racism and immigration as a driving force behind a conservative reaction.[18] As immigration-related issues rose to prominence in Europe, they could evoke many possible reactions. Some liberals might oppose immigration by people who rejected Western liberal values (as the Pym Fortuyn movement in the Netherlands). Economic conservative might support or oppose immigration because of the potential effects on employment or social welfare costs. Some liberals might support immigrants out of a desire for multiculturalism and new opportunities for the immigrants; some business sectors might favor immigration either because it benefits their sales or lessens their costs. Churches might embrace immigrants as part of their social concern for the needy (as Pope Francis has preached), while other religious actors might criticize immigrants for their values. There are real-life examples of each of these possibilities, which might lead to different political alliances.

In addition, political parties can position an issue into the framework of political competition. For example, the French ban on headscarves in 2004 and the ban on wearing the niqab in public places in 2011 were implemented by a conservative government, which provided political cues on these issues to their supporters and opponents. Party positions on other "new" issues, such as gay rights, GM foods, and global climate change, also connect these issues to broader political values. Thus, political parties can shape political cleavages by linking together diverse issues and articulating an alternative worldview.[19]

The Methodology of Studying Cleavages over Time

To track the evolution of political cleavages over time is a complex methodological matter, and there is no perfect solution. Creating measures of citizen positions on each cleavage is relatively straightforward in a cross-sectional study. The complication arises in longitudinal analyses. If identical questions are asked over time, the same method of index construction can be used. However, almost by definition the relevant political issues change over time and across nations, especially over long timespans such as this project. In the 1970s, for example, abortion policy was a significant measure of cultural positions in many parts of Europe; by 2009, public sentiment had changed and many nations had liberalized their abortion laws.[20] However, new gender-related issues of pay equity, sexual harassment, and same-sex marriage became salient issues on the cultural cleavage. Income inequality was a less salient economic issue in the 1970s, but it is now a central theme in terms of the state–market economic cleavage. So a survey that examines public issue preferences in 1979 necessarily should ask different questions than a survey in 2014 if it wants to capture the contemporaneous political divisions.

One solution to this quandary is latent variable analysis.[21] Instead of a constant set of issue questions, the items from each time point are examined in a dimensional model to identify the economic and cultural cleavages represented by these issues. I adopt this solution to study cleavages over time. I use Principal Components Analyses (PCA) to identify the economic and cultural cleavages as latent variables.

Studying a changing mix of issues over time should be an advantage, since the same set of questions over a several decade timespan is likely to include issues that are no longer relevant or whose meaning has changed over time. The principal investigators of each EES presumably selected issue questions that reflect the current political controversies at each time point. Although the questions may not coincide exactly with our theoretical interest in the two political cleavages, PCA can determine the fit. This methodology weights the relevance of each issue for the underlying cleavage, rather than treating them all as equally relevant. In summary, this approach presumes that the issues in each survey can be combined to reasonably represent the economic and cultural cleavages, and in comparable ways over time.

There are tradeoffs in the use of the PCA methodology. One strength is that it allows us to compare different models of the political space. For theoretical reasons, I have focused on the economic and cultural cleavages as defining the major bases of political competition. Some scholars still rely on a single Left–Right dimension. Lipset and Rokkan argued for four dimensions of cleavage. Oddbjörn Knutsen recently argued that five value dimensions are needed to understand electoral choices. But there is no magic number for the correct number of dimensions. Instead, there is a tradeoff between theoretical parsimony and empirical adequacy. What number of dimensions represents the ideal tradeoff between these two criteria? Alternative PCA models with different numbers of dimensions provide a method to see the empirical consequences of this tradeoff.

The indices produced from the PCA models are standardized variables, so it is not possible to compare the level of liberal/conservative positions over time. But comparing liberal/conservative cleavages over time might be problematic with any methodology, since the issue basis of comparison and the political context change.[22]

There is also a conceptual element in the choice of methodology. It involves how we think of concepts such as liberalism and conservatism. Let me use political tolerance as an example. A constant method would examine attitudes toward communists or homosexuals as indicators of tolerance, showing that contemporary publics are more tolerant than those of the past. An evolutionary method would say that tolerance involves acceptance of the contentious movements of the day. So instead of tracking attitudes toward communists (after the fall of communism), one should ask about tolerance of Muslims (Jihadists?) or anti-globalization protestors. Liberalism, in other words, is an evolving trait. Someone who expressed liberal views in the 1960s is likely to be a conservative by today's standards, even without changing any of their opinions. And the liberal of today is likely to hold views that may be considered conservative thirty years from now.

Both the constant and evolutionary definitions are justifiable on different grounds. I lean toward the latter as capturing what we generally mean about political cleavages, especially since the supply of party choices in elections will change with citizens' demands. Thus, this study's methodology follows the evolutionary definition of liberal and conservative positions.

To the best of my knowledge, the EES data are the most extensive cross-national, longitudinal evidence on the issue opinions—and potentially the political cleavages—in the established democracies in Western Europe. The project asked the same battery of issue questions across the nations in each EES to maximize cross-national comparability. I begin with the survey of the nine European Community (EC) member states in 1979; and then track the evolution of the economic and cultural cleavages to 2009 and 2014.

Issues and Cleavages in 1979

As citizens in the European Community prepared for the first direct elections to the European Parliament in 1979, the Eurobarometer surveyed public opinion on the policy issues facing these nine nations (see Appendix A for question wording).[23] Several questions asked about the role of government in regulating the economy, providing for social welfare, and other economic issues.[24] Other questions addressed the abortion issue, support for the military, and protection from terrorism as non-economic concerns. I added a general question on support for European unification to identify the cleavage ties of this issue.

I began the PCA with the most liberal identification of dimensions—those achieving the standard Kaiser's criterion of an Eigenvalue greater than 1.0. The left side of Table 2.1 describes the five dimensions from this unconstrained model. The first dimension clearly reflects the expected economic cleavage, with issues such as controlling multinationals, reducing income

Table 2.1. Citizen Issue Structures, 1979

Issue Questions	Unconstrained Dimensional Analysis					Two Dimensions	
	Economic	Regional	Nationalism	Terrorism	Gender	Economic	Cultural
Control multinationals	0.446	−0.011	−0.271	0.361	0.072	0.487	−0.285
Develop nuclear energy	−0.082	−0.021	0.733	−0.040	0.117	−0.162	0.554
Reduce income inequality	0.464	0.152	−0.189	0.305	0.196	0.592	−0.195
Increase penalties for terrorism	−0.010	−0.186	0.363	0.696	−0.227	−0.007	0.408
Expand public ownership of industry	0.785	0.029	0.054	−0.217	0.042	0.510	−0.222
Expand government management of economy	0.715	0.100	0.091	0.120	−0.148	0.548	−0.024
Stronger military defense	0.066	0.011	0.724	0.030	−0.161	−0.092	0.601
Women free to have abortion	0.027	−0.095	0.013	−0.003	0.860	0.199	−0.249
Equal representation for employees	0.580	0.133	−0.116	0.062	0.373	0.625	−0.274
More aid to 3rd world	0.163	0.780	−0.120	−0.052	−0.083	0.519	0.215
Stronger antipollution	0.052	0.281	−0.140	0.656	0.227	0.479	0.084
Protect free expression	0.315	0.289	−0.029	0.254	0.378	0.569	−0.021
Aid less developed regions	0.182	0.796	0.002	0.103	0.002	0.595	0.326
For European unification	−0.199	0.494	0.355	0.087	0.129	0.135	0.542
Eigenvalue for rotated dimensions	2.20	1.60	1.53	1.42	1.45	2.80	1.59
% Variance explained	15.7	11.4	10.9	10.1	10.3	20.0	11.3

Note: Table entries are coefficients from Principal Components Analysis with a Varimax rotation and pairwise deletion of missing data.

Source: 1979 European Election Study (Eurobarometer 11).

inequality, expanding public management of the economy, and greater employee representation within businesses. Given the long history of the economic cleavage in European politics and the institutionalization of this cleavage in European party systems, this cleavage clearly structures citizens' issue opinions.

However, there is much less coherence of the other issues into a single political cleavage. The second dimension includes the three items with a regional focus, spanning sub-national, European, and international activity. The third dimension reflects an unusual connection between support for a stronger military defense and developing nuclear energy. The fourth dimension combines stronger penalties for terrorism and support for anti-pollution efforts. The fifth dimension focuses on the one gender question: women's right to abortion.

These results suggest that a single cultural cleavage dimension was not fully apparent in the late 1970s, which is part of the reason to begin the study with the earliest data available.[25] New Social Movements were still developing; Green parties had not entered electoral politics as serious competitors. The path-breaking German *Grünen* was established in 1979, the Belgian ECOLO was founded in 1980, and AGALEV in 1982. While women's groups were mobilizing in the 1970s, much of their political impact lay ahead. By implication, the cultural cleavage would likely be even less structured if there were comparable survey evidence a decade earlier.

This multidimensional result provides a starting point for examining contemporary political cleavages. Economic issues stand alone on one dimension, never rising above a 0.40 coefficient for the other four components. The four additional dimensions are only weakly identified. The terrorism and gender dimensions barely surpass the Kaiser criterion for extracting a component.[26] If I constrain the analyses to only a three-dimensional solution, the issues on the fourth and fifth component start to overlap with other cultural items. A connection between cultural issues is not fully structured in 1979.

A theoretically guided analysis tests whether citizens' issue opinions confirm my prior expectations. The previous chapter argued that a traditional *economic cleavage* now competes with a separate *cultural cleavage* in most contemporary democracies. I constrained the Principal Components analysis to extract only two dimensions as seen on the right side of Table 2.1. The first component still represents various economic issues; the initial role of the state issues from the previous analysis, now joined by issues of economic aid to Europe's less developed regions and foreign aid to third world nations.

The second component now connects items that might be seen as favoring a strong state versus an alternative agenda. Those who want a stronger military defense and harsher penalties for terrorists are also positive toward European unification. For the combined Eurobarometer sample, among those who are

Citizens, Issues, and Political Cleavages

strongly favorable toward European unification, 60 percent support a stronger military defense, versus only 39 percent among those who are strongly unfavorable toward unification. In other words, in 1979 the public saw the European Community as a way to strengthen their nation—strength in unity. The contrasting opinions are support for women's right to an abortion, which has a weak negative coefficient on this cultural dimension. The weak negative coefficients for several of the economic issues imply a residual relationship between liberal cultural sentiments and liberal economic opinions.

A further question asks whether this structure for the pooled set of nations is relatively consistent across nations (also see Chapter 4). National social and economic conditions vary, and even more importantly the national policies and the salient issues of political debate vary. For example, Luxembourg residents may view multinational corporations in a different light than larger nations such as France or Germany. The British, Danes, and Irish might view unification differently than the founding nine member states. Shared governing in corporations has a different meaning in Germany because of existing co-determination policies than it does in Italy and the United Kingdom. Thus, each issue can have somewhat different relevance to the politics of each nation. In addition, although I focus on the economic and cultural cleavages, other sources of partisan division vary across nations. For example, a Lipset-Rokkan regional cleavage exists in nations such as Belgium and Britain. In short, we should not expect identical PCA structures across nations, even if the latent values are comparable. The question is whether these variations invalidate our efforts to define a shared European political space.

There are several methodologies to test this assumption of common cleavage dimensions.[27] I chose one of the simplest and most direct. In addition to the pooled cross-national PCA, I computed separate PCAs for each nation (Chapter 4). If the overall structure of opinions is essentially similar across pooled and individual nations, the scores from both PCA models should be highly correlated. For the nine member states, the average correlation of the scores on the economic cleavage across nations is very high (average $r = 0.89$), with less consistent but still strong correlations for the three 1973 accession states ($r = 0.73$). The cultural dimension is more varied, reflecting its still amorphous development. In the nine EU nations, the scales correlate strongly ($r = 0.75$), but only modestly for the three newer members ($r = 0.50$).

In summary, these findings point to the consistency of the economic cleavage across these democracies. Even with different party systems and different structures of interest group alignments, these issues form a common economic cleavage across all nine nations. This cleavage was a major factor in the creation of modern party systems and continues to be a central theme in electoral politics, so the clarity of this cleavage is not surprising. There is also an identifiable cultural cleavage, but it is still inchoate in 1979 Europe.

The potential elements of this cleavage are not strongly related among the citizenry, forming multiple dimensions. And the content of this cleavage varies more across nations. Citizen positions on these two cleavages provide the empirical foundation of this study.[28]

Issues and Cleavages in 2009

In the summer of 2009, citizens were again in the midst of an election campaign for the European Parliament.[29] It had been thirty years since the initial direct election in 1979, but this was the first EES that included questions on a range of national political issues.

In one sense, however, the passage of these three decades is fortuitous. The forces of social and political change that were emerging in the 1970s should be more apparent after this long interlude. The New Social Movements that were just emerging in the 1970s had become important political actors. For example, most EU nations had passed new environmental protection legislation and created new environmental ministries. The women's movement had reshaped social norms and legislation affecting women. As these societal and political changes occurred, they should have crystallized and politicized cultural divisions.

Another transformative force was the process of European integration and broader neo-liberal policies of economic globalization. Many economies experienced deindustrialization and its economic effects on displaced workers. One consequence was rising income inequality and government difficulties in regulating multinational corporations. These issues took on special salience after the start of the 2008 financial crisis. A further byproduct of globalization was the increase in non-EU immigration and refugee flight to Europe. These developments affected the citizenry, and ultimately the political process.

Thus, by 2009 I expected significant changes in political attitudes compared to 1979. First, the political agenda changed and many new cultural issues were now an important part of the political discourse. Issues of gay rights, expansion of gender equality, and immigration were more salient than in the prior period. Second, three decades of political debate on these cultural issues should create more structure and coherence to public opinion. For example, three decades of environmental policy debate should have informed public opinion on the topic. Recently formed far-right parties were also offering a dramatically different position on various cultural issues.

Table 2.2 presents the cleavage dimensions in the 2009 EES (see Appendix A for question wording).[30] The first noticeable change is the addition of new liberal and conservative cultural issues that were not as salient three decades

Citizens, Issues, and Political Cleavages

Table 2.2. Citizen Issue Structures, 2009

	EU9 Nations		EU15 Nations	
Issue Questions	Cultural	Economic	Cultural	Economic
Immigrants should adapt country's customs	0.643	−0.012	0.611	−0.065
Private enterprise solves economic problems	0.387	−0.382	0.357	−0.480
Prohibit same-sex marriages	0.512	−0.356	0.549	−0.262
State owns public services and industries	0.176	0.351	0.190	0.513
Women decide on abortion	−0.035	0.610	−0.128	0.455
Politics should not intervene in economy	0.347	−0.054	0.335	−0.045
Harsher sentences for lawbreakers	0.655	0.133	0.640	0.068
Redistribute income and wealth	0.307	0.442	0.332	0.539
Schools teach children obedience	0.590	0.133	0.608	0.047
Referendums for EU treaty changes	0.393	0.429	0.420	0.437
Women reduce work for family	0.453	−0.348	0.527	−0.178
Decrease immigration significantly	0.721	−0.034	0.730	−0.058
Attitude to European unification	0.349	0.084	0.277	0.118
Eigenvalue for rotated dimensions	2.85	1.31	2.81	1.42
% Variance explained	21.6	10.0	21.6	10.9

Note: Table entries are coefficients from Principal Components Analysis with a Varimax rotation and pairwise deletion of missing data.
Source: European Election Study 2009.

earlier. The EES included two issues on immigration, a new item on same-sex marriage, two additional gender-related questions, a question on sentencing law breakers, and one on educating children to obey authority. While the specific choice of items reflects the research priorities of the project, the shift toward cultural issues reflects the changing political discourse in these societies.

The left panel in the table presents results for the original nine EU member states, and the panel on the right presents results for the expanded EU15 membership. The two analyses yield fairly consistent results. Partly because of the large number of cultural items included in the issue battery, the first component represents the cultural cleavage, with immigration issues most clearly defining this dimension along with authority-related items and gender issues.[31] While there was some separation among various aspects of the cultural cleavage in 1979, the issues are strongly connected in the minds of Europeans in 2009.

The variety of issues that go together on this component speaks to the breadth of the cultural cleavage. Some issues, such as same-sex marriage and attitudes toward the family, might be derived from religious values, but this linkage is more tenuous for other cultural issues. Teaching students obedience and harsher penalties for criminals seems more directly linked to norms of authority relations. Immigration can evoke concerns about diversity but also illustrates other societal changes with economic and social effects. The fusion of these issues in the cultural cleavage reflects more than a single issue controversy or narrow value divide.

37

Political Realignment

The second dimension contains issues largely from the economic cleavage: private enterprise, state ownership of industry, and inequality in income and wealth. The item on using referendums to change EU treaties falls on this dimension, but reflects a somewhat complex issue of EU politics. The more direct question of respondents' attitudes toward European unification loads on the cultural cleavage.

It is worth a short digression to reiterate the interpretation of PCA coefficients in the context of the 2009 survey. The coefficients reflect how much each issue is related to the underlying latent concept, not the distribution of opinions. For example, immigration opinions are the clearest indicator of cultural values, tapping how one views the broader processes of social and political change occurring in Europe. Immigration opinions are often strongly felt, and the issue encapsulates many of the other aspects of the cultural cleavage: a challenge to national identity, economic disruption, erosion of traditional Christian values, and concerns about multiculturalism. Hence the high loadings of the two immigration issues on the cultural cleavage.

However, the PCA dimensional analyses do not signify the distribution of opinions on these issues. The vast majority of Europeans (75 percent) felt that schools should emphasize obedience, at the same time that a large majority (61 percent) support same-sex marriage. Even for the two immigration items, only a small minority strongly agree with both issue questions. Similarly, reducing income inequality and state ownership of industry are the two clearest measures of the economic cleavage—but a majority of Europeans favor one (reducing inequality) and a majority oppose the other (state ownership). The PCA results identify the structure of opinions but not the distribution of opinions.

In summary, the three decades between 1979 and 2009 witnessed the consolidation of a distinct cultural cleavage in the political space. New social interests connected by New Social Movements articulated a new postmaterial or GAL (green, alternative, libertarian) image of society. Political changes crystallized a TAN perspective (traditional, authoritarian, nationalist) that was the antithesis to the liberal culturalists. In addition, the economic cleavage continues to divide citizens over the role of the state and provision of social services. Europeans see these two cleavages as a parsimonious structure for understanding contemporary politics.[32]

Issues and Cleavages in 2014

The final time point is the 2014 European Parliament elections. A fundamental change in the cleavage structure in a short five-year span is unlikely. However,

Citizens, Issues, and Political Cleavages

Table 2.3. Citizen Issue Structures, 2014

Issues	Unconstrained Dimensions			Two Dimensions	
	Economic	Culture	Crime	Economic	Culture
State intervention in the economy	0.692	0.062	−0.089	0.695	−0.057
Redistribute wealth from rich to poor	0.717	−0.075	0.105	0.708	−0.047
Raise taxes for public services	0.344	0.609	−0.185	0.398	0.339
Same-sex marriage	0.039	0.710	0.074	0.104	0.600
Privacy rights even if they hinder efforts to combat crime	0.169	−0.121	0.780	0.158	0.373
A restrictive policy on immigration	0.168	−0.576	−0.382	0.114	−0.699
EU should have more authority over members economic policies	−0.003	0.170	0.547	0.014	0.470
Economic growth has priority over environmental protection	0.504	0.235	0.259	0.524	0.307
Eigenvalue for rotated dimensions	1.42	1.31	1.18	1.46	1.42
% Variance explained	17.7	16.3	14.7	18.2	17.7

Note: Table entries are coefficients from Principal Components Analysis with a Varimax rotation and pairwise deletion of missing data.
Source: European Election Study 2014, EU 15 nations.

the 2014 EES may capture more of the disruptions caused by the 2008 financial crisis involving the Eurozone and the terms of EU membership. Still, it is better to think of the 2014 survey as a partial replication of the 2009 analyses. The researchers selected a different set of issues and used a different question format. With these changes, is there a clear persistence in the economic and cultural cleavages?

The 2014 survey asked eight issue questions that seem to span the economic and cultural cleavages. For the EU15 member states, I repeated the same PCA methodology applied to the previous two surveys.

The first panels in Table 2.3 show the results when the number of extracted dimensions is defined by the standard Kaiser criterion. The first dimension is a clear expression of the economic cleavage, with high coefficients for state intervention in the economy, income redistribution, and economic growth over environmental protection. The second dimension contrasts the cultural issues of favoring same-sex marriage versus restricting immigration. The third dimension barely reaches the Kaiser criterion and includes support for the EU and a crime-related issue.

When the PCA is constrained to two dimensions, the second and third components merge into a single cultural cleavage. The issue of restricting immigrants now combines with support for the EU and combating crime versus support for same-sex marriage. Thus, the results of the 2009 and 2014 studies both present a common pattern of an economic cleavage and a cultural cleavage as defining the contemporary political space, despite differences in the issues, question format, and economic context of these two surveys.

Political Realignment

Cross-National Patterns

Economic and cultural orientations vary at the individual level (Chapter 3), and can vary as part of the national political culture.[33] For example, people in some nations may favor a more activist state on economic and welfare issues, while others prefer a more restricted government role. Cultural tendencies may similarly differ across nations as a function of their social experiences and basic value priorities. Prior research suggests a cultural divide between, Protestant, affluent Northern Europe and Catholic, conservative Southern Europe.[34] Therefore, I mapped the distribution of nations in each of the European Election Studies to identify such cultural patterns, and to assess whether national positions.

Figure 2.1 presents the national averages on the two cleavages in 1979. Differences across the EU9 nations are mostly distinguished by their positions on the economic cleavage. The British under the Thatcher government and the Germans who were moving toward a conservative Kohl government

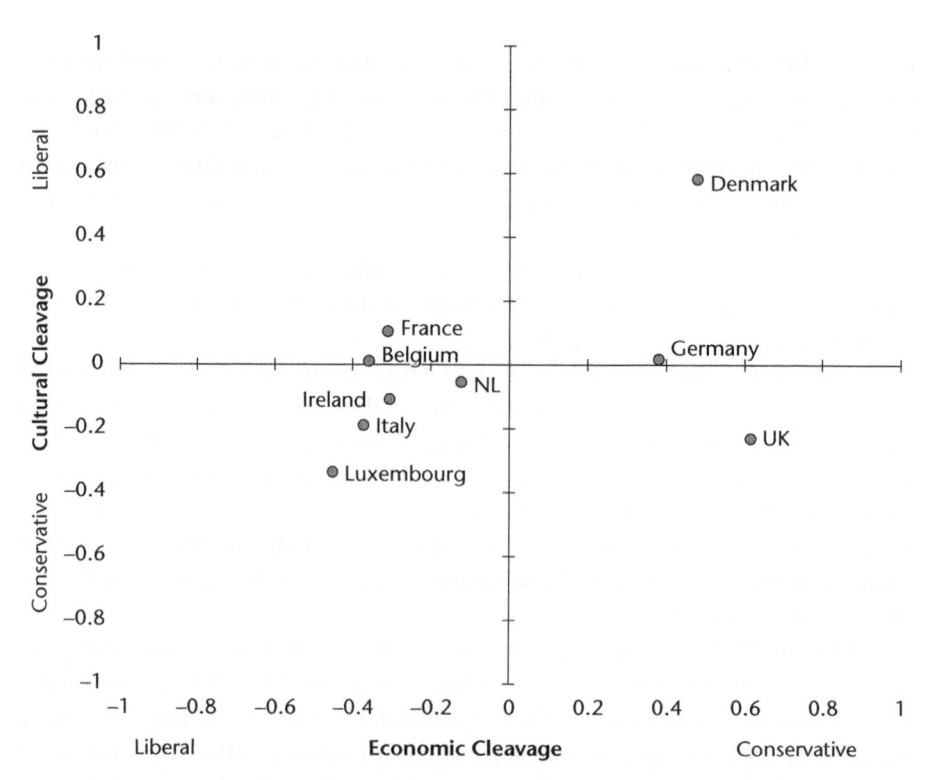

Figure 2.1. National Positions on Economic and Cultural Cleavages, 1979
Note: Figure entries are mean scores on the cleavage indices for each nation.
Source: 1979 European Election Study (Eurobarometer 11).

Citizens, Issues, and Political Cleavages

(in 1982) are both to the right of the average West European on economic issues—along with the Danes. Citizens in the other six member states position themselves to the left on the economic cleavage, which is generally consistent with other studies of this cleavage.[35] In contrast, most nations hover around the European average on the cultural cleavage, with only the Danes taking a distinctly more liberal position on this cleavage. Consequently, the cross-national differences on the economic cleavage in 1979 (eta = 0.37) are substantially larger than the differences on the cultural cleavage (eta = 0.24).

Figure 2.2 displays national scores on the two cleavages in the 2009 EES. This image is substantially different from the prior figure. Now the variation in national opinions is fairly modest along the economic cleavage. Germans still lean toward a conservative economic position, although the British public had shifted to the Left by the end of the Blair/Brown government.[36] More noticeable is the widening cultural difference between nations. Southern European publics tend to be more conservative on the cultural dimension, while Northern European nations—Sweden and Denmark especially—are

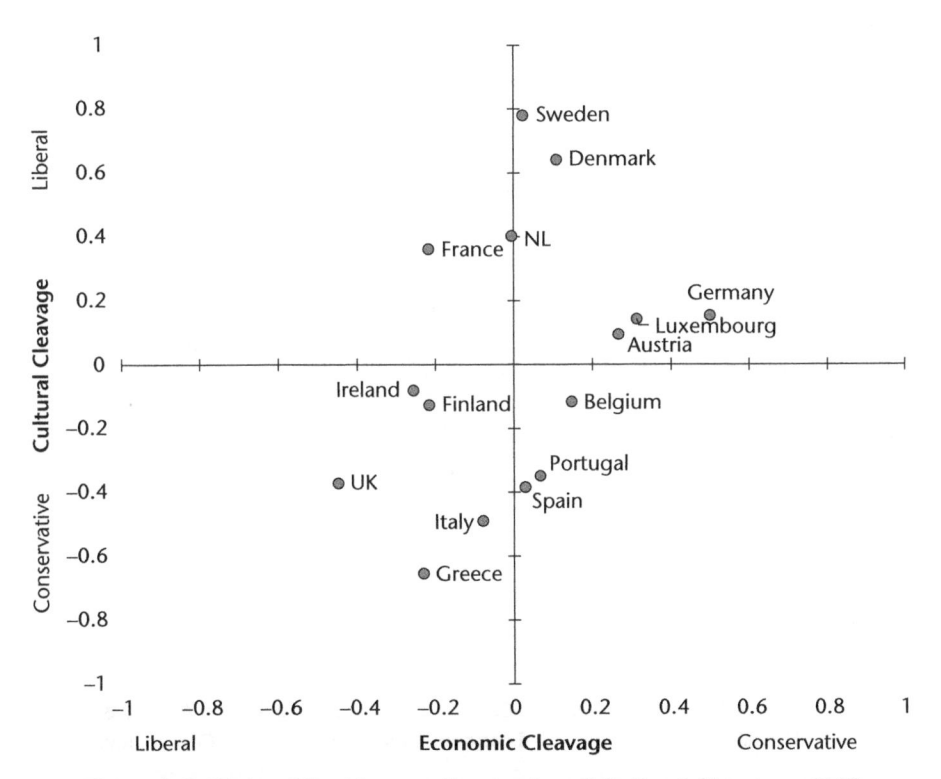

Figure 2.2. National Positions on Economic and Cultural Cleavages, 2009
Note: Figure entries are mean scores on the cleavage indices for each nation.
Source: 2009 European Election Study, EU15 nations.

Political Realignment

more liberal. As one specific illustration of the issue elements of this difference, 78.5 percent of Swedes support same-sex marriages, compared to only 39.9 percent of Italians and 33.1 percent of Greeks. The magnitude of the cross-national variation on the cultural cleavage now matches that on the economic cleavage (eta = 0.24 for both).

Finally, I replicated the analyses with the 2014 EES. Figure 2.3 displays a pattern that is more similar to 2009 than to 1979. There are modest national differences along the economic cleavage—ranging barely a scale point from most liberal to most conservative publics (eta = 0.20). In comparison, cross-national variation on the cultural cleavage remains large (eta = 0.28) and generally follows the previous North–South pattern.

In summary, over nearly the past half century, a new pattern of political cleavages has developed across European democracies. This is apparent in the structure of issue opinions at the individual level.[37] In the late 1970s, the economic cleavage was politically salient, but divisions along the cultural cleavage were just emerging at both the individual and national levels. Some analysts foresaw these divisions, but they were still to come.[38] Today, two

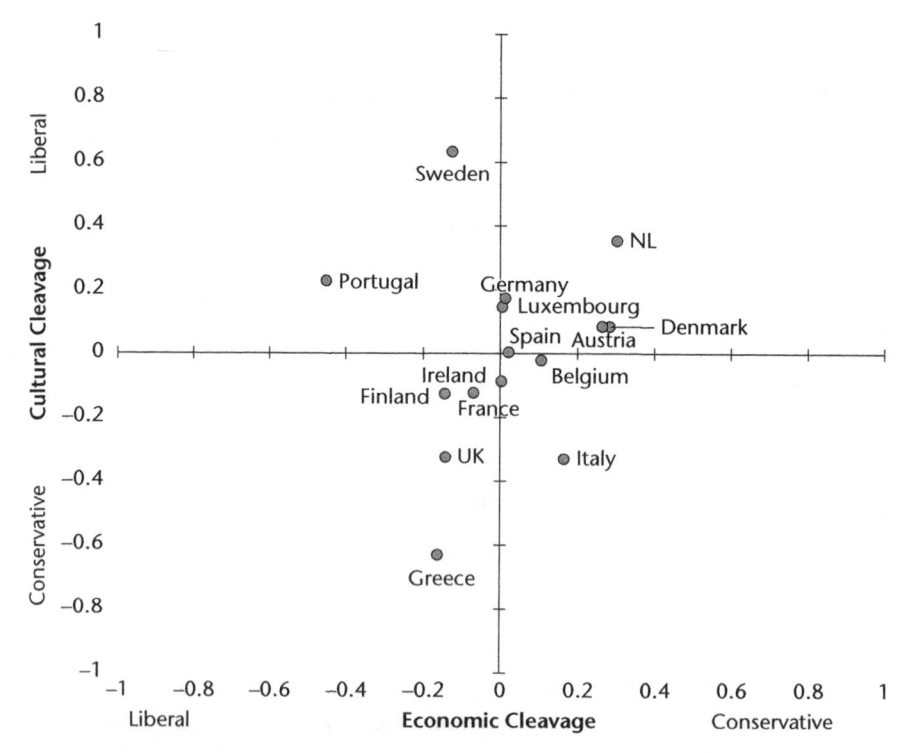

Figure 2.3. National Positions on Economic and Cultural Cleavages, 2014
Note: Figure entries are mean scores on the cleavage indices for each nation.
Source: 2014 European Election Study, EU15 nations.

clear issue cleavages—economic and culture—primarily structure citizen perceptions of the political space.

The Framework of Political Competition

According to Albert Einstein, "The supreme goal of all theory is to make the irreducible basic elements as simple and as few as possible without having to surrender the adequate representation of a single datum of experience."[39] In this vein, political scientists have debated the number of dimensions required to adequately describe political competition in contemporary European democracies.

A single issue might appear important in one election, to explain electoral results. However, most elections do not begin with a blank slate, but as a continuation of alternative worldviews fought over at the last election, with incremental adjustments. Thus, citizens' *issue opinions identify the broader cleavages* that structure political competition. In principle, there is no unique number of dimensions to political competition, and various scholars suggest different numbers of cleavages. The consideration of multiple frameworks is inevitable, and often necessary, depending on the theoretical question under study.[40] So the initial answer to Einstein's standard is that the number of basic elements is somewhere between one and "a lot."

This chapter has argued that an adequate and parsimonious description of citizens' political demands can be summarized with two issue cleavages.[41] The first is the economic cleavage that addresses the role of the state in society and the economy, the provision of social welfare benefits, and protection of those in need. The issues tapping this cleavage vary across surveys, but there is a common dimension in each of the three surveys. The economic cleavage was central to the formation of modern democratic party systems, and continues in evolutionary form in contemporary politics.[42]

The second dimension has evolved over the past several decades. As affluent democracies experienced unprecedented social modernization in the latter half of the twentieth century, new political demands emerged. Variously labeled as postmaterial, left-libertarian, or GAL issues, these themes began to coalesce into a new cleavage of political competition.[43]

This cultural cleavage was loosely structured in the 1979 EES, which predated the political prominence of citizen groups and political parties that articulated the liberal culturalist perspective. Later developing issues resulting from globalization and other changing social conditions were integrated into this cultural cleavage. Immigration, gay rights, and attitudes toward the EU are examples that stimulate vocal support by some parts of European societies, and vocal opposition by other sectors. By the time of the 2009 and 2014 surveys, this cultural cleavage structures citizens' issue opinions. These results are largely consistent with the findings from Hanspeter Kriesi and his colleagues, although now with more cross-national and longitudinal breadth.[44]

This evidence suggests that many recent contentious political events—Brexit, Trump's 2016 election, and the rise of far-right parties—reflect deeper cleavages that divide citizens and are not just reactions to current events. The controversies are examples of an ongoing cultural divisions related to modernization processes in affluent democracies. At issue is not just immigration, the expansion of gender equality, reactions to the Great Recession, or other specific issues—it is a cleavage between a view of a future society and a view of a past society that its supporters value. There were very negative areas of earlier European society, but there were also positive features that some citizens miss in the race to modernization. If we focus on the specific issue conflicts of the day, the ones that generate media headlines because they are provocative, we miss the forest by focusing on the trees.

Too often discussion of the cultural cleavage takes on a normative tone, especially on social media and on op-ed pages. I consciously minimize this evaluative tone in this study because I think it can blur our vision. (Just read Facebook posts *from both sides* after a major contentious event). The extreme poles of each dimension are not reflective of the entire European public. There are views—racism, violence, prejudicial intolerance, restricting freedoms, and other human rights—that go beyond the bounds of democratic politics and should be strongly criticized.

However, positions on the issues included in these opinion surveys can be legitimate on both sides, even if people disagree strongly. Democracy's value is that it provides a means to address such differences. The cleavage between agrarian and urban interests was not a competition between darkness and light. The historic religious cleavage in Western democracies was not, in my view, a cleavage between God and godlessness, although both sides considered themselves "in the right." These are examples of how societies debate their differing interests and values, and how the balance changes over time. Conflicting interests and preferences on the economic and cultural cleavages exist, and democratic politics can be a way to resolve them. With the time perspective offered by this chapter, one might modestly realize that many of the controversies of today will look differently in thirty years' time.

Notes

1. Daniel Bell, *The End of Ideology: On the Exhaustion of Political Ideas in the Fifties*. Glencoe, IL: Free Press, 1960, p. 373. Also see Robert Lane, The decline in political and ideology in a knowledgeable society, *American Sociological Review* (1966)

Citizens, Issues, and Political Cleavages

31: 649–62; Seymour Martin Lipset, A concept and its history: The End of Ideology. In Seymour Martin Lipset, ed., *Consensus and Conflict*. New Brunswick, NJ: Transaction, 1985.
2. Otto Kirchheimer, The transformation of the Western European party systems. In Joseph LaPalombara and Myron Weiner, eds., *Political Parties and Political Development*. Princeton: Princeton University Press, 1966.
3. Ronald Inglehart, *The Silent Revolution*. Princeton: Princeton University Press, 1977; Ronald Inglehart, The changing structure of political cleavages in Western society. In Russell Dalton, Scott Flanagan, and Paul Beck, eds., *Electoral Change in Advanced Industrial Democracies*. Princeton: Princeton University Press, 1984; Ronald Inglehart, *Culture Shift in Advanced Industrial Society*. Princeton: Princeton University Press, 1990.
4. Ronald Inglehart, *How People's Motivations are Changing and How this is Changing the World*. Cambridge: Cambridge University Press, 2017, ch. 6; Ronald Inglehart and Christian Welzel, *Modernization, Cultural Change, and Democracy: The Human Development Sequence*. New York: Cambridge University Press, 2005; Russell Dalton, *Citizen Politics: Public Opinion and Political Parties in Established Democracies*, 7th ed. Washington, DC: CQ Press, 2019, ch. 5.
5. Hanspeter Kriesi et al., *West European Politics in the Age of Globalization*. Cambridge: Cambridge University Press, 2008; Pablo Beramendi et al., eds., *The Politics of Advanced Capitalism*. Cambridge: Cambridge University Press, 2015; Jack Vowles and George Xezonakis, eds., *Globalization and Domestic Politics: Parties, Elections, and Public Opinion*. Oxford: Oxford University Press, 2016.
6. The public opinion surveys examined in this chapter are available from the website of the European Election Studies (http://europeanelectionstudies.net/).
7. Seymour Martin Lipset and Stein Rokkan, Cleavage structures, party systems, and voter alignments. In Seymour Martin Lipset and Stein Rokkan, eds., *Party Systems and Voter Alignments: Cross-national Perspectives*. New York: Free Press, 1967.
8. Zsolt Enyedi, The social and attitudinal basis of political parties: Cleavage politics revisited, *European Review* (2008) 16: 287–304; Hanspeter Kriesi, Restructuration of partisan politics and the emergence of a new cleavage based on values, *West European Politics* (2010) 33: 673–85; Oddbjørn Knutsen, *Social Structure, Value Orientations and Party Choice in Western Europe*. London: Palgrave, 2017.
9. Stephan Ansolabehere, Jonathan Rodden, and James Snyder, The strength of issues: Using multiple measures to gauge preference stability, ideological constraint and issue voting, *American Political Science Review* (2008) 102: 215–32.
10. Paul Goren, *On Voter Competence*. Oxford: Oxford University Press, 2012.
11. Kriesi et al., *West European Politics in the Age of Globalization*; Robert Rohrschneider and Stephen Whitefield, *The Strain of Representation: How Parties Represent Diverse Voters in Western and Eastern Europe*. Oxford: Oxford University Press, 2012.
12. Typically these are issues that in dimensional analyses are not significantly related to any broad cleavage dimension. The issue may be important, but standing alone it is unlikely to reshape political alignments and party systems.
13. Some might argue that the issue of European integration was a non-issue until recently. Political elites viewed a permissive consensus that allowed them wide

discretion in their actions. As Franklin and van der Eijk wrote: the giant issue of the EU "is not only sleeping, but has been sedated, so that Jack—in the shape of the mainstream parties—can run up and down the European beanstalk at will." Mark Franklin and Cees van der Eijk, *Choosing Europe: The European Electorate and National Politics in the Face of Union*. Ann Arbor: University of Michigan Press, 1995, p. 12. This might have applied to earlier periods. But as the EU giant grew, public attention to the issue also increased and became politicized in the 2000s.

14. Hanspeter Kriesi, Ruud Koopmans, Jan Duyvendak, and Marco Giugni, *New Social Movements in Western Europe*. Minneapolis, MN: University of Minnesota Press, 1985; Russell Dalton and Manfred Kuechler, eds., *Challenging the Political Order: New Social and Political Movements in Western Democracies*. New York: Oxford University Press, 1990.

15. Seymour Martin Lipset, The revolt against modernity. In Per Torsvik, ed., *Mobilization, Center-Periphery Structures and Nation-Building*. Bergen: Universitetsforlaget, 1981.

16. Kriesi et al., *West European Politics in the Age of Globalization*; Silja Häusermann and Hanspeter Kriesi, What do voters want? Dimensions and configurations in individual-level preferences and party choice. In Pablo Beramendi, Silja Häusermann, Herbert Kitschelt, and Hanspeter Kriesi, eds., *The Politics of Advanced Capitalism*. Cambridge: Cambridge University Press, 2015; Vowles and Xezonakis, eds., *Globalization and Domestic Politics*; Liesbet Hooghe and Gary Marks, Cleavage theory meets Europe's crises: Lipset, Rokkan, and the transnational cleavage, *Journal of European Public Policy* (2018) 25: 109–35.

17. Thomas Frank, *What's the Matter with Kansas? How Conservatives Won the Heart of America*. New York, 2004; Justin Gest, *The New Minority: White Working Class Politics in an Age of Immigration and Inequality*. Oxford: Oxford University Press, 2016; Katherine Cramer, *The Politics of Resentment: Rural Consciousness in Wisconsin and the Rise of Scott Walker*. Chicago: University of Chicago Press, 2016; Arlie Hochschild, *Strangers in Their Own Land: Anger and Mourning on the American Right*. New York: New Press, 2016; Goren, *On Voter Competence*.

18. Case Mudde, *Populist Radical Right Parties in Europe*. New York: Cambridge University Press, 2007; Wouter van der Brug and Joost van Spanje, Immigration, Europe and the "New Socio-cultural Dimension," *European Journal of Political Research* (2009) 48: 309–34.

19. Tim Bale, Cinderella and her ugly sisters: The mainstream and extreme right in Europe's bipolarizing party systems, *West European Politics* (2003) 26: 67–90; Tim Bale, Christoffer Green-Pedersen, André Krouwel, Kurt Richard Luther, and Nick Sitter, If you can't beat them, join them? Explaining Social Democratic responses to the challenge from the populist Radical Right in Western Europe, *Political Studies* (2010) 58: 410–26.

20. The 2009 EES found that four-fifth of Europeans endorsed a woman's right to choose, and many nations had liberalized their abortion laws. Thus, abortion rights were a less salient issue in most nations compared to the 1970s.

21. This is essentially the same methodology used in Kriesi et al., *West European Politics in the Age of Globalization*; Silja Häusermann and Hanspeter Kriesi, What do voters

Citizens, Issues, and Political Cleavages

want? Dimensions and configurations in individual-level preferences and party choice. In Pablo Beramendi, Silja Häusermann, Herbert Kitschelt, and Hanspeter Kriesi, eds., *The Politics of Advanced Capitalism*; Simon Bornschier, *Cleavage Politics and the Populist Right. The New Cultural Conflict in Western Europe.* Philadelphia: Temple University Press, 2010.

22. Another latent variable methodology assembles different questions into weighted measures of policy positions over time. The method places other assumptions on the data and comparability over time that are debatable. For examples see Shaun Ratcliff, Shawn Treier, Stanley Feldman, and Simon Jackman, The nature of ideological polarization in the American electorate. Paper presented at the annual meetings of the American Political Science Association, San Francisco, September 2017; Devin Caughey, Tom O'Grady, and Christopher Warshaw, Policy ideology in European mass publics. https://papers.ssrn.com/sol3/papers.cfm?abstract_id=2654216; James Stimson, Vincent Tiberj, and Cyrille Thiébaut, The evolution of policy attitudes in France *European Union Politics* (2012) 13: 293–316.

23. A significant advantage of the EES is that it presents a battery of issues with a common response format. Other studies typically combine issue questions asked throughout a survey with different response formats. A methods effect of question format or placement in the survey can distort relationships.

24. Kaiser's criterion extracts dimensions with an Eigenvalue greater than 1.0. I rotated the extracted dimensions using a Varimax method. I also explored an oblique rotation, but this generates essentially similar results with only weak correlations between the five dimensions in Table 2.1.

25. Romain Lachat and Martin Dolezal, Demand side: Dealignment and realignment of the structural political potentials. In Hanspeter Kriesi et al., *West European Politics in the Age of Globalization.* Cambridge: Cambridge University Press, 2008; Bornschier, *Cleavage Politics and the Populist Right.*

26. Their Eigenvalues in the unrotated analysis were only 1.15 and 1.03 respectively.

27. A common method is confirmatory factor analysis. However, this method looks for statistically significant differences in the structures of opinions. It does not test whether any structural differences produce significant differences in the scores for individuals, which is our primary concern. A higher coefficient for one item and a lower loading for another may produce differences in structure, but summated across all issues the resulting principal component scores might be equivalent.

28. The component scores from the PCA analyses are used as cleavage indices in the subsequent chapters. One advantage of the component scores is that they are weighted combinations of all the available issues, which diminishes the importance of any one issue. In addition, these latent variables produce scores that are more comparable over time even when the specific issues change.

29. Susan Banducci, Mark Franklin, Heiko Giebler, Sara Hobolt, Michael Marsh, Wouter van der Brug, and Cees van der Eijk, eds., *An Audit of Democracy in the European Union.* Florence: European University Institute, 2012. http://www.piredeu.eu/Database/DOCS/PIREDEU_Audit_of_Democracy_2012.pdf.

30. I present only the first two dimensions. An unconstrained principal components analysis identified three dimensions, with a separate gender dimension because of

the multiple gender-related questions in the survey. Russell Dalton, Party representation across multiple issue dimensions, *Party Politics* (2015) 23: 609–22.
31. The ordering of dimensions can be affected by the mix of questions in the issue battery, but whether a cleavage is the first or second dimension is largely irrelevant to the research that follows.
32. The broad patterns of change are consistent with other research: Kriesi et al., *West European Politics in the Age of Globalization*; Hanspeter Kriesi et al., *Political Conflict in Western Europe*. Cambridge: Cambridge University Press, 2012; Swen Hutter, Edgar Grande, and Hanspeter Kriesi, *Politicising Europe: Integration and Mass Politics*. Cambridge: Cambridge University Press, 2016.
33. Andrija Henjak, Political cleavages and socio-economic context: How welfare regimes and historical divisions shape political cleavages, *West European Politics* (2010) 33: 474–504.
34. Caughey, Grady, and Warshaw, Policy ideology in European mass publics, 1981–2014, find a similar tendency for Northern European nations to be more culturally liberal than the South. However, their emphasis on a strong North–South on the economic cleavage is less apparent in these analyses or the 2014 EES results in Figure 2.3.
35. Dalton, *Citizen Politics*, ch. 6.
36. Luxembourg also shows a significant shift. However, the 1979 sample comprised only 300 individuals and thus is a less reliable estimate.
37. I would downplay focusing on the location of any single nation in the cross-national figures because of changes in the questions asked and the specific national contexts at the time of the survey, but the overall patterns are clear.
38. Russell Dalton, Scott Flanagan, and Paul Beck, eds., *Electoral Change in Advanced Industrial Democracies*. Princeton: Princeton University Press, 1984.
39. Albert Einstein, On the method of theoretical physics. *Philosophy of Science* (1934) 1: 163–9.
40. Oddbjørn Knutsen, *Social Structure, Value Orientations and Party Choice in Western Europe*. London: Palgrave, 2017; Jonathan Wheatley, Identifying latent policy dimensions from public opinion data: An inductive approach, *Journal of Elections, Public Opinion and Parties* (2015) 25: 215–33; Dalton, Party representation across multiple issue dimensions; Ryan Bakker, Seth Jolly, and Jonathan Polk, Complexity in the European party space: Exploring dimensionality with experts, *European Union Politics* (2012) 13: 219–45.
41. At the same time, there are obviously other country-specific factors at work, such as regional–national divisions in Belgium, Britain, and Spain, or the East–West cleavage in unified Germany. These are important, but do not diminish the value of economics and culture as a common political framework. In addition, the literature discusses the statistical independence of these two dimensions: Lachat and Dolezal, Demand side. There is no definitive evidence because the relationship between both dimensions is partly a function of the selection of issues in a survey, and that changes over time. I used an oblimin rotation to estimate the correlation in the two-dimensional model. There was little change between 1979 ($r = 0.085$) and 2009 (0.087), but a stronger correlation in 2014 (0.204).

42. Vowles and Xezonakis, eds., *Globalization and Domestic Politics*; Rohrschneider and Whitefield, *The Strain of Representation*; Kriesi et al., *West European Politics in the Age of Globalization*.
43. Hooghe and Marks, Cleavage theory meets Europe's crises; Bakker, Jolly, and Polk, Complexity in the European party space.
44. Kriesi et al., *Political Conflict in Western Europe*; Kriesi et al., *West European Politics in the Age of Globalization*.

3

The Social Distribution of Cleavage Positions

Édouard studied philosophy at École Normale Supérieure in Paris, which led to a career as a writer. He is successful, liberal, and gay. His political loyalties in the 2017 French presidential elections clearly lay on the left. At the same time, many of his family openly supported Marine Le Pen in the elections. There is a sharp culture clash in the same family. This generational and economic clash exists in most affluent democracies. What makes Édouard unusual is that he wrote an autobiographical novel about his family's history.[1] His parents had limited education, and his father worked in the local manufacturing plant until he was injured on the job and placed on disability benefits. His father became angry as social benefits decreased, the plant closed down, the town struggled, immigration increased, and he felt marginalized in his own town. Édouard's youth was a battle with poverty and prejudice, and only fortuitous chance led him to an academic career and professional success. But he left behind a family mired in the other France, which might be similar to those in other affluent democracies. In 2017 many of these people saw Le Pen as a figure who would help invisible people like themselves (or Trump in the United States or Brexit in the UK). Édouard's story is painfully paralleled by J. D. Vance's family autobiography in the United States.[2] These works give a literary insight into the process of cultural/economic change and those who reject the changes.

I am neither endorsing the political views of Le Pen supporters nor Édouard Louis's broad criticism of contemporary French society; this example illustrates that people's social conditions often influence their political views in divergent ways. If we can describe the social distribution of opinions on political cleavages, we can better interpret the sources, meaning, and implications of those opinions.

Research examining the economic cleavage is rich and extensive. It provides a wealth of material from which to theorize on how citizens' social characteristics may shape their cleavage positions. Similarly, the emergence of a liberal cultural perspective, and more recently a conservative cultural position, generated more research on the social bases of the cultural cleavage.

This chapter locates citizens on the economic and cultural cleavage using several factors. Initially, I consider the social characteristics that might describe someone's social interests and their participation in distinct social group networks. While the results are not always novel, they provide a foundation for understanding these cleavages and how alignments have changed over time. Then the chapter considers the relationship between political values, such as Left–Right attitudes, postmaterial values, and political support and these two cleavages.

Political Cleavages and Social Structures

Seymour Lipset and Stein Rokan's study of social and political alignments maintains that cleavages identify the major competing interests in society, and this provides the basis for partisan alignments to represent those interests in politics.[3] Or in the common vernacular: Where a person sits socially determines where they stand politically. This section describes the social bases of the economic and cultural cleavages, and the realignment of social group positions over time.

The Economic Cleavage

There is an extensive research literature on the social bases of economic issues. The natural starting point is social class, but there are many different class definitions. The changing economic bases of advanced industrial societies have reshaped the traditional Marxist view of a dichotomous class structure. The separation of management from capital ownership and the expansion of the service sector have created an expanding new social stratum. Various authors describe this stratum as the "new middle class," "white-collar workers," the "salariat," or "socio-cultural professionals." Richard Florida identified a special subset of the new middle class as "knowledge workers," those who make their livelihood on the creation and use of information and are typically the vanguard of liberal cultural views.[4] The growth of government (and nonprofit) employment also produces a public sector that exists outside of the market and is thus subject to different economic contexts.[5] Especially relevant to our interests is Herbert Kitschelt's work.[6] He distinguishes between the market aspects of occupation, the skill levels involved, and the nature of the work experience. Evans and Tilley offer a similar expansion of the class framework to theoretically differentiate groups within the working class and middle class.[7] These latter two sources provide a template for our analyses to the extent they can be measured with the EES.

The EES asks a multi-category question on the respondent's occupation, but without the detail necessary to tap the finer class distinctions of previous class studies. The middle class is divided into several subcategories, such as executives, professionals, and white-collar workers. The working class can be divided by the skill level required by their job. Still, this should be sufficient to judge the broad relationship between occupation and the economic cleavage over time.

Prior research suggests that business owners and high-level professionals should lean toward market-oriented positions that benefit them individually. Conversely, the working class would favor more state control of the economy and society.[8]

Income is another standard measure of social status position. Research generally finds that high earners favor market-oriented policies, while low earners favor state intervention especially in providing social benefits and economic security for the less affluent. For example, Knutsen showed that income and occupation displayed almost the same correlation with Left–Right economic positions in a recent European Values Survey.[9] Income is not asked in either the 2009 or 2014 EES. Consequently, for the longitudinal comparisons, I use questions on subjective economic well-being that are asked in a somewhat comparable form in all three surveys.[10]

At least partly because education levels overlap with income and occupation, the highly educated traditionally leaned toward the conservative pole on the economic cleavage. Knutsen found this in an earlier analysis of the 1979 EES.[11] However, more recent analyses of the economic positions using cross-section surveys found weak correlations with education.[12] And historically, the better educated tend to support conservative parties, while the less educated supported Labour or social democratic parties; but this voting pattern has eroded over time.[13] So I would expect education effects to wane over time.

In theory, union membership should be another relevant measure of social status. Given the political position of most unions on the economic cleavage, their members should generally echo their support for state control of markets and greater welfare spending. The union membership question was not asked in the 1979 EES. By the time of the 2009 and 2014 surveys, the membership rates of unions had declined considerably from its post-WWII high. The distribution of union membership also shifted from manual workers in manufacturing to white-collar employment in public sector unions. So the historic influence of union membership might have attenuated over time.

The Cultural Cleavage

The cultural cleavage identified in Chapter 2 includes a diverse mix of issues, tapping themes of immigration, gender equality, gay rights, opinions of the European Union, and privacy versus social order. These issues contrast the agenda of progressive social interests versus a preference for traditional values and lifestyles that are challenged by social modernization and cultural change. Consequently, the social base of the cultural cleavage should be distinct from the economic cleavage.

Religious values and religiosity should affect several aspects of the cultural cleavage. One aspect of religiosity is subjective feelings of being religious, the importance of religion, and similar measures.[14] The second aspect of religiosity is participation in formal religions, such as attending church regularly, or belonging to a religious organization. Each of the EES surveys contains some measure of religiosity, albeit with different questions across the three waves.[15]

Stratos Patrikios and Georgios Xezonakis argued that globalization increased the strength of religious voting in nations with highly globalized economies.[16] I think this is a spurious relationship, and the driving force for contemporary religious voting is its linkage to the broader cultural cleavage. Given Christian morals and traditions in Western Europe, religiosity should be negatively correlated with issues such as gay rights, a progressive role for women, and other traditional lifestyle issues. These sentiments may also influence attitudes toward authority as part of the cultural cleavage. Conversely, secular citizens are typically more supportive of the libertarian aspects of the cultural cleavage. Recent analyses of similar value dimensions found that secular respondents were more liberal on libertarian–authoritarian attitudes, moral issues, and even attitudes toward immigrants.[17]

Social status characteristics also have potential relevance to the cultural cleavage. A long-established literature argues that manual workers hold conservative cultural values as a consequence of their social position and the social authority relations in their occupation and life experiences.[18] There is a complementary literature that addresses the cultural orientations of various middle-class occupations. Professionals in knowledge-related and interpersonal-oriented fields tend to be strong advocates for liberal cultural positions.[19] Conversely, business owners and managers are often embedded in hierarchic authority structures, focused on economic outcomes, and are more conservative in their cultural positions. The large mass of salaried white-collar workers seems to locate a middle position on the cultural cleavage.

Education has different implications for the cultural cleavage than for the economic cleavage. Educational level is often an indirect indicator of values that are related to the cultural cleavage: tolerance, acceptance of diversity, and openness to change. Norman Nie, Jane Junn, and Kenneth Stehlik-Barry saw higher education as the basis of a democratically enlightened citizenry, and education is a strongly linked to postmaterial values.[20] Highly educated individuals also have more social resources and occupy occupational positions that may diminish their concern about immigrants; higher SES individuals generally benefit most economically from globalization. Thus, contemporary

53

research generally shows that education has a stronger relationship with cultural values than with economic positions.[21]

As the cultural cleavage has grown in importance, this yields uncertain predictions of the overall partisan impact of social status.[22] If economic concerns predominate, then higher social status individuals may focus on their conservative economic tendencies. If cultural concerns predominate, this may moderate their traditional economic positions as they emphasize their liberal cultural positions. Consequently, it is unclear how the mix of contrasting views is reconciled when citizens have to make a single party choice on Election Day.

The forces of social modernization should also appear in age differences in political attitudes. The young are socialized in a new and changing world, and more readily accept new cultural norms. Thus, younger generations have more readily embraced environmental values, changing gender roles, and the diversity of individual lifestyles. In contrast, their elders often look back to a more tranquil past, or their images of a more tranquil past, when confronted by a society undergoing rapid cultural change. Thus, research shows that successive younger generations are more likely to have postmaterial values and libertarian orientations linked to these values.[23]

Two other social characteristics are potentially relevant to the cultural cleavage. Critical reactions to cultural change often seem strongest in rural areas where traditional lifestyles and values predominate.[24] Several recent qualitative works on rural populations in Europe and the United States provide insights into this cultural orientation.[25] Farmers may be among the best examples of this cultural view, and their opinions potentially generalize to a larger rural population. Conversely, urban life is more diverse and cosmopolitan, and thus may be more likely to endorse a liberal cultural agenda. Another possible factor is gender. Gender equality issues might attract women to locate themselves toward the liberal end of the cultural cleavage. However, Knutsen recently showed that women still tend to be more supportive of religious values, but there are only modest gender differences on other value dimensions.[26]

The Social Correlates of Political Cleavages

The changing social and economic conditions in affluent democracies should have affected the interests and values of various social groups. Thus, the changing cleavage structure should be visible in the political locations of social groups as they respond to these new social and political conditions. In a single election or a single nation, extraneous factors may come into play: the exceptional appeal of (or aversion to) a political leader, a political crisis or scandal, or similar events. To map the broad structure of political cleavages,

The Social Distribution of Cleavage Positions

this chapter focuses on the pooled patterns for European democracies (see Chapter 4 for country-level results). This pooled analysis should minimize the effects of extraneous factors and illustrate which political alignments have generally weakened or realigned.

I used the scores from the PCAs in Chapter 2 to calculate citizen positions on both cleavages; these scores are normally distributed and both cleavages are statistically independent.[27] This method also means that citizen positions are not dependent on a small number of issues, which can vary across time and nations, but reflect broader political values that transcend specific issues. Several recent studies have argued that multiple issue indices provide a more valid measure of the underlying cleavage positions and of citizens's political motivations.[28] Comparisons based on single issues or a sequential comparison of single issues are less reliable measures of opinions, and more subject to short-term influences.

Table 3.1 presents the correlations between socio-economic variables and scores on the economic and cultural cleavages. As hypothesized, social status traits are important for both the economic and cultural positions of Europeans. The Eta correlations for occupation are roughly comparable for both cleavages in 1979, and the economic cleavage correlation changes only modestly in the two more recent surveys. In contrast, the correlation between occupation and cultural cleavage increases markedly in 2009 and 2014. Education seems to follow a parallel course, with small differences on the economic cleavage across all three surveys. At the same time, the education gap for the cultural cleavage realigns and increases substantially in the two later EES surveys, with the better-educated holding distinctly liberal cultural positions. Higher education thus becomes a distinct marker of cultural liberalism.[29] Geoffrey Evans and James Tilley

Table 3.1. Social Status Correlates of the Economic and Cultural Cleavages

	1979		2009		2014	
Predictor	Economic Cleavage	Cultural Cleavage	Economic Cleavage	Cultural Cleavage	Economic Cleavage	Cultural Cleavage
Occupation*	0.11	0.14	0.14	0.27	0.08	0.25
Union member	–	–	−0.07	−0.20	0.06	0.09
Income quintile	−0.08	−0.07	–	–	–	–
Education	−0.03	−0.03	−0.06	0.34	−0.01	0.25
Subjective well-being	0.02	0.07	−0.09	0.14	−0.06	0.11
Age	−0.08	−0.12	−0.06	−0.25	−0.02	−0.21
Religiosity	−0.02	−0.24	−0.09	−0.31	–	–
Church attendance	–	–	−0.12	−0.27	−0.08	−0.15
Gender (female)	0.02	0.05	0.05	0.02	0.02	0.01
Large town	0.00	0.08	0.03	0.08	0.03	0.08

Note: Table entries are Pearson r correlations except for occupation (Eta correlation); positive values on cleavage indices are liberal positions. Dash means the variable was not available in the survey.

Sources: 1979, 2009, and 2014 European Election Surveys, established democracies.

have compiled a rich time series evidence for Britain, which shows a clear education gap on various cultural issues dating back to the 1960s and widening over time.[30]

To illustrate the realignment of occupational groups across these decades, Figure 3.1 presents the cleavage scores for occupation groups in both the 1979 and 2014 EES.[31] In 1979, occupational groups held fairly similar liberal/conservative views on both cleavages. Middle-class respondents—professionals, business owners, executives, and managers—expressed conservative views on economics and culture. In contrast, manual workers and the unemployed voiced liberal views on both cleavages. Even though the two scores are statistically independent, the distribution of both cleavage positions follows a Left–Right pattern.

By 2014 the economic cleavage has undergone a significant realignment.[32] Professionals, executives, and business managers have moderated their conservative views of the economic cleavage, perhaps a sign of a collectivist consensus eroding social class differences. Manual workers and the unemployed still favor a more activist state, but only slightly.

In contrast, class patterns on the cultural cleavage have shifted in significant ways. Professionals and executives are now very liberal on the cultural cleavage reflecting their advocacy on these issues and the separation of economics from culture. Many of these individuals would fall into what Richard Florida calls the creative class—a vanguard for cultural change. Equally important, the opposition to cultural change is now concentrated among business owners (the classic bourgeoisie),[33] farmers, manual workers, and the unemployed.

The EES codes occupation into broad categories, so we cannot examine the finer detail that would be required to test Florida's concept of the creative class or Kitschelt's framework of occupational categories. For the 2014 EES, however, I can expand the comparison to the occupation groups coded in the survey (Figure 3.2). The figure plots the average score of each occupational category on the cultural cleavage and the size of the bubble reflects the relative size of the group in the EU sample.

Students are, unsurprisingly, the most culturally liberal group in Europe, but they are closely followed by professional and middle-management executives. Top-level managers and desk-bound white-collar workers are also cultural liberals. Conversely, farmers, the retired, and shop owners are the most culturally conservative occupational groups. Homemakers are also cultural conservatives, as well as skilled and unskilled manual workers. A diverse set of factors—income, credentials, the content of work, and others—shape the cultural implications of occupation. And in overall terms, the class cleavage in contemporary Europe is much stronger on the cultural cleavage than for economic issues.[34] This is striking evidence of how class groups have realigned on the cultural cleavage to cut across the traditional working-class/middle-class divide.

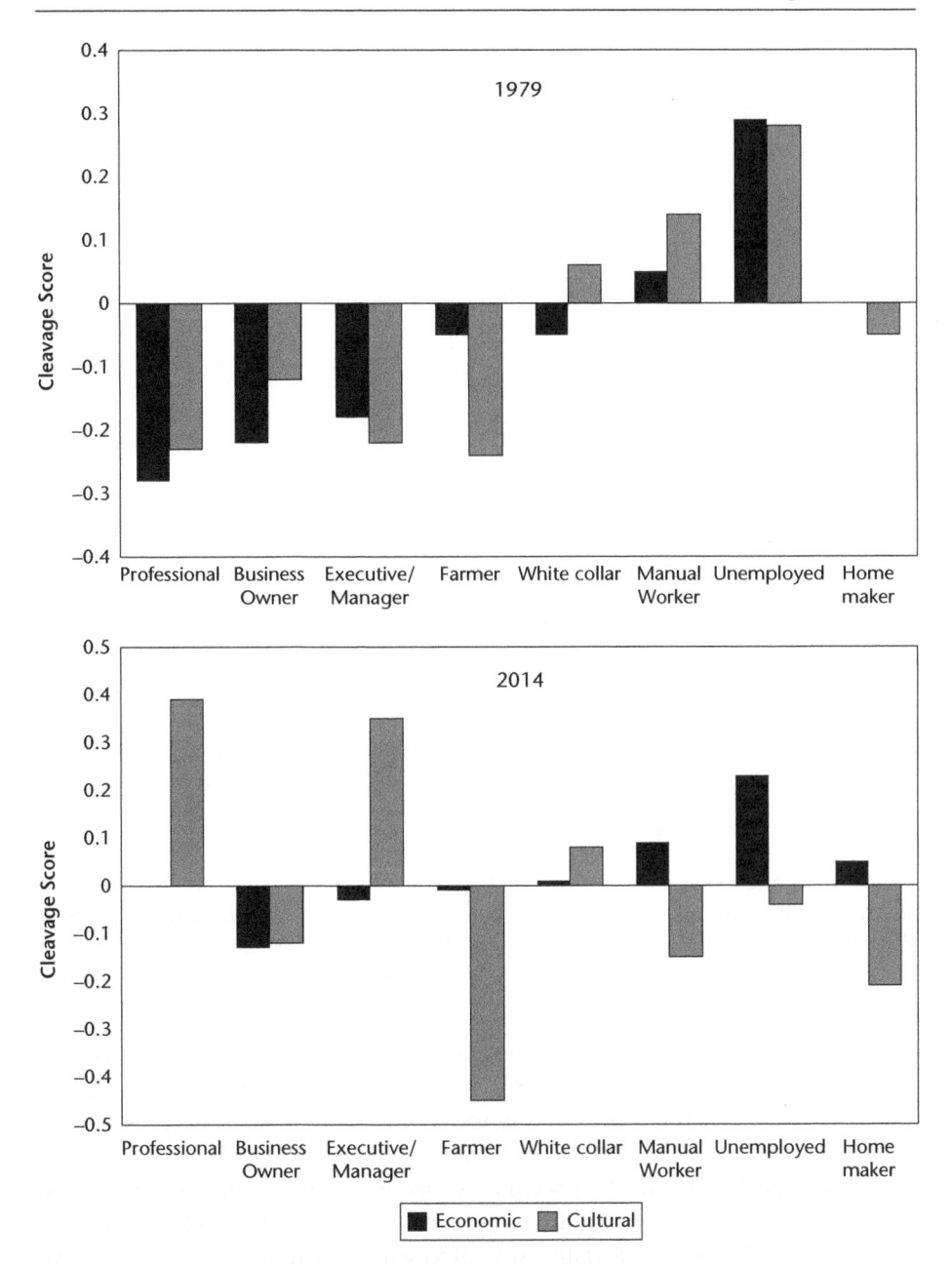

The Social Distribution of Cleavage Positions

Figure 3.1. Occupation and Cleavage Positions, 1979 and 2014

Note: Figure entries are mean scores on the cleavage dimensions; positive values are liberal positions.

Source: 1979 and 2014 European Election Study, established democracies.

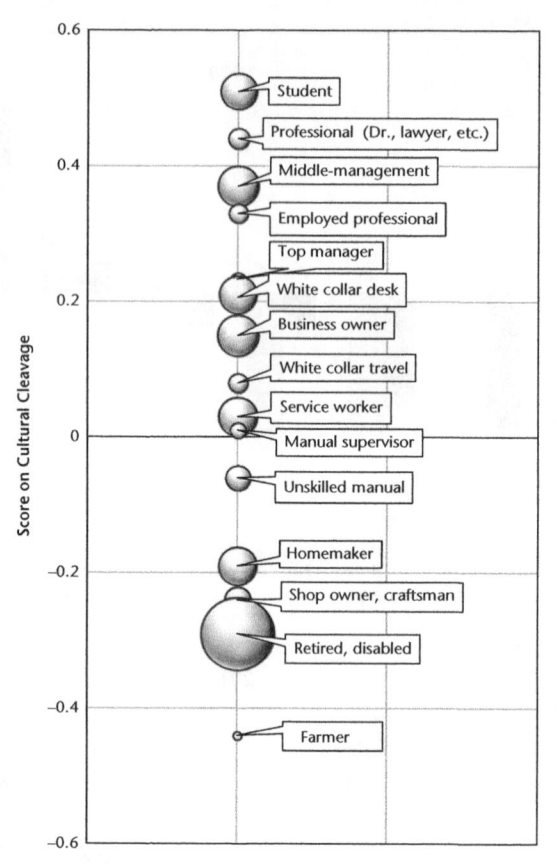

Figure 3.2. Detailed Occupation and Cultural Cleavage Position, 2014
Note: Figure entries are mean scores on the cultural cleavage dimensions; positive values are liberal positions. The size of the bubble reflects the size of the group in the EU15 sample.
Source: 2014 European Election Study, EU15 nations.

The lower half of Table 3.1 examines other theorized correlates of cleavage positions. Over this thirty-five year span, the age gap on the economic cleavage narrowed slightly, while differences on the cultural cleavage widened. Millennials are now one of the clearest social bases of liberal cultural attitudes. Another important correlate is secular versus religious orientations. Measured either in terms of feelings of religiosity or the frequency of church attendance, higher religiosity is substantially correlated with cultural attitudes in the two recent surveys.

To better illustrate citizen positions in this two-dimensional political space, Figure 3.3 plots the positions of several distinctive social groups on both cleavages in 1979 and 2014. In the 1979 survey, social class groups followed their long-standing Left–Right alignment along the economic cleavage.

Figure 3.3. Location of Social Groups in the Cleavage Space, 1979 and 2014

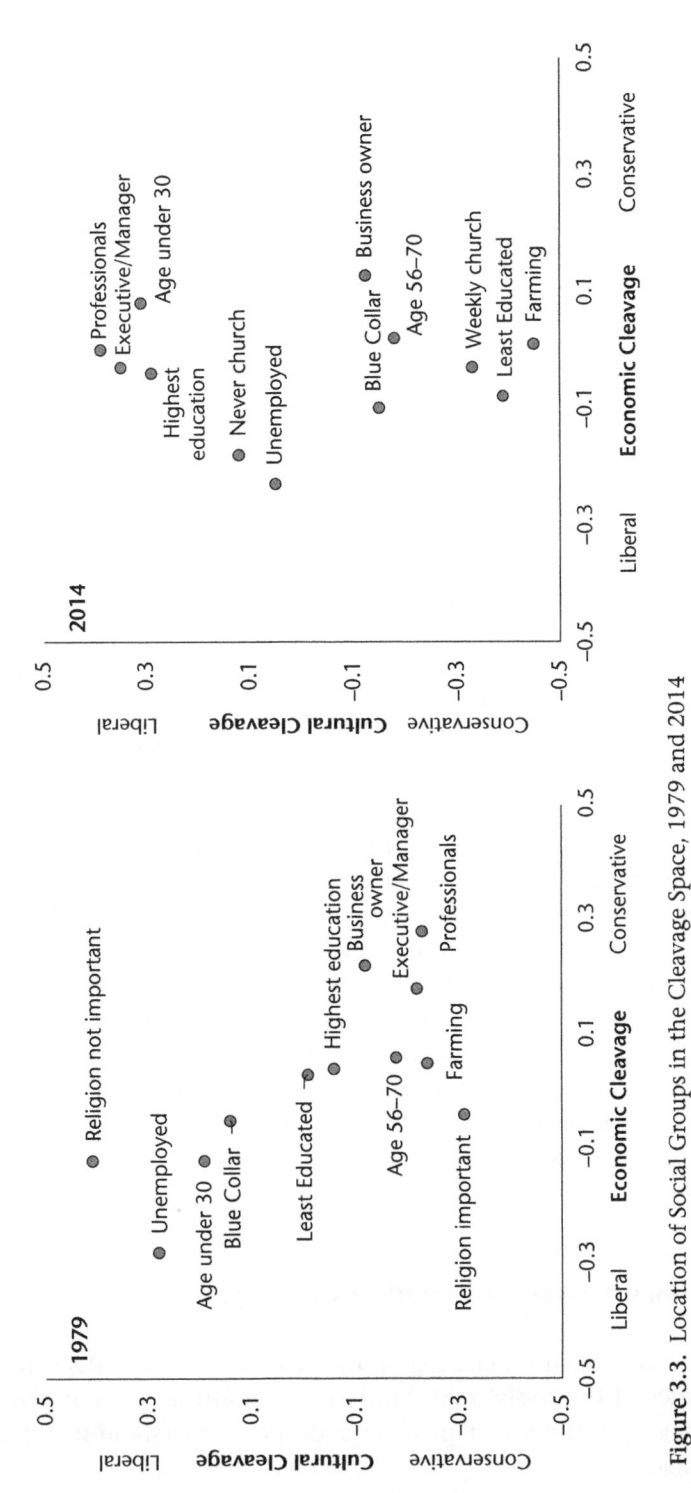

Note: Figure entries are mean scores for social groups on the two cleavage dimensions. The economic cleavage has been transformed from Figure 3.1 so that liberal positions appear on the left of the figure.

Source: 1979 and 2014 European Election Study, EU9 and EU15 nations respectively.

Executives, managers and professionals, and business owners all scored toward the conservative economic position, along with business owners. These middle-class groups also held conservative cultural positions as the two cleavages partially overlapped in political debates.[35] By 2014 there are only modest class-based differences in economic positions. Business owners lean toward market-oriented policies, while the other middle-class groups have moved toward the center on the economic cleavage. In both surveys, manual workers lean slightly toward a more liberal position on the economic cleavage. But these middle-class/working-class differences are quite modest by 2014.

At the same time, social status characteristics realign along the cultural cleavage. Several higher social status occupations—professionals, executives, and managers—shifted from opposition in 1979 to support for liberal cultural positions by 2014. In contrast, manual workers shifted from a liberal to a conservative position on the cultural cleavage—sharing the values of business owners.

One of the most marked changes is the increased polarization of educational groups along the cultural cleavage. The education gap was minimal in 1979, but the more highly educated are now strong advocates for modernization and the liberal social norms it encourages. The less educated are strong supporters of conservative cultural values.

The young and non-religious also lean more clearly toward liberal cultural values by 2014, with older and religious citizens at the other end of this cleavage. The religious cleavage is a long-term and fairly stable correlate of positions on the cultural cleavage.[36] The age gap actually widens over this timespan as generational change generates support for cultural liberalism.

Taken altogether, the shift in social group patterns over these thirty-five years indicates a significant realignment in the social base of political cleavages. Competition on the economic cleavage once structured political debate and party politics in Europe, but social divisions on this cleavage have narrowed. This is not to say that this cleavage is unimportant for party choice (see Chapter 7), but only that issue opinions are no longer strongly linked to social class positions.[37] Conversely, the widening social gaps along the cultural cleavage reshape the space of political competition and social group locations within this space.

The Attitudinal Correlates of Political Cleavages

Beyond social characteristics, cleavage positions should also reflect the values and attitudes of the individual. Moreover, the attitudinal correlates of citizens' cleavage positions can provide a deeper understanding of both political cleavages.

The Social Distribution of Cleavage Positions

A key theoretical question is whether either cleavage reflects images of the functioning of government and the democratic process more broadly. As contentious politics has become more common in affluent democracies, there are recurring waves of critical challenges to the government. The U.S. Tea Party and Occupy Wall Street movements were both critical of democratic governance, as well as voices for specific issue positions. The Anonymous movement in Spain, UKIP in Britain, or Syriza in Greece expressed anti-elite or anti-government positions that extended beyond their policy demands.

In addition, evaluations of governments and the democratic process can reflect citizens' images of who are the winners and losers politically, although this can be a complex calculation. The basic logic is that if citizens who favor an activist state see government policy moving in their direction, they will be more positive toward government. In contrast, if those with a market preference see public policy as less favorable to their positions, they will evaluate the government more critically. This might vary with the specific composition of the government in power, but the pooled EU analyses describe the broad cross-national images of the "winners" and "losers" and how this varies across the two political cleavages.

The EES includes several questions on support for democracy and governments. The first panel of Table 3.2 presents the correlations between satisfaction with the working of the nation's democracy and cleavage positions. In 1979, Europeans who were satisfied with the performance of the democratic system were more likely to hold conservative positions on both cleavages. For instance, among the most conservative quintile on the economic cleavage, about 60 percent were satisfied with the working of democracy, compared to only 40 percent among the most liberal quartile.[38] By 2009, however,

Table 3.2. Attitudinal Correlates of the Economic and Cultural Cleavages

	1979		2009		2014	
Predictor	Economic Cleavage	Cultural Cleavage	Economic Cleavage	Cultural Cleavage	Economic Cleavage	Cultural Cleavage
Satisfaction with democracy	−0.12	−0.12	−0.12	0.06	−	−
Government concern about citizens	−	−	−0.09	0.06	−0.07	0.21
Approve government record	−	−	−0.12	0.01	−0.09	0.08
Past economy positive	−	−	−0.08	−0.01	−0.05	0.19
Future economy positive	−	−	−0.01	0.04	−0.02	0.19
Left–Right position	0.29	0.32	0.21	0.27	0.28	0.29

Note: Table entries are Pearson r correlations; positive values on cleavage indices are liberal positions. A dash means the variable was not available in the survey.
Sources: 1979, 2009, and 2014 European Election Surveys, established democracies.

the pattern has changed—those most satisfied with government are still conservative on the economic cleavage, but they are now liberal on the cultural cleavage. This pattern might vary across nations according to policy histories and the partisan composition of the incumbent government (see Chapter 4), but an overall shift in these relationships has occurred across European democracies.[39]

Two other political support questions tap opinions in the 2009 and 2014 surveys. The relationship between political support and liberal economic positions remained relatively constant. Economic liberals were less likely to think that the government cared about the citizens or was performing well. The reasonable explanation is that economic liberals were reacting to the negative consequences of the recession, leading to critical evaluations of government performance. Conversely, cultural liberals express more support for the government on both questions. This relationship strengthens between the 2009 and 2014 surveys. Taken together, these two patterns suggest that Europeans generally see their government as leaning toward economic conservatism and cultural liberalism, and so governments were positively evaluated by those who held those positions.

The current literature on populism also links the economic problems following from the 2008 recession to the mobilization of economic discontents, such as the Occupy Wall Street protests in the United States or comparable economic protests across Europe.[40] The losers of globalization became vocal in politics and in a series of high profile election outcomes. In addition, the rationale that the economic losers in globalization are the base of New Right parties should show up in feelings of economic discontent.

The next two rows of Table 3.2 present the correlations of retrospective (past) and prospective (future) perceptions of the national economy with the two cleavage dimensions. These questions are only available in the 2009 and 2014 survey, but the results are still intriguing. In both surveys, people who have a positive view of the economy—past or future—tend to be economic conservatives. Their positive views of the market principle, as well as their generally higher socio-economic status, may carry over to their evaluations of economic performance. At the least, this is somewhat ironic in the context of the post-2008 financial difficulties in Europe, when market forces had failed.

In 2009 the relationships between perceptions of the economy and cultural positions are weak and vary in direction. By 2014, however, there are strong correlations for both past ($r = 0.19$) and future economic views ($r = 0.19$). In other words, the economic optimists embrace cultural liberalism. And when the financial crisis in Europe stimulated economic worries, concerned citizens seemed to link these sentiments to broader cultural clashes more than to the economic system. This merits future analysis with better longitudinal evidence.

Many studies use Left–Right as a summary of a person's position on the issues salient to them, and then extend this analysis to political parties and even governments.[41] A persistent question is the relative weight of various issues or political cleavages in determining Left–Right orientations. In a prior analysis of the 1979 EES, Ronald Inglehart found that Left–Right attitudes were strongly correlated with issues that tapped both economic and cultural topics. He concluded, "In other words, our strongest indicators of *both* dimensions seem to have the greatest impact on whether the individual views himself/herself as located on the Left or Right."[42]

Since then the research literature has continued to debate the relative weight of these two cleavages is structuring Left–Right orientations, and the EES provides a base for a more extensive longitudinal comparison. The last row in Table 3.2 shows strong correlations between Left–Right attitudes and both cleavages from 1979 until 2014, with some variability that might be attributable to the different issue questions in each survey. Even beginning in the late 1970s, cultural issues were a substantial aspect of the Left–Right continuum, very closely paralleling the relationship for the economic cleavage.[43]

At the same time, equal correlations between political cleavages and Left–Right do not mean that this balance applies evenly across the entire population. We expect some individuals to emphasize economic matters as the basis for their broader Left–Right positions, while others will place more stress on the cultural dimension.

The Social Roots of Cleavage Positions

The individual traits examined here inevitably overlap to some extent. Education levels are related to age and occupations. Religiosity is also correlated with age. To bring these distinct, but sometimes overlapping, influences together and determine their independent effects, I developed a multivariate model predicting cleavage positions.

Table 3.3 presents the results of ordinary least squares (OLS) regression analyses in all three EES surveys. Not all variables of interest are available in all surveys, but I assembled equivalent measures over time. I excluded Left–Right attitudes because the causal directions among these attitudes is ambiguous. In addition, Left–Right attitudes also reflect some of these same social characteristics and thus would subsume their impact in multivariate analyses. The models exclude economic perceptions because a comparable measure was not available for 1979.

I focus on the 1979 and 2014 results because the measures are more comparable and this displays the full longitudinal patterns. In 1979, economic orientations were only weakly tied to the social characteristics of citizens.

Political Realignment

Table 3.3. Multivariate Models Predicting the Economic and Cultural Cleavages

Predictor	1979 Economic Cleavage	1979 Cultural Cleavage	2009 Economic Cleavage	2009 Cultural Cleavage	2014 Economic Cleavage	2014 Cultural Cleavage
Managers	−0.02*	−0.03	−0.03*	0.03*	−0.02	0.03*
Business owner	−0.05*	−0.02	−0.04*	−0.01	−0.04*	−0.03*
Manual worker	0.01	0.05*	0.10*	−0.08*	0.01	−0.05*
Education	−0.04*	−0.05*	−0.03*	0.23*	0.01	0.14*
Subjective well-being	−0.01	0.06*	−0.04*	0.04*	−0.04*	0.06*
Age	−0.07*	−0.07*	−0.05*	−0.16*	0.01	−0.17*
Religiosity	−0.01	−0.23*	−0.10*	−0.24*	0.09*	−0.13*
Gender (female)	0.02	0.08*	0.08*	0.05*	0.02*	0.05*
Political support	−0.11*	−0.08*	−0.16*	0.12*	−0.05*	0.16*
Multiple R	0.15	0.29	0.24	0.48	0.13	0.37

Note: Table entries are standardized regression coefficients; positive values on cleavage indices are liberal positions. An asterisk denotes a relationship at 0.05 significance level.
Sources: 1979, 2009, and 2014 European Election Surveys, established democracies.

Professionals, business owners, and the more educated are slightly more conservative and the working class is more liberal. The strongest predictor is political support—satisfaction with the way democracy works—with satisfied citizens expressing more conservative economic attitudes.[44]

The predictors of cultural attitudes follow a different pattern in 1979. On the one hand, the social status and age tendencies are the same as on the economic cleavage, in part because of the partial overlap of liberal/conservative opinions on both cleavages in 1979. On the other hand, religiosity is a strong single predictor of cultural attitudes, even though only a single issue in the battery of items taps a religious topic (abortion).[45] The signs of culture clash were apparent even in 1979.

By the 2009 and 2014 surveys, relatively little had changed in terms of the economic cleavage. There was a slight, albeit insignificant, decline in the impact of social status measures on economic cleavage positions. And in general, weak social group differences in 1979 were repeated in these later surveys.

However, several social groups realigned along the cultural cleavage. Higher educated Europeans became distinctly more liberal on the cultural cleavage, rivaling the conservative impact of religiosity that worked in the opposite direction. Business managers (and professionals) began to lean toward cultural liberalism, and manual workers shifted toward cultural conservatism. The age gradient also widened, with the young shifting heavily toward cultural liberalism (see also Figure 3.2). Equally significant, political satisfaction was positively related to cultural liberalism in these two surveys, a reversal of the pattern in 1979. This produces a substantial realignment in the social base of the cultural cleavage that is focused on the advocates of social modernization, the better-educated, upper middle class, and the young—even while statistically controlling for the overlapping effects of each variable.

Social Positions and Political Cleavages

In 1979, a new cultural cleavage was emerging in Europeans' political thinking. Like prior cycles of social change and reactions to the modernization process, the issues of environmental protection, gender equality, expanding democracy, and social justice challenged the political status quo. But public opinion surveys at the time noted the inchoate nature of these issues, yet with the potential for a new political cleavage developing in the future. For example, my colleagues and I wrote:[46]

> Even if a process of political change has been set in motion, the long-term partisan consequences of this trend remain unclear. Part of this uncertainty arises because a distinct new basis of ideological cleavage has not yet emerged. Issue positions are not always consistently or coherently presented.... This situation may change as new parties and social groups emerge to represent and articulate these new issue interests and integrate them into a coherent ideological program.

At first, opinions on these new cultural issues often overlapped with traditional economic alignments.

Over time, however, this causal process developed. New Social Movements and new Green parties established this cultural cleavage as distinct from economic issues—and new issues were integrated into this cleavage. Counter groups mobilized to represent contrasting positions. As this study has demonstrated, by the new millennium the cultural cleavage is clearly evident in Europeans' political orientations. At the same time, many of the traditional concerns of the economic cleavage persist, often with new issue expressions of the underlying cleavage.

Tracking the positions of social groups over time and across the pooled set of European democracies provides a reference structure for understanding the broad impact of these modernization forces. Social groups are markers of the self-interests of individuals, such as the contrasting interest of class groupings. Social groups also identify the social networks to which individuals belong, and thus the political cues they experience. And more importantly, social groups can reflect the political values of their members that shape positions along both the economic and cultural cleavages.

The EES time series shows that a realignment in social group positions accompanied the emergence of the cultural cleavage. The traditionally conservative highly educated and those employed as professionals and managers moderated their economic positions; these groups became strong advocates for liberal cultural issues. Similarly, small age differences on the cultural cleavage widened over the thirty-five year span of the EES data. Millennials provide the strongest support for cultural themes such as gender equality, LGBTQ rights, tolerance of immigrants, and other issues. Cultural conservatives also are prominent among the religious sectors of society, while cultural liberals are decidedly more secular. Moreover, social groups are now more polarized on the cultural cleavage than the economic cleavage in all three EES surveys (Table 3.3).

The roots of this cultural cleavage are not short-term reactions to strife over EU policies, concerns about the post-2008 financial difficulties, or even reactions to a growing number of immigrants in Europe. Rather, these patterns mirror what should appear if the cultural cleavage represents the wider tensions between the advocates of liberal social modernization and the conservative reaction to defend a retrospective image of society.

While I expect these broad relationships between social position and cleavage position to continue going forward, this is different from the group bases of politics in Lipset and Rokkan's terms.[47] First, the traditional occupational, religious, and regional group networks provided an organizational base for previous cleavages. The typical British manual worker belonged to a labor union, spent time with his mates at the local pub, lived among his co-workers in council housing, and received political information and political cues through this network. Similarly, the typical Bavarian Catholic attended church each Sunday, belonged to Catholic social groups, perhaps had children in a Catholic school, and received information and political cues through this network. When Election Day approached, the unions, churches, and other institutionalized groups persuaded and mobilized their members on how they should vote. This model of a stable, bounded social community is fading in contemporary societies.

Second, the predictors of support for liberal cultural values tend to be concentrated in social groups that lack this fixed, institutional structure. For example, the younger generation supports liberal cultural values and senior citizens are cultural conservatives. But there are no national associations of millennials to organize social life, create institutionalized networks, and mobilize young voters. An organization to mobilize older citizens faces some of the same challenges, plus every year a significant number of their current members are leaving the electorate. Similarly, there are professional associations for business owners and various middle-class occupations, but these have less political sway than labor unions, and there is no association devoted to one of the most culturally liberal groups: the highly educated.

Thus, political cleavages are increasingly based on common issue interests rather than formal group alignments, because social group structures are more fluid and less institutionalized in contemporary society. As a result, cleavage alignments may be more susceptible to change if the political context changes, and thus less predictable than the group-based cleavages of the past.

And yet, the cultural cleavage today may not require a formal group basis like past cleavages. In more networked and sophisticated contemporary societies, the cleavage itself might create a political identity. New Social Movements and other citizen groups provide abundant political cues on the issues of the day. Facebook posts and Twitter feeds from like-minded friends are more constant than the communication networks of labor unions or churches. And an increasingly diverse media allow individuals to create an information environment that can frame their view of the world. These informal networks are becoming denser and denser, and can fulfill the theoretical requirements of defining interests and recognition of these interests that was part of the foundation of tradition, group-based social cleavages. If this occurs, issue-based cleavage politics can be less institutionalized but also more enduring.

Notes

1. Édouard Louis, *The End of Eddy: A Novel*. New York: Farrar, Straus and Giroux, 2017.
2. J. D. Vance, *Hillbilly Elegy: A Memoir of a Family and Culture in Crisis*. New York: Harper, 2016.
3. Seymour Martin Lipset and Stein Rokkan, Cleavage structures, party systems, and voter alignments. In Seymour Martin Lipset and Stein Rokkan, eds., *Party Systems and Voter Alignments: Cross-national Perspectives*. New York: Free Press, 1967.
4. Richard Florida, *The Rise of the Creative Class*. New York: Norton, 2002.
5. A question on employment in the public versus the private sector was only available in the 2009 EES.
6. Herbert Kitschelt, *The Transformation of European Social Democracy*. Cambridge: Cambridge University Press, 1994, ch. 2; Herbert Kitschelt and Philip Rehm, Occupations as a site of political preference formation, *Comparative Political Studies* (2014) 47: 1670–706; Herbert Kitschelt and Philip Rehm, What's the matter with America? An update on political realignment after the 2016 presidential election. Paper presented at the annual meeting of the American Political Science Association. San Francisco, August 2017.
7. Geoffrey Evans and James Tilley, *The New Politics of Class: The Political Exclusion of the British Working Class*. Oxford: Oxford University Press, 2017.
8. Knutsen, *Social Structure, Value Orientations and Party Choice in Western Europe*; Kitschelt and Rehm, Occupations as a site of political preference formation; Silja Häusermann and Hanspeter Kriesi, What do voters want? Dimensions and configurations in individual-level preferences and party choice. In Pablo Beramendi, Silja Häusermann, Herbert Kitschelt, and Hanspeter Kriesi, eds., *The Politics of Advanced*

Capitalism. Cambridge: Cambridge University Press, 2015; Kitschelt, *The Transformation of European Social Democracy*.
9. Knutsen, *Social Structure, Value Orientations and Party Choice in Western Europe*, ch. 3.
10. The 1979 survey asked if the respondent's family had difficulties making ends meet. The 2009 survey had respondents position themselves on a rich–poor scale. The 2014 survey asked whether respondents had difficulty paying monthly bills during the past year.
11. Oddbjørn Knutsen, Left–Right materialist value orientations. In Jan van Deth and Elinor Scarbrough, eds., *The Impact of Values*. Oxford: Oxford University Press, 1995.
12. Knutsen, *Social Structure, Value Orientations and Party Choice in Western Europe*, ch. 3; Martin Dolezal and Swen Hutter, Participation and party choice: Comparing the demand size of the new cleavage across arenas. In Hanspeter Kriesi et al., *Political Conflict in Western Europe*. Cambridge: Cambridge University Press, 2012, pp. 71–3.
13. Mark Bovens and Anchrit Wille, *Diploma Democracy: The Rise of Political Meritocracy*. Oxford: Oxford University Press, 2017; Thomas Piketty, Brahmin left versus merchant right: Rising inequality and the change structure of political conflict. WID.world working paper series, 2018/7 (www.piketty.pse.ens.fr/conflict).
14. Wolfgang Jagodzinski and Karel Dobbelaere, Secularization and church religiosity. In Jan van Deth and Elinor Scarbrough, eds., *The Impact of Values*. Oxford: Oxford University Press, 1995; Pippa Norris and Ronald Inglehart, *Sacred and Secular: Religion and Politics Worldwide*, 2nd ed. New York: Cambridge University Press, 2010; Knutsen, *Social Structure, Value Orientations and Party Choice in Western Europe*.
15. Religious denomination appears to have a lesser effect compared to religiosity, but denomination was not asked in all three EES.
16. Stratos Patrikios and Georgios Xezonakis, Globalization, religiosity and vote choice. In Jack Vowles and George Xezonakis, eds., *Globalization and Domestic Politics: Parties, Elections, and Public Opinion*. Oxford: Oxford University Press, 2016.
17. Kai Arzheimer and E. Carter. Christian religiosity and voting for West European radical right parties, *West European Politics* (2003) 32: 985–1011; Häusermann and Kriesi, What do voters want?; Knutsen, *Social Structure, Value Orientations and Party Choice in Western Europe*.
18. Theodor Adorno, Else Frenkel-Brunswik, Daniel Levinson, and Nevitt Sanford, *The Authoritarian Personality*. New York: Harper & Row, 1950; Seymour Martin Lipset, Democracy and working-class authoritarianism, *American Sociological Review* (1959) 24: 482–501; Kitschelt and Rehm, Occupations as a site of political preference formation.
19. Florida, *The Rise of the Creative Class*; Kitschelt and Rehm, Occupations as a site of political preference formation; David Broockman, Gregory Ferenstein, and Neil Malhotra, Wealthy elite policy preferences and inequality: The case of technology entrepreneurs. Manuscript: Stanford University Graduate School of Business, 2017; Dolezal and Hutter, Participation and party choice, pp. 71–3; Kitschelt, *The Transformation of European Social Democracy*, ch. 2.
20. Norman Nie, Jane Junn, and Kenneth Stehlik-Barry, *Education and Democratic Citizenship in America*. Chicago: University of Chicago Press, 1996; Ronald Inglehart, *Culture Shift in Advanced Industrial Society*. Princeton: Princeton University Press, 1990.

21. Knutsen, *Social Structure, Value Orientations and Party Choice in Western Europe*; Dolezal and Hutter, Participation and party choice, pp. 71–3; Romain Lachat and Martin Dolezal, Demand side: Dealignment and realignment of the structural political potentials. In Hanspeter Kriesi et al., *West European Politics in the Age of Globalization*. Cambridge: Cambridge University Press, 2008; Kitschelt and Rehm, Occupations as a site of political preference formation; Häusermann and Kriesi, What do voters want?
22. Herman van de Werfhorst and Nan Dirk de Graaf, The sources of political orientations in post-industrial society: Social class and education revisited, *The British Journal of Sociology* (2004) 55: 215–33; Lachat and Dolezal, Demand side; Häusermann and Kriesi, What do voters want?
23. Inglehart, *Culture Shift in Advanced Industrial Society*; also see, Ronald Inglehart and Christian Welzel, *Modernization, Cultural Change and Democracy*. Cambridge: Cambridge University Press, 2005; Knutsen, *Social Structure, Value Orientations and Party Choice in Western Europe*.
24. Axel Dreher, Noel Gaston, and Pim Martens, eds., *Measuring Globalization: Gauging its Consequences*. New York: Springer, 2008.
25. Justin Gest, *The New Minority: White Working Class Politics in an Age of Immigration and Inequality*. Oxford: Oxford University Press, 2016; Katherine Cramer, *The Politics of Resentment: Rural Consciousness in Wisconsin and the Rise of Scott Walker*. Chicago: University of Chicago Press, 2016; Arlie Hochschild, *Strangers in Their Own Land: Anger and Mourning on the American Right*. New York: New Press, 2016.
26. Knutsen, *Social Structure, Value Orientations and Party Choice in Western Europe*.
27. I replaced missing data with the sample mean scores in the initial calculation of principal component scores. If a respondent had missing data on half or more of the items, they were recoded as missing data on the PCA scores. This retains respondents with a few missing responses in the analyses. In the 2014 EU15 sample, for example, 3.2 percent of the total sample were coded as missing.
28. Häusermann and Kriesi, What do voters want?; Stephan Ansolabehere, Jonathan Rodden, James Snyder, The strength of issues: Using multiple measures to gauge preference stability, ideological constraint and issue voting, *American Political Science Review* (2008) 102: 215–32; Paul Goren, *On Voter Competence*. Oxford: Oxford University Press, 2012, ch. 4; Paul Goren, Harald Schoen, Jason Reifler, Thomas Scotto, and William Chittick, A unified theory of value-based reasoning and U.S. public opinion, *Political Behavior* (2016) 38: 977–97.
29. Also see Lachat and Dolezal, Demand side, pp. 246–8; Knutsen, *Social Structure, Value Orientations and Party Choice in Western Europe*, pp. 92–3.
30. Geoffrey Evans and James Tilley, *The New Politics of Class: The Political Exclusion of the British Working Class*. Oxford: Oxford University Press, 2017, ch. 4; Bovens and Wille, *Diploma Democracy*; Piketty, Brahmin left versus merchant right.
31. I recoded the more detailed occupation code in 2014 to conform as closely as possible to the simpler categories used in 1979.
32. The same basic pattern appears in 2009, but these data are not reported separately because of slight inconsistencies in the coding of occupation.
33. This category includes both business owners and shop owners who are separated in Figure 3.2.

34. Supporting evidence from the European Social Survey shows that higher status individuals are more likely to hold liberal positions on the issues of gay rights and immigration, while holding conservative positions on policies to reduce income inequality. Russell Dalton, *The Participation Gap*. Oxford: Oxford University Press, 2017, ch. 10.
35. Kitschelt coined the phrase "Left-Libertarian" to explain this new political position in the 1970s. This overlap is apparent in the principal component analyses in 1979.
36. Also see Lachat and Dolezal, Demand side, pp. 246–8.
37. A growing body of research argues that a broad consensus on the role of the state on economic issues has shifted attention to the performance of government rather than positional choices; for example, Harold Clarke et al., *Performance Politics: The British Voter*. New York: Cambridge University Press, 2008; Knutsen, *Social Structure, Value Orientations and Party Choice in Western Europe*. So even the economic uncertainties following the 2008 recession did not repolarize social classes on economic issues.
38. The causal direction of this relationship is ambiguous. Chapter 4 addresses this topic.
39. Another question asked only in 1979 assessed support for radical social change versus defending the status quo. Support for radical social change was substantially correlated with liberal positions on both the economic ($r=0.14$) and cultural cleavages ($r=0.17$).
40. Nicolò Conti, Swen Hutter, and Kyriaki Nanou, eds., Party Competition and Political Representation in Crisis: A Comparative Perspective, *Special issue of Party Politics* (2018) 24; Sara Hobolt and James Tilley, Fleeing the centre: The rise of challenger parties in the aftermath of the euro crisis, *West European Politics* (2016) 39: 971–91.
41. Ronald Inglehart and Hans-Dieter Klingemann, Party identification, ideological preference and the left–right dimension among western mass publics. In Ian Budge, Ivor Crew, and Dennis Farlie, eds., *Party Identification and Beyond*. New York: Wiley, 1976; Dieter Fuchs and Hans-Dieter Klingemann, The Left–Right schema. In M. K. Jennings and J. van Deth, eds., *Continuities in Political Action*. Berlin: deGruyter, 1989; Russell Dalton, David Farrell, and Ian McAllister, *Political Parties and Democratic Linkage: How Parties Organize Democracy*. Oxford: Oxford University Press, 2011, ch. 5; Robert Rohrschneider and Stephen Whitefield, *The Strain of Representation: How Parties Represent Diverse Voters in Western and Eastern Europe*. Oxford: Oxford University Press, 2012.
42. Ronald Inglehart, The changing structure of political cleavages in Western society. In Russell Dalton, Scott Flanagan, and Paul Beck, eds., Electoral *Change in Advanced Industrial Democracies*. Princeton: Princeton University Press, 1984, p. 80. This also produces an analytic problem when researchers use Left–Right positions as a surrogate for the economic cleavage. In a two-dimensional political space, a single item is insufficient to interpret the nature of political competition.
43. Only the 1979 survey to include Inglehart's index of postmaterial values, which is strongly related to both the economic cleavage ($r=0.25$) and the cultural cleavage ($r=0.23$).

44. Political support is measured by satisfaction with democracy in 1979 and 2009; the 2014 question asked whether the national parliament considers the public's concerns.
45. The models use subjective feelings of religiosity in 1979 and 2009, and church attendance in 2014.
46. Russell Dalton, Scott Flanagan, and Paul Beck, Political forces and partisan change. In Russell Dalton, Scott Flanagan, and Paul Beck, eds., *Electoral Change in Advanced Industrial Democracies*. Princeton: Princeton University Press, 1984, pp. 452–3.
47. Also see Liesbet Hooghe and Gary Marks, Cleavage theory meets Europe's crises: Lipset, Rokkan, and the transnational cleavage, *Journal of European Public Policy* (2018) 25: 109–35.

4

Political Cleavages across Nations

The European Union is one unit, except it isn't. In economic terms, the state's role in the economy varies widely across member states. Major portions of the economic infrastructure still have direct government involvement in several nations, while privatization has largely removed the government from these sectors in other nations. Welfare state provisions and other public services also diverge across the EU15.[1] The context for cultural issues is equally varied. A woman's right to abortion and the attached conditions vary across Europe, even after decades of policy reform. Provisions for law and order also differ, beginning with the structure of the legal system to the administration of justice. The percentage of immigrants in the population varies greatly across EU member states, as well as the characteristics of the immigrant population. And last, attitudes toward the EU and its policies also span a wide range across the 15 EU member states.

Yet, the previous (and subsequent) chapters largely focus on the EU nations as a group. In part, this reflects the characteristics of the data sources. With a broad time span, three surveys, and a changing political context, we can more reliably discuss European trends than the pattern in any single nation. In addition, this book has a broad theoretical interest. I expect that the evolution of political cleavages is common across the established democracies, even if the timing of the changes and the rate of change differs. Thus, the analysis of pooled European nations raises our vision to the broad patterns on the horizon.

To ensure the reader of the general consistency of the pooled European results, this chapter describes the basic patterns of political cleavages across the specific EU member states. To determine if the content of the economic and cultural cleavages is similar across nations, I compare the structure of issue opinions across EU member states. The chapter then examines the social correlates of cleavage positions across nations. In addition, I consider whether the contextual factors such as the structure of the economy or the religious composition of a society affect group alignments. The results should add more detail on how and why cleavage politics is evolving.

National Context and Issue Positions

I have argued that the evolution of political cleavages in Europe reflects a common, evolving political competition between the advocates and critics of social modernization. Yet many nation-specific studies focus on the particular events, politicians, or policies that shape the emergence of the cultural cleavage. For example, could Brexit have occurred without the remarkable ability of Nigel Farage to build UKIP into a viable political force, which prodded David Cameron to call for a Brexit referendum, with its surprising result? Did the coalitional politics of Austria's government give rise to the anti-establishment forces marshaled by Jörg Haider's Freedom Party; or was Jean Marie Le Pen's distinctive charismatic appeal responsible for the National Front's initial rise in France?

Ronald Inglehart and Pippa Norris are more skeptical of such nation-specific explanations for cultural conservative parties: "Observers commonly offer historical narratives, focused upon certain events and particular circumstances, to account for the rise of individual populist parties and leaders in each case. Nation-specific events such as these are proximate causes that help to explain why things worked out as they did within a given country—but they do not explain why the vote for populist parties across many countries has roughly doubled in recent decades."[2] They argued, as I have in previous chapters, that broader forces of societal change explain the pan-European patterns observed in this study.

At the same time, we should not expect absolute uniformity across nations. Some scholars claim that the characteristics of a nation—rather than a discrete event or political leader—shape the evolutionary pattern of political cleavages. For example, Silva Häusermann and Hanspeter Kriesi hypothesized that the state-market economic system might influence the structure of the economic cleavage across nations.[3] Economic views might be more polarized in highly competitive systems, and less so when the system emphasizes equality. Or, the salience of the income inequality issue might vary as a function of the actual inequality in a nation. They classified nations by the degree of state economic intervention and the emphasis on consumption versus investment. Despite their theoretical ideas, the issue cleavages in the 2008–9 European Social Survey (EES) displayed a similar structure for the economic cleavage across five different economic system types.

One might also postulate that a nation's cultural or social conditions would affect the composition of the cultural cleavage. Kriesi suggested that the religious traditions of a nation might affect the importance attached to various cultural issues.[4] Political discourse in conservative Catholic nations might be more polarized on issues related to church doctrines, such as policies toward abortion or same-sex marriage.[5] Similarly, Kriesi discussed whether conceptions of citizenship and concerns about EU sovereignty might shape attitudes toward immigration.[6] The project analyzed issue structures from election studies in six nations. They found some variance in cleavage patterns, but no clear distinction in the basis of these differences.[7]

A similar possibility is that the nation's historical relationship with the EU may influence views of the EU and the norms enshrined in their agreements. Similarly, attitudes toward globalization and EU standards might vary across small or export-dependent nations that rely on EU trade provisions, and larger, consumer nations.

These presumptions of similarities or differences in the structure of political cleavages can be tested by separate Principal Components Analysis (PCA) in each nation. Some cross-national variation is expected and inevitable, and these analyses assess the differences. At the same time, even with different weights for individual issues, the underlying commonality of the issues defining the economic and cultural cleavages should be apparent.

A different aspect of cross-national variation involves the correlates of cleavage positions. Features of the national context can influence political behavior in direct and indirect ways. For example, Oddbjørn Knutsen found that social class was an important predictor of economic values across European regions, but the strength of this relationship predictably varied across regions.[8] Knutsen also demonstrated that occupation and education had stronger and more consistent correlations with libertarian–authoritarian values across European regions. By describing specific national patterns for the structure of political cleavages and the correlates of cleavage positions we can assess the impact of such contextual influences.

Structure of the Issue Space across Nations

To make the empirical presentations more manageable, this chapter examines the fifteen member states in the 2009 and 2014 European Social Surveys. In 1979 the cleavage space was still forming. By the two later surveys, the current framework of Europe's cleavage structure was largely set.

The Cleavage Structure in 2009

The 2009 survey is the primary data source in this chapter. The survey includes a large battery of twelve issue questions and an additional question on support for the EU. This provides a rich and potentially varied basis of cross-national comparisons.[9] In addition, the EU15 nations span considerably more historical, social, and economic variation than the nine 1979 states.

Political Cleavages across Nations

The first empirical step determines how citizens link together specific issues to define both political cleavages. The dimensional structure is partly determined by the choice of questions and the diversity of themes that the principal investigators chose to include. From this set of questions, Chapter 2 extracted the two broad cleavages that structure contemporary politics. I repeated those same PCAs separately for each of the EU15 member states.

The PCA methodology and results are presented in Appendix B. To simplify the findings, Table 4.1 lists the three highest loading issues on the economic cleavage, and the four highest loading items on the cultural cleavage (where more questions were asked). In general terms, the economic and cultural cleavages described in Chapter 2 are clearly evident in almost every nation,

Table 4.1. The Primary Issues Defining Political Cleavages Across Nations, 2009

Nation	Top 3 Economic Issues	Top 4 Cultural Issues
Austria	Private enterprise, state ownership, income inequality	Decrease immigration, immigrant customs, harsh sentences, EU attitude
Belgium	Gay marriage, women limit work, economic intervention	Immigrants customs, teach obedience, decrease immigration, harsh sentences
Denmark	EU treaty, income inequality, state ownership,	Harsh sentences, decrease immigration, immigrant customs, teach obedience
Finland	State ownership, income inequality, EU treaty	Decrease immigration, immigrant customs, harsh sentences, teach obedience
France	State ownership, income inequality, EU treaty	Decrease immigration, immigrant customs, EU attitude, harsh sentences
Germany	State ownership, income inequality, private enterprise	Immigrant customs, decrease immigration, harsh sentences, teach obedience
Greece	State ownership, EU treaty, income inequality	Teach obedience, decrease immigration, gay marriage, harsh sentences
Ireland	Private enterprise, income inequality, economic intervention	Harsh sentences, teach obedience, EU treaty, decrease immigration
Italy	Economic intervention, state ownership, gay marriage	Decrease immigration, immigrant customs, gay marriage, women work
Luxembourg	Income inequality, state ownership, teach obedience	Decrease immigration, immigrant customs, EU attitude, harsh sentences
Netherlands	Teach obedience, economic intervention, state ownership	Harsh sentences, decrease immigration, immigrant customs, EU attitude
Portugal	Private enterprise, EU attitude, abortion	Decrease immigration, immigrant customs, EU treaty, teach obedience
Spain	Income inequality, abortion, state ownership	Decrease immigration, teach obedience, immigrant customs, private enterprise
Sweden	Income inequality, government ownership, EU referendum	Immigrant customs, decrease immigration, teach obedience, gay marriage
United Kingdom	Income inequality, government ownership, private enterprise	Decrease immigration, immigrant customs, harsh sentences, teach obedience

Note: See Appendix B for the complete Principal Components Analyses and the methodology.
Source: European Election Study 2009.

even if the specific composition of issues on each cleavage varies slightly. The four core issues on the government's role in the economy—income inequality, state ownership, private enterprise as a solution to the nation's problems, and political intervention in the economy—are frequently among highest loading issues on the economic cleavage. All but two nations (Belgium and Portugal) have high coefficients for at least two of these issues as high loadings, and half the nations have three. The PCA results are not invariant across nations, but we should not expect the content of the economic cleavage to include the exact same issues with the same weight in each nation. The value of the PCA model is that the latent variable has a common meaning albeit with different examples.

The cultural cleavage is most commonly linked to the issues of limiting immigration and immigrants adopting national customs. At least one of these two issues, and generally both, have high coefficients on the cultural cleavage. Several other markers of cultural positions are also common across most nations: teaching obedience in the schools, harsher penalties for criminals, and same-sex marriage. In overall terms, the national results follow the pooled EU results in Chapter 2. All of the listed cultural issues in Table 4.1 are consistent with the definition of the cultural cleavage in previous chapters.

Another notable result is the lack of a clear cleavage position for attitudes toward the EU (see Appendix B). Much has been written on the impact of globalization and the EU's role in social change in Europe, but its linkage to other issues and thereby broader political cleavages is highly variable. In several nations with different political histories—Austria, Denmark, Germany, Luxembourg, the Netherlands, and the UK—support for the EU is tied to liberal cultural values. Yet in other nations—Finland, Greece, Ireland, and Sweden—support for the EU is linked to liberal economic values. In several other nations, support for the EU is seen as a conservative economic position. These findings suggest that there is no single EU-wide interpretation of the meaning and costs–benefits of EU membership, which should vary across nations. Thus, attitudes toward the EU are not a clear driver of cultural conservativism across Europe.

As another means to validate the similarity of pooled and national level PCA results, I calculated individual scores from the country-level PCAs and then compared them to the scores from the pooled analyses of Table 2.2. I matched the appropriate dimensions from the pooled and nation-specific PCAs.[10] This method determines if the measurement of these two cleavages yields basically similar results across nations. For all EU15 nations, the two scores are correlated at 0.79 for the economic cleavage and 0.90 for the cultural cleavage.[11] The economic cleavage is less robust, but fewer items define this dimension. There is little variation in these correlations across the subsets of the original six member states, the EU9 nations, or the EU15 nations.

Political Cleavages across Nations

The Cleavage Structure in 2014

To validate the findings from the 2009 EES, I turned to the 2014 survey. The survey covers the same fifteen EU member states The survey only includes a battery of eight issue questions, and several of these have ambiguous meanings. For example, is the tradeoff between the economy and environmental protection an economic issue or a cultural issue? Is EU authority over economies a cultural indicator of responses to a loss of national sovereignty or support for strong economic policies? Even with these limitations, the broad framework of the economic and cultural cleavages was apparent in the pooled PCA results (Table 2.3), and we expect a similar pattern across individual nations.

The PCA methodology and results are presented in Appendix B. To follow the model for the 2009 EES, Table 4.2 lists the three highest loading issues on

Table 4.2. The Primary Issues Defining Political Cleavages Across Nations, 2014

Nation	Top 3 Economic Issues	Top 3 Cultural Issues
Austria	State intervention, taxes/services, EU economic authority	Environment vs. economy, privacy, gay marriage
Belgium	State intervention, redistribution, economy vs. environment	EU authority, immigration, taxes/services
Denmark	Taxes/services, redistribution, economy vs. environment	Privacy, EU authority, immigration
Finland	Redistribution, taxes/services, state intervention	Immigration, EU authority, gay marriage
France	Redistribution, state intervention, gay marriage	EU authority, taxes/services, economy vs. environment
Germany	Redistribution, state intervention, economy vs. environment	Gay marriage, immigration, EU authority
Greece	Redistribution, economy vs. environment, EU authority	Gay marriage, immigration, taxes/services
Ireland	State intervention, economy vs. environment, redistribution	EU authority, immigration, privacy
Italy	State intervention, redistribution, economy vs. environment	Immigration, gay marriage, EU authority
Luxembourg	EU authority, taxes/services, state intervention	Redistribution, economy vs. environment, immigration
Netherlands	State intervention, redistribution, taxes/services	EU authority, immigration, gay marriage
Portugal	State intervention, economy vs. environment, redistribution	Gay marriage, immigration, EU authority
Spain	Redistribution, economy vs. environment, state intervention	Privacy, immigration, gay marriage
Sweden	Taxes/services, redistribution, state intervention	Immigration, gay marriage, privacy
United Kingdom	Taxes/services, state intervention, redistribution	EU authority, immigration, privacy

Note: See Appendix B for the complete Principal Components Analyses and the methodology.
Source: European Election Study 2014.

the economic cleavage, and the three highest loading items on the cultural cleavage. In general terms, the economic and cultural cleavages described in Chapter 2 are clearly seen in almost every nation, although the composition of issues on each cleavage varies slightly.

In all but two nations, the three issues with the highest loading on the economic component all deal with economic matters. The most common items are the redistribution of wealth (14 nations) and state intervention in the economy (13 nations). Among the three items with the highest loadings, about nine-tenths clearly reflect some economic theme.

The patterning of issues on the cultural cleavage is less distinct, in part because of the ambiguous meaning of some of the issues. For instance, EU authority over the economy loads on the cultural dimension in eleven nations. Even though it explicitly cites the economic domain, the national sovereignty aspect seems more prominent. Yet, Austrians, Greeks, and Luxembourgers interpret this issue as part of the economic cleavage. Similarly, in most nations, the tradeoff between the environment and economy is more strongly linked to the economic cleavage, but this a cultural theme in Austria and France. Thus the direct comparability of the cultural measures varies slightly more than for the economic cleavage, but the content of the cultural cleavage still focuses on cultural issues across the EU15.

The mix of issues in defining national cleavages in 2009 and 2014 is inevitable because the salient economic and cultural problems in each nation will vary. Indeed, this is a potential strength of the latent variable approach in focusing on common underlying values, while allowing some variability in the measurement of these values. The dominant pattern is the similarity of citizen perceptions of the issue space across nations in both 2009 and 2014. This is similar to Häusermann and Kriesi's results with a different set of issue questions.[12] National differences exist, but at the margins. This similarity provides further justification for treating these two cleavage dimensions as comparable measures across European publics.

Social Characteristics and Cleavages

Each EU member state varies in the economic priorities of the incumbent government, as well as their experiences with the 2008 recession and subsequent economic effects. Their cultural characteristics are as equally diverse. For example, the immigrant experience is widely different, both in the number and composition of the immigrant population and in the government's official policies toward immigrants. The social conditions of citizens also differ across these fifteen nations. Thus, the average cleavage position of citizens varies across these nations (Figure 2.2).

Our interest now turns to whether the similar economic and cultural cleavages across nations belie a different social base for these cleavages. Prior research suggests that contextual factors might affect the social correlates of opinions, although the evidence on such contextual effects is mixed.[13] The theories of potential differences are probably more numerous than the degrees of freedom in the cross-national comparisons. I start by estimating predictive models for all fifteen EU nations, and then explore more specific hypotheses that replace national labels with conceptual categories.

This section focuses on the 2009 EES because a richer set of issues measures cleavage positions, and this allows us to focus on detailed relationships and interactions in more depth. In broad terms, however, the 2014 results are similar to those presented here.

Table 4.3 shows the OLS regression model linking citizens' social characteristics to their positions on the economic cleavage in each nation; this replicates the regression model for the pooled set of EU15 nations (Table 3.3). The bottom panel in the table presents the EU15 pooled results as a reference point. We should expect some sampling variation across nations rather than identical coefficients, as well as national effects. The question is whether basic contrasts are apparent in these analyses.

The sheer number of coefficients in the table presents a challenge in drawing conclusions. One approach is to prioritize the comparison by focusing the most important predictors of cleavage positions, discounting differences on less important predictors. The strongest three predictors of economic positions based on the pooled model are political support ($\beta = -0.16$), manual workers ($\beta = 0.10$), and religiosity ($\beta = 0.10$). The coefficients for political support vary in strength across nations, but only one nation (Spain on political support) displays a statistically significant coefficient with the opposite direction. This might be a function of Spain's post-2008 financial problems eroding political support among economic conservatives. Manual workers lean toward liberal economic views in all nations except one (France). In all but one nation (Luxembourg), manual workers are more liberal than business owners (managers vary more than manual workers, but owners are also a small share of the sample). The size of this class cleavage varies substantially, however, with the largest gap in Finland (an owner versus manual worker difference of 1.03) and the smallest in Greece (0.28). Finally, religiosity is negatively related to economic liberalism in every nation except Portugal. So if we are primarily interested in the direction of the strongest predictors, the cross-national patterns are broadly similar. If we are concerned about the magnitude of effects, there are more significant differences even for the strongest predictors.

Table 4.4 presents parallel national models for the cultural cleavage. As shown in Chapter 3, the three strongest predictors are religiosity ($\beta = -0.24$ for the EU15 model), education ($\beta = 0.23$), and age ($\beta = -0.16$). In every nation,

Table 4.3. Multivariate Models Predicting the Economic Cleavage by Nation

Predictors

Countries	Managers	Business owner	Manual worker	Education	Well-being	Age	Religiosity	Gender	Political Support	Intercept	Multiple R
Austria	0.03	-0.48*	0.42*	-0.00	-0.12*	-0.017*	-0.04*	0.16*	-0.09*	-13.76	0.21
Belgium	-0.20	-0.03	0.26*	-0.00	0.13*	0.003	-0.01	0.16*	-0.14*	4.08	0.29
Denmark	-0.28*	-0.14	0.15*	0.00	-0.05	-0.004*	-0.05*	0.19*	-0.19*	-7.73	0.36
Finland	0.11	-0.70*	0.33*	-0.00	-0.08*	0.001	-0.06*	0.33*	-0.28*	1.68	0.32
France	-0.22	-0.35	-0.09	-0.01	-0.04	-0.001	-0.03*	0.04	-0.24*	-1.44	0.31
Germany	-0.09	-0.45	0.02	-0.00	-0.11*	-0.002	-0.03*	0.14*	-0.35*	-5.62	0.26
Greece	0.10	-0.17	0.12	-0.01*	0.05	0.007*	-0.09*	-0.08	-0.15*	13.61	0.28
Ireland	-0.39*	-0.17	0.17*	-0.02*	-0.10*	-0.006*	-0.01	0.23*	-0.16*	-11.38	0.25
Italy	-0.24	-0.20	0.14	-0.01	-0.03	-0.005*	-0.03*	0.15*	-0.15*	-10.8	0.29
Luxembourg	-0.03	0.18	0.22	-0.04*	-0.11*	-0.004*	-0.03*	0.06	-0.20*	-8.14	0.27
Netherlands	-0.32*	-0.64*	0.10	0.00	-0.06*	0.002	-0.04*	0.01	-0.17*	3.66	0.28
Portugal	-0.03	-0.56*	0.09	-0.01	-0.10*	-0.011*	0.00	0.18*	-0.13*	-22.29	0.30
Spain	0.03	-0.35	0.11	-0.00	0.01	-0.005*	-0.06*	0.33*	0.10*	-10.34	0.38
Sweden	-0.20	-0.42	0.35*	-0.00	-0.09*	-0.003	-0.00	0.22*	-0.34*	-6.36	0.35
United Kingdom	-0.07	-0.06	0.35*	-0.02	-0.07*	-0.007*	-0.04*	0.24*	-0.07	-13.67	0.27
All EU15	-0.15	-0.24	0.23	-0.01	-0.03	-0.003	-0.03	0.17	-0.18	-6.42	0.24
(st. error)	0.04	0.06	0.02	0.002	0.01	0.001	0.00	0.02	0.01	0.987	
Standardized β	-0.03	-0.04	0.10	-0.03	-0.04	-0.05	-0.10	0.08	-0.16		

Note: Table entries are unstandardized regression coefficients; positive values on cleavage indices are liberal positions. * denotes significant at 0.05 level.

Sources: 2009 European Social Surveys, established democracies.

Table 4.4. Multivariate Models Predicting the Cultural Cleavage by Nation

	Predictors									
Countries	Managers	Business owner	Manual worker	Education	Well-being	Age	Religiosity	Gender	Political Support	Intercept	Multiple R
Austria	0.07	−0.01	−0.49*	0.08*	0.02	−0.014*	−0.05*	0.24*	0.14*	−28.19	0.34
Belgium	−0.16	−0.32*	−0.38*	0.01	0.03	−0.007*	−0.05*	0.00	0.08*	−13.44	0.36
Denmark	0.17	0.35	−0.31*	0.02*	−0.04	−0.007*	−0.08*	0.05	0.04	−12.17	0.38
Finland	0.06	−0.08	−0.25*	0.02*	0.01	−0.011*	−0.07*	0.23*	0.29*	−21.95	0.54
France	0.08	0.13	−0.29*	0.04*	−0.01	−0.017*	−0.08*	−0.01	−0.10*	−32.77	0.45
Germany	0.09	0.05	−0.20*	0.04*	0.03	−0.013*	−0.05*	0.08	0.11*	−25.27	0.46
Greece	−0.05	0.16	−0.11	0.02*	0.03	−0.013*	−0.10*	0.09	−0.16*	−25.62	0.42
Ireland	0.17	0.38*	0.03	0.03*	−0.04	−0.012*	−0.07*	0.08	0.05	−23.41	0.36
Italy	0.23	−0.09	−0.04	0.01*	0.05*	−0.010*	−0.06*	0.10	−0.03	−19.90	0.42
Luxembourg	0.06	0.19	−0.54*	0.04*	−0.04	−0.008*	−0.05*	0.05	0.10*	−16.18	0.48
Netherlands	−0.12	−0.06	−0.29*	0.04*	−0.01	−0.004*	−0.07*	0.17*	0.14*	−8.24	0.55
Portugal	−0.08	0.26	−0.07	0.01*	0.01	−0.003*	−0.05*	0.11*	0.14*	−5.99	0.38
Spain	0.27	−0.14	−0.05	0.03*	0.04*	−0.008*	−0.06*	0.19*	0.14*	−16.71	0.54
Sweden	0.40*	−0.29	−0.14	0.01*	−0.06*	−0.010*	−0.06*	0.08	0.17*	−19.18	0.37
United Kingdom	0.06	−0.08	−0.12	0.08*	0.01	−0.013*	−0.04*	−0.08	0.12*	−25.74	0.49
All EU15	0.13	−0.08	−0.20	0.04	0.03	−0.01	−0.08	0.10	0.14	−17.72	0.48
(st. error)	0.04	0.05	0.02	0.001	0.01	0.00	0.03	0.02	0.01	0.893	
Standardized β	0.03	−0.01	−0.08	0.23	0.04	0.16	−0.24	0.05	0.13		

Note: Table entries are unstandardized regression coefficients; positive values on cleavage indices are liberal positions. * denotes significant at .05 level.
Sources: 2009 European Social Surveys, established democracies.

the unstandardized coefficients for religiosity are negative and statistically significant. Similarly, education is positively related to liberal cultural positions in every nation. Age patterns are also substantial and consistent across nations, with older Europeans favoring conservative cultural positions. The other notable pattern is the consistent conservative leanings of manual workers across all but one nation (Ireland).[14]

One consistent pattern is the greater predictive power for cultural views compared to economic positions. In all fifteen nations, the Multiple Rs for the cultural cleavage are larger. So even if the cultural cleavage has coalesced more recently, it now taps basic social divisions more clearly than the economic cleavage. Chapter 3 found a similar pattern for the pooled 2014 EES.

Contextual Effects

The mass of coefficients in the nation-specific regression analyses (135 for each cleavage) admittedly makes it difficult to summarize all the cross-national patterns in these results. An even more powerful comparison exchanges the proper nouns of nation states with conceptual traits that may shape the structure of the political space. For example, prior research suggests that the structure of the economic system and the composition of the citizenry might affect the correlates of opinion. I test this logic with two comparisons. First, theory presumes that competitive economic systems might intensify class differences in economic orientations, while class differences might be moderated in egalitarian systems. Following Hanspeter Kriesi's research, the egalitarian economic systems are the three Scandinavian nations in the EES: Denmark, Finland, and Sweden; the competitive systems are Britain, Ireland, and Germany.[15]

Second, the social base of the cultural cleavage should reflect the religious values prevalent in the society. Religiosity may have a weaker influence on cultural positions in predominately secular societies, while it would have stronger effects in traditional, Catholic societies. I contrasted the three secular, Protestant nations of Denmark, Finland, and Sweden with the more traditional Catholic/Orthodox Mediterranean states of Greece, Italy, Portugal, and Spain. The grouped comparisons can also determine whether these contextual variables have differential effects for the other predictors in the regression models.

Table 4.5 displays the multiple regression models predicting cleavage positions for these three sets of nations. In terms of comparing competitive and egalitarian nations, there are generally small differences in the structure of the economic cleavage across these two sets of nations. The primary difference is

Table 4.5. Predicting Cleavage Positions by National Traits

| | Competitive | | Egalitarian | | | |
| | | | Secular/Protestant | | Catholic | |
Predictors	Economic	Culture	Economic	Culture	Economic	Culture
Managers	−0.20	0.15	−0.22	0.28	−0.13	0.16
	(0.11)	(0.09)	(0.09)	(0.09)	(0.12)	(0.10)
Business owner	−0.01	−0.01	−0.30	−0.03	−0.28	0.11
	(0.13)	(0.11)	(0.05)	(0.14)	(0.12)	(0.09)
Manual worker	0.33	−0.18	0.38	−0.36	0.07	−0.02
	(0.05)	(0.04)	(0.15)	(0.04)	(0.04)	(0.03)
Education	−0.02	0.05	−0.01	0.03	−0.01	0.01
	(0.01)	(0.01)	(0.01)	(0.01)	(0.01)	(0.01)
Well-being	−0.06	−0.02	−0.11	0.03	−0.01	0.02
	(0.02)	(0.02)	(0.02)	(0.02)	(0.01)	(0.01)
Age	−0.008	−0.009	−0.003	−0.009	−0.003	−0.007
	(0.001)	(0.001)	(0.001)	(0.001)	(0.001)	(0.001)
Religiosity	−0.03	−0.04	−0.03	−0.10	−0.02	−0.07
	(0.01)	(0.01)	(0.07)	(0.01)	(0.01)	(0.01)
Gender	0.27	0.01	0.29	0.05	0.10	0.17
	(0.05)	(0.04)	(0.04)	(0.04)	(0.03)	(0.03)
Political support	−0.20	0.14	−0.26	0.07	−0.15	0.07
	(0.03)	(0.02)	(0.03)	(0.03)	(0.02)	(0.02)
Intercept	−15.97	−17.69	−5.41	−17.87	−5.44	−13.69
	(2.64)	(2.11)	(2.54)	(2.47)	(2.13)	(1.72)
Multiple R	0.29	0.39	0.35	0.44	0.18	0.40

Note: Table entries are unstandardized regression coefficients (and standard errors); pairwise deletion of missing data. The categorization of nations is described in the text.
Source: European Election Study, 2009.

that business owners are actually more economically conservative in the three egalitarian nations, but managers/executives and manual workers hold similar positions in both models.[16]

The second contrast compares secular/Protestant Scandinavia to Catholic Mediterranean nations. The primary predictors of cultural positions are relatively similar across both sets of nations. In the Scandinavian nations, religiosity and age have stronger effects on cultural positions compared to the other two groups of nations. The largest variation is for gender differences. Perhaps because of restrictions on women's roles in Southern Europe, women lean more strongly toward a liberal cultural position in these nations (or men are more culturally conservative). The other notable differences are for the economic variables. There is a starker contrast between managers and manual workers in secular/egalitarian Scandinavia than in Mediterranean nations.

The overall patterns show a similarity in the direction of effects for most predictors across these three sets of nations. Most of the inconsistencies in the regression models involve variables with weaker coefficients. In contrast to the prior theorizing, the largest effects for both economic and cultural predictors tend to occur in egalitarian Scandinavia, where theory suggests weaker effects on both cleavages (based on the Multiple R for both cleavages). Such multilevel comparisons deserve more attention, and perhaps justify pooling different surveys together to expand the empirical base for comparisons. However, these preliminary comparisons for the 2009 EES suggest broad consistency in the correlates of cleavage positions across established European democracies.

Commonalities and Differences

There are undoubtedly substantial differences between the social position and life conditions of a manual worker in Southern Europe and another in Germany. Similarly, the expectations of a very religious individual in Sweden likely differs from a very religious citizen of Ireland. This chapter asked how such country-level differences compare to the shared worldview of citizens and social groups across Europe.

The chapter first examined the structure of political cleavages across nations. A common economic and cultural cleavage structure is evident, even if the weight given to issues on each cleavage varies slightly.[17] The economic cleavage is determined by a mixed set of economic issues that reflect common political orientations, just as the cultural cleavage is now defined by a predictable set of other issues. To some extent, this commonality is greater than might be expected because social and political conditions vary substantially across the EU15 nations. For example, government policies toward immigrants and the composition of the immigrant population vary considerably, yet this is a clear and common marker of positions on the cultural cleavage. The role of the government in the economy also varies across the EU nations, yet Europeans broadly see this as an important element of economic cleavage. In short, the mix of issues might vary across nations, but the basic content of the economic and cultural cleavages seems comparable across Europe. Thus, the pooled analyses represent a reasonable mix of what exists at the national level.

The second theme of the chapter was a comparison of the social correlates of cleavage positions across the EU15 nations. Again, the broad pattern describes a similarity in the primary predictors of both the economic and cultural cleavage. Similar age differences in cultural orientations, for example, are found across Europe, just as class differences in economic orientations are widely observed. I do not doubt that there are many important differences between the political views of a German manual worker and a Spanish worker, for example, but they generally share a common economic position relative to business owners in their respective nation. The same pattern applies to secular and religious differences in the cultural cleavage.

Political Cleavages across Nations

Moreover, without more detailed analyses and multi-level modeling, it is difficult to determine whether the observed cross-national differences are real or a function of an underspecified model that excludes other relevant characteristics. The most obvious factor is the political context. The cues of political parties and interest groups can reinforce or moderate social differences on political issues.[18] The composition of the government and recent government actions can also shape opinions, such as the varied relationship between political support and cleavage positions in Table 4.4. These topics can be examined with denser data collections for more nations and more time points.

No single pooled model will be a perfect fit to all the cases included in the analysis. But that is not the objective. Rather, this chapter has shown that the pooled structure of the political space defined by the economic and cultural cleavages represents an adequate and parsimonious summary of the nature of political competition in the nations of contemporary Europe.

Notes

1. This chapter focuses on the original nine EU states joined by Austria, Finland, Greece, Portugal, Spain, and Sweden.
2. Ronald Inglehart and Pippa Norris, Trump and the populist authoritarian parties: *The Silent Revolution* in reverse, *Perspective on Politics* (2017) 15: 9.
3. Silja Häusermann and Hanspeter Kriesi, What do voters want? Dimensions and configurations in individual-level preferences and party choice. In Pablo Beramendi, Silja Häusermann, Herbert Kitschelt, and Hanspeter Kriesi, eds., *The Politics of Advanced Capitalism*. Cambridge: Cambridge University Press, 2015.
4. Hanspeter Kriesi, Restructuring the national political space. In Hanspeter Kriesi et al., *Political Conflict in Western Europe*. Cambridge: Cambridge University Press, 2012.
5. Knutsen, *Social Structure, Value Orientations and Party Choice in Western Europe*.
6. Hanspeter Kriesi, Contexts of party mobilization. In Hanspeter Kriesi et al., *West European Politics in the Age of Globalization*. Cambridge: Cambridge University Press, 2008, pp. 33–4.
7. Romain Lachat and Martin Dolezal, Demand side: Dealignment and realignment of the structural political potentials. In Hanspeter Kriesi et al., *West European Politics in the Age of Globalization*. Cambridge: Cambridge University Press, 2008. This might be a function of different questions being asked across time and nations. Knutsen's analysis of the European Social Survey showed that class polarization was highest in Nordic systems that are lower in social status inequality, but the religious cleavage was sharper in Mediterranean nations.
8. Oddbjørn Knutsen, *Social Structure, Value Orientations and Party Choice in Western Europe*. London: Palgrave, 2017, ch. 3.
9. The 2014 European Election Study also might be impacted by the immediate financial crisis in Europe, and the 2014 survey had only eight issue questions so measuring the economic and political cleavage is built on a thinner base.

Political Realignment

10. The ordering of the economic and cultural cleavages sometimes differed across nations.
11. The least congruent countries were Belgium and Portugal.
12. Häusermann and Kriesi, What do voters want?
13. Kriesi, Restructuring the national political space; Lachat and Martin Dolezal, Demand side. Knutsen, *Social Structure, Value Orientations and Party Choice in Western Europe*.
14. One area deserving more attention is the varied polarity of the coefficients for political support. With more cases one might explore whether the composition of the government, political history, or another factor explains these differences.
15. Kriesi, Contexts of party mobilization; Häusermann and Kriesi, What do voters want?
16. Less expected are the relatively larger group differences on the cultural cleavage. The middle-class/working-class gap on the cultural cleavage is wider in the three egalitarian nations.
17. I also compared the PCA analyses for three distinctive groups of nations defined by their economic system and their religious norms (see Table 4.4). These analyses showed general consistency across these different contexts.
18. See Chapter 7 on how the degree of party polarization affects the relationship between cleavage positions and party vote choice.

5

Elites, Issues, and Political Cleavages

In 1979 Marjorie (Mo) Mowlam was hired as a young political science professor at the University of Newcastle-upon-Tyne. She was raised in England but had received her Ph.D. in political science from the University of Iowa. Mowlam was a Labourite at heart and had earlier worked for Labour MP Tony Benn. She was active in feminist causes and supported Britain's campaign for nuclear disarmament. She started attending local Labour Party meetings in Newcastle and worked on the 1983 Labour campaign. But she was a fish out of water since the local party was dominated by male, blue-collar, union workers, and union officials. A young, blonde, feminist with a Ph.D. from a U.S. university didn't quite fit, and so she was passed over when she first sought office.

In 1987 the MP for the Redcar constituency, an official for the National Union of Blastfurnacemen, decided to retire. Under prodding by the national party, the local Labour Party selected Mowlam as its candidate and she won the election. She represented a different sort of Labour MP. Women constituted only a very small fraction of the MPs, it was still a gentlemen's club on both benches. Many of her policy positions did not conform to the majority of her party. But eventually she rose through the ranks, became a member of Tony Blair's cabinet, and for a time was one of the most popular politicians in Britain.[1]

Mowlam's experience illustrates some of the changes that occurred within the political parties that parallel the citizen patterns described in previous chapters. She was a leading Labour politician and top elected official when she retired as a cabinet minister and Chancellor of the Duchy of Lancaster in 2001. By conventional political science standards, however, she was hard to place on the traditional Left–Right scale. She was a liberal on both the economic and cultural cleavages, but an unconventional mix of both that sometimes put her at odds with other Labour Party supporters who thought only in terms of economic issues.

This chapter examines the opinions of party elites to determine how the supply of political choices in Europe has evolved over time. Did the political views of party elites change over time as in the Mowlam example as elites also adjusted to social modernization? In 1979, 1994, and 2009, the European Election Studies (EES) interviewed Candidates to the European Parliament (CEPs). The surveys asked candidates about their positions on the same issues as in the citizen surveys.

I first examine the structure of elite issue opinions to see if a two-dimensional cleavage structure is also apparent among elites. Then, the chapter describes the correlates of cleavage positions among elites. Many of the demographic forces that shape public opinion may also influence the views of party elites. Citizen-elite similarities in the correlates of cleavage positions can potentially strengthen voter-party linkages. I also map the distribution of national elites on both political cleavages.

Issues and Cleavages in 1979

The 1979 election for the European Parliament was a historic event. It was the first direct election of the parliament's members, and the first true transnational election in history. The EES sampled candidates drawn from the party lists, and 742 CEPs were interviewed during the late spring of 1979.[2]

I am not interested in the EP elections per se. Rather, these data offer a rare opportunity to compare the opinions of top-level party elites cross-nationally. In most cases, the parties' nomination procedures for the EP elections followed their procedures for national parliamentary elections. In addition, the historic nature of the direct elections and the growing importance of the European project meant that a wide range of party leaders ran for election—François Mitterrand, Willy Brandt, Leo Tindemans, Georges Marchal, Benito Craxi, and others—and won seats in the European Parliament. The result is a sample of the top stratum of European political elites: 78 percent had held party office, and 61 percent had held elective office.

The CEP survey included the same fourteen issues asked in the 1979 citizen survey (Chapter 2). I used Principle Components Analysis (PCA) to identify whether an economic cleavage and cultural cleavage structure elite opinions as for citizen opinions.[3] The PCA extracted two broad components for political elites, similar to the results from the citizen study.[4] The left side of Table 5.1 presents the results for the elite sample in all nine member states, and the right side repeats the results from the citizen survey.

The first component in the CEP study connects several economic issues: controlling multinationals, reducing income inequality, expanding public management of the economy, greater employee representation, and aid to Europe's regions and the developing nations. The general pattern of the economic cleavage is similar across both samples. Since the economic cleavage was a formative influence on European party systems and continues to

Elites, Issues, and Political Cleavages

Table 5.1. Elite and Citizen Issue Structures, 1979

	Elites		Citizens	
Issue Questions	Economic	Cultural	Economic	Cultural
Control multinationals	0.693	0.363	0.487	0.285
Develop nuclear energy	−0.310	−0.483	−0.162	−0.554
Reduce income inequality	0.704	0.262	0.592	0.195
Increase penalties for terrorism	−0.123	−0.592	−0.007	−0.408
Expand public ownership of industry	0.238	0.766	0.510	0.222
Government to manage economy	0.514	0.544	0.548	0.024
Stronger military defense	−0.184	−0.760	−0.092	−0.601
Women to decide abortions	0.129	0.608	0.199	0.249
Equal representation for employees	0.471	0.371	0.625	0.274
More aid to third world	0.717	0.175	0.519	−0.215
Stronger antipollution	0.717	0.092	0.479	−0.084
Protect free expression	0.536	0.085	0.569	0.021
Aid less developed regions	0.708	−0.141	0.595	−0.326
For European unification	0.185	−0.637	0.135	−0.542
Eigenvalue	3.53	3.22	2.80	1.59
Shared variance percentage	25.2	23.0	22.0	11.3

Note: Table entries are coefficients from Principal Components Analysis with a Varimax rotation and pairwise deletion of missing data.
Source: Candidates for the European Parliament Study, 1979; 1979 European Election Study (Eurobarometer 11).

structure political competition, its existence in elite issue positions is not surprising.[5]

The second component is a mix of cultural items. The conservative pole includes support for national defense, stronger penalties against terrorism, and opinions toward European unification.[6] As with the public sample, European unification is seen as strengthening the member states. The liberal cultural pole is defined by support for a woman's abortion rights and a weaker loading for employee representation.

In overall terms, citizen-defined and elite-defined perceptions of the political space are broadly similar. Both groups of Europeans see a similar two-dimensional structure of political competition. Elite opinions are more structured than citizen opinions. This shows in the higher coefficients for most issues in the elite PCA, and higher shared variance for both components. This is typical in opinion analyses comparing citizens and elites.[7] And while the two components are distinct in both PCAs, elites are more likely to interconnect both cleavages to reflect a Left-libertarian versus Right-authoritarian framework.[8]

Issues and Cleavages in 1994

Linked to the 1994 elections, a new project team surveyed candidates for the Europe Parliament.[9] None of the general public surveys included a comparable

Table 5.2. Elite Issue Structures, 1994

Issue Questions	Economic	Cultural
Diminish income inequality	0.783	0.182
Tougher action against criminals	0.013	−0.797
Government to have greater role in economy	0.725	0.242
Women to be free to decide on abortion	0.286	0.615
More state protection of environment	0.628	0.074
More state protection individual rights	0.568	0.112
Stronger limits on immigration	−0.363	−0.661
Maintain current welfare level	0.621	0.380
Decriminalize marijuana	0.224	0.722
Attitude towards European integration	−0.019	0.081
Eigenvalue	2.62	2.21
Shared variance percentage	26.2	22.1

Note: Table entries are coefficients from Principal Components Analysis with a Varimax rotation and pairwise deletion of missing data.

Source: Candidates for the European Parliament Study, 1994, EU12 nations. Weighted by party vote share.

battery of issue questions. So I examine elites to see the evolution of elite opinions since the 1979 survey. The EES asked for opinions on nine issues questions that span both economic and cultural themes, adding a general question on support for European integration. The issue questions were asked in every nation except Sweden, with 1256 candidates from over 100 political parties.

Table 5.2 presents the PCA of candidates' issue opinions. The slightly different mix of issues in 1994 produces two cleavage dimensions similar to the 1979 CEP survey.[10] A first component includes economic issues such as income inequality, the government's role in managing the economy, and maintaining current welfare benefits. Even with different issues and different coefficient values, this economic cleavage is similar to the 1979 results.

The second component is a distinct cultural cleavage. The conservative pole includes the issues of tougher action against criminals and stronger limits on immigration. The connection of immigration to a conservative cultural position is not inevitable, but it is certainly explainable. Immigration from outside the EU had grown because of the breakup of the Soviet Union, the Balkan wars, and the general process of economic globalization. In addition, immigrants are a clear marker of how society is changing in unfamiliar ways and thus the topic is easily linked to other aspects of the cultural cleavage. In contrast, a liberal cultural orientation taps the issues of abortion rights for women and decriminalization of marijuana. The coefficients for these four issues are equally high values, but with opposite polarity. Elites draw a clearer distinction between both cleavages compared to 1979, with each issue strongly related to only one dimension.[11]

Issues and Cleavages in 2009

The 2009 European Parliament elections were the first after the onset of the financial crisis in 2008. The three largest EP party groups lost votes in the election, presumably as a reaction to the crisis, and the representation of Green parties and far-right parties increased. It was in this context that the EES surveyed 1236 candidates for the European Parliament in the EU15 member states.[12]

As for the general public in 2009, the EES asked elites to give their opinions on a comparable battery of issue questions. Reflecting the changing times, an item on same-sex marriage and questions on women's roles highlighted the shift toward cultural issues across Europe. The battery also included two immigration questions while none were asked in the 1979 survey. In addition, a familiar set of issues tapped sentiments on the economic cleavage.

Table 5.3 presents the results of a PCA testing for an economic and cultural cleavage structuring these issue opinions.[13] The left side of the table presents the elite results, the right side displays the general public results from Chapter 2.

Because of the increased number of cultural issues, the cultural cleavage emerges as the first component in both samples. Among elites, the cultural cleavage strongly connects issues such immigration, same-sex marriage, women's rights, and attitudes towards lawbreaking. One could argue that these are distinct issues, and there is little reason for attitudes toward immigrants to be linked to same-sex marriage or a woman's right to choose an abortion, or teaching

Table 5.3. Elite and Citizen Issue Structures, 2009

	Elites		Citizens	
Issue Questions	Cultural	Economic	Cultural	Economic
Immigrants should adapt to country's customs	0.723	−0.207	0.611	−0.065
Private enterprise best to solve economic problems	0.407	−0.734	0.357	−0.480
Prohibit same-sex marriages	0.774	−0.052	0.549	−0.262
State should own public services and industries	−0.093	0.804	0.190	0.513
Women free to decide on abortion	−0.574	0.148	−0.128	0.455
Politics should not intervene in the economy	0.300	−0.577	0.335	−0.045
Harsh sentences for lawbreakers	0.707	−0.129	0.640	0.068
Redistribute income and wealth	−0.235	0.748	0.332	0.539
Schools teach children to obey authority	0.676	−0.155	0.608	0.047
Referendums should decide EU treaty changes	0.419	0.555	0.420	0.437
Women should reduce paid work for family	0.709	−0.052	0.527	−0.178
Decrease immigration significantly	0.844	−0.037	0.730	−0.058
Attitude to European unification	0.411	0.439	0.277	0.118
Eigenvalue	4.28	2.69	2.81	1.42
Shared variance percentage	32.9	20.6	21.6	10.9

Note: Table entries are coefficients from Principal Components Analysis with a Varimax rotation and pairwise deletion of missing data.
Source: European Election Study 2009, Candidate and Citizen surveys, EU15 nations.

respect for authority in the schools. In the minds of elites and many citizens, these items reflect a common worldview of cultural conservatism—an earlier time when these topics were not political issues because societal norms were different. Such is the nature of the contemporary culture clash.[14]

The economic items in the 2009 survey form a clear second dimension. Endorsement of private enterprise, opposition to state ownership of public services, and opposition to income redistribution are all strongly interrelated. However, opinions toward to the EU are now linked to both the cultural and economic cleavages, which perhaps is a sign of the Union's expanding political role since 1979.

Over these three decades the greatest change is the emergence of a clear cultural cleavage in the issue opinions of EU elites, and presumably members of most national parliaments. Both the cultural and economic cleavages are highly structured in elite belief systems, as noted in the high percentage of shared variance on both components. Furthermore, compared to 1979, there is a greater separation between the two cleavages.[15] Thus, since the early 1990s the structure of the political space among political elites has been framed by the economic and cultural cleavages, and new cultural issues have been integrated into this existing structure.

The Correlates of Cleavage Positions

Candidates to the European Parliament are obviously very different from the average European in their social and economic backgrounds. For instance, only a sixth of the 1979 Parliament were women. Almost two-thirds came from middle-class families based on their father's education. They represent the very top level of politically engaged individuals, regardless of their political position or party. The British delegation, for example, included the 9th Duke of Wellington,, two barons and two baronets, and a handful of life peers—not quite an average group of blokes.[16] Thus comparing the distribution of opinions across standard demographic variables leaves little room for variation. Even by the 2009 survey, about four-fifths of CEPs reported at least some level of college education, the median age was 49 years, only a tenth self-identified as working class, and two-thirds were male.

Still, the cleavage positions of political elites should reflect their own experiences, their own group affiliations, and other social traits. So paralleling Chapter 3, this section explores the potential social bases of elite cleavage positions. I repeat the methodology used in studying the general public; the PCA models produce component scores for elites in all three surveys.[17] The issues in each year differ, but I believe that the underlying dimensions represent the same two broad cleavages. With the relatively small national

Elites, Issues, and Political Cleavages

samples in 1979, the analyses have to look at broad patterns rather than detailed comparisons. A more fundamental problem is that some of the CEP's social characteristics are unavailable in the 1979 survey.[18]

Candidates for the European Parliament in 1979

To an extent, one might expect elite attitudes to reflect their social position, perhaps attenuated by their high social and political status. But many of the correlates of attitudes in the general public surveys may carry over to elites. Table 5.4 presents the correlations between some basic social characteristics and both political cleavages in 1979. The CEP's former occupation before entering politics shows a substantial correlation with their positions on both cleavages. In addition, the father's reported occupation has an even stronger relationship with cleavage positions, indicating the persistence of class alignments. The better educated are slightly more conservative on economic issues, but liberal on cultural issues.

The top panel in Figure 5.1 shows that class follows a general liberal-conservative pattern on both cleavages. Elites from upper middle-class occupational backgrounds—business owners, professionals, managers, and executives—have conservative positions on both the economic and cultural cleavages. In contrast, white-collar workers and the working class lean toward the liberal pole on both cleavages. Class patterns for elites thus echo the pattern for the general public in 1979 (see Figure 3.1). Overall, there is a conservative-liberal consistency across class groupings.

Generation can be an important marker of broader societal trends influencing the political positions of succeeding generations of elites.[19] There are only

Table 5.4. Social Status and Elite Cleavage Positions, 1979

	1979	
Predictor	Economic	Cultural
CEP's occupation*	0.25	0.27
Father's occupation*	0.31	0.30
Education	0.04	−0.06
Age	0.03	−0.19
Church attendance	0.14	−0.42
Gender (female)	−0.03	0.19
Left–Right	0.49	0.63

Note: Table entries are Pearson r correlations except for the respondents and their father's occupation (Eta correlation); positive values on cleavage indices are liberal positions.

Sources: 1979 Candidates for the European Parliament survey, EU9 nations.

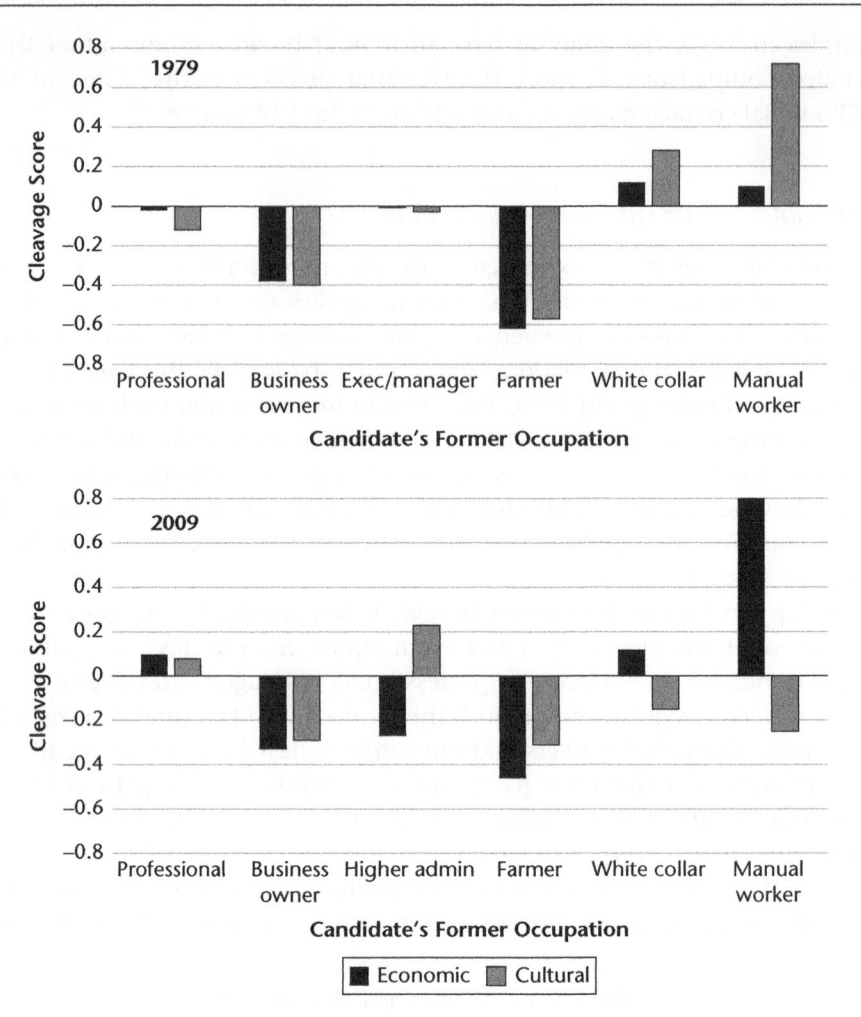

Figure 5.1. Elite Occupation and Cleavage Positions, 1979 and 2009

Note: Figure entries are mean scores on the economic and cultural cleavages. Positive values are liberal positions.

Source: 1979 and 2009 Candidates for the European Parliament Surveys.

modest differences in economic positions between younger and older CEPs. However, older elites are substantially more conservative on the cultural cleavage. To the extent that the cultural cleavage represents the tension between modernization trends and a retrospective view of a past society, this is what should be expected.

This cultural clash appears even more clearly in the relationship between religiosity and both cleavages. Those who attend church more regularly hold distinctly conservative positions on the cultural cleavage. The only issue on the cultural cleavage with an explicit religious connection is abortion. And

Elites, Issues, and Political Cleavages

even when this item is excluded from the cultural cleavage measure, there is still a sizeable negative relationship (r = .−29).[20] So although religion is related to cultural orientations, religion is tapping broader orientations toward authority, security, and traditional values.

Gender differences in political values can be complex. Women voters have historically supported conservative parties, ostensibly because of their concern about traditional values, the importance of the family, and security concerns. However, in terms of political cleavages, the expectations are somewhat different. Gender differences on the economic cleavage are not statistically significant. Women are significantly more liberal on the cultural cleavage.

Finally, the 1979 CEP study asked respondents to position themselves on the standard Left–Right scale. Paralleling the findings for the general public in 1979, overall Left–Right positions are strongly related to both the economic and cultural cleavages. The relationships are notably stronger than for the European public (Table 3.2), which is typical in elite-public comparisons. Even at this earlier time point, the cultural cleavage is very strongly linked to the overall ideological identity of elites.

Candidate for the European Parliament in 1994 and 2009

The 1994 and 2009 surveys can show how the political orientations of political elites changed from the CEPs in 1979. By these two later surveys, the EP had institutionalized its status in Europe, attracting politicians focused on European careers. Their political role and lifestyle in Strasbourg and Brussels put them on par with the members of many national parliaments. And their political views stood as reasonable articulations of their party's policies.

Many of the CEPs had long non-political careers, and so the EES asked about their occupation before becoming a full-time politician. The first row of Table 5.5 shows a strong relationship between occupation and the economic cleavage, and a sizeable relationship for the cultural cleavage in the 2009 survey. In addition, a subjective social-class question in 2009 displays a strong relationship with the economic cleavage, and a weak correlation with the cultural cleavage.

More insightful, however, is the pattern across specific occupational groups. The lower panel of Figure 5.1 presents occupational differences on both cleavages in 2009 to maximize the time distance from the 1979 results in the top panel.[21] Business owners, higher administrators, and farmers show distinctly conservative positions on the economic cleavage, with manual workers leaning heavily toward liberal economic positions. Professionals and white-collar workers have ambivalent economic views; a similar pattern was apparent in the 1994 CEP survey (not shown).

95

Political Realignment

Table 5.5. Social Status and Elite Cleavage Positions, 1994 and 2009

Predictor	1994 Economic Cleavage	1994 Cultural Cleavage	2009 Economic Cleavage	2009 Cultural Cleavage
CEP's occupation*	0.14	0.13	0.30	0.23
Subjective class	–	–	0.42	0.09
Education	−0.11	0.04	−0.10	0.10
Age	−0.06	−0.02	0.08	−0.25
Church attendance	−0.17	−0.42	−0.22	−0.34
Religiosity	–	–	−0.22	−0.34
Gender (female)	0.19	0.17	0.06	0.21
Urban residence	–	–	0.06	0.17
Satisfied with democracy	−0.31	−0.21	−0.42	0.18
Satisfied EU democracy	−0.11	−0.21	−0.42	0.26
Left–Right	0.54	0.56	0.58	0.56

Note: Table entries are Pearson r correlations except for occupation (Eta correlation); positive values on cleavage indices are liberal positions. A dash means the variable was not available in the survey.

Sources: 1994 and 2009 Candidates for the European Parliament Surveys, EU12 and EU15 nations respectively; weighted by party vote share.

The cultural cleavage shows a clear realignment of group positions. By 2009, manual workers joined business owners and farmers in favoring a conservative cultural position. In contrast, professionals, and higher administrators express more liberal cultural values than in 1979. The simple middle-class versus working-class divide seen in the top panel of Figure 5.1 no longer appears.

Educational patterns in both CEP surveys mirror this result. There is a weak tendency for the better educated to be more conservative on economic cleavage in both 1994 and 2009. At the same time, the better educated elites are more liberal on the cultural cleavage, and this correlation increases between the 1994 and 2009 surveys. Cultural liberalism has a middle-class, highly educated base. Given the elite status of CEP members, the ability to identify the residual influence of socio-economic traits is somewhat surprising.[22]

Another sign of social change involves the relationship between age and political cleavages positions. In 1979 both of the age patterns were modest. In the 1994 survey, there is still a weak age pattern on the both cleavages, but older elites are becoming more culturally conservative. By 2009, there is a strong pattern of older elites leaning toward conservative cultural values—an indicator of their reaction to cultural change. Older elites in 1994 and 2009 display a substantially weaker tendency toward a liberal position on the economic cleavage.

Gender differences on the economic cleavage remain muted. Women CEPs lean slightly toward economic liberalism and even more strongly toward cultural liberalism when compared to 1979. The cultural pattern is stronger among CEPs than among the general public (compare to Table 3.3).

Another common demographic marker of attitudes is the rural/urban divide. I expected more liberal opinions in urban areas than in rural areas, which might be reflected in the attitudes of CEPs. The complication is that the EP elections use a PR system where candidates are not formally dispersed through the nation. Still, Table 5.5 shows that candidates in the 2009 study who live in urban areas are more liberal on the economic cleavage, and even more so on the cultural cleavage. This harks back to Lipset and Rokkan's similar discussion of the rural/urban cleavage as a historical cleavage in Europe.[23]

One of the most significant results comes from comparing cleavage positions with satisfaction with the function of the national and EU government. My presumption is that satisfaction reflects how elites think the government is responding to their own issue concerns. The contrast is striking. In 1994, economic and cultural conservatives both tended to be dissatisfied with the functioning of government, albeit modestly so.

By 2009, economic conservatives who favor an unfettered market economy are distinctly more satisfied with both their national and EU governments. In contrast, liberal culturalists are more positive about government performance. In terms of these European elites in overall terms, this reveals their perceptions of the course of public policy in Europe—a conservative trend on economic matters and a liberal trend on cultural issues.[24] Unfortunately, no comparable measure exists in the 1979 CEP survey to determine if this relationship has changed over time.

The last row in Table 5.5 presents the relationships between Left–Right orientations and the two cleavage dimensions. Both correlations are very strong in each survey even though the two cleavages are statistically unrelated to each other because of the PCA methodology. Using the two cleavage positions to predict Left–Right orientations in 2009, for example, explains two-thirds of the total variance (R=0.80). So both cleavages have relatively equal weight on the Left–Right identities of these elites.

In summary, it appears that social polarization on the cultural cleavage has increased over time. A realignment in the liberal positions of professionals, the better-educated, and younger elites—counterbalanced by a conservative shift by the working class—has created a new group bases for these issues. Moreover, this shift in the class alignment of political elites parallels the changes observed for the European general public (Chapter 3). One might speculate on the causal direction of these patterns. Is this a bottom-up pattern of changing public values influencing elite views, or a top-down pattern of elites sending political cues to prompt citizens to change? Undoubtedly there is a bit of both, and I lack the empirical evidence to answer this question. So perhaps the broadest conclusion is that the social alignments of both citizens and elites are responding to social modernization in similar ways.

Political Realignment

Cross-national Patterns

A final perspective comes from plotting elite positions on the economic and cultural cleavages for each nation. This is more problematic than for the general public samples because the CEP samples are much smaller. In addition, not all parties agreed to participate in the surveys, which can distort national means even in the party weighted results. With caution, this information is useful.

I begin with the 2009 survey because it benefitted from thirty years of experience in interviewing elites, and the party coverage is more representative. The sample sizes are larger in each nation as well. The expansion to the EU15 nations also gives more breadth to the cross-national comparisons. There is abundant evidence that the political culture of Northern Europe and Scandinavia tends to be more liberal in cultural terms, while Mediterranean Europe is more conservative.[25] Other studies point to the contrast between nations with competitive versus egalitarian economic norms (see Chapter 4). Do such patterns emerge among CEPs?

Figure 5.2 plots the national means on the economic and cultural cleavage for elites in 2009.[26] Too much emphasis should not be placed on the location

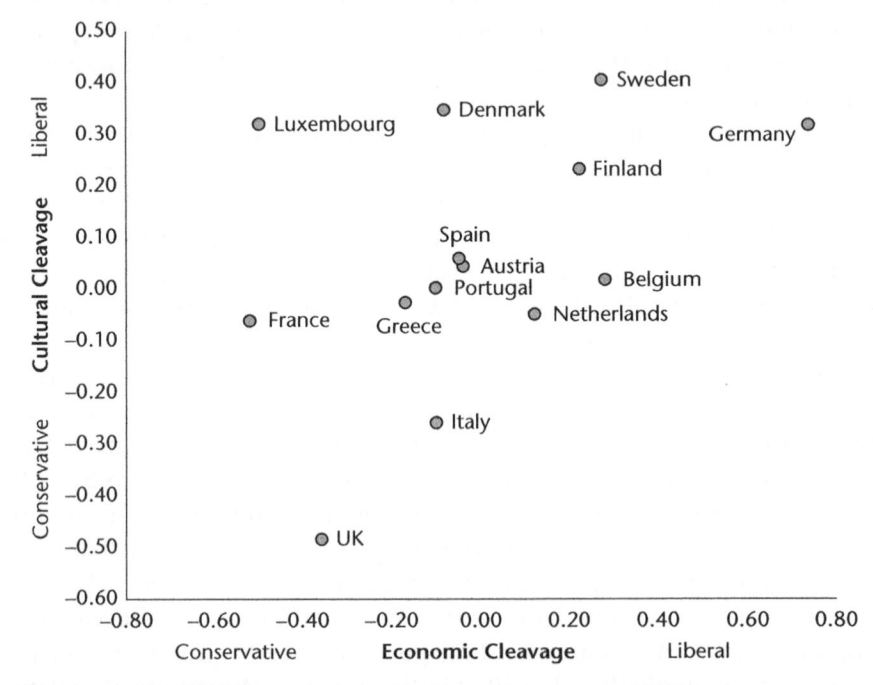

Figure 5.2. National Differences in CEP Cleavage Positions, 2009

Note: Figure entries are mean scores on the economic and cultural cleavage. Positive values are liberal positions.

Source: 2009 Candidates for the European Parliament Survey. Weighted by party vote shares.

Elites, Issues, and Political Cleavages

of any one nation, because of the uncertain representativeness of the CEP samples. Perhaps the most notable pattern is the cross-national dispersion on both the economic and cultural cleavages.[27] The four nations with the most economically conservative elites are France, Luxembourg, Britain, and Greece. In contrast, the four nations with the most economically liberal elites are in Germany, Belgium, Sweden, and Finland.

The three Scandinavian nations stand out for their liberalism on the cultural dimension which is consistent with their respective publics (Figure 2.2). Conversely, British, Irish, and Italian elites lean toward the conservative cultural positions much as the general public in these nations. To a partial degree, elites' cultural positions lean toward a North–South pattern or between Catholic and Protestant nations.

Figure 5.3 presents the comparable results for ten EU nations in 1994.[28] Sweden did not ask the issue batteries in 1994. The Portuguese elites are an outlier on both dimensions, which led to their exclusion.[29] Among the nations in the figure, there is more cross-national variation on economic positions than on the cultural cleavage. Party elites in Spain, the UK, Germany, Italy, and France lean toward economic liberalism, while the Dutch elites are

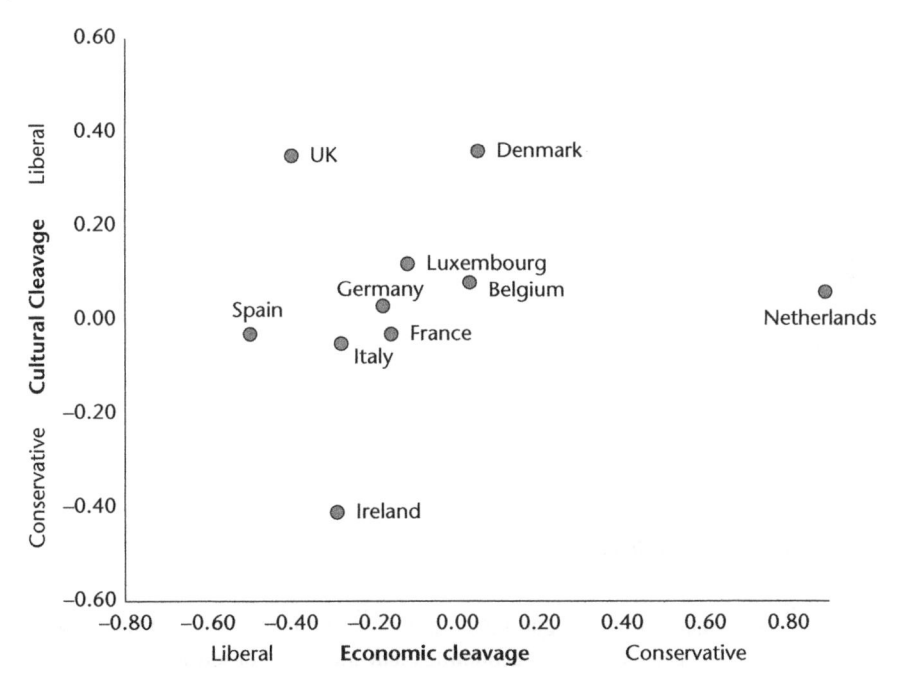

Figure 5.3. National Differences in CEP Cleavage Positions, 1994

Note: Figure entries are mean scores on the economic and cultural cleavages. Positive values are liberal positions.

Source: 1994 Candidates for the European Parliament Surveys. Weighted by party vote shares.

Political Realignment

the most economically conservative. There is also a tendency for elites from Catholic nations to be more conservative on the cultural cleavage than the Protestant nations of the UK and Denmark. Still, these national results should be viewed with caution because they depend on the small number of respondents and some parties are missing, which can affect the overall result.

Finally, Figure 5.4 presents the cross-national patterns from the 1979 CEP study.[30] In these comparisons, Danish elites are outliers on both cleavages. However, this pattern is also reflected in the Danish general public results in 1979 (Figure 2.2). The cultural liberalism of Danish elites and the citizenry seems consistent with other studies, and the 1979 election saw a shift toward the conservative economic position of the non-socialist coalition in reaction to the negative state of the economy. The other nations are clustered more tightly with about the same variation along the economic and cultural cleavage.[31] Again, the cross-national patterns do not seem to be based on religious traditions or levels of economic development.

Admittedly, it is difficult to compare the continuity in the positions of party elites in each nation over these three time points. In part, the representativeness

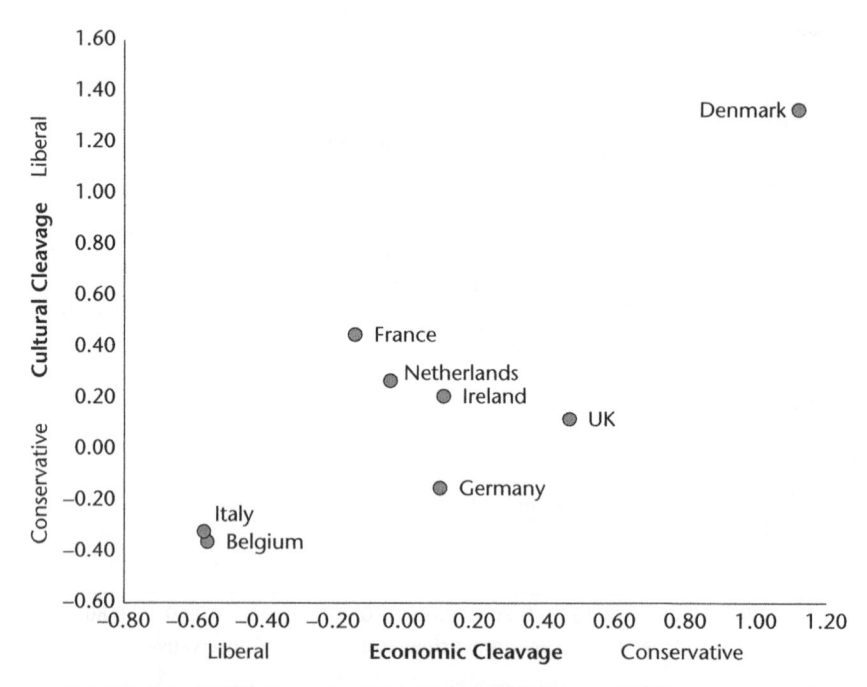

Figure 5.4. National Differences in CEP Cleavage Positions, 1979

Note: Figure entries are mean scores on the economic and cultural cleavages. Positive values are liberal positions.

Source: 1979 Candidates for the European Parliament Surveys. Weighted by party vote shares.

of elite samples varies, with a modest number of interviews and some parties not participating. This is one reason why I focus on pooled elite analyses that draw upon the full sample. In addition, party positions have really changed in some instances, possibly reflecting the policies of the parties in power, the national context, or a conscious realignment of the party's identity. Such causal explanations are, however, difficult to judge empirically with the data at hand. Therefore, we should refocus attention on the 2009 results whose evidence is most reliable. This survey shows wide national variation on both the economic and cultural cleavages among party elites that seems to mirror the citizenry in these nations (See Chapter 4).

Citizens and Elites

Life as a member of the European Parliament is demanding, but also rewarding. For twelve sessions a year they meet in Strasbourg, with its wonderful Quartier des Tanneurs, the cathedral, and numerous historic churches. I can verify that the food in this picturesque Alsatian city is exceptional, especially if one is on an expense budget. Then they pack up the offices in the Louise Weiss building and head off to Brussels for additional sessions and meetings with representatives of the other EU institutions. The salary and benefits of MEPs are generous, especially considering the workload. It is a heady life, but what about the people back home who elected these representatives to the European Parliament?

There are many reasons to expect similarities between European citizens and political elites. Democracy implies that citizens elect elites who share their political beliefs and can represent them in the political process. Elites became active in their chosen parties, presumably, because they share the values embedded in the party and its programs.

However, elites are, well, elite. In social status, political experience, and a host of other factors the CEPs are very different from the average European. Their social status, life style, and other factors can potentially distance members of the European Parliament from their own social roots, and the life experiences of their voters. Robert Putnam's law of increasing disproportionality holds that as one moves to ever higher elite status, the differences from the average citizen increase.[32] And candidates for the European Parliament are high-level party elites.

The similarities between citizens and elites begin with their perceptions of the political space. Both groups see issues combining in similar ways to identify the economic and cultural cleavages. Both groups also display the evolution and crystallization of the cultural cleavage between 1979 and 2009.

Political Realignment

There is a common two-dimensional political space for citizens and elites, although CEPs see a clearer structure because of their political engagement.

Perhaps more surprising is the similarity in the correlates of cleavage positions across citizens and elites, despite the law in increasing disproportionality. Not only are the class correlates of cleavage positions comparable across both groups, they also follow the same realignment pattern across time. The Left–Right alignment of occupation groups in 1979 shifts with some middle-class elites moving toward a liberal culturalist position, while elites from a working-class background move toward a conservative cultural position. This realignment in political cleavages over this three-decade span is seen in citizen surveys that track this gradual evolution over time, and now we see parallel evidence at the elite level.[33]

Another similarity is the importance of religiosity as a predictor of cultural values among citizens and elites over time. There is also a strong age gradient in cultural attitudes for both citizens and elites. These relationships are further evidence that the cultural cleavage reflects broad orientations that contrast traditional images of society against a liberal modernist version. This cleavage has crystallized over time, as political alliances link newer issues into the cultural cleavage.

Elite attitudes can illuminate the content of current public policy. For example, CEPs exhibit very strong relationships between their own cleavage positions and their evaluations of the performance of the democratic system in their respective nations. Elites and citizens who favor conservative economic policies are more positive in their performance evaluations in 2014, while liberal culturalists are also more positive. One might view this as a summary of the course of public policy across the EU.

At the same time, there are important differences to highlight. The highly structured belief system of elites indicates that these cleavages define the lines of political competition in Europe today. If people respond to the political supply of choices provided by parties and elites, this implies that the party choices now are clearly framed by these two cleavages (see Chapter 6).

And even though the social correlates of cleavage positions are similar for citizens and party elites, the distribution of social positions vary substantially. The elite bias of the CEPs mean they accentuate the views of the upper middle class, the affluent, and the well-educated. These compositional differences may make CEPs less representative of the distribution of opinions in their nation. For example, Wouter Schakel and Armen Hakhverdian used a series of mass-elite surveys for the Netherlands to explore this topic, and found a widening representation gap between the better and less well educated on multicultural issues.[34] This same distancing of elites from the average citizen may be occurring across the EU (see Chapter 8).

Elites, Issues, and Political Cleavages

In summary, both citizens and elites similarly see the contemporary space as defined by both cleavages. They also show the same evolutionary process to current cleavage alignments in broad terms. This leads to the question of whether citizens use these cleavage positions to select parties to represent them within the political process.

Notes

1. Julia Langdon, *Mo Mowlam*. New York: Little Brown, 2001.
2. The Inter-university Consortium for Political and Social Research distributes the 1979 CEP survey (ICPSR 9033). Some of the demographic variables were restricted to protect the confidentiality of the respondents. The principal investigators generously gave me access to the unrestricted data. Also see note 10 on restrictions in the 1979 survey.
3. To ensure the overall representativeness of the elite sample, the data are weighted by the party weight variable provided in the dataset. This weight ensures that elites from each nation are represented in proportion to the nation's population size, and parties are represented in proportion to their vote share in the most recent national election. This also minimizes the effects of small parties whose candidates responded in higher proportions.
4. A third component barely met the minimum standard for extraction (Eigenvalue = 1.04), with nuclear power and penalties for terrorism having high loadings. Russell Dalton, Political parties and political representation: Party supporters and party elites in nine nations, *Comparative Political Studies* (1985) 18: 267–99.
5. The environmental protection variable loads on the economic dimension as well. This might be because the question calls for state action on the environment, and the distribution is highly skewed toward positive replies, which restricts the variance and relationship with other issues.
6. In the 1970s the major terrorist threats were domestic radicals, such as the Red Army Faction: the Baader-Meinhof group in Germany and the Brigate Rosse in Italy.
7. Philip Converse, The nature of belief systems in mass publics. In David Apter, ed., *Ideology and Discontent*. New York: Free Press, 1964; Philip Converse and Roy Pierce, *Political Representation in France*. Cambridge: Harvard University Press, 1986.
8. Oblimin solutions that allowed a correlation between the two dimensions showed a significantly larger correlation for the elite sample (r=0.31) than for the citizen sample (r=0.09). On Left-libertarian perspective see Herbert Kitschelt, Left-Libertarian parties: Explaining innovation in competitive party systems, *World Politics* (1988) 40: 194–234.
9. Lieven de Winter et al., *European Candidates Study 1994*. GESIS Data Archive, Cologne. ZA3077. The Swedish sample was not asked the same issue battery, so it is not included in these analyses.
10. A third dimension barely exceeds Kaiser's Criterion (Eigenvalue=1.07), so I constrained the result to two dimensions. The results are quite similar to

Political Realignment

Thomassen and Schmitt's analyses of this same survey, except they included several EU-related questions that produced a third European-national dimension. Jacques Thomassen and Hermann Schmitt, Policy representation, *European Journal of Political Research* (1997) 32: 165–84.

11. However, an Oblimin rotation shows that positions on the two dimensions are still significantly correlated (r=0.296).
12. For further information on the survey see: Hans Giebler and Bernhard Weßels, *2009 European Election Candidate Study: Methodological Annex*. GESIS Data Archive, Cologne. ZA37352. https://www.gesis.org/. The data are available as: Bernhard Weßels, et al 2011. *European Parliament Election Study 2009, Candidate Study*. GESIS Data Archive, Cologne. ZA5048. https://www.gesis.org/.
13. A third dimension barely exceeds Kaiser's Criterion (Eigenvalue=1.04) so I constrained the result to two dimensions. Russell Dalton, Party representation across multiple issue dimensions, *Party Politics* (2017) 23: 609–22.
14. This also partially reflects how political discourse and the positions of political actors shaped these connections; see Chapter 6; Ronald Inglehart and Pippa Norris, Trump and the populist authoritarian parties: *The Silent Revolution* in reverse, *Perspective on Politics* (2017) 15: 443–54. But there are also contrary examples; Pim Fortuyn founded his party in the Netherlands on the basis that increased immigration conflicted with liberal values that endorsed same-sex marriage and women's rights. And in some nations early opposition to immigrants centered among communist parties because of their concern for competition to their working-class supporters.
15. The assumption of orthogonality in the PCA is more accurate in 2009. In Oblimin solutions that allowed the two dimensions to be related, the correlation was a significantly weaker than in 1979 (r=0.11) and comparable to the citizen sample (r=0.09).
16. https://en.wikipedia.org/wiki/List_of_members_of_the_European_Parliament_for_the_United_Kingdom,_1979–84
17. The models in Tables 5.1 to 5.3 are used to create economic and cultural cleavage scores. In each year about a sixth of the sample did not respond to the issue questions, and are coded as missing data. Preliminary analyses did not detect a strong ideological or national pattern in these non-responses.
18. Neither the original principal investigator nor the ICPSR has a dataset with all the restricted variables that were original excluded to protect respondent confidentiality. These include questions on national party, age, gender and other demographics. However, I was able to recover some of the required variables from an intermediary dataset.
19. Russell Dalton, Generational change in elite political beliefs: The growth of ideological polarization, *Journal of Politics* (1987) 49: 976–97.
20. I repeated the PCA analyses excluding the abortion question, and computed new scores for the economic and cultural cleavages. The cleavages are not as clearly defined without the abortion question, but follow similar patterns.
21. The 1994 survey coded occupation categories differently, which limits direct comparisons.

Elites, Issues, and Political Cleavages

22. The 2009 survey also asked CEPs about their membership in various interest or affinity groups. Liberal economic positions were more common among members of labor unions, professional associations, and environmental groups. In contrast, liberal cultural positions were more common among members of environmental groups, women's groups, and labor unions.
23. Seymour Martin Lipset and Stein Rokkan. Cleavage structures, party systems, and voter alignments. In Seymour Martin Lipset and Stein Rokkan, eds. *Party Systems and Voter Alignments: Cross-national Perspectives*. New York: Free Press, 1967.
24. The EU seems linked to the cultural positions because it is viewed as a source of these changes, even by elites. For example, a question in the 1994 survey question asked if the candidate felt at home in any EU country; those answering affirmatively are cultural liberals (r=0.17). Another question asked if the CEPs thought the EU was a threat to the cultural identity of their nation. In 1994, those who saw such a cultural threat are cultural conservatives (r=−0.33). By 2009, these two sentiments are even more closely bound together (r=−0.63)!
25. Ronald Inglehart, *Culture Shift in Advanced Industrial Societies*. Princeton: Princeton University Press, 1990; Ronald Inglehart and Pippa Norris, *Rising Tide: Gender Equality and Cultural Change Around the World*. Cambridge: Cambridge University Press, 2003.
26. The number of respondents with full data ranges from 8 (Ireland) to 230 (United Kingdom). Because of the very low number of interviews, Ireland is not included in the figure.
27. Nation is more strongly correlated with the economic cleavage (Eta=0.40) than for the cultural cleavage (Eta=0.32).
28. Significant parties that are not surveyed in 1994 sample include the French PCF, Fine Gael and Labour in Ireland, and the PS in Portugal. The party coverage is even less complete in 1979.
29. The Portuguese elite sample scored −0.55 on the economic cleavage and −0.92 on the cultural cleavage. This was well beyond the range of other nations on both cleavages. In addition, the Portuguese data are based on only 22 cases with full data, and lacking elites from the large Socialist Party.
30. The number of respondents with full data ranges from 9 (Ireland) to 150 (Germany). There was only a single elite respondent with full data in Luxembourg, and so this nation is not included in the figure.
31. Nation is more strongly correlated with economic cleavage positions (Eta=0.42) than for the cultural cleavage (Eta=0.34).
32. Robert Putnam, *The Comparative Study of Political Elites*. Englewood Cliffs, NJ: Prentice-Hall; 1976.
33. Romain Lachat and Martin Dolezal, Demand side: Dealignment and realignment of the structural political potentials. In Hanspeter Kriesi et al., *West European Politics in the Age of Globalization*. Cambridge: Cambridge University Press, 2008.
34. Wouter Schakel and Armen Hakhverdian, Ideological congruence and socio-economic inequality, *European Political Science Review* (2018) (doi.org/10.1017/S1755773918000036).

Part II
Political Cleavages and Party Alignments

Part II

6

Political Cleavages and Political Parties

The Danish Progress Party was founded in 1972 by tax lawyer, Mogens Gilstrup, to protest against high taxes and the Danish government's expansive role in the society and economy. Gilstrup had a very unconventional perspective on politics. For example, in a system with high taxes and high levels of social services, he proudly proclaimed that he paid no taxes because he considered it a flawed system. The party's program for the 1973 elections proposed cutting salaries for civil servants, the abolition of the foreign service, and an end to civil servants' pensions since they didn't really work in the first place. Progress wanted to phase out the personal income tax and dramatically reduce government spending. The party proposed replacing the defense budget with a 50 Krona coin; if the Russians invaded, someone could call Moscow to surrender.[1] After all, how much could the Danish military really do to stop the Russians?

One could imagine that such political rhetoric would spell electoral death, especially in a liberal society such as Denmark. Instead, Progress won 15.9 percent of the votes and 28 seats in parliament. In its first election, it became the second largest party in the Danish Folketing. After a couple more elections, the party expanded its platform to oppose immigration, especially by Muslims. My point is that Progress was a conservative party of a different sort that formed more than three decades ago. Its "progress" was to turn back the clock on the progress of modernization.

The Progress Party is a dramatic example of the fluidity and increased political choice occurring in the Danish party system. Moreover, this happened in Denmark—and other nations—when the European Union was still the European Community consisting of only nine nations, immigration into Europe was limited, neo-liberal economic policies were still developing, and even before the first Green parties emerged in Europe. In other words, extreme conservative parties on the cultural cleavage existed before the 1990s.

This chapter uses three surveys of Candidates for the European Parliament (CEPs) in 1979, 1994, and 2009 to locate parties in the political space, and track the evolution of party positions across Europe and across time.[2] In simple terms, what partisan choices did European publics face as they made their way to the polls on Election Day, and how have these choices changed over time?

Changes in the Party Supply

The positions of political parties in the policy space defined by the economic and cultural cleavage identify the supply of party choices available to voters. Presumably, the dispersion of parties throughout this space creates greater choice—and policy direction—for voters on Election Day, especially if voters hold a mix of different policy preferences. To map this party space over time and nations is a challenging task because the empirical evidence is limited, and the academic speculation is quite extensive.

The three CEP surveys asked the candidates their opinions on issues similar to those asked in the EES citizen surveys. Each year a different set of political issues identify an economic and a cultural cleavage. Even with their direct involvement in politics and presumably more sophisticated understanding of the issues, the structure of political cleavages is quite similar for CEPs and the European public (Chapter 5).

These three elite surveys can identify party positions on both cleavages over time. I calculate a party's location as the average of its candidates' positions on the economic and cultural cleavage indices created in Chapter 5. Several previous studies have used this method to define party positions on the Left–Right scale, and I extend this to the two cleavage dimensions.[3] Party positions are available for most significant parties at each election and provide evidence on the evolution of party supply over time.[4] Most of the analyses in this chapter weight parties by their vote share to diminish any distortion from small fringe parties in the CEP surveys.

What might we expect for party positions in the political space defined by the economic and cultural cleavages? The Downsian spatial model sees parties as aligned on a single Left–Right dimension.[5] Thus, a party might move in a liberal or conservative direction as a strategic decision to appeal to voters, and this is seen as a driving force in electoral competition.[6] Electoral research often presents the Left–Right scale as a surrogate for the economic cleavage.[7] This cleavage was enshrined in the identity of Labour, Social Democratic, Socialist, and Communist parties—or their Conservative opposition on the other end of the continuum. The logic of party strategies and the alternatives for parties were fairly constrained in this one-dimensional world.

During this earlier period, party scholars often saw cultural issues as secondary, reflecting the traditional values of the religious cleavage in Europe in opposition to the secular and modernizing values of liberal parties. Some

Political Cleavages and Political Parties

nations had significant regional cleavages, but these were typically localized and less of a national framework of competition. The emergence of New Left parties was still on the horizon.

As Europeans gave increasing attention to cultural issues, I have argued that this altered the popular demands placed on the party system. More voters adopted distinctly liberal cultural positions, or conservative cultural positions, separate from their economic views.[8] The creation of a two-dimensional space from the one-dimensional Left–Right structure alters the logic of party competition. As a new orthogonal cleavage develops, parties have incentives to differentiate themselves on this cultural cleavage.[9] A leftist party on the economic cleavage has the choice to adopt a liberal or conservative position on the cultural cleavage—and similarly for conservative economic parties. Since the voters provide the political demands, when the demands disperse so should the parties.

However, established parties already have a traditional voter clientele, network ties to these communities, and party identifiers. This existing political base can be an impediment to innovation. For example, as environmental issues gained public attention, the established Left was often hesitant to represent these issues for fear they would alienate their working-class voters who saw environmentalism as threatening their jobs, while conservative business interests saw environmentalism as a threat to their profits. Feminist movements generated a similar quandary for established parties on the Right and Left. Some established parties obviously did shift their positions, but there was substantial inertia.

Herbert Kitschelt provided a rich study of how Social Democratic parties addressed these challenges in the 1980s.[10] In his view, moderate leftist parties lost their vision and popular appeal in the 1970s–1980s, and as a result, some of these parties were attracted to liberal cultural movements and their agendas. But the question was how to respond in complex two-dimensional party space. The parties explicitly or implicitly faced a decision that involved interaction among multiple factors: the linkages between the party and the labor movement, the popular demands for liberal cultural policies, existing competition from other leftist parties such as the Communists, the electoral potential for a Green or New Left party to win representation, and their own party's ultimate goals in terms of policy or power maximization.

Thus, the Social Democratic parties across Europe initially responded in diverse ways to the emerging cultural cleavage. The German SPD is a good example because it vacillated between different strategies in successive *Bundestagswahlen* from 1983 to 1990 and beyond. In one election, the party moved toward the center on the economic cleavage to attract middle-class voters, in the next election it moved toward a culturally liberal position to usurp the issues of the Greens.

Political Realignment

If the Social Democrats or other established parties did not respond to changing public issue demands, this created the potential for new partisan contenders to develop. These initial challenges primarily came from Green or New Left parties that articulated a clear culturally liberal agenda. To be successful, new challengers have to break through the impediments to entry. Among other factors, this involves differentiating themselves sufficiently from the other contenders to be identified as a new political choice. The Greens' anti-party stance, unconventional political style, and alternative political agenda allowed them to differentiate themselves from other parties and attract young cultural liberals to their cause.[11]

As these parties entered parliament or threatened to, this brought increased attention to these issues which could further shift public demands. It also led to many moderate leftist parties moving toward a libertarian cultural position—in part because of the party elites' own ideology, and as a vote maximization strategy because the size of the working class was decreasing and the size of the well-educated, professional middle-class was increasing.

Writing at the beginning of the 1990s, Kitschelt states: "Social democrats are no longer primarily the political agents of blue-collar workers, but forge a socioeconomic coalition that includes different segments of the labor market."[12] He saw the major leftist parties as adopting a Left-libertarian position in which strong ties to labor unions became a liability for these parties. Moreover, Kitschelt felt that Social Democrats were well-advised to move toward a more libertarian and more capitalist position which involve a substantial transformation in electoral coalitions. Once this occurred, he believed that this strategy would diminish the importance of welfare-state policies of the economic cleavage. Kitschelt also assumed that the established middle-class conservative parties would respond with Right-authoritarian policies. Political competition would then be framed by Left-libertarian parties competing against Right-authoritarian parties.

However, this off-diagonal alignment of party positions across the two cleavages creates new political tensions that were underdeveloped in some earlier discussions of electoral change. Such an alignment opens the space for other parties to compete to represent "unoccupied" areas of the political space. Timothy Hellwig offered two contrasting strategies for the traditional leftist parties.[13] A *convergence model*, such as that described by Kitschelt, argues that majority support of neo-liberal policies would pressure economically liberal parties (e.g., Social Democrats and Labour parties) to move toward the median voter at the center on the economic cleavage. A *compensation model*, in contrast, would have economically liberal parties advance policies to mitigate the negative effects of economic change on the economic losers of modernization. Liberal parties would address the new sources of inequality and economic insecurity that are consistent with their historic ideological positions. Such policies could polarize the economic cleavage and require new representatives, such as *Die Linke* in Germany or reformed post-communist parties in other European party systems.

In addition, by the start of the millennium, conservative reactions to the cultural cleavages were becoming more apparent. Just as the moderate leftist parties were pulled to more educated middle-class voters, the same forces existed on the right. If Leftist parties accepted environmental reform—which most did—and expansion of gender rights—which most did—these policies further increased the party void for citizens who did not support these reforms. So moderate conservative parties faced a similar dilemma of convergence or compensation that faced moderate leftist parties. Just as with the rise of Green/New Left parties, the solution might involve the emergence of new parties to articulate under-represented demands. In short, analyses of party change based solely on economics or only on cultural issues is only a partial representation of reality.

The advantage of the CEP surveys is that they can track the evolution of this process over time through the issue opinions of party elites. The closest approximation of a one-dimensional party space is likely to be found in the 1979 survey (or even more clearly had there been a survey a decade earlier). By the time of the 1994 CEP survey, the progressive forces of cultural liberalism were reshaping European party systems. The potential strategies that Kitschelt, Hellman, and others had suggested were becoming a reality for cultural liberalism. By the next CEP survey in 2009, culturally conservative parties had entered the party systems of many West European nations. This seemed to occur both because the political context had changed as a byproduct of globalization, social modernization, and other societal changes, and because the existing parties were adjusting their political positions in a two-dimensional political space which opened the potential for new culturally conservative parties.

In short, party systems expanded to fill the two-dimensional political space. As one illustration, among the nine EU member states in 1979, the effective number of parties competing in national elections increased from approximately 38 circa 1979 to around 52 by the 2014 European Parliament elections.[14] As the number of dimensions of political competition increased, the number of parties to represent this space inevitably increased.

However, the exact pattern of party behavior on both cleavage dimensions and the relationship between the two dimensions remain debated research questions.[15] Had parties widely diffused through the two-dimensional space, or had a Left-libertarian versus Right-authoritarian cleavage became the dominant structure of European party systems? The analyses here track the pattern of party change across European party systems taken together. This diminishes the idiosyncrasies of any single nation or a specific party's position to see the broad patterns of change for the established democracies of Europe.

The Party Space in 1979

The economic cleavage is a distinct part of how CEPs perceive the structure of political competition in the 1979 EP election (Chapter 5). The cultural cleavage was still forming and partially overlapped with economic concerns. The next step is to translate these measures of elite issue opinions into the party alignments. Which parties took distinctive positions on the economic cleavage and which were distinctive on the cultural cleavage?

I calculated cleavage scores for the individual CEPs using the 1979 PCA analyses (Table 5.1) and then computed each party's score as the average of their candidates' scores.[16] To provide more reliable estimates of party positions, I examine only parties with at least three respondents to the survey (47 parties). Even with these cautious steps, there is substantial sampling variability in a data point based on a few cases. One cantankerous politician or one party dissident can have a sizeable effect on the overall party position. For this reason, Appendix C validates this methodology with a comparison to the Chapel Hill Experts Study (CHES).[17] Still, one should not place too much weight on the placement of any single party but look at the larger picture across all parties.

Figure 6.1 aligns the political parties in this two-dimensional space in 1979. A party's score on the economic cleavage locates it along the horizontal axis, and its score on the cultural cleavage locates it on the vertical axis. The size of each bubble represents the party's vote share in the 1979 EP elections.

The importance of the economic cleavage across EU9 party systems is quite apparent. Some of the major parties are identified in the figure, and they are generally aligned along the horizontal axis. The British Conservatives and French RPR are to the far right on the economic cleavage, while the British Labour Party, Dutch PvdA, German SPD, and Danish Social Democrats are all to the left of center, although only slightly so.[18]

There is some variance along the cultural cleavage; elites from several large social democratic parties were adherents of liberal cultural positions even before the emergence of Green/New Left parties. In part, this may reflect their own beliefs as the party elites changed from representing working-class occupations to also attracting members of the well-educated middle class.[19] It was easier for these elites to see the potential for new support among young, liberally oriented, middle-class voters who were more concerned with cultural issues because the elites shared these values. In fact, several of the New Left parties of the 1980s were splinter groups from the larger Social Democratic party. And one of the most liberal parties on this cleavage is the Danish Social Democrats.[20] In overall terms, CEPs from the larger leftist parties were almost as liberal on the economic cleavage and the cultural cleavage; more liberal than many of their own supporters (see Chapter 8).

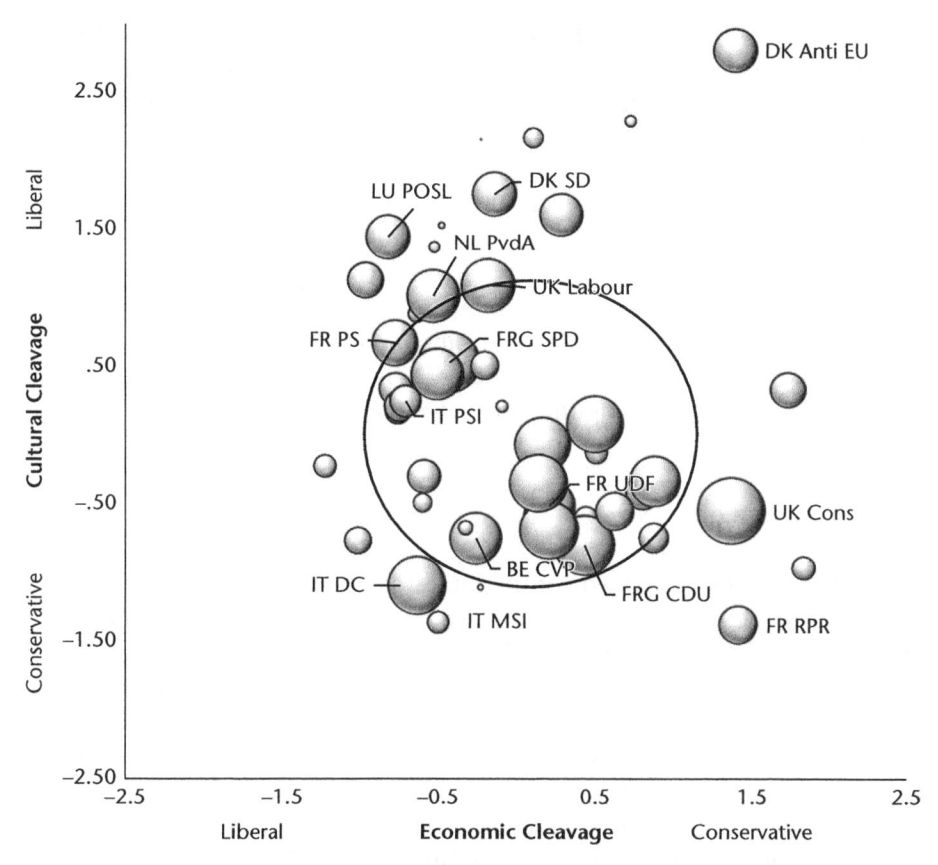

Figure 6.1. Party Locations on the Economic and Cultural Cleavages, 1979

Note: Figure entries are mean scores of party elites on the economic and cultural cleavages; the size of each bubble reflects the party's vote share in the election. (N = 47). The circle represents +/−1.0 standard deviation from the center point.

Source: Candidates for the European Parliament survey, 1979.

In contrast, cultural conservatism often was represented by religious parties such as the Italian Christian Democrats, the Belgian Christian People's Party, and the German Christian Democratic Union. These conservative groups occupied moderate positions, the majority are located within one standard deviation of the center point, and none of these parties scored below −1.50 on the cultural dimension.

In summary, the party supply in 1979 offered modest economic choices as the major parties had reached a general consensus on the role of the state in the economy. Even social democratic parties were no longer campaigning on the nationalization of industry. The traditional working-class hard-Left party position had almost disappeared. Leftist parties mostly varied on alternative means to reach generally accepted goals, such as social welfare provisions and government management of the economy. Economically conservative parties, such as Margaret Thatcher's Conservative Party, held more distinctly conservative economic positions stressing the importance of market forces.

The parties also displayed significant division on cultural issues. This is primarily a contrast between socialist and social democratic parties that adopted liberal cultural positions to attract middle-class voters, and Christian parties that held moderate cultural conservative positions (along with a concern for working-class social support in several Catholic nations). To an extent, Kitschelt's description of a Left-libertarian versus Right-authoritarian cleavage seemed to apply in this election.[21] These results provide the baseline for examining how party alignments evolved to the present.

The Party Space in 1994

The 1994 EP elections marked another milestone for Europe.[22] The collapse of the Soviet Union reshaped the European political landscape and potentially reshaped the party landscape in the EU. Now there were twelve member states with the accession of Spain, Portugal, and Greece. By 1994, the impact of neoliberal economic policies was becoming more apparent, the first wave of postcommunist immigration was increasing racial and ethnic diversity in Western Europe, and the 1987 Single European Act and the 1992 Maastricht Treaty widened and deepened the EU's involvement in society. The long-term processes of social modernization had continued since the 1979 EP study: the further secularization of European society lessened the social base of religious parties, occupational structures shifted from working-class to middle-class jobs, and a liberal cultural agenda had made policy progress.

In that context, the 1994 CEP study was more ambitious than the 1979 survey in its party coverage and in the size of the elite samples. This survey thus provides a fuller picture of party alignments. I again use the average of party candidates' scores from the PCA (Table 5.2) to position parties in a two-dimensional political space.

Figure 6.2 depicts party alignments in 1994. Three additional nations and larger sample sizes mean there are more parties represented in the space (N = 69). A compact group of social democratic and socialist parties now forms a cluster of parties that are liberal on both cleavages. This includes parties such as the Belgian Socialists, the Dutch PvdA, the French Socialists, and the German SPD. Indeed, *these parties are often more culturally liberal than economically liberal*; their positions also overlap with several Green parties. The Social Democratic and Green parties differ in their political positions in specific nations, but both party groups overlap in the aggregate (see Chapter 7).

Political Cleavages and Political Parties

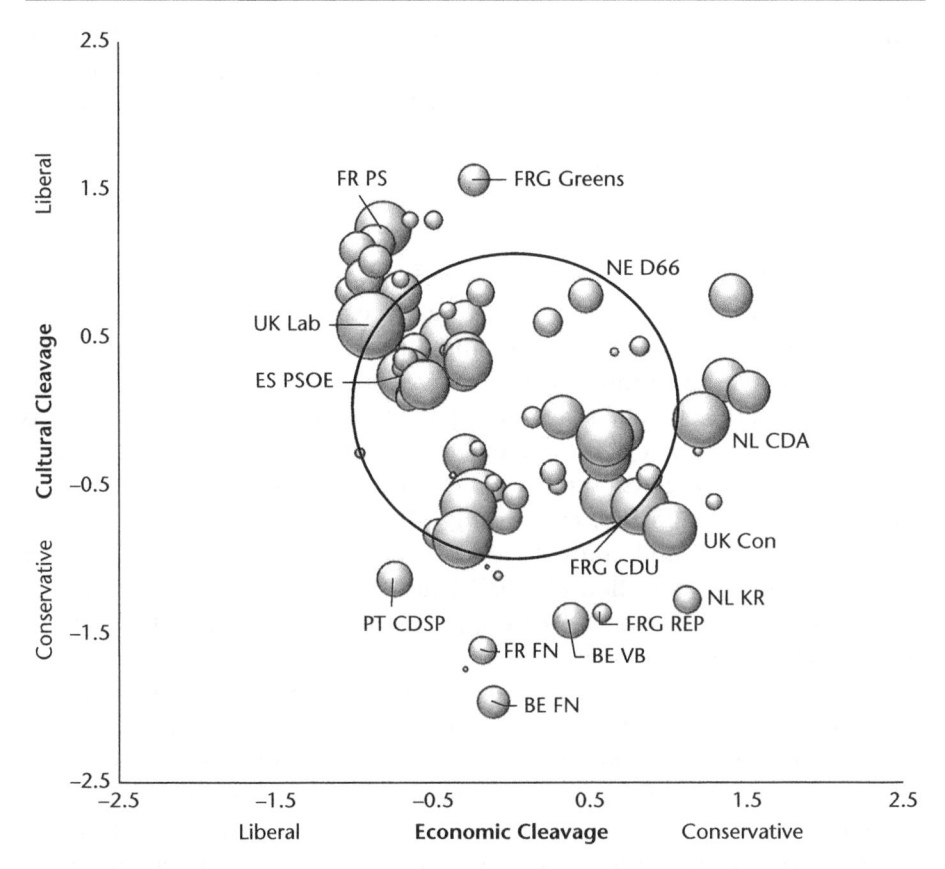

Figure 6.2. Party Locations on the Economic and Cultural Cleavages, 1994

Note: Figure entries are mean scores of party elites on the economic and cultural cleavages; the size of each bubble reflects the party's vote share in the election. (N=69). The circle represents +/−1.0 standard deviation from the center point.

Source: Candidates for the European Parliament survey, 1994, EU15 (without Sweden).

The figure also shows a distinct cluster of parties holding conservative positions on both the economic and cultural dimensions. Compared to 1979, however, many of these parties have moderated their cultural positions. Fading electoral support for some traditional religious parties decreases their partisan base, such as the religious depillarization in the Netherlands and the passing of the Italian Christian Democrats. In addition, other parties moderated their cultural positions for strategic reasons as they also catered to changing policy preferences among middle-class voters.

The other notable feature of the figure is the emergence of distinctly conservative parties on the culture cleavage. The French National Front, the Belgian National Front, the Belgian Flemish Block, and the German Republikaner were established after the 1979 election. These parties gave voters in their respective

Political Realignment

nations a clear conservative choice on cultural issues. The French National Front, for example, was more than a half-point more culturally conservative than any party in the 1979 survey. As with the Green parties earlier, the extreme positions of these parties and their alternative populist style probably helped them differentiate themselves from the existing parties and mobilize new support. These culturally conservative parties generally held centrist positions on the economic cleavage, so voters from all economic views might be attracted by their conservative culturalism.[23]

Of course, one might ask the chicken and the egg question. What came first, did political entrepreneurs establish these parties and thereby redefine the conservative pole on cultural issues—or were conservative voters already there and the new parties supplied them with partisan representation? Both options are probably true to a degree, but I lean toward the latter explanation. One of the byproducts of the PCA methodology is that it constructs political spaces with similar characteristics, even using different political issues.[24] That is, both the economic and cultural cleavage indices have an average score of 0.0 and a standard deviation of 1.0.[25] Thus, the distribution of CEPs in the political spaces of 1979 and 1994 are approximately the same, centered on the average candidate as the origin point.

This means there is no net shift toward cultural conservatism as measured between the 1979 and 1994 analyses because the PCA constructs a standardized political space. In the 1979 survey, the most culturally conservative CEPs represented religious parties: 26 percent from the German CDU/CSU, 27 percent from the Italian Christian Democrats, and a smattering of smaller religious parties and others. As these established parties moderated their views, and possibly as a reaction to changes in political debates, cultural conservatives coalesced into new political parties with distinctly conservative positions. Among CEP elites with the very conservative culture scores in 1994, votes were spread across the party spectrum: 16 percent for the Belgian VB/VU, 11 percent for the Italian Popular Party (PPI), 9 percent for the Portuguese CDS/PP, 8 percent for the French National Front, 6 percent for the Dutch SGP/CU, 3 percent for the small German Republikaner party, and so forth.

The Party Space in 2009 and Beyond

The most recent survey of EP candidates was done for the 2009 election. This contest took place after the first onslaught of the 2008 financial crisis, but before the series of economic problems—sovereign debt crisis, Eurozone conflicts, and other matters that produced Europe's wider financial crisis.

This CEP survey included more nations and more elite respondents, providing a more robust empirical base. I follow the same procedures as for 1979 and

Political Cleavages and Political Parties

1994; calculating scores for candidates on both cleavages, and then a party average score when the survey interviewed at least three party candidates. The cross-national coverage now expands to the EU15 nations.[26]

Figure 6.3 presents the party space as represented by CEPs in 2009. If anything, the economic cleavage has become more distinct—perhaps because of the financial crisis or the renewal of hard left parties. Now economically conservative parties are counterbalanced by (reformed) communist parties on the extreme left; the French PCF, the German *Linke*, the Italian reformed Communists, and the Luxembourg *Linke*. For the first time across the three CEP surveys, there are parties to the left of the −1.50 point on the economic cleavage. I doubt this is a function of measurement since the economic issues in the 2009 survey are not significantly different from earlier surveys. Social Democratic and Green parties still hold center-left positions on the

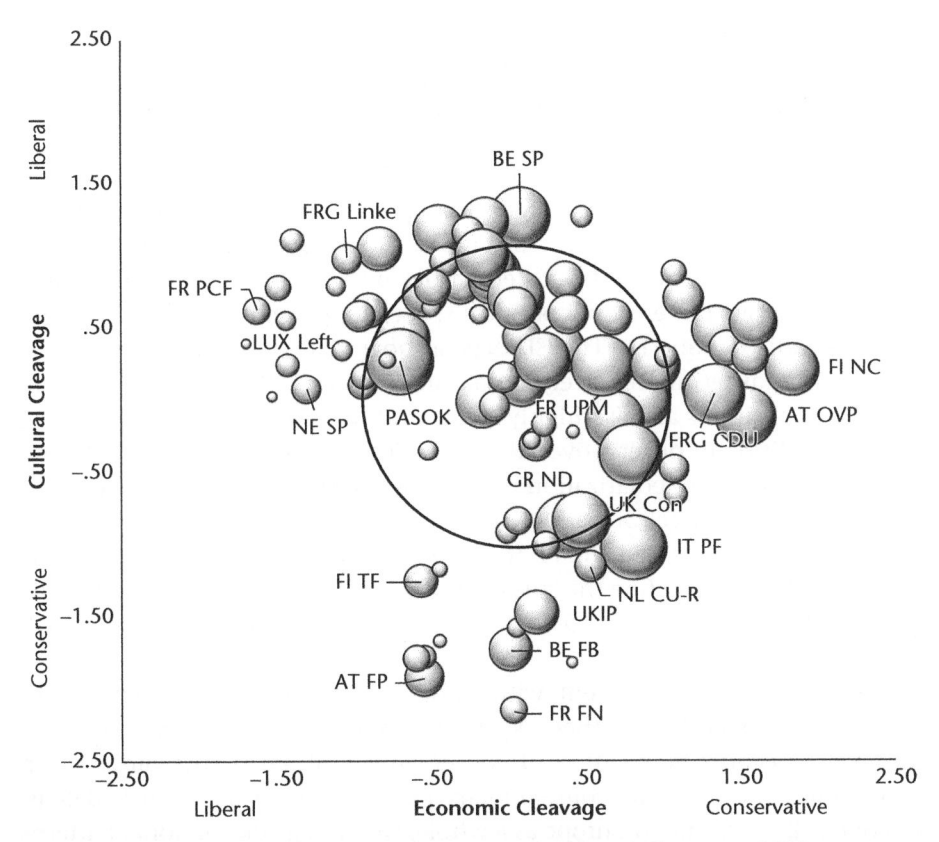

Figure 6.3. Party Locations on the Economic and Cultural Cleavages, 2009

Note: Figure entries are mean scores of party elites on the economic and cultural cleavages; the size of each bubble reflects the party's vote share in the election. Only parties with at least 1 percent of the vote (N=94). The circle represents +/−1.0 standard deviation from the center point.

Source: Candidates for the European Parliament survey, 2009, EU15.

economic cleavage and liberal positions on the cultural cleavage. For example, the German SPD and the British Labour party hold more distinctly liberal positions on the cultural dimension than on the economic dimension, and this is repeated in several other nations. This appears to be the culmination of the Social Democratic journey away from its working-class base and historic economic positions to emphasizing issues appealing to other demographic groups.

Now we also see a more heavily populated cluster of culturally conservative parties. The addition of new EU member states expands this group; such as the Austrian Freedom Party, the Finnish True Finns, and Swedish Democrats. New conservative options were also expanding in earlier EU member states. UKIP did exceedingly well in the 2009 EP election, and the PVV was becoming a political force in The Netherlands. Berlusconi's Italian People of Freedom party won a plurality in the EP election. In short, by 2009 the supply of culturally conservative parties had grown in total numbers and spread across Europe. A significantly larger number of parties scored below −1.50 on the cultural dimensions, representing more of Europe's citizens. Party systems had apparently adjusted to the changing times.

Comparable party elite data were not collected for the 2014 European elections. It is possible, however, to triangulate results from the 2009 CEP survey, the 2010 CHES, and the 2014 CHES to approximate party positions in 2014.[27] The party experts located parties on a set of policy issues, which can define a two-dimensional political space comparable to the CEP studies (see Appendices C and D). The CHES data show that party alignments on the economic cleavage are relatively similar in 2009 and 2014 (data in appendices). Party positions are also highly stable on the cultural cleavage. However, by 2014 additional conservative cultural parties are attracting significant voter support, and party polarization along the cultural cleavage increases.[28] For example, the Greek XA and Syriza anchor opposite poles of the cultural dimension; Podemos and the PP frame the cultural alignment in Spain; the Greens and the AfD define the cultural poles in Germany. In other words, the pattern of change from the 1994 to 2009 CEP studies continued in the 2014 European elections.

These results are consistent with prior descriptions of party change in Europe, now extended another decade and to more nations.[29] However, the ambivalent economic position of conservative cultural parties differs from some other analyses. The contemporary party systems vary in their details, of course. By focusing in Europe as a whole, we average out national patterns for a more global view of electoral change. The overall pattern shows a dispersion of parties throughout the two-dimensional cleavage space the political realignment of some established parties and through the creation of new parties.

Party Traits and Cleavage Positions

The classic Lipset and Rokkan discussion of political cleavages and party systems emphasized the stability of these alignments; the so-called "frozen cleavage" description.[30] But Lipset and Rokkan also acknowledged that party systems were beginning to thaw. There has been increased turnover and fragmentation of party systems, which includes both the departure or rebranding of older parties and the creation of new party contenders.[31] The press of new issues, or the actions of competing parties, may also prompt parties to change their political views and political alignment, even if the name remains the same.

Consequently, this section describes some of the correlates of party positions to better understand the factors that shape party locations as well as the content of these party positions. The analyses test theories of party supply that may reflect the mechanisms producing the patterns observed here. Since I am most concerned with contemporary party alignments, I focus on the two most recent CEP surveys where the empirical base is firmest.

One standard metric for judging party positions is the Left–Right dimension.[32] This is a common framework in elite and mass discourse about parties, and researchers discuss Left–Right as a shorthand for summarizing parties' political stances. Left–Right is also a powerful political identity in shaping voter choice. However, politics in two or more dimensions raises the question of the policy content of these ideological positions. Does Left mean support for social programs and the working class, or cultural issues of support for immigrants, gay rights, and gender equality? In most research, the answer is ambiguous or finessed at least partially because the Left–Right scale is the most widely used measure of party positions.

The CEP data show how parties' Left–Right identity is related to their economic and cultural positions. The surveys asked candidates to locate themselves, their party, and their party's voters on the same Left–Right scale used in public opinion surveys. The first panel of Table 6.1 displays the correlation between these Left–Right scores and party cleavage scores in the 1994 and 2009 CEP studies.[33]

Party scores on both cleavages are very strongly related to all three Left–Right measures. The small differences between the 1994 and 2009 CEP studies may be a function of the passage of time, the varied set of issues in both surveys, or the addition of three more nations in 2009. These strong correlations are even more notable because the economic and cultural scores are essentially uncorrelated because of the PCA methodology, even when individual candidates' scores are aggregated into party scores. Thus, a party's Left–Right identity is not just a merger of liberal views on both cleavages versus conservative views on both cleavages (e.g., Left-libertarian

Political Realignment

Table 6.1. The Correlates of Parties' Economic and Cultural Positions

Correlates	1994 Economic	1994 Cultural	2009 Economic	2009 Cultural
CEP Left–Right	0.63*	0.80*	0.69*	0.70*
Party Left–Right	0.58*	0.77*	0.69*	0.66*
Voter Left–Right	0.57*	0.78*	0.68*	0.64*
Year party formed	0.24*	0.05	0.27*	−0.29*
EP vote share	−0.12*	0.01	−0.33*	0.06
Satisfied with working of democracy	−0.29*	0.09	−0.43*	0.21*

Note: Parties are weighted by EP vote share except for the EP vote share relationship; asterisks marks significant correlations (p<0.05).
Source: Party aggregates calculated from Candidates for the European Parliament survey 1994 and 2009, EU15.

versus Right-authoritarian). Rather, Left can mean *either liberal economic or liberal cultural positions or both*. And the reverse for Right parties. In other words, the Left–Right identity of a party can come from either or both cleavages, which means assumptions that simply equate Left–Right with the traditional socio-economic cleavage are inaccurate.[34]

Another way to understand current party alignments is through changes in the supply of party choices over time. Very culturally conservative parties—typically labeled far-right or populist right parties—have proliferated in recent decades as seen by comparing party spaces in 1979 and 2009. In addition, an earlier wave of cultural liberalism as Green and New Left parties formed in the 1970s–1980s. Even if some parties no longer compete, the residue of this history should be detectable in contemporary party systems.

I measure this evolution of party supply by correlating the year a party was formed with its position on the economic and cultural cleavages (Table 6.1). In 1994 and 2009, younger parties tend to be more liberal on the economic cleavage—reflecting the expansion of Green, New Left and reformed Communist parties in recent decades. In contrast, there is an insignificant correlation for the cultural cleavage in 1994, which grows to a strong negative relationship by 2009. This can be traced to the emergence of new conservative and far-right parties on cultural issues.

Figure 6.4 illustrates this relationship for the 2009 study where this pattern is clearest. Still-existing parties that formed prior 1940 now generally lean toward liberal cultural norms. Certainly, there were cultural conservative parties in the past—fascist parties in interwar Europe, extreme-right parties in postwar Europe, Christian-based parties stressing traditional values, peasant parties, and others.[35] But most of the culturally conservative parties from this earlier period lost electoral support as European societies modernized and cultural norms shifted toward liberal positions. This pattern changes in recent decades, however. Most of the very culturally conservative parties

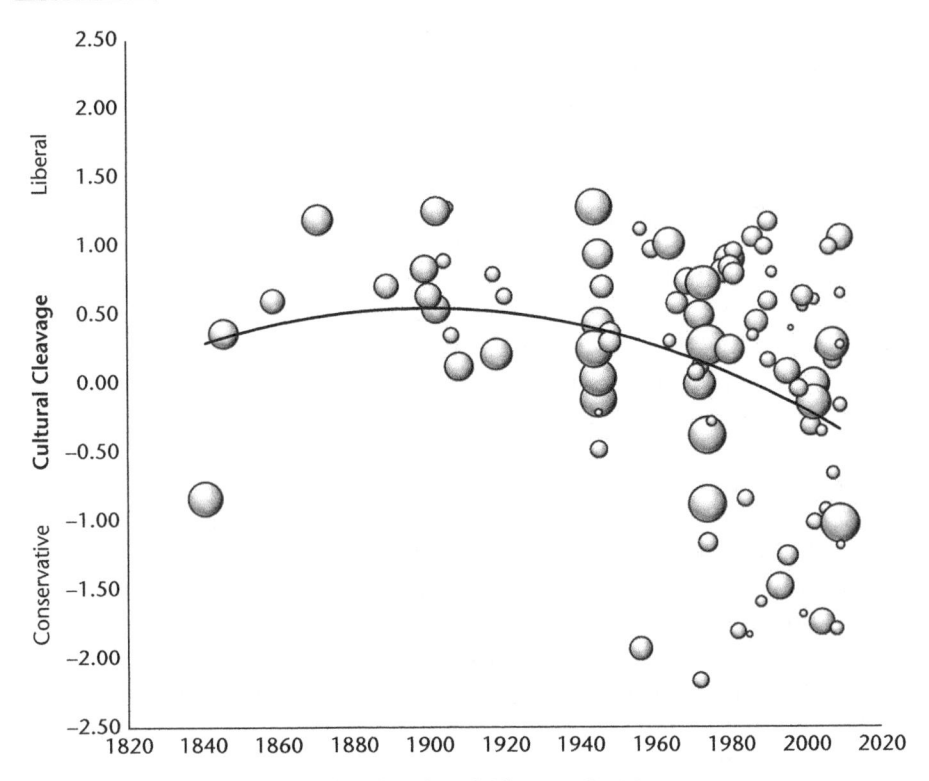

Figure 6.4. Year Party Formed and Cultural Cleavage Position

Note: Figure entries are mean scores of party elites on the cultural cleavages by the year of party formation; the size of each bubble reflects the party's vote share in the election. (N=92). Positive values are liberal positions.

Source: Candidates for the European Parliament survey, 2009, EU15.

today have formed since 1980, which produces a curvilinear time pattern.[36] Conversely, the figure also shows that the 1970s and 1980s were formative periods for liberal cultural parties such as the Greens and New Left parties. These counter trends widened the polarization gap on the cultural cleavage.

A parallel analysis of party positions on the economic cleavage shows a shift toward economic conservatism among recently formed parties (data not shown). This trend is less distinct and partly reflects the high level of economic liberalism among older leftist parties that formed during the social democratic mobilization in the early 1900s (labor, socialist, and social democratic parties). Among the sixty contemporary parties formed since 1960, there is barely a relationship between year of founding and economic positions ($r = -0.12$).

Party size may be another marker of political positions. The Green/New Left parties advocating new liberal cultural positions and recent culturally conservative parties are generally small parties seeking representation in already established party systems. While there are occasional exceptions—such as the Austrian Freedom Party and Berlusconi's Forza Italy—the new conservative cultural parties also tend to have smaller vote shares. One might term this the elephant hypothesis. If party systems are inhabited by large "elephant" parties generally located near the middle of the political space, a new "mouse" has to find a niche away from the elephants to live and prosper. In less zoological terms, new parties generally begin small as they seek out potential voters, craft their political message, and develop an organizational base for election campaigns. New parties also generally form at the borders of the political space, where there are unrepresented issues; but there are fewer voters the further a party is placed from the political center.

Table 6.1 shows that the largest parties are located toward the conservative pole on the economic cleavage in both years, especially in the 2009 survey. Presumably, this pattern reflects the fragmentation of economically liberal parties (communist, social democratic, New Left), as several large economically conservative parties moved even further to the Right. In contrast, the larger parties tend to be cultural liberals as small culturally conservative emerged to represent this constituency in recent years. This implies that the cultural cleavage was a greater disruptive force on the Left than on the Right.

Another way to identify the base and political orientations of parties is in terms of their images of government and the performance of government.[37] Are economically liberal parties generally positive toward the working of the democratic system, or more critical? And how do relationships vary across both cleavages? I presume that satisfaction with the government reflects party elites' perceptions of how the government is responding to their issue positions. To capture this process, I averaged CEP's evaluations of the government for each party.

As in Chapter 5, the contrast is striking. In 1994, economically liberal parties—as reflected in party elites' opinions—tend to be less satisfied with the functioning of government ($r=-0.29$), but cultural liberals are slightly more satisfied ($r=0.09$). In 2009, economic liberal parties are even more strongly dissatisfied with the working of democracy in their country. For many of these economically liberal candidates, the financial crisis was a failure of the market economy because of government policies. In contrast, liberal culturalists are more positive about government performance. At least in terms of these elites, and presumably their parties, this indicates their perceptions of the course of public policy in Europe. Thus, the individual patterns for CEPs found in Chapter 5 carry over to party positions when aggregated.

Changing Party Supply

In the modern era, party systems are unlikely to be frozen. The tremendous social and economic changes occurring in affluent democracies prompt parties to respond and adapt, because the lack of responsiveness can produce irrelevance or new party competitors. This is especially likely in multiparty systems with low barriers to entry.

This study has argued that party competition now occurs within a framework defined by the economic and cultural cleavages. This chapter demonstrated how the supply of party choices has changed over the past several decades. In 1979, the economic cleavage was the primary basis of party competition. At the same time, a party alignment on the cultural dimension was forming and became more distinct from economic positions by the 1994 survey. By then, liberal cultural parties, such as Greens and New Left parties, represented these positions in many national parliaments. In addition, several established social democratic parties adopted more liberal cultural views. By 2009, these patterns of partisan realignment were even more evident. Reinvigorated post-communist parties in several nations articulated liberal economic positions, and conservative parties advocated market-based policies—thereby increasing party polarization on the economic cleavage. At the same time, new culturally conservative parties—with generally centrist views on the economic cleavage—further polarized the supply of party choices on the cultural cleavage.[38]

Additional study is necessary to disentangle the factors that produced these changes. However, three things seem important. The first is a centrist movement by many established leftist parties on the economic cleavage. These parties tempered their economic positions in an attempt to attract new middle-class voters as their working-class base decreased in size (and their own elites became more upper middle class). The efforts of New Labour in Britain, Gerhard Schröder's Neue Mitte in Germany, or Bill Clinton's Third Way in the United States illustrate this pattern. The parallel rightward shift by conservative parties shifted government economic policies in a neoliberal direction.

A second factor is a change in cultural positions by some established parties. The most obvious example is the movement of many traditionally leftist parties to a culturally liberal position. This was also prompted by efforts to appeal to middle-class voters who held liberal cultural views. The rise of Green and New Left parties on their flank changed the electoral calculus of these parties. Thus, Herbert Kitschelt's description of a Left-libertarian party cluster in Europe is partially correct.[39] At the same time, some culturally conservative parties, like the German CDU/CSU, moderated their conservative cultural positions, possibly also in reaction to shifting societal norms. The expansion of women's rights and gay rights in Europe, for example, often came with conservative support or at least tolerance.

These two factors raise questions about the theoretical dichotomy between the convergence and compensation models of party change.[40] Parties do not face a simple choice along the economic policy dimension, but have to position themselves in a multidimensional space. The German SPD, for example, could simultaneously converge toward the center on the economic cleavage, while pursuing a more polarized liberal position on the cultural cleavage. The party wanted to retain manual workers with a modestly liberal economic program, while simultaneously appealing to liberal middle-class voters on cultural issues. Geoffrey Evans and James Tilley presented longitudinal evidence that described how the British Labour Party moved in tandem with the changing electorate to a more centrist position on the economic cleavage and a more liberal position on the cultural cleavage.[41] Most other large leftist parties in Europe struggled with this same strategic choice that could mix convergence and polarization across different cleavages.

Moreover, there is complementary evidence that these policy differences between parties are communicated to the citizenry through the party messaging in election campaigns. Edgar Grande and his colleagues presented intriguing evidence of the differential emphasis on economic and cultural issues across party families.[42] Communist parties emphasize economic themes; social democratic parties straddle the themes of economic liberalism and cultural liberalism. In contrast, Green parties emphasize cultural liberalism in their campaign messages, while far-right parties stress conservative cultural themes. This use of different cleavage themes in election campaigns signals where voters should go to find their primary interests best represented. With more extensive longitudinal data we might be able to track these mass-elite processes in more detail.

The third factor affecting party supply is the emergence of new political parties, especially in cultural terms. New parties articulated issues that forced the established parties to respond, at least to minimize the electoral challenge of these parties, and thereby changed the context of political competition. Left alone, the established parties would predictably have shown greater policy inertia. Instead, social democrats and socialist parties faced an incentive to address environmental, gender and other issues that they had long avoided. Traditional conservative parties confronted by new culturally conservative parties started to discuss immigration and other cultural issues to lessen potential electoral losses. Politics is now a multidimensional competition among multiple parties, and the totality of available choices affects the potential for diverse views to find partisan representation.

Evidence of the inertia of established parties comes from a comparison of party positions in 1994 and 2009. Admittedly, the number of parties available

Political Cleavages and Political Parties

to compare across both elections is fairly small—a first indicator of the fluidity of contemporary party systems. For example, of the 69 parties in the 1994 CEP survey, only about a half can be matched with the same or an equivalent party in 2009. This is due to turnover in the parties competing in both elections, and to a smaller degree, a sufficient sample size in both CEP surveys to merit inclusion.

Comparing party positions based on fairly small numbers of party elites in both years should generate a large sampling error. Comparing party locations based on a different set of candidates answering questions about two different sets of issues separated by 15 years of intervening policy debate is a high wire act. Thus, I present these data with some trepidation and the expectation of substantial volatility in party positions. I encourage the reader to proceed with caution.

Figure 6.5 shows the continuity in party locations for the economic cleavage on the left and the cultural cleavage on the right. There is a sizeable correlation in parties' economic positions in both years (r=0.75), and adjustments for measurement and sampling error would undoubtedly increase this relationship.[43] Most of the change occurs for parties that were economically liberal in 1994, who moderated their economic position in the 2009 survey.

There is even greater partisan stability on the cultural cleavage (r=0.88). Continuing parties became more culturally liberal between 1994 and 2009 in relation to the total political space, so the supply of conservative cultural party choices decreased among these parties.[44] This creates a political space that new parties might colonize. In summary, the moral and ethical aspects of cultural issues may make them more resistant to change than more easily negotiated economic positions.

These tentative results suggest that the expanding diversity in party supply on the cultural cleavage arose primarily through the formation of new parties. The figure shows that very few continuing parties held conservative cultural positions (less than −1.0) in either 1994 or 2009, and they generally have small vote shares. Yet, by 2009 many significant culturally conservative parties existed in these party systems. As a result, the supply of party system choices diversified more from new parties entering political competition than from the established parties adjusting their broad identity in a response to changing times.

From the predominately economic variation in party positions in postwar Europe, contemporary party systems now offer a wide range of economic choices and a wide (or wider) range of choice on the cultural cleavage. This has been a long-term evolution of party choices, and it is not clear that the evolutionary process has reached its completion. But Europeans today have more partisan outlets to express their policy views.

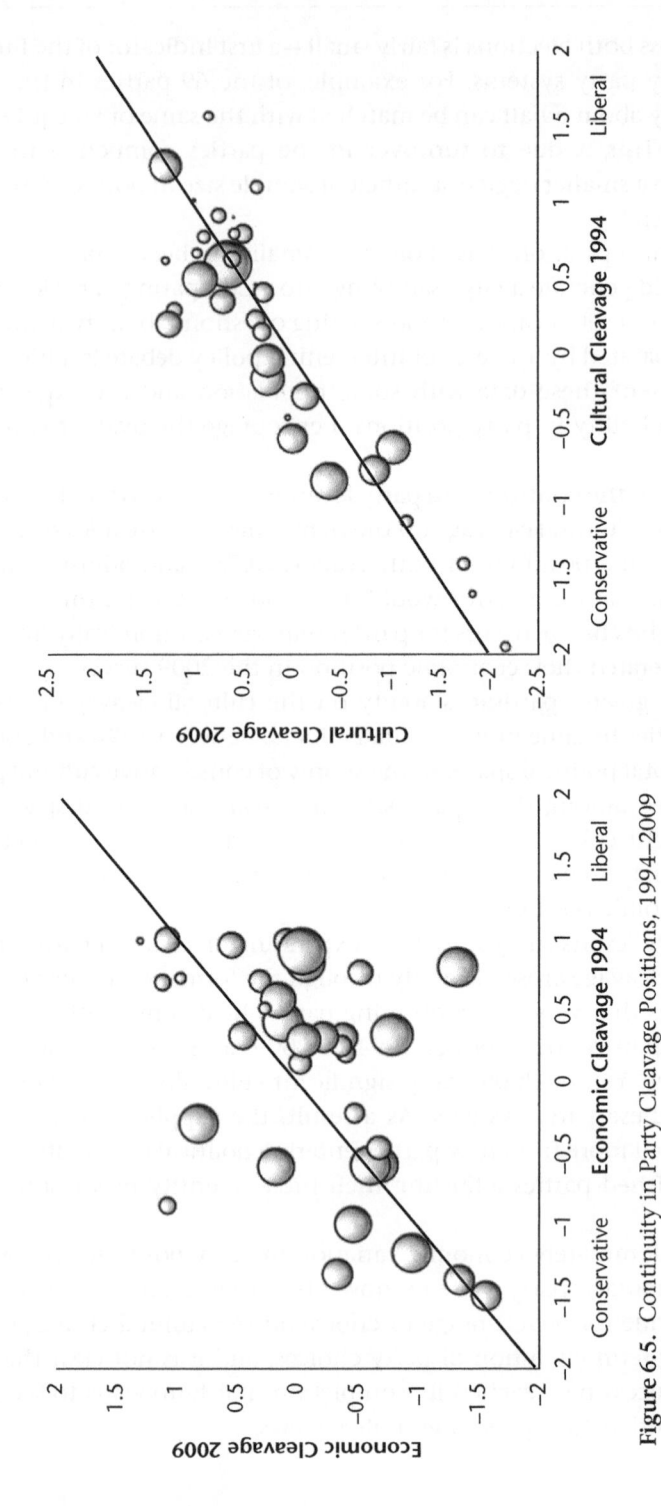

Figure 6.5. Continuity in Party Cleavage Positions, 1994–2009

Note: Figure presents parties that are included in both CEP surveys; the size of the bubble reflects the party vote share in 1994. Positive values are liberal positions on both cleavages.

Source: Aggregated party scores from CEP 1994 and 2009 studies. N=39.

Notes

1. An alternative version is that the defense department would be replaced by a telephone answering machine with the message: "We surrender."
2. The 1979 survey is available from the ICPSR at the University of Michigan (ICPSR 9033). The other two studies were acquired from the GESIS archive in Germany: 1994 (ZA3078) and 2009 (ZA5048).
3. Jacques Thomassen and Hermann Schmitt, Policy representation, *European Journal of Political Research* (1997) 32: 165–84; Warren Miller et al., eds., *Policy Representation in Western Democracies*. Oxford: Oxford University Press, 1999; Russell Dalton, Party representation across multiple issue dimensions, *Party Politics* (2017) 23: 609–22.
4. To balance caution against practical research needs, I only examine parties that had at least three candidates in the survey. The maximum number of parties fulfilling these requirements were: 56 parties in 1979 (44 with at least 1 percent of the popular vote); 91 in 1994 (70 with at least 1 percent of the popular vote), and 108 parties in 2009 (88 with at least 1 percent of the popular vote). See Appendix D for list of parties and their cleavage scores. Part of the increase in the number of parties is because the EU expands from 9 to 12, to 15 member states. The effective number of parties per nation also increased over time.
5. Anthony Downs, *An Economic Theory of Democracy*. New York: Harper, 1957; Samuel Merrill and Bernard Grofman, *A Unified Theory of Voting: Directional and Proximity Spatial Models*. Cambridge: Cambridge University Press, 1999; Michael McDonald and Ian Budge, *Elections, Parties, Democracy: Conferring the Median Mandate*. Oxford University Press on Demand, 2005.
6. James Adams, The causes and the electoral consequences of party policy shifts in multiparty elections, *Annual Review of Political Science* (2012) 15: 401–19; Lawrence Ezrow, *Linking Citizens and Parties*. Oxford, Oxford University Press, 2010.
7. Seymour Martin Lipset and Stein Rokkan, Cleavage structures, party systems, and voter alignments. In Seymour Martin Lipset and Stein Rokkan, eds., *Party Systems and Voter Alignments: Cross-national Perspectives*. New York: Free Press, 1967; Ronald Inglehart and Hans-Dieter Klingemann, Party identification, ideological preference and the Left–Right dimension among Western mass publics. In Ian Budge, Ivor Crewe, and Dennis Farlie, eds., *Party Identification and Beyond*. London: Wiley, 1976; Oddbjørn Knutsen, *Social Structure and Party Choice in Western Europe: A Comparative Longitudinal Study*. Houndsmills, Basingstoke: Palgrave Macmillan, 2004.
8. This is especially likely because the Principal Components Analyses disperses citizens equally on both cleavages in each survey, with the origin point representing the average voter.
9. Gary Cox, Centripetal and centrifugal incentives in electoral systems, *American Journal of Political Science* (1990) 34: 903–35; Kenneth Shepsle and Ronald Cohen, Multiparty competition, entry and entry deterrence in spatial models of elections. In James Enelow and Melvin Hinich, eds., *Advances in the Spatial Theory of Voting*. Cambridge: Cambridge University Press, 1990; Gary Cox, Multicandidate spatial

competition. In James Enelow and Melvin Hinich, eds., *Advances in the Spatial Theory of Voting*. Cambridge: Cambridge University Press, 1990.
10. Herbert Kitschelt, *The Transformation of European Social Democracy*. Cambridge: Cambridge University Press, 1994.
11. Herbert Kitschelt, *The Logics of Party Formation: Ecological Politics in Belgium and West Germany*. Ithaca, NY: Cornell University Press, 1989; Herbert Kitschelt and Staf Hellemansm, *Beyond the European Left: Ideology and Political Action in the Belgian Ecology Parties*. Durham, NC: Duke University Press, 1990.
12. Kitschelt, *The Transformation of European Social Democracy*, p. 6.
13. Timothy Hellwig, *Globalization and Mass Politics: Retaining the Room to Maneuver*. New York: Cambridge University Press, 2015; Timothy Hellwig, The supply side of electoral politics. In Jack Vowles and Georgios Xezonakis, eds., *Globalization and Domestic Politics*. Oxford: Oxford University Press, 2016.
14. Calculated from data at Michael Gallagher's Electoral Studies website: https://www.tcd.ie/Political_Science/staff/michael_gallagher/ElSystems/Docts/effno.php.
15. Hanspeter Kriesi et al., eds., *West European Politics in the Age of Globalization*. Cambridge: Cambridge University Press, 2008; Simon Bornschier, The new cultural divide and the two-dimensional political space in Western Europe, *West European Politics* (2010) 33: 419–44; Robert Rohrschneider and Stephen Whitefield, *The Strain of Representation: How Parties Represent Diverse Voters in Western and Eastern Europe*. Oxford: Oxford University Press, 2012, ch. 4; Jack Vowles and George Xezonakis, eds., *Globalization and Domestic Politics: Parties, Elections, and Public Opinion*. Oxford: Oxford University Press, 2016; Ryan Bakker, Seth Jolly, and Jonathan Polk, Complexity in the European party space: Exploring dimensionality with experts, *European Union Politics* (2012) 13: 219–45; Ronald Inglehart and Pippa Norris, Trump and the populist authoritarian parties: *The Silent Revolution* in reverse, *Perspective on Politics* (2017) 15: 443–54.
16. Appendix D presents the party scores on both cleavages for all three CEP surveys.
17. Other comparisons of elite opinions and expert opinions of party Left–Right positions can be found in Russell Dalton and Ian McAllister, Random walk or planned excursion? Continuity and change in the Left–Right positions of political parties, *Comparative Political Studies* (2015) 48: 759–87.
18. The Danish Progress Party described at the start of this chapter is not presented because it is an excessive outlier, earning a 4.66 score on the standardized economic cleavage, which is two and half times further right than the nearest party.
19. On the SPD in Germany see Hermann Schmitt, *Neue Politik in alten Parteien: Zum Verhältnis von Gesellschaft und Parteien in der Bundesrepublik*. Opladen: Westdeutscher Verlag.
20. The outlier in the upper right is the Danish People's Movement against the EC. The movement opposed membership in the European Community because it favored a broader internationalist agenda, social justice and other issues that aligned it with liberal cultural positions.
21. Kitschelt, *The Transformation of European Social Democracy*.
22. Hermann Schmitt and Jacques Thomassen, eds., *Political Representation and Legitimacy in the European Union*. Oxford: Oxford University Press, 1999.

23. Cas Mudde, *Populist Radical Right Parties in Europe*. New York: Cambridge University Press, 2007; Jan Rovny, Where do radical right parties stand? Position blurring in multidimensional competition, *European Political Science Review* (2013) 5: 1–26.
24. This is also a limitation of the method because we cannot calculate absolute change between surveys since the component scores are standardized at each time point.
25. In 1979, the standard deviations were: economic cleavage (1.02) and cultural cleavage (1.04). In 1994, the standard deviations were: economic cleavage (0.997) and economic cleavage (0.995).
26. In a separate figure (not shown) I mapped the party space for the EU9 nations. The patterns are quite similar to these with less density because there are fewer parties.
27. Bakker, Jolly, and Polk, Complexity in the European party space.
28. Also see Sarah Hobolt and James Tilley, Fleeing the centre: The rise of challenger parties in the aftermath of the Euro crisis, *West European Politics* (2016) 39: 971–91.
29. Romain Lachat and Hanspeter Kriesi, Supply side: The positioning of political parties in a restructuring space. In Hanspeter Kriesi et al., *West European Politics in the Age of Globalization*. Cambridge: Cambridge University Press, 2008; Bornschier, The new cultural divide and the two-dimensional political space in Western Europe. Also see Rohrschneider and Whitefield, *The Strain of Representation*; Kitschelt, *The Transformation of European Social Democracy*.
30. Lipset and Rokkan, Cleavage structures, party systems, and voter alignments.
31. Alessandro Chiaramonte and Vincenzo Emanuele, Toward turbulent times: Measuring and explaining party system (de-)institutionalization in Western Europe (1945–2015), *Rivista Italiana di Scienza Politica* (2018) 27: 1–23.
32. Downs, *An Economic Theory of Democracy*; Dieter Fuchs and Hans-Dieter Klingemann, The Left–Right schema. In M. Kent Jennings and Jan van Deth, eds., *Continuities in Political Action*. Berlin: deGruyter, 1989; Dalton, Farrell and McAllister, *Political Parties and Democratic Linkage*.
33. The relationships in Table 6.1 weight parties by their vote share in the respective EP election to give more weight to larger parties. The party vote share correlation is the exception and uses unweighted data. I excluded parties with less than 1 percent of the vote.
34. The same conclusion applies at the individual level (Table 5.4 and 5.4).
35. A new project is tracing the distribution of various party families over the past decade: Giacomo Benedetto and Simon Hix, The rise and fall of Social Democracy, 1918–2017. Paper presented at the annual meetings of the American Political Science Association, San Francisco, 2017. Overall figures are at: Simon Oxenham, The rise of political apathy in two charts, *Nature* (June 6, 2017) https://www.nature.com/news/the-rise-of-political-apathy-in-two-charts-1.22106.
36. The Multiple R for the non-linear relationship is R=0.33.
37. Christopher Anderson and Aida Just, Legitimacy from above: The partisan foundations of support for the political system in democracies, European *Political Science Review* (2013) 5: 335–62; Robert Rohrschneider and Stephen Whitefield, Critical parties: How parties evaluate the performance of government, *British Journal of Political Science* (2017). doi.org/10.1017/S0007123416000545.

38. An important caveat is that the views of party elites might not represent the actual policies of the parties, and there should be some distinction. However, the CHES data and other evidence for recent elections show a strong relationship between the thoughts of party elites and the parties policies.
39. Kitschelt, *The Transformation of European Social Democracy*.
40. Hellwig, The supply side of electoral politics; Lawrence Ezrow and Timothy Hellwig, Responding to voters or responding to markets? Political parties and public opinion in an era of globalization, *International Studies Quarterly* (2014) 58: 816–27.
41. Geoffrey Evans and James Tilly, *The New Politics of Class: The Political Exclusion of the British Working Class*. Oxford: Oxford University Press, 2017.
42. Edgar Grande, Simon Maag, Alena Kerscher, and Regina Becker, Framing Europe: Are cultural-identitarians frames driving politicization? In Swen Hutter, Edgar Grande, and Hanspeter Kriesi, eds., *Politicizing Europe: Integration and Mass Politics*. Cambridge: Cambridge University Press, 2016, p. 197.
43. Such as computing the sampling error of a typical sample of CEPs within a party, and the measurement error in a correlation based on only 35 cases sampled in this manner.
44. By comparison, for the same set of parties the CEPs' self-placement on the Left–Right scale is correlated at $r=0.95$ over the 1994–2014 time span, $r=0.89$ for placement of their party, and $r=0.90$ for placement of their party's voters. Even though the content of Left–Right might change over time, the identity itself seems to endure. See Dalton and McAllister, A random walk or a planned excursion.

7

Electoral Choice—Voter Demand and Party Supply

Dutch citizens faced a difficult electoral choice in 2017. Almost thirty parties competed in the parliamentary election, and thirteen won seats in the Tweede Kamer. The range of viable party choices was exceptional because of the low threshold for representation in the Dutch system. The new parliament has several leftist parties, including the Labor party (PvdA), the Socialist Party, and Green Left. Several religious parties won seats. The conservative People's Party for Freedom and Democracy (VVD) had the largest vote total, followed by Geert Wilders' far-right Party for Freedom (PVV). Parliament also includes a Party for the Animals (PvdD), a party for senior citizens (50PLUS), and several other small parties.

There is strong evidence that issues matter in elections, and thus cleavages derived from these issues should also matter. But voting choices are influenced by multiple factors. Electoral research argues that because of the complexity of politics, many voters use heuristics, such as party identification and social group cues, to guide their voting choices. However, these political cues might be an imprecise reflection of issue preferences. For example, a Dutch PvdA partisan (traditionally a manual worker) might habitually support the party and pay less attention to specific policy issues in an election. Alternatively, if political alignments are changing, as in contemporary Europe, many voters might have difficulty identifying which party most closely reflects their views—especially in a complex political environment such as The Netherlands. Or voters may be pulled toward (or away from) a party because of the personal qualities of the party leader or the party's past governing performance.

This chapter examines the extent to which the economic and cultural cleavages structure voting choice across European party systems. Citizens and political elites perceive a common political space, but are individual voters able to link their own preferences to an appropriate party representative? Equally important, have these relationships changed over time. Social modernization may have lessened voters' concern about the issues of the economic cleavage, while increasing attention to cultural issues. One also expects that distinct population subgroups give different weight to the two cleavages as they make their electoral choices. I use longitudinal comparisons from the European Election Studies to address these points.

I first discuss the methodological challenges in linking citizens' cleavage positions to voting choice. Then I describe the relationship between citizens' cleavage positions and their party choices. The chapter concludes by discussing the results and their implications for political competition in contemporary democracies. The results describe how the changes in the structure of political competition described in previous chapters have impacted on electoral choice in affluent democracies.

Voting in a Two-dimensional Cleavage Space

One of the challenges in comparing voting choices across multiparty systems is the diversity of party options. With thirteen parties winning seats in the Dutch parliament and a small handful in Britain, how does one compare voting decisions across such diverse systems? One possible solution has been to focus on party families as a common standard. That is, compare the bases of support for social democratic, green, conservative, or far-right parties across the EU. There is an extensive literature on such comparisons.

Figure 7.1 shows a potential problem with the party-family approach. The figure plots a set of party families based on the Candidates for the European Parliament (CEP) survey in 2009 (also see Chapter 6). Members of a party family tend to cluster in their expected location in the two-dimensional political space. Communist parties position themselves to the far left on the economic cleavage; green parties are at the liberal end of the cultural cleavage; far-right parties are at the opposite end of the cultural cleavage.

However, there is considerable variation within families on these two broad cleavages. All but one Social Democratic party leans toward the liberal end of the cultural dimension, but these parties span a substantial range along the economic cleavage. Green parties display even broader range on the economic cleavage. Conservative and Christian Democratic parties also cover a wide span of the political space. Far-right (or nationalist) parties, as coded by the EES, even include a party with a moderate cultural position and a conservative economic position.[1] In other words, a vote for the British Labour Party does not imply the same policy choices as a vote for the Dutch PvdA. Thus, comparing voting for different members of party families across nations is

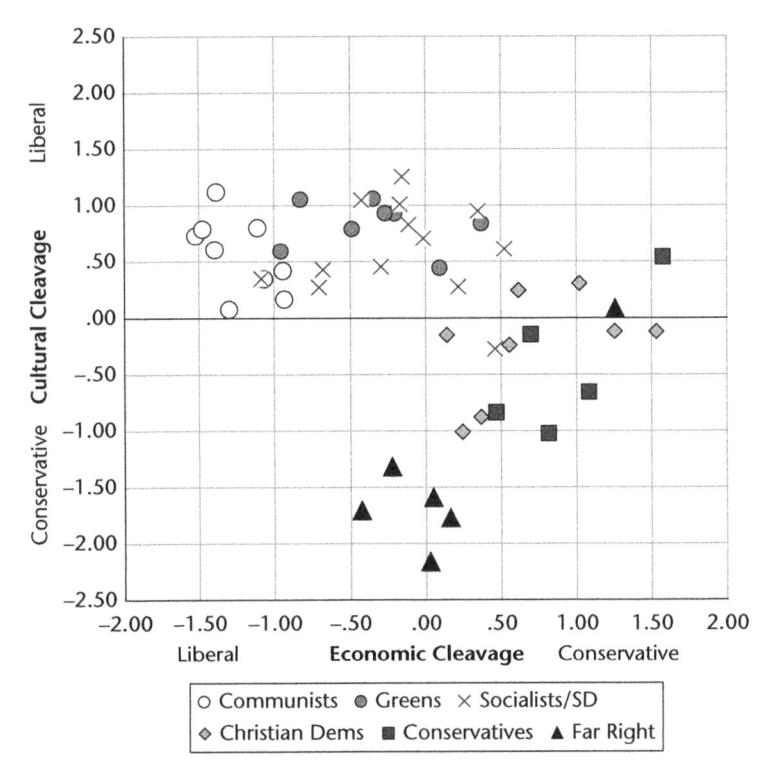

Electoral Choice—Voter Demand and Party Supply

Figure 7.1. Location of Party Families in the Political Space

Note: Figure entries are average scores on the economic and cultural cleavages of party candidates by nation grouped into their respective party family.

Source: Candidates to the European Parliament Survey, 2009.

problematic because this overlooks the considerable variation within families. Party family is only an approximation of a party's political positions.

Another complication occurs if we want to compare party choices relative to the available options in a nation. Multinominal logistic regressions can describe voters' choices across all parties. However, this methodology treats parties as discrete categories rather than acknowledging the varied choices along the dimensions of political competition. A Dutch voter choosing between the VVD and CDA has a narrower choice range than one considering the VVD and D'66 because this is a wider policy gap in a two-dimensional space.

In addition, the complexity increases in cross-national analyses. Since the supply of party choices varies across nations, our methodology should recognize the variation in political positions that are the basis of electoral choice. The supply of choices also can affect the importance of each cleavage. For instance, the existence of a reformed communist party is likely to increase the effect of economic orientations on voting because a more distinct choice is available.

135

Conversely, a party representing a very liberal cultural position or conservative cultural choice might strengthen the influence of this cleavage for voting behavior. The overall polarization of the party system also may have an effect. For example, the British majoritarian system focused on two large parties likely attenuates the effects of vote predictors compared to a system with highly polarized choices as in The Netherlands.[2]

A common solution to this challenge is to simplify the choice to a single dimension, such as the Left–Right scale.[3] This method has merit because it recognizes the ideological differences between parties. A pair of voters who choose between two proximate parties on the Left–Right scale are making more similar choices than two voters who pick a far-right and far-left party.[4] This method is also common because party Left–Right positions are available from multiple sources, and can easily be correlated with the Left–Right positions of voters. Electoral studies repeatedly find a strong correlation between voters' self-position and their party choice in Left–Right terms.[5] Moreover, the polarization of parties on this dimension affects the strength of this relationship.[6]

Yet, the previous chapters illustrate the complex and multiple meanings of Left–Right orientations in terms of the economic and cultural cleavages. Although mass and elite scores on both cleavages are statistically independent, positions on both cleavages are strongly related to overall Left–Right orientations. This may be evidence that Left–Right orientation is a "super issue" summarizing an individual's overall political preferences.[7] However, the exact mix of factors defining Left–Right positions for individual citizens and parties—and hence the interpretation of Left–Right relationships—is ambiguous because of the indeterminate mixing of issues and cleavages.

As a solution to this problem, analyses must consider party choices on both the economic and cultural cleavages. The first step is to score each party on the two issue cleavages. The next step correlates the citizen's positions on the economic and cultural cleavage to their party choices defined in the same terms. This captures the reality of voters making a choice not just on economic matters or on cultural issues, but on a mix of both.

Numerous studies have demonstrated that voter positions on the economic cleavage have a strong influence on voting choice over time.[8] Despite the tremendous societal changes over these past several decades, competition along the economic cleavage remains important, even if the issue composition of this cleavage changes. With the possible exception of regional, linguistic, or other niche parties, economic concerns remain a central theme in most party programs.

Recent research sometimes seems to breathlessly proclaim the rise of a new cultural cleavage as a framework for voting choices. Yet, the cultural cleavage already existed in the 1970s for both citizens and elites, albeit in a less distinctive form (see Chapters 1 and 2). As these societies changed, additional issues were incorporated into the cultural cleavage. In addition, the formation of new liberal and conservative cultural parties expands the party choices available to voters.[9] In France and Germany, for example, the presences of Green and far-right parties (the FN and AfD) gives a clearer expression of cultural cleavage, which can increase the impact of cultural positions on voting choice.

By linking voters' attitudes and social traits to their voting choice, we can determine the relative electoral importance of the economic and cultural cleavages. The multiple EES surveys also indicate any changes in the importance of each cleavage over time. The findings should demonstrate the course European electoral systems have traversed over the past three decades, and perhaps the path that lies ahead.

The Correlates of Voting Choice

In many ways, the simple act of voting is not so simple. Voters should sort between alternative information sources and collect information on the available choices. Past voting behavior and partisan attachments also guide voter choices. The traits of the leading candidates is another factor to consider. In a multiparty system, as in the Dutch party system at the start of this chapter, the complexity of voter decision-making is magnified by the number of party options a voter should consider.

I am not trying to develop a comprehensive model of all the factors affecting voting choice. Instead, I concentrate on the causal chain that begins with social structure, leads to voter positions on the economic and cultural cleavages, and then to voting for a specific party to represent these political views. This focuses our attention on voter-party fit for these two cleavages.

Because voting behavior in EP elections are considered second-order elections with different voting dynamics, the analyses use reported vote choice in the previous national election rather than the European Parliament vote.[10] I created two variables as each party's score on the economic and cultural cleavages using the CEP survey (Figures 6.1 to 6.3).[11] For example, CEPs for the Dutch PvdA have a liberal +0.17 score on the economic cleavage and a liberal +1.25 on the cultural cleavage in 2009. Conversely, PVV elites score −0.61 on the economic cleavage and −1.39 on the cultural cleavage. Scoring the parties in terms of their cleavage positions provides a broadly comparable measure across nations. This pair of party scores is available for the 1979 and 2009 European elections.

Each possible party choice in a nation is given two scores: one is the party's position on the economic cleavage, and the second is the party's position on the cultural cleavage. Thus, there are two dependent variables measuring party cleavage positions instead of the single Left–Right measure used in most previous studies of ideological voting.

The most direct analysis is the bivariate relationship between voters' positions on each cleavage and their chosen party on the cleavage (Table 7.1). In 1979, there were strong correlations between the voters' own cleavage positions and their party choices as measured on both the economic cleavage (r = 0.35) and the cultural cleavage (r = 0.37). The results for the economic cleavage are not surprising since this has been a persistent cleavage in European party systems. The cultural cleavage was still developing in 1979, although it tapped clear cultural issues: support for the strong military, harsh penalties against terrorist and opinions toward abortion. And even with a restricted party supply on the cultural cleavage, the correlation between voters' cultural opinions and party choice was substantial.

As a reference point, the table also includes the correlation between voter's Left–Right position and their party choices coded on both political cleavages. These relationships are a bit stronger than for either cleavage dimension, which may reflect the nature of Left–Right orientations as summarizing existing issue opinions. This broadens the content of the Left–Right measure but blurs the interpretation of these relationships. In addition, in 1979 there was moderate cross-correlation between the economic and cultural cleavages that is captured by Left–Right orientations.[12] That is, citizens' economic positions also affected party choice in cultural terms (r = 0.17) and citizens' cultural positions affect choices in economic terms (r = 0.15). This is because party choices on both cleavages partially follow a left-libertarian and right-authoritarian pattern in 1979.

The table's next two columns extend these analyses to the 2009 election. A different set of issues measures positions on both cleavages, and the electorates and the CEPs are thirty years distant from the 1979 election. The

Table 7.1. Voter Cleavage Positions and Party Choice

	Party Cleavage Positions							
	1979 EES		2009 EES		2009 EES, CHES		2014 EES, CHES	
Citizen Positions	Economic Cleavage	Cultural Cleavage	Economic Cleavage	Cultural Cleavage	Economic Cleavage	Cultural Cleavage	Economic Cleavage	Cultural Cleavage
Economic	0.35	0.17	0.30	0.04	0.26	0.05	0.23	0.18
Cultural	0.15	0.37	0.01	0.38	0.07	0.36	0.11	0.39
Left–Right	0.41	0.43	0.39	0.36	0.33	0.36	0.31	0.30

Note: Table entries are Pearson's correlation coefficients. Data weighted by EU population size.

Sources: European Election Study, 1979, 2009, and 2014; Candidates for the European Parliament Study, 1979 and 2009; Chapel Hill Expert Study, 2010 and 2014.

voter-party link for the economic cleavage is slightly lower, despite the fact that these nations had just experienced the first economic shocks following the 2008 financial crisis. Conversely, the cultural link is almost identical to the results for 1979 despite the broadening of the issue base for the cultural cleavage and the emergence of new party choices on this cleavage. The results speak to the continuity of cleavage-based voting choices rather than substantial changes over this 30-year time span.

To validate these relationships, I extended the analyses with the Chapel Hill Experts Survey (CHES). I used the CHES to calculate cleavage scores for parties from the 2010 and 2014 surveys (see Appendix C). This tests the robustness of the prior voting choice results because CHES relies on academic experts to identify the parties' issue positions and asks different issue questions than those in the EES citizen and candidate surveys.

The third panel of Table 7.1 shows the agreement between voters and their party on both cleavage dimensions based on the 2010 CHES measures. The direct correlations for both cleavages are slightly lower, which might be a consequence of the different measurement methods. And yet, the same basic pattern of economic and cultural linkage continues. The CHES and the CEP estimates of party positions show that the cultural cleavage is somewhat more important as a predictor of voting choice across European publics.

The final panel in the table extends these analyses to 2014 using the CHES measures of party positions. Voter positions on the economic and cultural cleavages continue to show substantial correlations with party preferences. The effect of economic opinions reaches its low point in the series ($r = 0.23$), which is surprising given the presumed impact of the 2008 financial crisis and its byproducts. But it is also possible that immediate controversies over the euro, sovereign debt, and fiscal performance shifted attention away from the larger ideological controversies embedded in the economic cleavage.[13] For instance, voters in Portugal, Ireland, Greece, and Spain were concerned with more immediate economic problems, while citizens in Germany had different economic concerns in reaction to the financial crisis. Conversely, the influence of cultural opinions remains strong, especially in comparison to the economic cleavage.

In summary, citizens' positions on the economic and cultural cleavages both show a substantial and persisting correlation with party preferences over the past three decades. Splicing together different data sources suggests that the impact of the economic cleavage may have weakened over the 1979–2014 time span. Any change is modest and may be a complex reaction to the financial crisis in 2009 and beyond. At the same time, the evidence suggests that that the cultural cleavage is not a recent feature of European electoral behavior, and may be a growing factor in voters' choices.

Cross-national Variation in Cleavage Voting

This chapter has concentrated on the overall European patterns of political cleavage based voting choice because the EES are most valuable in describing such broad patterns. But party competition, even in EP elections, is largely a national level process.

Although I expect that both cleavages are relevant across the EU member states, the weight of each cleavage may vary. For example, nations differ in how citizens position themselves on each cleavage dimension, with Northern Europe more liberal on cultural issues than Southern Europe. Do these patterns systematically affect the electoral importance of the cultural cleavage? Similarly, much has been written on how the structure of the economy and the economic policy regimes vary across Europe, potentially affecting the strength of the economic cleavage.[14] The supply of party choices and the polarization of parties might also affect the relevance of each cleavage to voting behavior.

The EES can extend the analyses to voters in each nation. I utilize the 2009 and 2014 CHES studies (rather than the CEP surveys) to measure party positions. The CHES has information for more parties, which is important in measuring party supply within each nation.[15] In several nations, the CEP survey lacks some significant parties, or too few candidates responded to reliably measure party positions. Where information on parties from both sources exists, however, they strongly agree (Appendix C).

Table 7.2 presents the correlations between voters' cleavages positions and their party choice in each nation. The average correlations across the EU14 nations are effectively indistinguishable from the EU-wide results in Table 7.1. Citizen positions on the cultural cleavage are more strongly related to voting choice than for the economic cleavage. Moreover, there is little change in the average correlation between 2009 and 2014.

One also sees substantial cross-national variation in the importance of citizens' cleavage positions as predictors of voting choice. In 2009, for example, the correlations for the economic cleavage vary from 0.02 (Belgium) to 0.41 (Sweden); the cultural correlations vary from 0.10 (Ireland) to 0.53 (The Netherlands).

This variation in correlations is not surprising since in any single election nation-specific issues come into play, as well as other campaign effects. Such variation is inevitable. But there are also systematic patterns across both surveys. For instance, Swedish voters are the most polarized on the economic cleavage in both elections, and the British are among the weakest in displaying economic effects in both years.[16] In general, nations with strong economic correlations in one election tend to display strong economic correlations in the next; and the same for the cultural cleavage—even though the specific issues defining the cleavage vary between 2009 and 2014.

Table 7.2. Voter Cleavage Positions and Party Choice by Nation

	2009		2014	
Nation	Economic Cleavage	Cultural Cleavage	Economic Cleavage	Cultural Cleavage
Austria	0.30*	0.52*	0.13*	0.38*
Belgium	0.02	0.20*	0.29*	0.23*
Denmark	0.32*	0.45*	0.35*	0.47*
Finland	0.34*	0.44*	0.34*	0.40*
France	0.35*	0.38*	0.22*	0.53*
Germany	0.29*	0.29*	0.28*	0.30*
Greece	0.27*	0.47*	0.23*	0.28*
Ireland	0.22*	0.10*	0.06	0.20*
Italy	0.24*	0.35*	0.01	0.32*
Netherlands	0.29*	0.53*	0.28*	0.36*
Portugal	0.22*	0.15*	0.09*	0.02
Spain	0.33*	0.41*	0.26*	0.25*
Sweden	0.41*	0.30*	0.53*	0.50*
United Kingdom	0.04	0.40*	0.15*	0.43*
EU14 average	0.26	0.36	0.23	0.33

Note: Table entries Pearson's correlation coefficients. Asterisk denotes significance at p < 0.01.

Sources: 2009 and 2014 European Election Surveys for voter information; 2010 and 2014 Chapel Hills Expert Surveys for party scores.

The demand-supply framework of this study suggests two broad explanations for the cross-national patterns. On the supply side, one might presume that a polarized public produces more polarized voting choices. To an extent, this is moderated by the PCA's production of standardized scores. The EU pooled calculation of scores allows some dispersion of citizens on each cleavage across nations. However, the cross-national variation is very slight, and there is only a negligible and statistically insignificant relationship with the strength of the party correlations (e.g., r = 0.19 in 2009 for the economic cleavage).

A more likely explanation falls on the supply side of the parties that compete in each nation. The number of parties, or preferably the effective number of parties, may affect the supply of policy choices available to voters and thereby the importance of policy voting. With more parties and presumably more varied choices, voters can find clearer expression for their preferences. However, prior research indicates that the number of parties is a poor surrogate for the political diversity of party choices.[17]

There is stronger evidence that the extent of a party systems' ideological polarization is a more direct predictor of the strength of ideological voting.[18] When the political parties are focused on economic competition and hold distinctly different positions on the economic cleavage, this simplifies and encourages economic-based voting choices. Similarly, if parties are clearly identified with distinct positions on the cultural cleavage and translate this into campaign rhetoric and voter appeals, this should facilitate culturally based voting choices. In highly polarized party systems with many diverse parties—such as Denmark, Finland, France, Sweden, and The Netherlands—there may be diverse choices on both cleavages.

For each of the nations in the 2009 EES, I calculated a measure of party polarization on both the economic and cultural cleavage (Appendix E). The indices use the location of each party on the cleavage based on the CHES scores, weighted by the size of the party's vote share in the election. This polarization index measures the dispersion of party choices along each cleavage, somewhat analogous to a standard deviation of a distribution.[19]

Figure 7.2 illustrates the relationship between the level of party polarization on the economic and cultural cleavages along the horizontal axis and the strength of cleavage-based voting on the vertical axis. The circles in the figure represent the correlations for economic cleavage voting in 2009. There is a modest positive relationship with party polarization and the strength of economically based voting (r = 0.26). In retrospect, this likely reflects the long, persisting effect of economic issues on modern party systems. Even if the British Labour Party or Swedish Social Democrats have moved away from their prior

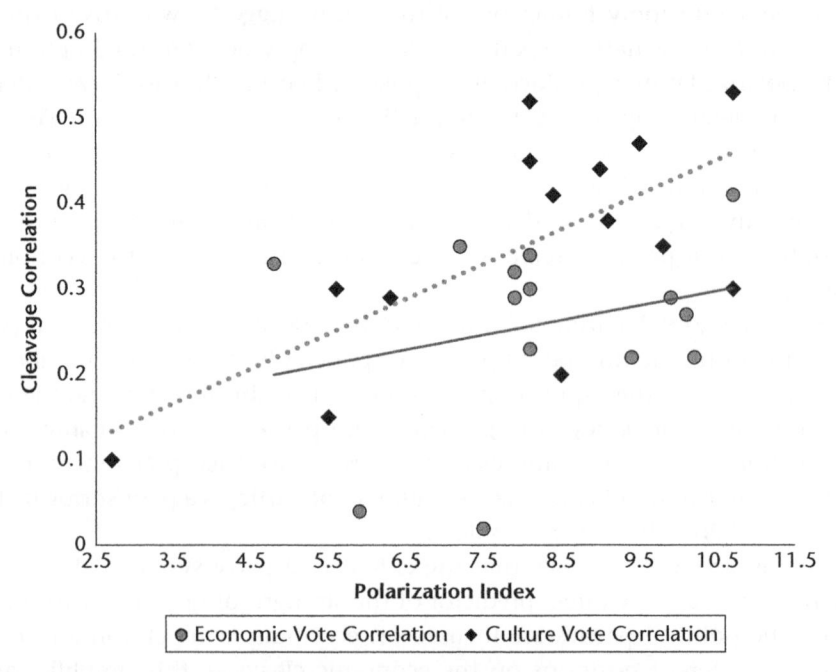

Figure 7.2. Party System Polarization and Strength of Cleavage Voting

Note: Figure entries are correlations between citizens' economic and cultural cleavage positions and their party vote choice scored on each cleavage.

Source: European Election Survey, 2009.

economic policies, there is a persisting economic identity from their political history. Political parties' economic images probably lag behind political reality.

In contrast, the diamonds in the figure represent the correlation between citizens' cultural positions and party choices. The cultural polarization of the party system is very strongly related to the strength of culturally based voting (r = 0.76). For example, the Dutch party system shows the greatest polarization on the cultural cleavage and the strongest correlation for culturally based voting. Ireland has the least polarized party system, and also the weakest cultural correlation for voting. As a "new" cleavage with relatively recent entrants into party competition, the parties at either end of the cultural cleavage often define their identity through this cleavage—Green and New Left parties contrasting with far-right parties—making this more visible to voters. In contrast, the old parties are often trying to reinvent themselves by downplaying their heritage, even as they adopt positions on the cultural cleavage.

With only a small set of nations, we cannot systematically test multiple theories of contextual factors.[20] Yet these findings and the cross-national literature on Left–Right voting lead to the conclusion that the nature of party supply—as represented by the polarization index—is a significant factor affecting the strength of cleavage voting across nations. With a choice of party positions on a cleavage, voters can more easily find a party that shares their views; without choice, policy voting is constrained.

Multivariate Modeling

The expanding supply of party options gives citizens more voice on the policies facing their nation, but it also complicates the voter's decision because there are potential tradeoffs between party positions on both cleavages. Elections are not like restaurant menus where a voter can choose their favorite from column A, and another favorite from column B. In most elections voters only get one choice. Other factors beyond the economic and cultural cleavages also influence electoral choices. Political cleavages may not fully mediate the demographic location of voters. Social class, religiosity, or generation may influence vote choice independently of cleavage positions. Trust in government or evaluations of economic conditions may similarly exert an independent impact on voting decisions.

This produces a complicated methodological challenge. Ideally, the analysis should explicitly consider the tradeoff between a party's economic position and its cultural position in making a voting choice. The objective should be to maximize total proximity to the chosen party if both cleavages are weighed equally. But nearly all prior analyses have examined both cleavages separately,

Political Realignment

rather than as a two-dimensional choice. The best-fit party on the economic cleavage may not be the best fit on the cultural cleavage. How do voters make this tradeoff?

As a first step in addressing this question, I follow the methodology of separate multivariate analyses while recognizing the limitations.[21] Two multiple regressions predict voter choice in terms of party locations on the economic cleavage and the cultural cleavage. As control variables, the model includes occupation, education, age, religion, generation, and other demographic traits considered in prior chapters. The asymmetric effects of political support were apparent in predict citizen's cultural positions (see Chapter 3), and the model considers whether this continues for voting choices on both cleavages. Finally, the model adds retrospective and prospective judgments of the economy to see if performance judgments of government have effects independent of cleavage positions.

Table 7.3 presents the results of these multiple regressions for the 1979, 2009, and 2014 European elections. Citizen positions on the economic cleavage understandably have the strongest relationship in explaining vote choice when the parties are categorized in terms of their position on this cleavage. Voters' cultural cleavage positions have the strongest relationship when parties are categorized in terms of their cultural positions. Moreover, there are significant cross-cleavage effects. For example, voters with liberal positions

Table 7.3. Multivariate Models Predicting Party Preferences

	1979		2009		2014	
Vote Predictors	Economic Cleavage	Cultural Cleavage	Economic Cleavage	Cultural Cleavage	Economic Cleavage	Cultural Cleavage
Economic position	0.33*	0.16*	0.28*	0.05*	0.19*	0.16*
Cultural position	0.12*	0.32*	0.18*	0.41*	0.13*	0.36*
Managers	−0.01	−0.01	−0.01	−0.01	−0.01	−0.02
Business owner	0.03	−0.06*	0.01	−0.03	0.02	−0.01
Blue collar	0.01	0.10*	0.03	0.04*	0.03*	−0.02*
Education	−0.04*	−0.05*	−0.01	−0.02	−0.01	0.01
Subjective well-being	−0.04*	0.01	−0.06*	−0.02	−0.06*	−0.01
Year of birth	0.02	−0.02	0.04*	−0.07*	−0.09*	−0.03*
Religiosity	0.07*	0.19*	−0.05*	−0.08*	0.09*	0.02
Gender (female)	0.01	0.01	0.00	0.03	−0.07*	0.01
Political support	−0.12*	0.06*	−0.11*	0.10*	−0.16*	0.04*
Retrospective economy	–	–	0.00	0.02	0.01	0.06*
Prospective economy	–	–	0.07*	0.01	0.12*	−0.07*
Multiple R	0.40*	0.47*	0.41*	0.46*	0.39*	0.43*

Note: Table entries are standardized regression coefficients; positive values on cleavage indices are liberal positions. Pairwise inclusion of missing data. Asterisk denotes significance at $p < 0.05$.

Sources: 1979, 2009, and 2014 European Election Surveys for voter information; 1979 and 2009 Candidates for the European Parliament studies for party scores, and Chapel Hills Expert Surveys for 2014 party scores.

on the cultural cleavage are also more likely to vote for parties defined by their economic liberalism—even though both cleavages began as independent dimensions. This reflects a partial clustering of party choices along a left-libertarian versus a right-populist axis.[22]

More relevant to the question of electoral change is the pattern of relationships for the economic and cultural cleavage over time. Citizens' positions on both cleavages are important predictors of voting choice, but their weight changes across elections. The economic cleavage has the strongest effect on vote choice in the 1979 election, and then the coefficients decrease in the 2009 and 2014 surveys. Europe's financial difficulties at the time of the 2009 and 2014 surveys did not stimulate broad economic orientations, which is also seen in the simple bivariate results. In contrast, the importance of the cultural cleavage increases slightly over time. Consequently, from a pattern of the essential equality of effects in 1979, the cultural cleavage is almost twice as important as a predictor of party choice in 2014.

Other attitudinal measures also show notable results. Those who express more support for the government or political system tend to vote for economically conservative parties and culturally liberal parties. This reflects the same biases that were evident in predicting citizen and CEP positions on both cleavage dimensions (Chapter 3). The people who are satisfied with government favor conservative economic policies and liberal cultural policies—and parties that represent that mix.

Because of the financial difficulties Europe experienced after the 2008 downturn, I included retrospective and prospective economic evaluations to the models. In some ways, the results echo the pattern for political support. In 2009 and 2014 those who were optimistic about the economy favored conservative economic positions, while leaning toward liberal cultural positions. Pair with the political support findings, the general implication is that European governments that were pursuing such a conservative-liberal mix of policies were garnering more public support.

Finally, most of the demographic controls have weak effects, and often with shifting relationships over time. Only the large size of the EES survey makes these coefficients statistically significant if not substantively significant. Only one of the demographic coefficients is greater than $\beta = 0.10$.

The Effects of a Changing Issue Agenda

One of the subthemes of this study has been the rising salience of cultural issues in affluent democracies.[23] Interest in the issues of a political cleavage presumably magnifies the effects of cleavage positions on voting choice.[24] Spatial voting models assume that voters see party differences along a salient cleavage more distinctly, as if the dimension is elongated to increase the gap between parties while leaving party distances the same on the other dimension.[25] For example, for someone more concerned with issues on the cultural cleavage, party positions on the economic cleavage might appear less distinct, and vice versa. Thus, voters should emphasize the salient cleavage in determining their party choice because they see these differences more distinctly.

The 2009 EES asked respondents to name the most important issue facing their nation. I coded the most important problems into scales for economic issues or cultural issues.[26] I hypothesized that the salience of either set of issues would increase the weight of the relevant cleavage on voting choice.

Table 7.4 replicates the previous model of voting in the 2009 election, controlling for the salience of economic issues or cultural issues.[27] The findings reinforce the general presumption about issue salience, especially for the cultural cleavage. The right side of the table shows that when cultural issues are highly salient, a person's cultural orientations are a very strong predictor of their party choice ($\beta = 0.48$) and economic orientations are irrelevant ($\beta = 0.04$). To these individuals, the party system is almost one-dimensional in cultural terms. The only other variable with a substantial relationship with party choice in this model is political support. And even for citizens who give less salience to cultural issues, cultural positions are still the predominant influence on voting choice. Culture matters.

The same effects exist in more muted tones for the economic cleavage. Economic issues are mentioned much more frequently as a national problem,

Table 7.4. Issue Salience and Models of Party Choice

Vote Predictors	Economic Cleavage		Cultural Cleavage	
	Low Salience	High Salience	Low Salience	High Salience
Economic position	0.25*	0.31*	0.06*	0.04
Cultural position	0.21*	0.15*	0.35*	0.48*
Managers	−0.00	−0.01	−0.01	0.00
Business owner	0.01	0.01	−0.04*	−0.03
Blue collar	0.04*	0.02	0.05*	0.02
Education	−0.02	0.00	−0.03*	0.00
Subjective well-being	−0.04*	−0.08*	−0.00	−0.02
Year of birth	0.05*	0.03*	−0.06*	−0.07*
Religiosity	−0.04*	−0.05*	−0.09*	−0.05*
Gender (female)	0.01	0.00	0.03	0.01
Political support	−0.12*	−0.10*	0.09*	0.12*
Retrospective economy	−0.01	0.02	0.03*	0.01
Prospective economy	0.06*	0.08*	0.00	0.01
Multiple R	0.40*	0.43*	0.40*	0.53*

Note: Table entries are standardized regression coefficients; positive values on cleavage indices are liberal positions. Pairwise inclusion of missing data. Asterisk denotes significance at $p < 0.05$.

Sources: 2009 European Election Surveys for voter information; 2009 Candidates for the European Parliament Study for party scores.

and so the variance between low and high salience is not as stark. As the salience of economic problems increases, however, so does the strength of the relationship between voters' economic positions and their party choices. There is also a decrease in the importance of cultural positions as economic salience increases. In both of these conditions, cultural position exerts a significant relationship with party choice, even when the parties are arrayed in terms of the economic positions.

If one extrapolates these patterns across time, they imply that the public's attention to these cleavages will affect their relative importance for electoral choice. Perhaps in a time of economic turmoil, cultural cleavages will diminish, but even when economic issues are highly salient the effects of cultural positions remain substantial. In contrast, when cultural issues are more salient, this seems to diminish the relevance of the economic cleavage. The same might apply to subgroups of the population that hold a distinct interest in one cleavage or the other, such as class differences in attention to the economic cleavage or religious/secular differences in the salience of the cultural cleavage.

Electoral Choices

Far from the thesis of frozen party systems, this study had told a cumulative story of electoral change over several decades: from citizen attitudes to party alignments to voting choices. Chapters 2 and 3 described the distribution of citizen opinions on the economic and cultural cleavages, and how opinions have realigned over time. A similar realignment in elite cleavage positions occurred for the established parties, and new parties increased the supply of party options. Finally, this chapter described the strong influence of citizens' cleavage positions on their voting choices. Both the economic cleavage and the cultural cleavage now frame electoral competition in European party systems.

The diversity of party positions across the economic and political cleavages has increased the options available to voters and presumably improves political representation. The Dutch voters described at the beginning of this chapter now have more options in finding a party that shares their views. Agreement is never perfect since many factors are involved in the election, but the increasing number of choices should give voters more opportunity to find a compatible party. This should benefit the democratic process.[28]

Yet, the development of diversified party systems also creates new challenges. Policy voting in a one-dimensional Left–Right party system was relatively straightforward. One looks left and looks right, and picks the closest party unless other factors come into play. The proximate choice is less obvious in a multidimensional space.[29] The optimal party choice on one cleavage might conflict with the optimal party choice on the other cleavage, even with many parties spread throughout the space. Instead of looking left and looking right for the adjacent policy choices, a multidimensional space means a 360-degree comparison which might lead to many possible choices. Diversity in choice is generally positive, but this adds to the complexity of party strategy and voter choice.[30]

When political scientists persistently lament the limited sophistication of mass publics, this two-dimensional space may create an additional challenge. Some social psychologists argue that complex choices can lead to less accurate choices and dissatisfaction.[31] In a well-known marketing study, Sheena Iyengar and Mark Lepper concluded: "the presence of choice might be appealing as a theory, but in reality, people might find more and more choice to actually be debilitating."[32] In their case, they were studying consumer purchasing behavior, but this can carry over into politics. More choice might not satisfy people and might even lead to political indecision. Other social psychologists have noted that the diversity of choice might actually decrease the odds of making the "right" choice if there is information overload. In a two-party system, the blind voter has a 50 percent chance of making the "right" choice; in a ten-party system the odds decrease. These complications may be especially likely for citizens who are not politically sophisticated. I am not saying that voting is like buying a jar of jam, but there are elements of human cognition that span consumer behavior and political behavior that merit more attention.

This complexity increases if we accept that the salience of both cleavages is not constant across all voters. Voters who are most interested in cultural issues, for example, likely perceive a party space that accentuates party differences on this cleavage. And similarly for the economic cleavage. While this might help voters simplify their choices, it violates what Donald Stokes called the axioms of common reference and fixed structure.[33] This complexity increases if we assume that political parties also give different weight to the economic and cultural cleavage in their basic platforms and campaigns. This means there is no single shared electoral experience, but different images of the party choices for different segments of the electorate.

These patterns also imply a greater methodological complexity for empirical studies of voting choice in such multidimensional systems. Previous statistical models typically explain voting choice in terms of a single dimension or a series of categorical comparisons. Both are flawed in a multidimensional political world, especially if we wish to make cross-national comparisons. A very large literature discusses contemporary party systems in terms of multiple dimensions, but a paucity of empirical research that adequately models the complexity of choice in these systems or the implications of this complexity for the political process.

Some implications are clear, however. The factors discussed here lead to expectations that voting choices will become more fluid. The social group base of each cleavage that might provide stability is less developed for these two cleavages. The cross-pressures of two distinct cleavages further increase the potential for electoral change. In addition, the inevitable change in the salience of each dimension is another factor that can increase electoral change. And with a more fluid electoral space for the voters, there is a complementary tendency for party alliances to be more fluid. A more fragmented, fluid system increases the complexity of coalition formation and governing.

Notes

1. This was the Danish People's Party. The 2010 Chapel Hill Expert Survey also codes the party as very conservative on the economic cleavage, but also more conservative on the cultural cleavage although not as extreme as most nationalist parties.
2. Russell Dalton, Left–Right orientations, context, and voting choice. In Russell Dalton and Christopher Anderson, eds., *Citizens, Context and Choice: How Context Shapes Citizens' Electoral Choices*. Oxford: Oxford University Press, 2011.
3. Andre Freire, Bringing social identities back in: The social anchors of Left-Right orientation in Western Europe, *International Political Science Review* (2006) 27: 359–78: Russell Dalton, David Farrell, and Ian McAllister, *Political Parties and Democratic Linkage: How Parties Organize Democracy*. Oxford: Oxford University Press, 2011, ch. 6; Ian Budge, Hans Keman, Michael McDonald, and Paul Pennings, *Organizing Democratic Choice: Party Representation Over Time*. Oxford: Oxford University Press, 2012; Timothy Hellwig, *Globalization and Mass Politics: Retaining the Room to Maneuver*. New York: Cambridge University Press, 2015.
4. Anthony Downs, *An Economic Theory of Democracy*. New York: Harper & Row, 1957.
5. Cees van der Eijk, Hermann Schmitt, and Tanja Binder, Left–Right orientations and party choice. In Jacques Thomassen, eds., *The European Voter: A Comparative Study of Modern Democracies*. Oxford: Oxford University Press, 1995; Martin Kroh, The ease of ideological voting: Voter sophistication and party system complexity. In Hans-Dieter Klingemann, ed., *The Comparative Study of Electoral Systems*. Oxford: Oxford University Press, 2009; Dalton, Left–Right orientations, context, and voting choice.
6. Russell Dalton, The quantity and the quality of party systems: Party system polarization, its measurement and its consequences, *Comparative Political Studies* (2008) 41: 899–920; Dalton, Left–Right orientations, context, and voting choice.
7. Ronald Inglehart, *Culture Shift in Advanced Industrial Society*. Princeton: Princeton University Press, 1990.
8. Oddbjørn Knutsen, *Social Structure, Value Orientations and Party Choice in Western Europe*. London: Palgrave, 2017; Silja Häusermann and Hanspeter Kriesi, What do voters want? Dimensions and configurations in individual-level preferences and party choice. In Pablo Beramendi, Silja Häusermann, Herbert Kitschelt, and Hanspeter Kriesi, eds., *The Politics of Advanced Capitalism*. Cambridge: Cambridge University

Press, 2015; Romain Lachat, The electoral consequences of the integration-demarcation cleavage. In Hanspeter Kriesi et al., eds., *West European Politics in the Age of Globalization*. Cambridge: Cambridge University Press, 2008.
9. Knutsen, *Social Structure, Value Orientations and Party Choice in Western Europe*; Häusermann and Kriesi, What do voters want?; Simon Bornschier, *Cleavage Politics and the Populist Right. The New Cultural Conflict in Western Europe*. Philadelphia: Temple University Press, 2010.
10. To maximize the sample size, the 2009 analyses combine party vote in the national election and voting intention among non-voters.
11. These party scores were calculated only when at least three CEPs were interviewed for the party.
12. For example, cultural attitudes were significantly correlated with party locations on the economic cleavage ($r = 0.15$), even though PCAs construct these two indices to be orthogonal in both the citizen and CEP samples.
13. Nicolò Conti, Swen Hutter, and Kyriaki Nanou, eds., "Party Competition and Political Representation in Crisis: A Comparative Perspective," Special issue of *Party Politics* (2018) 24; Enrique Hernández and Hanspeter Kriesi, The electoral consequences of the financial and economic crisis in Europe, *European Journal of Political Research* (2016) 55: 203–24; Liisa Talving, The electoral consequences of austerity: Economic policy voting in Europe in times of crisis, *West European Politics* (2017) 40: 560–83.
14. Herbert Kitschelt and Philipp Rehm, Party alignments: Change and continuity. In Pablo Beramendi, Silja Häusermann, Herbert Kitschelt, and Hanspeter Kriesi, eds., *The Politics of Advanced Capitalism*. Cambridge: Cambridge University Press, 2015; Häusermann and Kriesi, What do voters want?
15. The CHES data are available for voters from more parties (N = 109) in the 2009 EES than for parties covered by the CEP study (N = 79). The major omission is that CHES did not include Luxembourg in 2010. Also see Appendix C for a comparison of CEP and CHES indices.

    I matched the 2010 CHES data to the parties in the 2009 EES. Given the high correlations found in Chapter 6, even the passage of one year seems to make a minor difference since party cleavage positions are relatively stable. The 2014 CHES is an even closer time match to the EES public survey.
16. Geoffrey Evans and James Tilley provide confirmation of the British results. They show a clear narrowing of economic influences on the vote over time, while cultural issues have a stable or increasing influence up through the 2010 election. Geoffrey Evans and James Tilley, *The New Politics of Class: The Political Exclusion of the British Working Class*. Oxford: Oxford University Press, 2017, ch. 7.
17. Dalton, The quantity and the quality of party systems; Dalton, Left–Right orientations, context, and voting choice.
18. Dalton, The quantity and the quality of party systems; Dalton, Left–Right orientations, context, and voting choice.
19. See Appendix E on the calculation of the polarization indices.
20. I replicated the 2009 polarization results in the 2014 election and found comparable results: economic cleavage ($r = .28$), cultural cleavage ($r = .77$).

21. My thanks to Carl Berning for exploring a Structural Equation Model (SEM) that simultaneously predicts voter choice on both cleavages. Without considering the measurement model element of SEM, Berning finds that voter positions on the economic and cultural cleavages do not fully mediate the effects of demographics and other voter traits (as in Table 7.3). In addition, the direct effects of citizen cleavage positions are roughly comparable for the 2009 EES. To address the limitations of two separate OLS regressions, we are collaborating to fully develop this SEM model in further research. Another possibility is an iterative estimation process between two separate models until total fit is maximized.
22. Herbert *Kitschelt, Left-libertarian* parties: Explaining innovation in competitive party systems, *World Politics* (1988) 40: 194–234; Herbert Kitschelt, *The Transformation of European Social Democracy*. Cambridge: Cambridge University Press, 1994, ch. 2.
23. Ronald Inglehart cites research showing the changing salience of economic and cultural issues in party platforms across a set of affluent democracies from 1950 to 2010. Ronald Inglehart, *Cultural Evolution: How People's Motivations are Changing and How this is Changing the World*. Cambridge: Cambridge University Press, 2018, Figure 10.6.
24. Zoe Lefkofridi, Markus Wagner, and Johanna Willmann, Left-authoritarians and policy representation in Western Europe: Electoral choice across ideological dimensions, West *European Politics* (2014) 37: 65–90; Nonna Mayer and Vincent Tiberj, Do issues matter? In Michael Lewis-Beck, ed., *The French Voter*. Basingstoke, UK: Palgrave Macmillan, 2004.
25. Donald Stokes, Spatial models of party competition, *American Political Science Review* (1963) 57: 368–77; James Enelow and Melvin Hinich, *The Spatial Theory of Voting: An Introduction*. Cambridge: Cambridge University Press.
26. I excluded responses that did not clearly reference either set of issues or that narrowly referred to the EP elections, such as comments on the tenor of the campaign or media coverage. Since up to three responses were possible, each scale runs from 0 to 3.
27. Because more people list economic issues, I distinguish between those who list one or fewer economic issues versus two or three. For the cultural issues I collapsed variable to no mention and one or more issues mentioned.
28. The contrasting example is party systems that are aligned along a single political dimension and so limit electoral choice. If we accept that citizen positions roughly conform to a bivariate normal distribution on the economic and cultural cleavages, party systems that do not reflect this distribution will leave a large proportion of the public distant from any party. The US case is one example (see Chapter 9).
29. Donald Stokes' seminal work on spatial voting similarly observed: "A troublesome problem in applying a more general model to the real world is that of defining some kind of distance function over all pairs of points [parties] in the space. The need for such a function is less acute in the one-dimensional case, because an approximate ordering of distances between points can be derived from the strong ordering of points in the space. However, the points of a multidimensional space are no longer strongly ordered, and it may not be possible to compare the appeal of two or more

parties for voters located at a given point by measuring how far from the point the parties are." Stokes, Spatial models of party competition, p. 371.
30. Anna-Sophie Kurella and Jan Rosset, Blind spots in the party system: Spatial voting and issue salience of voters face scare choices, *Electoral Studies* (2017) 49: 1–16; Anwen Elias, Edina Szöcsik, and Christina Zuber, Position, selective emphasis and framing: How parties deal with a second dimension in competition, *Party Politics* (2015) 21: 839–50.
31. Sheena Iyenga, *The Art of Choosing*. New York: Hachett, 2010; Barry Schwartz, *The Paradox of Choice: Why More Is Less*. New York: Harper Collins, 2004.
32. Sheena Iyenga and Mark Lepper, When choice is demotivating: Can one desire too much of a good thing? *Journal of Personality and Social Psychology* (2000) 79: 995–1006.
33. Stokes, Spatial models of party competition.

8

Congruence and Representation

In September 2015, British MP and Labour's Deputy Leader Tom Watson gave a closing speech at the Labour Party's annual conference in Brighton. The party was torn by internal divisions and conflicts over the recent selection of Jeremy Corbyn as party leader. The Parliamentary Labour Party was deeply divided over Corbyn's policies, from his stated opposition to ever using Britain's nuclear weapons to his controversial views on a host of traditional Labour issues. Yet, Watson's speech proclaimed that Corbyn was the people's choice, and told the conference: "From unity comes strength. That's why we're stronger now, as we prepare to leave Brighton, than we were when we arrived. We speak with one voice. We are One Labour."[1]

One of the goals of representative democracy is to match like-minded voters and parties. However, political parties, especially Jeremy Corbyn's, don't speak with a single consistent voice on all policy matters. And neither do their voters. Voters can hold positions on a range of issues, and thus have to do the mental calculus to decide which party best represents their views overall. Some British voters may have cast their 2017 ballot because of Corbyn's economic policies (or cultural cleavage position)—or despite them. British millennials, for example, were strong opponents of Brexit, yet they supported the Labour Party in 2017 despite Corbyn's waffling on EU membership. Some people might vote for Labour because they have always voted for "their" party, even when the party leaders changed the party's political goals.

This chapter concentrates on the representation of voter preferences through the electoral decisions examined in the Chapter 7. To what degree do voters and their chosen party share common political preferences? Voting is an individual-level phenomenon. Political representation is primarily a collective outcome of elections. We judge effective representation by the degree to which citizen preferences are accurately represented by the parties elected to represent their voters in the governing process.

This chapter's analyses go beyond prior research in two major ways.[2] First, instead of the common measurement of political representation in terms of the Left–Right scale, I compare citizen and elite *cleavage positions* to judge agreement in a two-dimensional space.[3] The Left–Right framework is a reasonable way to begin studying representation by simplifying the complications for party strategy, voter decision-making, and researchers' empirical study. However, political competition now involves multiple policy controversies that are only partially overlapping. Examining voter-party congruence in multidimensional terms moves research beyond the simplified Downsian framework.[4]

Second, the chapter separates the macro and micro aspects of political representation. Research normally asks: How well do parties represent the collective position of their voters? To what degree does the position of the average party voter correspond to the position of their chosen party? If parties are close representatives of their voters in these macro terms, then this implies an effective transmission of citizens' views into parliamentary representation.

In addition, there is a micro-level aspect of representation that considers how well each citizen's political views are represented by their chosen party.[5] The average of all party voters may be a poor representation of how well individual voters are represented. If parties cast a wide net for voters, following a catch-all electoral strategy, the average party voter might be close to the party's position but there is a wide variation in micro-level representation. In contrast, a party with a more focused electoral base may be more congruent.

A strong link between the political views of the public and political elites is one of the essential principles of democratic political systems. Previous research points to the strong macro-level congruence of voters and parties in Left–Right terms, and consequently argues that the representation process works successfully. Yet, the structure of political competition is becoming more complex as new issues enter the political agenda and new parties engage the voters. This chapter asks whether expanding representation beyond a single unidimensional Left–Right framework changes our understanding of this process.

Studying Macro-level Representation

The structure of parliamentary systems gives political parties a special position in the representation process. In most European democracies, parties are the dominant actors in elections; selecting candidates, securing campaign funding, organizing the campaign, and attracting votes for the party "team."[6] Most parliamentary elections now use some variant of a proportional representation (PR) electoral system, and the public casts their ballot directly for a party rather than an individual candidate in most nations. This system generally produces a responsible party government model in which parties are the key representatives of the public's policy preferences.

Congruence and Representation

The process of aggregating voters' positions within a party also addresses the persistent question about whether citizens make informed electoral choices.[7] Voters face the challenge of collecting and evaluating information at election time, judging the past actions of the parties and their claims for the future. Such reasoned decision-making should lead individuals to select a party that closely represents their political views. This is the basic principle of representative democracy. At the same time, one can easily imagine conditions that will widen the gap between voters and parties: party identifiers may habitually vote for their preferred party even if it distances itself from their political views, voters may be attracted to a party because of a charismatic leader that outweighs policy congruence, or some voters might simply not make well-informed choices. Thus, the degree of voter-party congruence is a measure of the effectiveness of representative democracy.

This implies we should judge democracy by its collective outcomes as well as the individual choices that make up these outcomes. The collective decisions that come from elections are often better than the judgments of any single individual because they cumulate the knowledge of the whole community. Some voters might be biased in one direction, some in the opposite direction; some are well informed, others pay only limited attention to politics. However, when cumulated together, the total information brought to the collective decision should generate representative outcomes.[8]

Even well-intentioned and informed voters may face challenges in making a reasonable choice, however. The actions (or inactions) of party elites may complicate the voters' efforts to determine which party best represents their opinions. Some party representatives may make vague or even conflicting statements on a policy issue, so the parties' precise position may be difficult to assess. This is especially likely in parties with decentralized decision-making and multiple elites who claim to be party representatives. Ultimately, however, the degree of congruence is a measure of the strength of this link in the party government chain, even if voter-party congruence is inevitably imperfect.

Most cross-national representation studies use the Left–Right scale to study voter-party congruence, measuring party positions by elite attitudes, expert surveys, party manifestos, or citizens' perceptions of the parties.[9] Previous analysis of the 2009 EES across the EU27 nations found a very strong relationship between party voters' average Left–Right score and the Left–Right position of their chosen party ($r = 0.85$).[10] Research showing consistently high congruence between party voters and their parties' Left–Right position generates optimistic evaluations of the functioning of representative democracy.

However, Jacques Thomassen cautioned that representation research may have a blind corner because many scholars "assume that representativeness on the left–right dimension automatically implies representativeness on a range of other issues as well."[11] Thomassen discussed how the emergence of new cultural and social issues that cut across traditional Left–Right party alignments might not be as well represented.[12] Indeed, there is a growing scholarly consensus that contemporary political competition involves multiple policy controversies that are only partially overlapping.[13]

The previous chapters support Thomassen's position. A two-dimensional space based on economic and cultural competition provides a richer, albeit still parsimonious, depiction of the major political controversies shaping electoral politics in contemporary Europe. So our examination of political representation will be based on this framework.

Measuring Congruence

This chapter examines voter-party congruence based primarily on the 2009 European Election Study (EES). The main rationale is the large survey of Candidates to the European Parliament (CEPs) that identifies party positions on the economic and cultural cleavages (Chapter 5). The 2009 EES also provides comparable information on citizens in the EU member states, using the same issue questions to maximize citizen-elite comparisons. In addition, the chapter compares overall congruence on both cleavages to the patterns in the 1979 European election.

For each party, I constructed a mass-elite party dyad as the unit of analysis. To determine the citizen half of the dyad I combined voters in the 2009 election and non-voters who preferred a specific party to maximize the number of partisans.[14] The average scores of each party's supporters on the economic and cultural cleavages define this side of the dyad.

For the candidate half of the dyad, I calculated the average scores for party candidates to the European Parliament. At least three candidates were required for a party to be included in the dyad. Such small N aggregations warrant caution because sampling error alone blurs the underlying relationships. But these data represent the most consistent measures of party positions across citizens and parties for a large number of parties.

To estimate the congruence between partisans and party elites on each cleavage, I use two measures. One measure of representation is *political responsiveness*.[15] Responsiveness presumes that the relative positions of party supporters should be closely related to the positions of the parties. In other words, liberal voters should be represented liberal parties, and conservative voters by conservative parties. Responsiveness is normally measured by a simple regression coefficient (b) from an Ordinary Least Squares model:

Party elites' mean position = a + b (party voters' mean position)

Congruence and Representation

An unstandardized b = 1.0 means that each unit shift in voter sentiments is exactly matched by an equal shift in party elite positions. A b coefficient greater than 1.0 means that parties accentuate the opinion differences between voter groups: party elites are more polarized on the issue than are party voters. A b less than 1.0 indicates parties are under-responsive to their voters.[16]

The second measure of representation is *centrism*, which is the absolute difference between the average of party supporters' positions and the average of partisan candidates' positions on each cleavage.[17] Centrism is analogous to saying that party elites locate themselves near the average cleavage positions of their supporters. This measure has the advantage that it can be calculated for both cleavages separately, and for the two distances in the two-dimensional space.

Party Voters and Party Elites

One of the best ways to envision the representation process is to plot the position of voters and parties on each political cleavage as a measure of responsiveness. Figure 8.1 thus compares the position of party voters and party elites on the economic cleavage. Each dot in the figure represents a party dyad. The horizontal axis plots the mean score of each party's supporters on the economic scale; the vertical axis plots the mean score of each party's EP candidates. The figure shows very high congruence between party voters and party candidates on the economic cleavage (r = 0.73). This is nearly the same level of agreement (r = 0.85) as exists on the overall Left–Right scale for the EU27.[18]

Party elites tend to be more polarized than their own supporters on the economic cleavage. That is, parties with liberal economic positions are often more liberal than their own voters, and conservative parties are more conservative than their voters. The regression line (b = 1.25) means that for each 1.0 unit difference for party voters on the X-axis, party elites differ by 1.25 units along the Y-axis. In other words, many parties "over-represent" their voters on the economic cleavage.[19] For instance, the average voter for the German Linke has a liberal 0.69 score on economic cleavage, but party elites locate themselves at a more liberal 1.14 score. Conversely, CDU/CSU voters average a −0.77 position on the economic cleavage, but the party elites score themselves at −1.33. One can see this variation in reference to the 45-degree line that marks equal scores on both dimensions.

This "over-representation" pattern is typical in representation research based on the Left–Right scale.[20] Perhaps such over-representation occurs because the identities of many political elites are more closely linked to their party's historic economic position. Such intense views may also motivate

Political Realignment

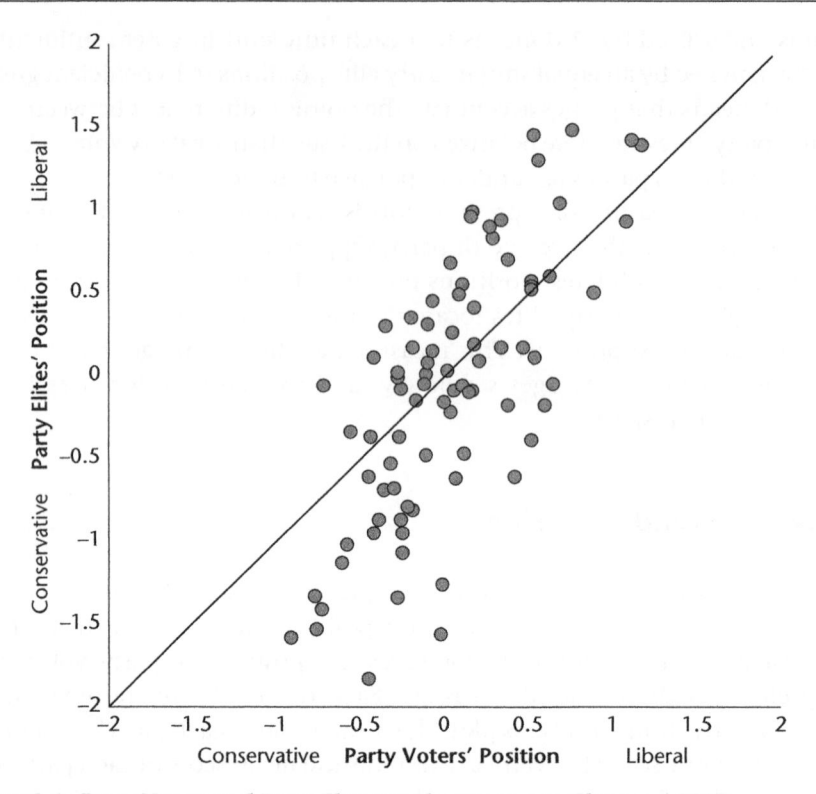

Figure 8.1. Party Voters and Party Elites on the Economic Cleavage, 2009

Note: Figure entries are mean scores for party voters and party candidates on the economic cleavage. (N=82). Positive values represent liberal economic positions.

Source: Party dyads from 2009 European Election Study and 2009 Candidates to the European Parliament Study. Constructed by the author.

people to pursue a political career. The distinct positions of party elites also send a signal of the party's intent to prospective voters.

On cultural issues, the parties are highly responsive to their supporters (Figure 8.2). The positive slope (b = 0.87) indicates that party elites are about as polarized as their party supporters; a regression line would run parallel to and slightly above the 45-degree line in the figure. Compared to the economic cleavage, there is a relatively even dispersion of party-voter dyads above and below the 45-degree line across most of the range of party choices. Together, this broader distribution of voter and elite positions produces a stronger correlation than for the economic cleavage (r=0.83).

At the conservative end of the cleavage (predominately new far-right parties), party elites tend to be much more conservative than their voters. For example, the Vlaams Belang party (Flemish Interest) in Belgium is distinctly more conservative (−1.74) than its bloc of party supporters (−0.39). The same

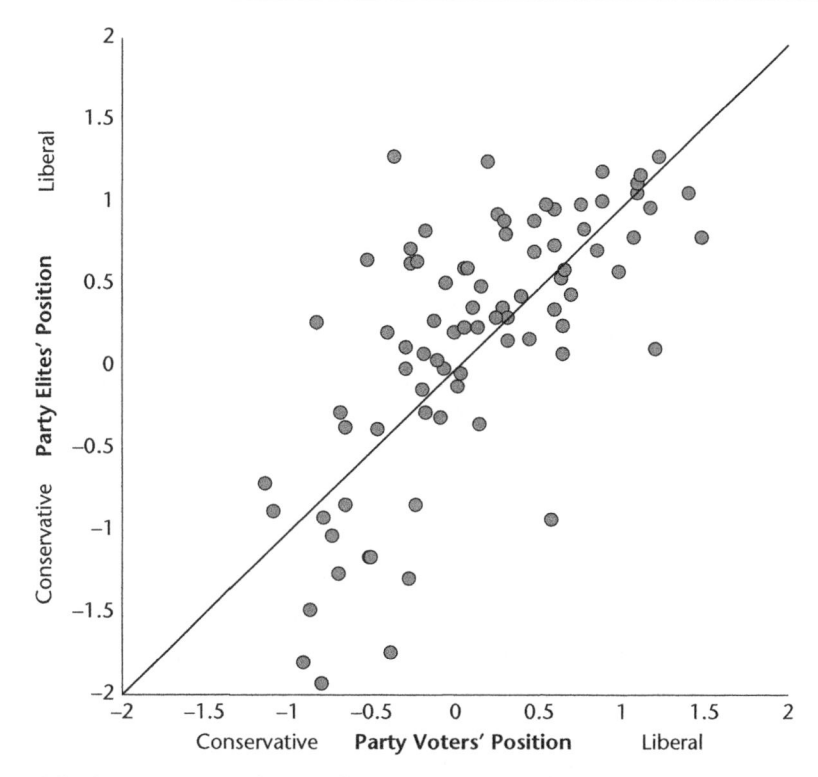

Figure 8.2. Party Voters and Party Elites on the Cultural Cleavage, 2009

Note: Figure entries are mean scores for party voters and party candidates on the cultural cleavage. (N=82). Positive values represent liberal cultural positions.

Source: Party dyads from 2009 European Election Study and 2009 Candidates to the European Parliament Study. Constructed by the author.

applies to the Austrian Freedom Party, the Dutch PVV, the British UKIP, and several other extreme culturally conservative parties. Some of the same factors polarizing party elites on the economic cleavage may be at work at this end of the cultural cleavage.

A Look Back in Time

The 2009 EES provides a detailed picture of voter and party alignments in contemporary Europe. It is a robust data source to describe contemporary party alignments.

However, examining the continuity and evolution of political cleavages requires a time dimension. The 1979 European election provides this baseline.[21] There are limits to these data in terms of constructing dyads. The number of EU member states was smaller, there were fewer parties competing

Political Realignment

in these nations, and the sampling of party elites was less comprehensive. This produces less precision in our measurements, but it is the best available evidence linking party elites and their voters in the early history of the EU.

The first panel of Figure 8.3 presents the relationship with party voters and party elites in terms of the economic cleavage. There is a strong relationship across these dyads (b=0.88, r=0.50). Liberal voters generally are represented by liberal parties, and vice versa. This figure also shows a pattern of "over-representation" among economically conservative parties, which are half to a full point more conservative than their voters. There is less bias among economically liberal parties.

The second panel displays the equivalent relationship for the cultural cleavage. The relationship produces a very strong correlation for the dyads (r=0.70). There is also a slight pattern of over-representation in this relationship at both the liberal and conservative ends of the cleavage (b=1.10).[22]

Both figures speak to the continuity of party competition along the economic and cultural cleavages. The statistics for the cultural cleavage are similar in both years. This reinforces the argument that the cultural cleavage has evolved over time, rather than rising as a new cleavage fueled by globalization, immigration, and other more recent phenomena. If there is a novelty in these findings, it is the weaker representational linkage for the economic cleavage in 1979. The economic cleavage and traditional party alignments are present, but with less structure than in 2009. The timing of the 1979 election may be a factor; it occurred as conservative parties, such as British Labour and the German CDU/CSU, were adopting new neo-conservative economic programs, and as the oil-shock recession of the mid-1970s was reshaping economies in the West.

The rest of this chapter focuses on the 2009 results to describe contemporary party competition. However, the overall conclusion is that both political cleavages have a long-standing base in European party politics.

Centrism

Another way to envision the representation process is by examining the absolute agreement between voters and their respective parties, which is measured by centrism. Centrism is easily measured in a unidimensional party space as the distance between voters and their party on the Left–Right scale. It becomes more complex in our analyses. First, our analyses use latent variable measures of positions on the economic and cultural cleavages that were constructed separately for citizens and party elites. In one sense, there is a common metric; but this metric is adjusted by the Principal Components Analysis to have a standardized distribution for each sample. (Appendix F considers a different methodology of pooled analysis, and discusses the implications.)

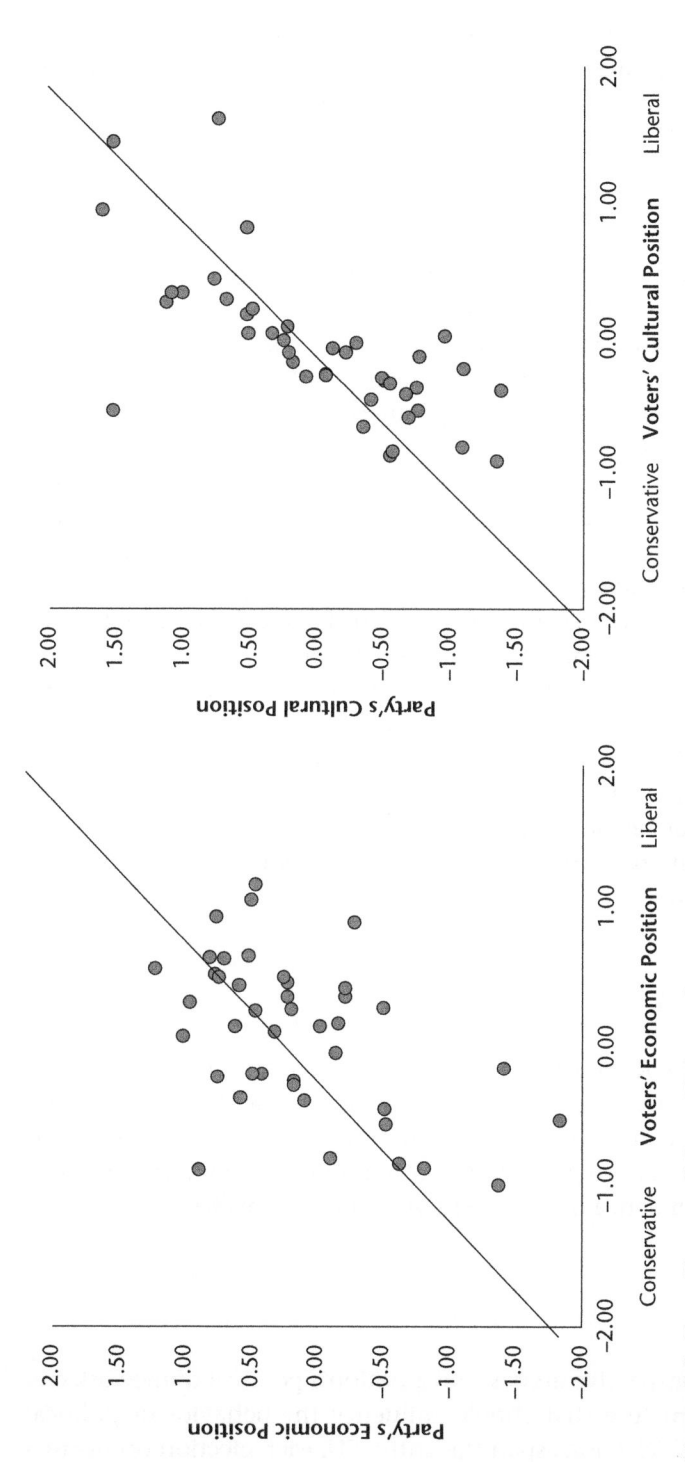

Figure 8.3. Party Voters and Party Elites on the Economic and Cultural Cleavages, 1979

Note: Figure entries are mean scores for party voters and party candidates on the cultural cleavage. (N=42). Positive values represent liberal cultural positions

Source: Party dyads from 1979 European Election Study and 1979 Candidates to the European Parliament Study. Constructed by the author.

The two-dimensional space of party competition raises another issue. One measure of centrism calculates the Euclidian distance between party voters and their chosen party in the two-dimensional space.[23] Another measure is the so-called city block statistic, which treats distances as right angles similar to walking along city blocks instead of as the crow flies. I use the Euclidean method in this chapter, and also calculate the distance separately for the economic cleavage and the cultural cleavage.[24]

In overall terms, the average distance between party voters and their chosen party in the two-dimensional space is 0.69, or about two-thirds of one standard deviation in the standardized space. The *average centrism* scores are very similar (economic mean=0.45; cultural mean=0.43); the *median centrism* scores vary more because elites are more polarized on the economic cleavage than on the cultural cleavage (economic median=0.40; cultural median=0.30).

The centrism measures can show whether voter-party congruence on one cleavage is systematically related to congruence on the other. That is, some parties are good representatives in general, and some poorly represent their voters. This pattern would produce a positive relationship between the two centrism scores. Alternatively, some parties might focus on the economic (or cultural) cleavage and maximize the fit to their voters on these issues, while directing less attention to the other cleavage. This would suggest a negative relationship between the two cleavage centrism statistics.

In actuality, there is virtually no relationship between the centrism scores on both cleavages (r=−0.05).[25] It appears that parties adopt a mix of strategies—some focus on one cleavage, while others focus on the other, or both—so the aggregate pattern appears random. I explore this topic more in the analyses that follow.

Predicting Centrism

What factors affect the level of voter-party congruence on the economic and cultural cleavage, as well as overall congruence in the two-dimensional political space? There are two sets of possible predictors. First, the varied political context of nations may influence congruence. Second, specific party characteristics may influence the representative linkage. This section considers both factors.

National Context

An institutionalist perspective argues that a nation's political framework creates an incentive structure that should influence the behavior of political parties.[26] Although EP elections span the entire EU, each election occurs in a national context with specific political histories, electoral rules, incumbent governments, and a unique combination of political parties. Our question is whether specific frameworks encourage voter-party congruence.

Research often argues that the composition of a nation's party system is linked to the degree of voter-party congruence. The standard hypothesis is that more party choices, and presumably more diverse party choices, should produce a closer fit between voters and their parties.[27] The effective number of electoral parties (ENEP) varied widely in the 2009 election from 2.9 in Spain to 7.7 in the Netherlands.[28]

A more direct measure of the diversity of party choices is the polarization of parties across the political spectrum. If political parties are dispersed along the economic (or cultural cleavage), this provides more distinct choices for voters.[29] More diverse choices should translate into a stronger voter-party linkage.[30] To test this hypothesis, I use the polarization indices for the economic and cultural cleavages constructed with the CHES party expert data (see Appendix E).

Finally, the socio-economic development of a nation may influence representation. More affluent and educated publics are presumably better able to understand the complex world of politics and make appropriate voting choices. These same societies may also have more stable party systems. I test this thesis using the United Nations' Human Development Index that combines national income, education levels, and longevity.[31]

Table 8.1 presents the correlations between the national traits and the size of the voter-party centrism gap for the economic cleavage, cultural cleavage, and total distance. While the contextual hypotheses seem plausible, institutional

Table 8.1. Predictors of Aggregate Voter-Party Congruence

Predictors	Economic Distance	Cultural Distance	Total Distance
Contextual Factors			
Effective number of parties	0.29*	−0.11	0.11
Economic polarization	0.04	–	0.06
Cultural polarization	–	0.08	0.13
Human Development Index	0.19	−0.17	0.02
Party-level Factors			
Party economic position	−0.35*	–	−0.04
Party economic position squared	0.63*	–	0.32*
Party cultural position	–	−0.22*	−0.17
Party cultural position squared	–	0.43*	0.23*
Vote percent in 2009	0.06	−0.02	0.05
Year party formed	−0.19^	0.06	−0.08
Mass party organization	0.07	0.05	0.12
Party family	0.42*	0.55*	0.41*

Note: Table entries are Pearson's correlations, except for party family which are Eta correlations. *Correlation significant at p<0.05, ^ at p<0.10.

Source: Party dyads from 2009 European Election Study and 2009 Candidates to the European Parliament Study. Constructed by the author.

factors have a limited influence on voter-party congruence in the 2009 EES. Only one of the twelve correlations shows a statistically significant correlation with voter-party distances. The effective number of parties is positively related to a larger voter-party gap on the economic cleavage, but then has a negative statistically insignificant correlation for the cultural cleavage.

Party system polarization slightly increases congruence on the economic and cultural cleavages. However, parties toward either pole on both cleavages tend to be more extreme than their own voters, which now appears in these distance measures.

The Human Development Index (HDI) has a contrasting pattern for both cleavages, although none of the relationships is statistically significant. The representation gap on the economic cleavage is larger in nations with higher HDI scores, and smaller on the cultural cleavage in higher HDI nations.

There are substantial national differences in these various measures of voter-party agreement.[32] But these nominal differences are not systematically related to distinct features of the political context or party system as examined here. This is, in a sense, a positive finding because it implies that representation is not closely tied to the specific institutional arrangements.

Party Traits

Contextual factors may have limited impact on voter-party congruence because these effects are constant across parties, and the variation in congruence primarily occurs at the party level. The challenge of representation actually begins at the party level as like-minded voters and parties to identify each other and establish an electoral bond.

Much of the party-level research on congruence emphasizes the clarity of party cues as essential in allowing voters to find a party that shares their political views.[33] This clarity can be produced in many ways. One measure of party clarity is its political ideology or identity that cues voters. For example, parties at the ideological extremes offer distinct political programs, and thus voters more easily know where they stand—and can stand with them if they agree.[34] For example, the Communist Party of France or the French National Front implies a clearer policy profile than the Union for a Popular Movement (UMP) or En Marche. Similarly, Bonnie Meguid has argued that niche parties—green, radical right, and ethnoterritorial parties—are more closely linked to their voters because of their distinct political profiles.[35] Thus, the position of parties at the poles a political cleavage, or a party family, might influence congruence.[36]

The size of a political party also may affect the clarity of its position and thus its responsiveness to voters, although the direction of effects is unclear. On the one hand, large parties might provide more information on their policy positions to the voter. But with size also comes the potential for intraparty disagreements, and an inertia to new issue demands. Conversely, smaller parties might feel compelled to be more responsive to their voters to maintain their existence, but they might also be more labile in their positions because of their small political base. In addition, the strategic voting literature argues that when a person is concerned about the electability of their chosen party, they may vote for a larger party that is more likely to win the election or gain legislative seats.[37] This process might erode the voter-party congruence for small parties because of such defections.

Previous research results for party size are mixed. For example, Mattila and Raunio used the 1994 EP study to show that larger parties were less responsive to their voters on EU issues.[38] In contrast, previous analyses of the 1979 and 2009 EES studies found that party size had weak and varied effects on issue congruence.[39] Party size (vote share in the 2009 EP election) can test whether party size affects representation.

The length of time a party has competed in elections also might influence the clarity of party positions and thus voter-party congruence. Established parties have a track record that may enable voters to better identify the parties' positions as well as committing a party to match their positions. In comparison, new parties often evolve their positions over successive elections as they expand their programs beyond their initial formative issues.

Finally, several studies suggest that centralized and well-organized parties are more effective in presenting a single coherent party message that facilitates voter-party congruence. In contrast, decentralized parties may speak with many voices.[40] This logic builds on a long tradition emphasizing the efficiency of oligarchy or centralized structures in managing political parties.

The Evidence

I collected measures to test party-level hypotheses of voter-party congruence.[41] The lower half of Table 8.1 tests these hypotheses. The most striking result is the effect of party positions along each cleavage. As shown in Figures 8.1 and 8.2, parties that locate themselves at the extreme liberal or conservative position on either cleavage generally are more distant from their voters than centrist parties. This is another illustration of the "over-representation" of voter positions at the political extremes, which yields larger vote-party gaps.

This is seen more clearly in Figure 8.4 that plots each party's position on the two cleavages along the horizontal axis, and the size of the centrism gaps on the vertical dimension. The non-linear patterns are quite striking. When party elites are very conservative on either cleavage (−1.5), the predicted line estimates that party voters are significantly more moderate on the economic cleavage (toward the center by 0.5) and on the cultural cleavage (more centrist

Political Realignment

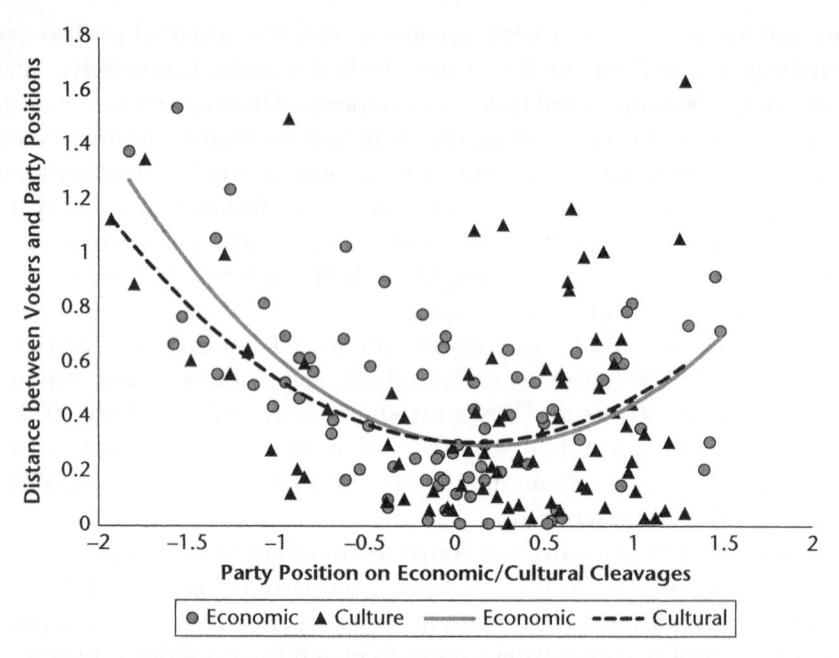

Figure 8.4. Voter-Party Representation Gap by Party Cleavage Position

Note: Figure entries are scores for party candidates on both cleavages on the horizontal axis and voter-party distances on the vertical axis. The lines are polynomial regression estimates for economic and cultural cleavages (N=82).

Source: Party dyads from 2009 European Election Study and 2009 Candidates to the European Parliament Study. Constructed by the author.

by about 0.6). An even stronger pattern of voter moderation exists on the liberal end of each cleavage.

Why are these voters supporting a party that is so distant from their own position? Some voters may misperceive their chosen party or not feel that more moderate alternatives represent their views. Sophisticated voters may also support a more extreme party in the expectation that their preferences will be only partially represented in negotiated policy outcomes, so they back a more extreme party. Orit Kedar showed that this pattern is especially likely in proportional representation elections.[42]

Party family is an indirect measure of political extremism as well as tapping the primary identity of a party. A well-known belief in American politics says that because of party histories and identity, the left (Democrats) own the economic cleavage and the right (Republicans) own the cultural cleavage.[43] If this extends to Europe, we might expect that Labour and Social Democratic parties will focus on representing their voters' position on the economic cleavage. Conservative and Christian Democratic parties may focus on the

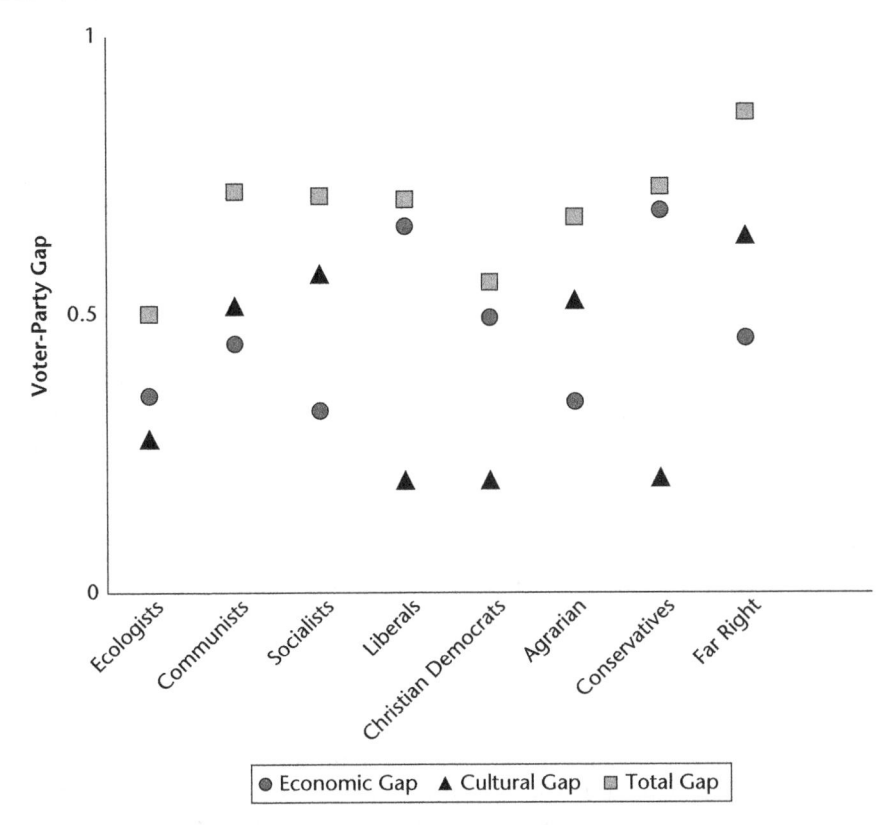

Figure 8.5. The Representation Gaps for Party Families

Note: Each marker indicates the average centrism gap for the parties belonging to the party family for the respective issue dimension.

Source: 2009 European Election Study, party voter and candidate dyads.

cultural cleavage. Green parties share a liberal cultural identity, with far-right parties at the other end of this cleavage. Partisan reality is complex.

As expected, Leftist parties—Social Democrats, Communists, and Greens—are close to their voters on the economic cleavage (see Figure 8.5). Conversely, the largest voter-party gaps on the economic cleavage occur for diverse groups of conservative parties that represent centrist, nationalist, liberal traditions.[44] Thus, it appears that party responsiveness for the economic cleavage reflects the traditional identity of leftist parties that formed around these issues—for voters and elites.

The cultural cleavage presents a mirror image. Liberals, Christian Democrats, Conservatives are relatively close to the conservative position of their voters on the cultural cleavage. Greens are close to their liberal voters. All four of these party families have built their identities around cultural themes. The mix of parties with the largest representation gap on the cultural cleavage is also illuminating. Five of the ten largest gaps are for socialist or communist parties; in these cases, the party elites are distinctly more liberal than their own voters.[45]

This contrast between both cleavages illustrates the strategic challenges facing political parties today. For example, social democratic parties show the closest match to their voters on the economic cleavage of any party family, but this is paired with a larger than average gap on cultural issues. As these parties moved away from their traditional working-class constituency in the pursuit of liberal cultural voters, the cultural gap to their working-class voters increased. Similarly, rightist parties are responsive to their voters on the cultural cleavage, but this comes at the cost of a significantly wider gap on economic issues. In a multidimensional space, many parties seem to emphasize one cleavage, and suffer on the other as a consequence.[46]

The outliers from this pattern are far-right parties. Despite their dramatic emergence in European party systems and their claim to represent the forgotten voter, the voter-party gaps on both the economic and cultural cleavage are substantial. Thus, the total voter-party distance is the largest of any party family. Perhaps it is the populist style of many of these parties, rather than their policy programs, that attract the disenchanted.

Another possible explanation for these patterns is a different perception of the political space across party families. Donald Stokes and a host of public choice scholars have demonstrated that if we allow the salience of dimensions to vary across actors, then distances to parties can vary greatly.[47] To some extent, this is inevitable in a multidimensional political space. However, the 2009 results tend to run counter to these expectations. If higher salience for a cleavage implies that party positions are accentuated, this should increase the gap between voters and their parties on the cleavage. But the pattern is in the opposite direction: Social Democratic parties are closer to their partisans on economic cleavage; Green parties (on the left) and Christian Democratic parties (on the right) are closer to their voters on the cultural cleavage. Thus, it is probably the very process of differential salience that more closely binds many voters to specific parties.[48]

Beyond these two variables, none of the other party characteristics have consistent, statistically significant effects across issue dimensions. Traits such as the age of the party or its overall size have weak and inconsistent effects across issue dimensions. A mass party organization is not correlated with the voter-party gap on either cleavage.[49] Thus, the objective characteristics of a political party matter less for voter-party congruence than a party's political views.

Each Voter and Their Party

The previous analyses follow Hanna Pitkin's dictum that representation is a collective property of the political system—matching voter groups to parties and governments.[50] This led to the comparisons of how well parties represent their voters in aggregate. However, another perspective comes from the standpoint of each citizen. A voter can ask: How closely does my chosen party reflect my political views? Rather than aggregating to all party voters, this section explores the representation process at the micro level.

The contrast between macro and micro definitions of voter-party congruence has several implications for how we think about democratic representation. While aggregate models may assess the overall representativeness of a political system, a micro-level model illustrates how this impacts on individual citizens. As Matthew Golder and Jacek Stramski stated, "From the perspective of each individual citizen, this is arguably the main conceptualization of congruence that matters—each citizen wants to know how far the representative is from her preferred position."[51] Previous analyses have examined this topic based on the Left–Right scale, and we extended this research to the representation gaps on the two political cleavages.[52] Public policies may be based on averages, but the impact of government policy varies across individuals. These individual effects can be lost in aggregate analysis.[53]

Political Representation at the Micro-level

Our approach parallels what Golder and Stramski call a "many to one" measure of representation. The many are the individual voters of a party, and the one is the party's position in the political space.[54] The calculation is straightforward, as the total distance between the voter and their chosen party and the distance on each cleavage.

Partisans have about the same individual representation (centrism) gap on the economic cleavage (mean=0.85) as on the cultural cleavage (mean=0.80).[55] The total average distance between a voter and their chosen party is inevitably larger (mean=1.30), which is a substantial gap in a space constructed with standardized measures. This means that many voters see their chosen party as only weakly representing their policy views.

To some degree, these results may partially reflect the methodology. The analyses imposed a fixed structure on party competition in these nations. Individual voters may give different weights to the issues, focus their attention on only one political cleavage, or even act as single-issue voters. The collective representation of the party space is also a construction we impose on these comparisons. The configuration of the two-dimensional space undoubtedly varies somewhat across nations. However, a parallel analysis of congruence on the single Left–Right scale found that many voters deviate by a substantial margin from their preferred party even when the voters define the party's position.[56] Moreover, depending on methodology, between a quarter and a half of voters select a party that is *not the closest to them* on the Left–Right scale. The Downsian model of voting for the closest party seems to falter when applied to individual voters.

Through the miracle of aggregation, democratic representation seems to function quite well in contemporary European party systems. But if the frame of reference shifts to the individual, the total individual-level representation gap is about double what the data show for party dyads. This leaves many individuals feeling quite distant from their chosen party. One can imagine how these voters feel about the other parties, especially if their party is in the opposition.

Predicting Micro-level Representation

Many factors might systematically affect how closely individuals are to their preferred party. One set of factors might be attributes of the individuals themselves, such as their level of political interest or information. The attributes of parties also might influence congruence levels. The following analyses examine both sets of potential predictors.[57]

Issue Salience. The large literature on issue voting routinely demonstrates that the salience of issues magnifies their impact as a predictor of voting choice (see Chapter 7). One might extend this logic to political representation. If voters are very concerned about economic issues, they might focus their attention on the party that best represents their views along the economic cleavage; and similarly for voters concerned with cultural issues. There is little empirical evidence of how issue salience affects voter-party congruence at the individual level. As an initial test, I used the most important problems cited by voters into a scale of economic or cultural issue salience.[58]

Political Sophistication. Political sophistication helps citizens understand the complexities of the political world. Thus, we might expect that political interest and sophistication would affect the size of the representation gap. The representation gap should be smaller among the politically sophisticated, while the less sophisticated should make less accurate political choices.[59] I use political interest and educational levels to capture the skills and motivations driving political sophistication.

Party Identification. A party identification binds individuals to a specific party, even possibly overlooking short-term policy differences with the party. The implications for the representation gap are unclear, however.[60] On the one hand, partisans might be more likely to vote for "their" party, even if they feel another party better represents their position in an election—thus producing a larger representation gap. On the other hand, partisans may be more susceptible to the psychological processes of persuasion and projection that would promote congruence—thus producing a smaller representation gap as they adopt their party's positions. If non-partisans are issue voters, they may display an even smaller representation gap.

Party Characteristics. For party characteristics, I focus on many of the same factors that potential effect the representation gap for aggregated party dyads. A central theme is that the *clarity of party positions* helps voters identify party positions and select a proximate party.[61] An indicator of clarity is the party's actual policy position. Several recent individual-level analyses of the 2009 EES show that ideologically extreme parties generally display a closer fit to the position of individual voters.[62] These parties' more distinct positions enable like-minded voters to identify the party as sharing their preferences. However, the first part of this chapter demonstrated that politically extreme parties are often more polarized than their own voters, and so their aggregate representation gap is larger. One can test these alternatives by comparing how party positions along the economic and cultural cleavages affect micro-level congruence.

Another surrogate for clarity is the age of the party. Established parties have a track record that may enable voters to better identify the parties' positions as well as committing to a party that matches their positions. In comparison, new parties often evolve their positions over successive elections as they expand their party platforms.

The ideological clarity thesis also holds that niche parties with distinct political identities—Communist, Green parties, regional parties, and far-right parties—offer clear political profiles to potential voters, which should maximize representation.[63] In contrast, large parties that follow catch-all strategies to increase their vote share would produce a more diffuse party position, and thus a wider variance in the political views of their supporters.

The Evidence

The top panel of Table 8.2 presents correlations between citizen attributes and the micro-level representation gap. In broad terms, these traits have little impact on representation gaps. While some correlations are statistically significant because of the large EU15 sample size, the substantive effects are trivial. For instance, the salience of economic issues in the election is unrelated to the economic representation gap (r=0.00), just as the salience of cultural issues is essentially unrelated to the cultural representation gap (r=−0.03).

Political Realignment

Table 8.2. Predictors of Individual-Level Representation Gap

Predictors	Economic Distance	Cultural Distance	Total Distance
Individual Factors			
Economic issues salience	0.00	−0.03*	−0.02
Cultural issues salience	0.01	0.04*	0.03*
Political interest	0.02	−0.01	0.00
Education	0.02*	−0.07*	−0.03*
Party identification	−0.03*	0.03*	0.00
Party Factors			
Economic position—polynomial	0.17*	–	0.11*
Cultural position—polynomial	–	0.16*	0.09*
Party family	0.09*	0.18*	0.10*
Year party formed	−0.04*	−0.03*	−0.04*
Vote percent in 2009	0.02	0.01	0.03*

Note: Most table entries are Pearson's correlations; party positions are Multiple R from a polynomial regression, party family are Eta correlations. *Correlation significant at p<0.05.

Source: Voter-party comparison from 2009 European Election Study and 2009 Candidates to the European Parliament Study (N~10,000).

Similarly, political sophistication as measured by political interest or education has limited influence on the size of the representation gap on either cleavage. Although some of these correlations are statistically significant, none exceed a 0.10 value. Moreover, some effects run in counter directions; the better educated have a smaller representation gap on the cultural cleavage (r=−0.07), but a slightly larger gap for the economic cleavage (r=0.02). Previous analyses of the representation gap on the Left–Right dimension came to largely similar conclusions on the small effect of sophistication measures.[64]

The micro-level representation gap is also relatively independent of attachments to a political party. People with strong party attachments have a slightly smaller representation gap on the economic cleavage, but a slightly larger gap on the cultural cleavage. Neither difference is substantively noteworthy.

The lower half of the table describes how characteristics of the political parties may affect these representation gaps. Just as for the macro-level representation gap (Figure 8.3), party positions on each cleavage show a larger representation gap is at the poles of each cleavage, and smaller at the center of the cleavage. The non-linear relationships for the economic cleavage and the cultural cleavage are noticeably larger than the influence of the voter's own traits in the top of the table.

As with the macro results, because it combines both the identity of a party and its centrist/extremist position, party family also has a strong relationship with the micro-level representation gap. The patterns also broadly replicate the previous macro-level findings. When a party says it is a Green party or a Christian Democrat party, for example, this sends a clear signal to the voters.

Other party traits display more modest relationships. Newer parties are slightly closer to their own supporters. New parties have to attract voters, presumably by highlighting issues that produce this new voter base. For example, the German Linke and AfD both gained initial voter support by offering a distinct, and underrepresented, policy profile. The implication for established parties is less clear. Is the representation gap for older parties larger because these parties are less responsive to their voters (party inertia), or because adherents of these parties have changed their views but prior loyalties produce continuing party support (partisans' inertia)? And, a party's vote share in the 2009 election was essentially unrelated to the size of the representation gap.

In summary, the level of micro-level representation appears to be more a function of where you live (the characteristics of the party system) and the type of party you support, than a voter's personal characteristics. And in overall terms, the individual voter is relatively distant from their preferred party on both cleavages.

Cleavage Politics and Political Representation

Every three, four, or five years, the citizens of various European nations have one opportunity to select the Member of Parliament or political party that will represent them in policy making and governing. Thus, accurate and effective political representation is essential in ensuring that the public's preferences are carried forward into the democratic process.[65] Without a strong representational linkage, the other elements of democracy—parties, election campaigns, voting, and popular governance—are merely decorations. This chapter has studied how well political parties reflect the policy views of their supporters.

The effectiveness of representation depends on how it is defined. Most previous studies have described very high congruence between the blocs of party voters and their chosen parties in terms of overall Left–Right positions. This chapter extends these analyses to citizen representation on the economic and cultural cleavages. In terms of aggregate groups of party voters, there is strong voter-party congruence on the economic cleavage. Party systems are still aligned with the socio-economic conflicts existing in Western Europe.

The new cultural clashes over globalization, immigration, gender issues, and authority patterns polarize both citizens and party elites. Specific issues may show a wider representation gap, especially on gender issues.[66] But on the broad cultural cleavage, there is a very strong relationship between voter blocs and their respective parties. Together, these results suggest that in

173

comparison to the average European, party elites are more polarized than their voters on the economic issues of the past, and less so on the issues of the new cultural cleavage.

These results add to the evidence about the functioning of representation in Western European democracies. Although this pattern reaffirms previous findings, it is still striking that with all the talk of limited voter sophistication, complex policy choices, and volatile party systems, voters can generally find a party that represents their economic positions so well. If one allowed for the complexity and inevitable imperfections of the empirical data used in this chapter, the relationships would be even stronger.[67] This leads to the common conclusion that electoral representation functions fairly well in contemporary European democracies.

Beyond voter-party agreement at the macro level, an alternative approach considers representation from the perspective of individual citizens. People judge representation by how well their chosen party reflects their own opinions. This study shows that aggregate voter-party agreement coexists with substantial individual-level distance from one's chosen party—almost a full standard deviation on both the economic and cultural cleavages. Mathematically, this is almost inevitable. However, the magnitude of the individual-level representation gap is considerable, especially compared to the range of cleavage positions across parties.

Moreover, this is not just a function of our focus on issues and political cleavages. Research on Left–Right agreement similarly finds large representation gap, and nearly half of all voters do not select a party that is actually closer to them in Left–Right terms. This large representation gap may explain why studies of national elections and European Parliament elections found that nearly half of voters do not feel represented by the party for which they actually voted.[68] In short, the patterns describe here seem to reflect the general nature of the representation process rather than the distinct circumstances of these cleavages or the 2009 EP election.

The chapter further explored the factors that might explain the individual-level representation gap. National institutional conditions have only a modest effect on representation. This is a good thing because it means that democratic representation is not closely bound to specific institutional arrangements. Furthermore, the traits of individual voters have only a weak relationship with the individual-level representation gap.

In contrast, the supply of party choices seems more important in structuring political representation. Parties with distinct positions at the liberal or conservative poles of each cleavage are less congruent with their supporters than centrist parties. Strong political views on the part of party leaders may make them less responsive to their own voters. They are selling an ideology, rather than marketing what potential supporters want. This is also apparent in comparing representation patterns across party families. In other words, the degree to which parties represent the citizenry is heavily dependent on the choices that the parties supply, which seems only modestly related to citizen demands based on our overall findings.

In addition, the sharp contrast between high levels of congruence at the aggregate level and a much wider representation gap at the individual level seems to be a common characteristic of contemporary elections. These results suggest that we need to go deeper into the process of political representation than just calculate congruence between the average voter and their party. Something important is lost by aggregation. To the individual, this missing element might shape their images of how well they are represented in the political process. If many voters feel dissatisfied with the party offerings, it is little consolation to know that the average partisan is close to their respective party. Instead, a voter would ask: does the party represent me. For many individual voters, the answer is no.

What is perhaps surprising is the generality of the individual-level representation gap across the citizenry. Political interest, education, partisanship and other factors had little impact on the gap between voters and their chosen party. The choice of a party has a much larger impact on the size of the representation gap than do the characteristics of the individual voter. These results are a caution to the epistocratic claim that less educated and politically engaged citizens are unable to make reasonable choices about which party best represents their views.[69] Individuals can follow many routes to making reasonable choices, and these decisions apparently are not heavily based on political sophistication.

In summary, this study illustrates a paradox in democratic representation studies. Aggregate studies conclude that democratic elections are a very effective means of representation, yet individual citizens see the shortfalls in party representation as described here. Both are important political realities and the pattern is similar on the economic cleavage and cultural cleavage. Thus, how we define and measure representation strongly affects our conclusions about the effectiveness of party representation in European democracies.

Notes

1. Tom Watson, Speech by Tom Watson to Labour Party Annual Conference, *Labour Press*, 2015. http://press.labour.org.uk/post/130199981519/.
2. Portions of this chapter draw upon my previous study of issue congruence in the 2009 EP elections; Russell Dalton, Party representation across multiple issue dimensions, *Party Politics* (2017) 23: 609–22; Russell Dalton, Citizens' representation in European Parliament elections, *European Union Politics* (2017) 18: 188–211. There are

several important differences from this chapter. The earlier studies examined party congruence in all 27 EU member states. The representation gap is larger in the new democracies, and the structure of opinions varies somewhat from the established democracies. In addition, the earlier studies use a different methodology to define and measure political cleavages.

3. There are some earlier multidimensional analyses. On the 1979 EP election: Russell Dalton, Political parties and political representation: Party supporters and party elites in nine nations, *Comparative Political Studies* (1985) 18: 267–99. On the 1994 EP election: Jacques Thomassen and Hermann Schmitt, Policy representation, *European Journal of Political Research* (1997) 32: 165–84; Mikko Mattila and Tapio Raunio, Cautious voters—supportive parties, *European, Union Politics* (2006) 7: 427–49. On the 2009 EP election: Rory Costello, Jacques Thomassen, and Martin Rosema, European parliamentary elections and political representation, *West European Politics* (2012) 35: 1226–48; Dalton, Party representation across multiple issue dimensions.
4. Anthony Down, *An Economic Theory of Democracy*. New York: Harper & Row, 1957.
5. Matthew Golder and Jacek Stramski, Ideological congruence and electoral institutions, *American Journal of Political Science* 54 (2010) 54: 90–106.
6. Russell Dalton, David Farrell, and Ian McAllister, *Political Parties and Democratic Linkage: How Parties Organize Democracy*. Oxford: Oxford University Press, 2011, ch. 3.
7. Dalton, Farrell, and McAllister, *Political Parties and Democratic Linkage*, ch. 5.
8. James Surowiecki, *The Wisdom of Crowds; Why the Many Are Smarter than the Few and How Collective Wisdom Shapes Business, Economies, Societies, and Nations*. New York: Doubleday, 2004; Bernard Grofman and Scott Feld, Rousseau's general will: A Condorcetian perspective, *American Political Science Review* (1998) 82: 567–76.
9. John Huber and G. Bingham Powell, Congruence between citizens and policymakers in two visions of liberal democracy, *World Politics* (1984) 46: 291–326; Dalton, Farrell, and McAllister. *Political Parties and Democratic Linkage*; Ian Budge, Michael McDonald, Paul Pennings, and Hans Keman, *Organizing Democratic Choice: Party Representation Over Time*. Oxford: Oxford University Press, 2012; Robert Rohrschneider and Stephen Whitefield, *The Strain of Representation: How Parties Represent Diverse Voters in Western and Eastern Europe*. Oxford: Oxford University Press, 2012.
10. Dalton, Party representation across multiple issue dimensions.
11. Jacques Thomassen, The blind corner of political representation, *Representation* (2012) 1: 13–27.
12. Also see Henry Valen and Hanne Marthe Narud, The conditional party mandate: A model for the study of mass and elite opinion patterns, *European Journal of Political Research* (2007) 46: 293–318.
13. Ronald Inglehart, The changing structure of political cleavages in Western society. In Russell Dalton, Scott Flanagan, and Paul Beck, eds., *Electoral Change in Advanced Industrial Democracies*. Princeton: Princeton University Press, 1984; Ronald Inglehart, *Culture Shift in Advanced Industrial Society*. Princeton: Princeton University Press, 1990; Lisbeth Hooghe, Gary Marks, and Carol Wilson, Does left/right structure party positions on European integration? In Gary Marks and Marco Steenbergen,

eds., *European Integration and Political Conflict*. Cambridge: Cambridge University Press, 2004; Ryan Bakker, Seth Jolly, and Jonathan Polk, Complexity in the European party space: Exploring dimensionality with experts, *European Union Politics* (2012) 13: 219–45; Dalton, Party representation across multiple issue dimensions.
14. At least 20 partisans is the minimum for the voter side of the dyad; the median number of partisans in the dyads is 94.
15. G. Bingham Powell and Lynda Powell, The analysis of citizen–elite linkages. In Sidney Verba and Lucian Pye, eds., *The Citizen and Politics*. Stanford, CA: Greylock, 1978; Dalton, Party representation across multiple issue dimensions.
16. The intercept term, a, measures the bias of party elites compared to party voters. For instance, at the lowest value on citizen issue positions, does the regression equation predict a lower or higher value for party elites?
17. Christopher Achen, Measuring representation, *American Journal of Political Science* (1978) 22: 475–510; Bernhard Weβels, System characteristics matter. In Warren Miller et al., eds., *Policy Representation in Western Democracies*. Oxford: Oxford University Press, 1999.
18. Dalton, Party representation across multiple issue dimensions.
19. A comparison across all EU27 nations found a much stronger relationship for economic issues (b=1.82), but a varied relationship across subsets of the cultural cleavage. The voter-party slope for immigration and authority measures (b=1.18) was stronger than for gender issues (b=0.88). See Dalton, Party representation across multiple issue dimensions.
20. Dalton, Political parties and political representation; George Rabinowitz, Stuart MacDonald, and Ola Listhaug, New players in an old game: Party strategy in multiparty systems, *Comparative Political Studies* (1991) 24: 147–85: Orit Kedar, When moderate voters prefer extreme parties: Policy balancing in parliamentary elections, *American Political Science Review* (2005) 99: 185–99; James Adams, Samuel Merrill, and Bernard Grofman, *A Unified Theory of Party Competition: A Cross-National Analysis Integrating Spatial and Behavioral Factors*. New York: Cambridge University Press, 2005.
21. Dalton, Political parties and political representation.
22. The outlier in the figure is the Luxembourg Liberal Party whose four candidates are much more culturally liberal than party voters. The figure does not include the Danish Progress Party because of its extreme value on the economic cleavage (as noted in Chapter 6), but it was included in the statistical analyses.

    Both regression coefficients are statistically significant, but because of the small N the standard errors are relatively large (economic=0.17, cultural=0.24) so the differences in coefficients is not statistically significant.
23. This is done using a common Euclidian spatial model: Total distance^2=(distance on economic cleavage)^2+(distance on cultural cleavage)^2.
24. These measures are the absolute value of the difference between voters and party candidates.
25. Other analyses of party representation in the EU27 found similar patterns. Left–Right centrism was only correlated at r=0.03 with socio-economic centrism, r=0.14

for cultural issues, and r=0.02 for gender issues. Dalton, Party representation across multiple issue dimensions.
26. Matt Golder and Benjamin Ferland, Electoral systems and citizen-elite ideological congruence. In Erik Herron, Robert Pekkanen, and Matthew Shugart, eds., The *Oxford Handbook of Electoral Systems*. Oxford: Oxford University Press, 2018; Lawrence Ezrow, *Linking Citizens and Parties*. Oxford: Oxford University Press, 2010.
27. Dalton, Farrell, and McAllister. *Political Parties and Democratic Linkage*, ch. 5; also Weβels, System characteristics matter.
28. The structure of the electoral system is often considered, but all EU elections were conducted under some form of proportional electoral system. District magnitude can also affect the number of parties and voters' decision making, but its effect is largely captured by the effective number of parties.
29. The polarization of party systems is only weakly correlated with the effective number of parties competing in elections, Russell Dalton, The quantity and the quality of party systems, *Comparative Political Studies* (2008) 41: 899–920.
30. Weβels, System characteristics matter; Mattila and Raunio, Cautious voters—supportive parties.
31. The data are available from the United National Development Program: http://hdr.undp.org/en/data. I used data from the year before the 2009 election.
32. The eta correlations between nation and centrism measures are: economic cleavage 0.46; cultural cleavage 0.37; total centrism 0.45.
33. Dalton, Political parties and political representation; Weβels, System characteristics matter; Rohrschneider and Whitefield, *The Strain of Representation;* Agnieszka Walczak and Wouter van der Brug, Representation in the European Parliament, *European Union Politics* (2013) 14: 3–22.
34. Walczak and van der Brug, Representation in the European Parliament; Mattila and Raunio, Cautious voters—supportive parties.
35. Bonnie Meguid, *Party Competition between Unequals*. Cambridge: Cambridge University Press, 2008.
36. Other research argues that voters who want policy change will select parties more extreme than themselves to ensure that the new government's policies will actually deviate from the status quo: Merrill, Grofman, and Adams, Assimilation and contrast effects in voter projections of party locations, *European Journal of Political Research* (2001) 40: 199–221; Kedar, When moderate voters prefer extreme parties. This would be the reason that might produce a larger voter-party gap at the political extremes.
37. Michael Alvarez, Frederick Boehme, and Jonathan Nagler, Strategic voting in British elections, *Electoral Studies* (2006) 25: 1–19; Andre Blais and Richard Nadeau, Measuring strategic voting: A two-step procedure, *Electoral Studies* 15 (1996): 39–52.
38. Mattila and Raunio, Cautious voters—supportive parties.
39. Dalton, Party representation across multiple issue dimensions; Dalton, Political parties and political representation.
40. Dalton, Political parties and political representation; Rohrschneider and Whitefield, *The Strain of Representation*, ch. 6.

41. The clarity of a party's position is its extremism on each cleavage. The EES coded party family to more directly tap the niche party thesis. A party's size is measured by its vote share in the 2009 EU election. Party age is the year the party was formed. The party structure variable is the index of mass party organization in Rohrschneider and Whitefield, *The Strain of Representation*, ch. 6. This index combines expert judgments of the locus of decision making in the party, the significance of the membership base, and the party's links to affiliate groups.
42. Kedar, When moderate voters prefer extreme parties; also Adams, Merrill, and Grofman, *A Unified Theory of Party Competition*.
43. Richard Scammon and Ben Wattenberg, *The Real Majority: An Extraordinary Examination American Electorate*. New York: Coward-McCann, 1968; also see Chapter 9.
44. The parties with the largest voter-party gap on economic centrism are: Dutch People's Party for Freedom and Democracy, Finnish National Coalition Party, Danish People's Party, Flemish Liberals and Democrats, Dutch PVV, Dutch PvdD, British Liberal Democrats, Swedish Center Party, Portuguese Democratic Union Coalition, and the British Green Party.
45. The parties with the largest gap on cultural centrism are: Belgian Socialist Party, Dutch Pvd, Flemish Interest, Italian Reformed Communist Party, Freedom Party of Austria, Panhellenic Socialist Movement, Danish People's Movement against the EU, Luxembourg Socialist Workers Party, Finnish Social Democratic Party, and the Dutch PVV.
46. Anna-Sophie Kurella and Jan Rosset, Blind spots in the party system: Spatial voting and issue salience of voters face scare choices, *Electoral Studies* (2017) 49: 1–16; Anwen Elias, Edina Szöcsik, and Christina Zuber, Position, selective emphasis and framing: How parties deal with a second dimension in competition, *Party Politics* (2015) 21: 839–50.
47. Donald Stokes, Spatial models of party competition, *American Political Science Review* (1963) 57: 368–77; James Enelow and Melvin Hinich, *The Spatial Theory of Voting: An Introduction*. Cambridge: Cambridge University Press.
48. Edgar Grande, Simon Maag, Alena Kerscher, and Regina Becker, Framing Europe: Are cultural-identitarians frames driving politicization? In Swen Hutter, Edgar Grande and Hanspeter Kriesi, eds., *Politicizing Europe: Integration and Mass Politics*. Cambridge: Cambridge University Press, 2016.
49. However, my analyses of Left–Right agreement in the 2009 elections and Rohrschneider and Whitefield's research finds party organization affects agreement on the overall Left–Right scale. Dalton, Party representation across multiple issue dimensions; Rohrschneider and Whitefield, *The Strain of Representation*, ch. 6.
50. Hanna Pitkin, *The Concept of Representation*. Berkeley: University of California Press, 1967, pp. 216–25.
51. Golder and Stramski, Ideological congruence and electoral institutions, p. 92.
52. Also see Dalton, Citizens' representation in European Parliament elections; Walczak and van der Brug, Representation in the European Parliament.
53. One possible complication is that voters may not perceive "their party" as having the same position as stated by party elites. Research shows that voters tend to perceive greater consistency with their preferred party for reasons independent of

ideological agreement. On the one hand, partisans might project their own position onto their preferred party to be consistent, even if they are unsure. On the other hand, perceptions of a party's position may persuade individuals to adjust their own position to fit.
54. Golder and Stramski, Ideological congruence and electoral institutions.
55. The median distances are slightly smaller but still similar for the economic cleavage (median=0.72) and the cultural cleavage (0.69) and total distance (1.22).
56. Dalton, Citizens' representation in European Parliament elections.
57. For more extensive analyses of the representation gap in unidimensional Left–Right terms, see Dalton, Citizens' representation in European Parliament elections. This section draws heavily on those findings.
58. I excluded responses that did not clearly reference either set of issues or that narrowly referred to the nature of the EP election, such as the tenor or media coverage of campaign (also see Table 7.4).
59. Walczak and van der Brug, Representation in the European Parliament.
60. Rohrschneider and Whitefield, *The Strain of Representation*.
61. For example, see Ana Belchior, Explaining Left–Right party congruence across European party systems: A test of micro-, meso-, and macro-level modalism, *Comparative Political Studies* (2013) 46: 352–86; Dalton, Citizens' representation in European Parliament elections; Rohrschneider and Whitefield, *The Strain of Representation*; Walczak and van der Brug, Representation in the European Parliament.
62. Walczak and van der Brug, Representation in the European Parliament; Belchior, Explaining Left–Right party congruence across European party systems.
63. Belchior, Explaining Left–Right party congruence across European party systems; Meguid, *Party Competition between Unequals*.
64. Dalton, Citizens' representation in European Parliament elections, p. 201.
65. Pitkin, *The Concept of Representation*; G. Bingham Powell, *Elections as Instruments of Democracy: Majoritarian and Proportional Visions*. New Haven: Yale University Press, 2000.
66. Dalton, Party representation across multiple issue dimensions.
67. Converse and Pierce, *Political Representation in France*, Appendix C.
68. Bernard Weßels and Hermann Schmitt, Meaningful choices: Does parties' supply matter? In Jacques Thomassen, ed., *Elections and Democracy*. Oxford: Oxford University Press, 2014; Christopher Anderson, Electoral supply, median voters, and feelings of representation in democracies. In Russell Dalton and Christopher Anderson, eds., *Citizens, Context and Choice*. Oxford: Oxford University Press, 2011.
69. Christopher Achen and Larry Bartels, *Democracy for Realists: Why Elections Do Not Produce Responsive Government*. Princeton: Princeton University Press, 2016; Jason Brennan, *Against Democracy*. Princeton: Princeton University Press, 2016.

9

The American Experience

In 2016, the United States experienced what some experts claim is the most unusual presidential election in its modern history. The Democrats picked the first woman to run as a major-party candidate, while the Republicans selected a far-right populist who is the first modern candidate never to have held an elected office. With battles in 140-character bursts, the tenor of the campaign was unusual, to say the least. At times it seemed more like a reality TV program than a presidential election. The pundits expected Hillary Clinton to shatter the glass ceiling of politics.[1] Politicians, pollsters, and Clinton's partisans were shocked by her loss in the election, just as much Donald Trump's supporters celebrated that the polls and predictions had been wrong.

Many of the election post-mortems focused on the unusual aspects of the campaign—especially the prominence of cultural issues and economic dissatisfaction. Clinton focused her appeal on identity groups defined by race, ethnicity, and gender. Trump countered with a populist and nationalist appeal to conservative Americans who felt societal change had marginalized them in economic and/or cultural terms.

In the shadow of the Brexit vote in the United Kingdom and the success of far-right parties in several European democracies, Trump's victory was seen as the emergence of a similar cultural cleavage in the United States. My colleague, Michael Tesler, and other scholars argued that racial identities and racial policy were deciding factors in the election.[2] Others saw sexism and misogyny as the reason why former Obama voters swung to the Trump column.[3] Some reports cited economic and cultural frustrations of those marginalized by globalization for the surprising outcome.[4] In short, the culture wars had come to America.

Descriptions of cultural clashes as a brand new phenomenon overlook modern American political history. In many ways, the United States was an early adapter of cultural politics, which came to prominence in the 1960s and 1970s. In the half-century (and before) leading up to the 2016 election, the cultural cleavage ebbed and flowed with political circumstances and the political choices supplied by the party system. Some scholars argued that the 1992 presidential election was the "first electoral cultural war."[5] Patrick Buchanan's speech at the Republican National Convention was the declaration of war, with the Bush and Clinton campaigns emphasizing their cultural differences. Others claimed that the 2000 Bush versus Gore campaign was the crystallization of the red state/blue state realignment of American politics.[6] These political forces exist in American politics much as they are changing party alignments in Europe.

This chapter tracks the evolution of political cleavages in the United States from the early 1970s to the 2016 election. In institutional terms, the United States is an exceptional case because of its presidential form of government, the two-party system, and its economic and cultural history. The historic racial divisions in the United States are another unique factor to its politics. Yet the economic forces of globalization and deindustrialization also occurred in the United States, as did the progressive social movements on race, gender, and other issues. This chapter provides a more detailed historical record of one nation that goes beyond the European comparisons in prior chapters. The final analytic section concentrates on the impact of the economic and cultural cleavages on voting choice in 2016, including comparisons of primary election candidates to show how candidate supply affected the importance of both cleavages. In short, the chapter expands our comparisons to this important political case to show that the framework of economic and cultural cleavages reaches beyond Europe.

American History and the Cultural Cleavage

While I focus on contemporary politics, one could easily argue that the American polity was built on a foundation of economic *and* cultural issues.[7] Our study, however, begins with the Aquarian decade of the 1960s. Warren Miller and Teresa Levitin, for example, wrote about the changing political alignments that emerged in the 1960s. *The New Politics and the American Electorate* described the impact of new cultural cleavages in American politics:

> Even more widely evident, and perhaps more threatening to established values than the student protests, were the counterculture values that questioned the work ethic, patriotism, authority, conventional religion, and moral values.... For many Americans, the New Politics that encompassed these new issues and themes brought more dissension and more reaction to the dissension, more protest and the legitimation of that protest, more evidence of radical and revolutionary beliefs and behaviors, more sense that the social fabric was unraveling than anything they had ever experience.[8]

This wave of cultural liberalism challenged the status quo on issues of civil rights, gender equality, environmental equality, opposition to the war in Vietnam, and other cultural issues. Following Newton's Third Law, this produced a counter-movement by culturally conservative political actors. George Wallace's third-party campaign in 1968 was a racist and anti-progressive movement that won 9.9 million popular votes, 46 electoral votes, and 5 states.

Richard Scammon and Ben Wattenberg's book, *The Real Majority*, argued that the two major parties had become polarized on their election appeals—the Democrats owned the economic cleavage and the Republicans owned the cultural cleavage—but the majority of Americans held a centrist position on both cleavages.[9] These authors described forces that were becoming integrated into party alignments through candidates such as George Wallace and Richard Nixon's Southern Strategy on the Right, and Gene McCarthy, Robert Kennedy, and George McGovern candidacies on the Left. Rick Perlstein's *Nixonland* provides a rich, detailed account of the rise of the culture wars in the 1960s that involved violent and sometimes deadly clashes between two sides.[10] Each side viewed themselves as saving the nation and their opponents as a threat to the Republic. The many parallels to contemporary US politics are striking, except that in some areas the 1960s were an even darker period for American democracy.

Ronald Reagan's populist and culturally conservative message in 1980 led to a retrenchment of progressive reforms enacted by previous administrations. This cycle continued over the next several decades, with different names on the conservative side.

After George W. Bush's election as president in 2000, Thomas Frank wrote a best-selling book that linked the Republicans ascendance to a widening cultural divide in America.[11] He saw the experience of his home state of Kansas as showing how the forces I have described as social modernization were leaving parts of America behind and encouraging cultural conservatism by a frustrated working class. Several academics, of course, disagreed and many liberal politicians ignored the signs.

More recently, a set of ethnographic studies of rural America describe the same cultural divide.[12] Rural Wisconsin residents, for example, often rejected the liberal values of M&M (Milwaukee and Madison) and felt government did not exist to help them address their needs, but to benefit others. Many of these Wisconsinites voted for Obama and his promise of change in 2008, and then frustrated again, voted for Tea Party Governor Walker (three times) and Trump in 2016. Thus, the theme of cultural change and conservative reaction has been a recurring theme of modern American politics, even if current commentary sometimes overlooks this history and treats everything as new and different.

A full electoral history of these five decades would describe the ebb and flow in the importance of issues and cleavages to the American public. The supply of party choices on both cleavages also changed across time. In every contested Republican primary since 1972, a clear-cut cultural conservative has run for the party's nomination. And in most elections, a cultural liberal ran to represent the Democratic Party in the presidential election.

Several recent empirical studies of American electoral politics have emphasized the two-dimensional framework used throughout this book. For example, Stanley Feldman and Christopher Johnston's analysis of party alignments at the start of the millennium concluded: "a unidimensional model of ideology provides an incomplete basis for the study of political ideology. We show that two dimensions—economic and social ideology—are the minimum needed to account for domestic policy preferences."[13] Longitudinal analyses of the American National Election Study (ANES) series describe the economic and cultural cleavages as a long-term basis of political division among the American public.[14]

The Democrats and Republicans face a complex challenge to balance the economic and cultural cleavages at election time. Because of the majoritarian electoral system and the dominance of the two major parties, there is limited political space for a Green or New Left party to represent cultural liberals, or for a new far-right populist party. In contrast, European PR electoral systems facilitated an increasing number of parties to represent divergent views. The solution in the United States is for political activists to take over an existing party. The political views of party activists suggest a shift in the political insiders of each party. Based on surveys of party national convention delegates from 1992 to 2008, the traditional values and populist wings of Republican Party generally increased, moving the party to the right on cultural issues. Conversely, Democratic Party activists moved away from centrist positions and toward more progressive cultural policies.[15] These trends existed a half century before the "historic" 2016 election.

Time series data from the ANES track public positions on the issues of both cleavages over time, and their perceptions of the parties' positions. The data are limited, however. The ANES lacks independent evidence on party positions such as is often found in European election studies, and the set of issue questions is uneven. However, this is the best source for analyses over time. In addition, a continuous series of opinion surveys provide detailed longitudinal analyses that were was not possible with the European Election Studies.

Party Alignments over Time

One way to start the analyses is to track how the positions of the Democratic Party and Republican Party have evolved on several key measures. This can describe how the supply of party choices available to voters has changed over time. I begin with the broadest measure of the "Liberal" to "Conservative" images of the parties. These terms are common political markers in America.[16] Candidates are described as tending in one direction or another. Media reports describe public policies using these terms. And election results are often described as a shift in a liberal or conservative direction depending on the outcome. It is a common metric that most people hear and use.

The extensive research literature on electoral realignment or sorting in the United States often intuits the position of parties from the positions of partisans.[17] Or, it relies on aggregated party scores based on party platforms or roll call votes in Congress.[18] One of the unfortunate aspects of this research is the absence of long-term valid evidence on party positions, and how they may have changed over time. I think these alternative measures miss the full picture of how parties present themselves to the public at election time.

I turn to another source of party positions: the American public. In each election survey since 1972, the ANES has asked citizens to locate the parties on the Liberal–Conservative (Left–Right) scale. These are the parties' political images as perceived by the public, rather than the messages the party sent or tried to send. Moreover, cross-national research shows that the public's Left–Right placement of political parties has an extremely strong correlation with party placements by experts or party elites (also see Appendix C).[19] Admittedly, the content of the Liberal and Conservative labels changes over this time span—this is a central theme of this study—but these broad orientations summarize the political discourse at each time point.

Figure 9.1 tracks the self-location of citizens and their positioning of the presidential candidates since 1972.[20] The median Americans locate themselves very close to the midpoint of the scale (4.30 on average) in each election. There is virtually no change in the public's median position over this 44-year time span. This contrasts with the regular claims that various campaigns reflect a distinct leftward or rightward shift by the public. Continuity is more apparent than change.

Much more noticeable is the change in the party supply over time. The McGovern candidacy in 1972 was the Democrats' celebration of political liberalism and electoral failure. Americans saw Jimmy Carter in 1976 as the most centrist of the Democratic candidates across this time series. Since then, the public views the party's candidates as trending toward a more liberal position. Obama in 2012 and Clinton in 2016 are seen as almost as liberal as McGovern. A linear trend line shows a half-point leftward shift by the Democrats over the full time span.

Conversely, in the eyes of the public (but probably not the pundits and experts), the Republican candidates have followed a fairly constant position over time. The Reagan candidacy registers as a slight shift to the right, which

Political Realignment

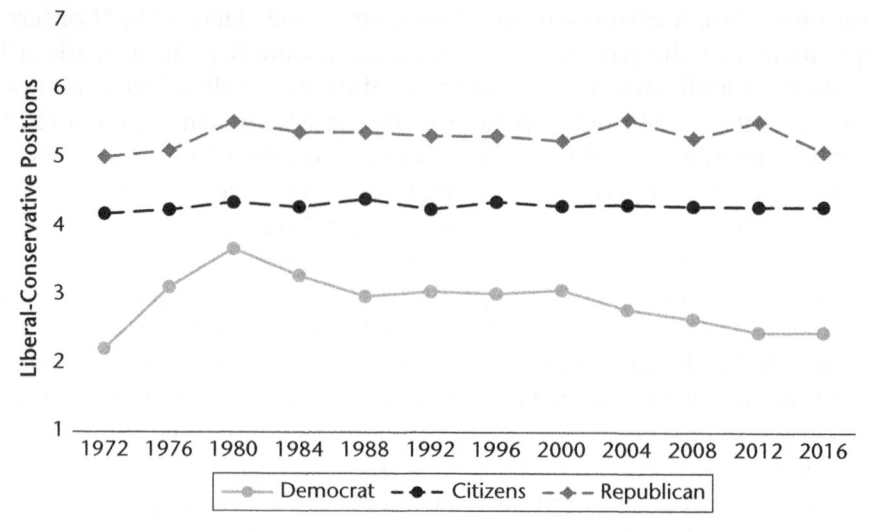

Figure 9.1. Positions of Citizens and Presidential Candidates on Liberal–Conservative Scale

Note: Figure values are median scores on the 7-point scale.

Source: ANES cumulative file and 2016 ANES. Only in-person interviews.

moderates by his re-election in 1984. The Bush candidacy in 2004, and Romney in 2012, show a similar rightward shift. But most surprising, in 2016 the American public sees Donald Trump as the most moderate Republican candidate since Richard Nixon at the start of the time series!

The other notable result from this figure is the size of the gaps from the median voter to the Democratic or Republican candidate. With the exception of Reagan's two victories in 1980 and 1984, the median citizen is closer to the Republican candidate in all the other elections since 1972.[21] On average, the public views Republican candidates as nearly a half-point closer than to the Democrats, which is a substantial lead in terms of this scale. Across the twenty-four comparisons over these twelve elections, the second closest match between citizens and a candidate is Trump in 2016.

One possible explanation for 2016 is that voters did not know where to place Trump's very unconventional campaign on the conventional Liberal–Conservative continuum. However, the percentage of the public that located Trump either at the neutral midpoint or said "don't know" was only 2 percent higher than for Hillary Clinton. Skeptics might cite research highlighting the public's limited political sophistication, which might have led people to miss the obvious conservative signals from the Trump campaign.[22] I discount this general indictment of the public, and it does not explain why this applies uniquely to the Republican candidate in 2016.

An alternative, almost heretical, explanation is that Americans are accurately reporting on how they view the party candidates and their overlap with these candidates across this time series. The combination of Trump's unorthodox populist rhetoric on economic and cultural matters may have convinced voters that he was not straying from Republican Party orthodoxy in significant ways. And to an extent, these perceptions constitute the reality for citizens who have to decide on their voting choices based on their perceptions.

Parties and Economic Issues

We can give more meaning to the trends in parties' Liberal–Conservative images by tracking specific issues. Similar to the Liberal–Conservative scale, the ANES asked people to position themselves and the candidates on several issue scales. The number and content of these issue scales vary widely over time as politics changed or the interests of the principal investigators shifted. Questions on the busing of schoolchildren or foreign relations with the Soviet Union stopped being relevant, for example, and new questions were added.

Three issues seem to tap the core concept of the economic cleavage as it has been used in this study, and which are asked fairly regularly. The first asks whether the government should be the guarantor of a good job and standard of living or should this be the individual's responsibility.[23] This is a fairly stark choice for a person to make, but it reflects some of the policy debates that structure party choice.

The top panel of Figure 9.2 shows that Americans slightly lean toward the individual responsibility alternative, but only slightly, echoing the individualism of the American political culture. The position of the median citizen changes little over time. From 1972 to 2008, the public is fairly close to the position of the Republican candidate. Only in the last two contests do the Republican candidates move markedly to the right. Conversely, the Democratic candidates are generally more distinctly liberal than the American public by a substantial margin. The two largest gaps were McGovern in 1972 (2.48 difference) and Obama in 2012 (1.81). In fact, the only election when the public places the Democrat closer to their own position than the Republican is 2016—and even here the difference between the two major party contenders is very small (0.15).

Another example of the economic cleavage is the tradeoff between increasing public services versus reducing public spending.[24] Americans seem to react to the behavior of the government in Washington in a thermostatic manner.[25] As Bill Clinton pursued a more expansive agenda, the public shifted slightly to less public spending in 1996, and then during the Bush administration toward more public spending. The pendulum shifts back in a conservative direction under Obama. Americans generally see the Democratic candidates as

Political Realignment

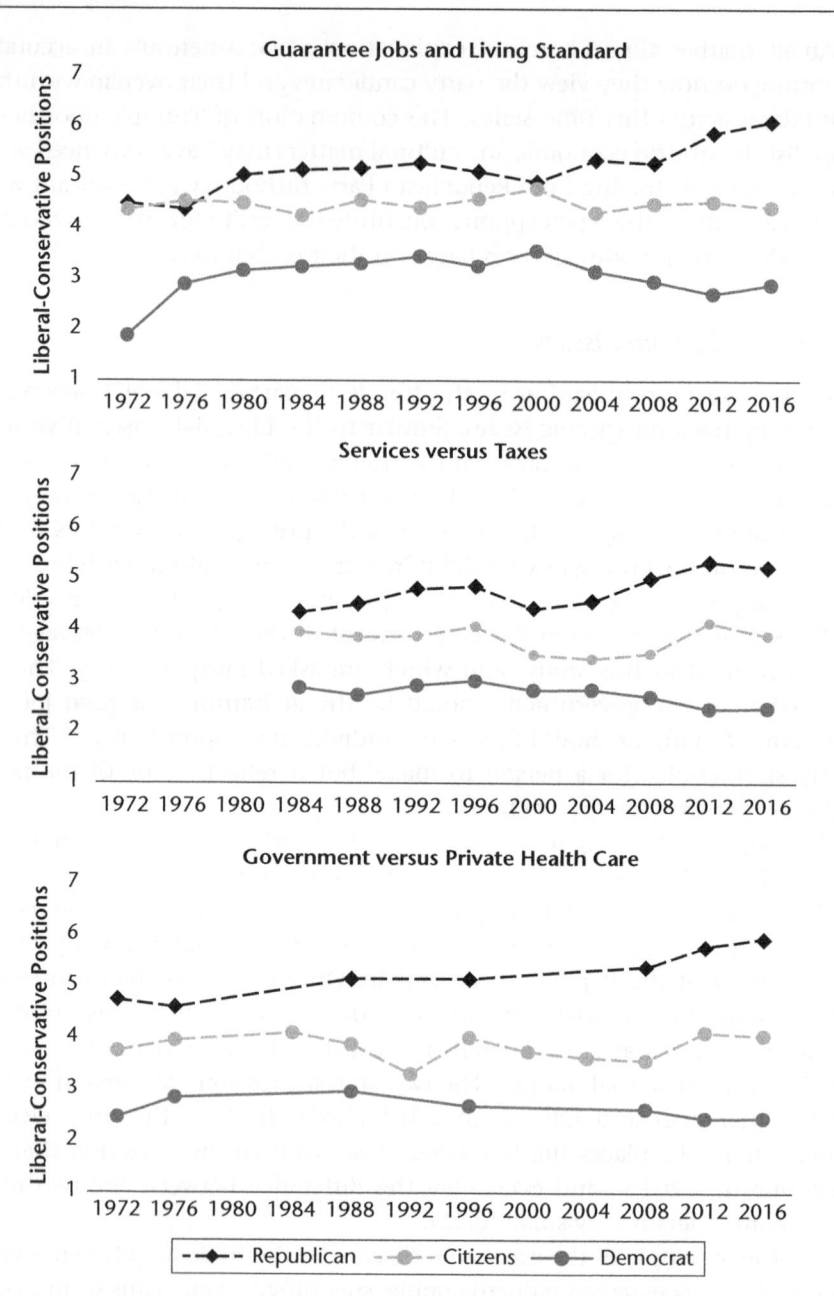

Figure 9.2. Public's Positioning of Presidential Candidates on Economic Issues

Note: Figure entries are median scores for placement of presidential candidates and self-placement.

Source: American National Election Studies cumulative file and 2016 ANES. Only in-person interviews. Surveyed time points noted by line marker.

fairly similar across the years on this issue, and the change in party supply occurs as the Republicans move almost steadily toward the position of less public spending. However, only in 2000 and 2004 is the Democratic candidate located closer to the median citizen than the Republican candidate.

The final example is the provision of health care by the government or by private providers.[26] This has been an enduring concern of the Democrats since the Truman administration, with partial progress over the years through programs such as Medicare and Medicaid. From the 1970s through the 1990s there are modest differences between to two parties, and the median citizen is slightly closer to the Republican candidates. In 1992 public opinion shifts in a liberal direction, and this provided an incentive for Bill Clinton's failed attempt to enact universal health care. The public moves back to a centrist position in 1996, which more or less continues until a slight conservative shift as a backlash to Obamacare. However, the figure indicates that successive Republican candidates move steadily rightward starting in the 1970s, which distances the Republican Party from the median voter.

As expected, the pattern of party images is slightly different on each issue. The starting point and degree of change in party perceptions varies. Across all three issues, however, the perceptions of the Democrats become more liberal between 1988 and 2016 (the longest time span on all three issues). And people see the Republicans becoming more conservative. Thus, Americans recognize the increasing polarization of the presidential candidates and see a widening gap between themselves and either party. And in both 1988 and 2016, both parties are about equally distant from the median citizen.

Parties and Cultural Issues

Perhaps one sign of the evolution of the cultural cleavage is the paucity of comparable issue scales on cultural themes across the ANES time series. Questions at the start of the time series, such as school busing or urban unrest, are not asked in recent years. Conversely, the new issues, such as environmental protection, immigration, and gay or transgender rights, lack a long time series using the same 7-point comparative format. Thus, the parties' placements on cultural issues are limited to attitudes toward abortion, government assistance to blacks, and (possibly) defense spending.

An important aspect of the cultural cleavage involves gender rights and the role of women in society and politics.[27] The best available measure asks about women's right to abortion (the top panel in Figure 9.3).[28] Since 1980, the public shows a slight trend toward the liberal end of the scale, with most Americans favoring no legal restrictions on abortion, or allowing it in case of rape, incest, or when a woman's life in danger. Throughout the time series, Democratic presidential candidates are closer to the median American than

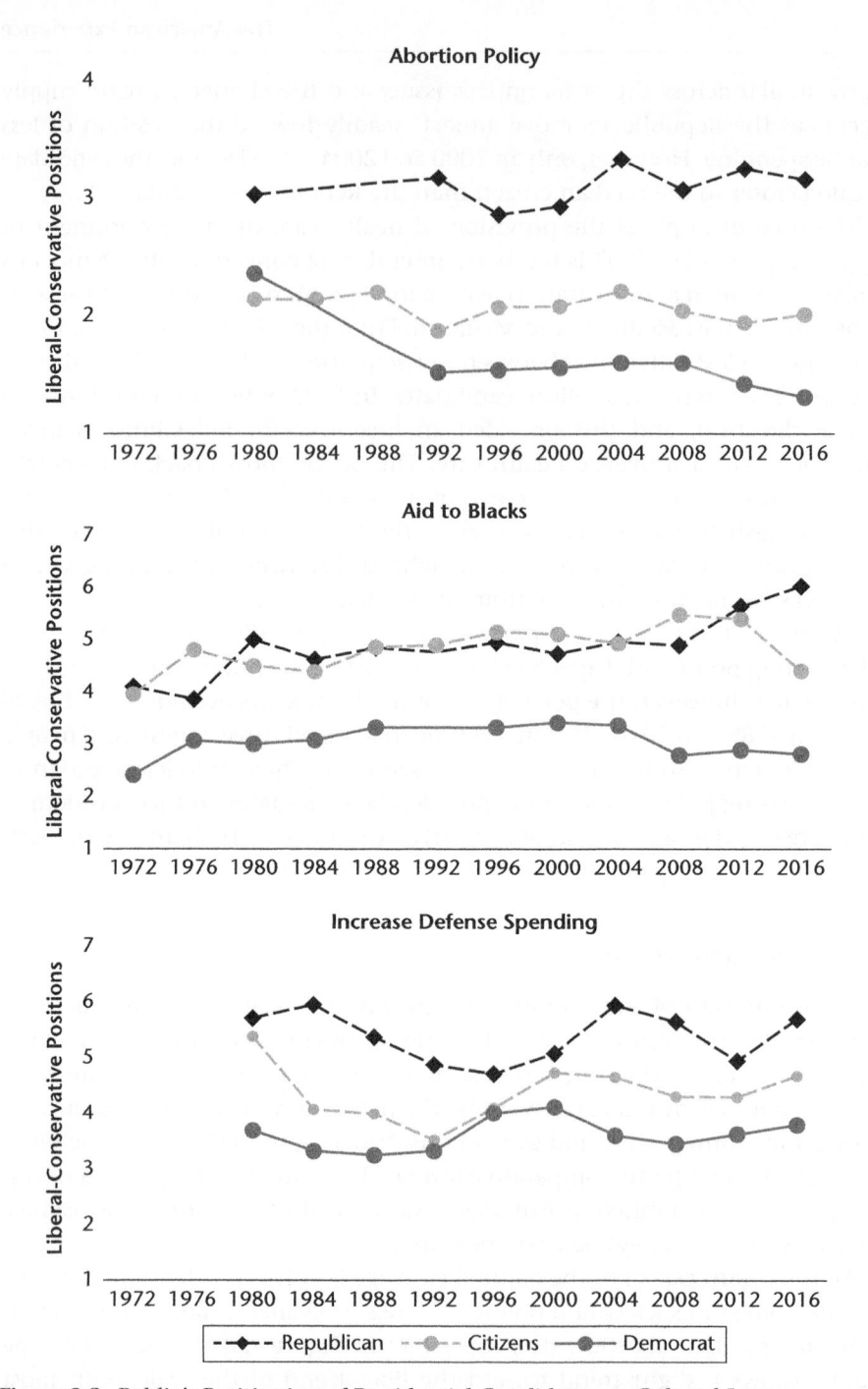

Figure 9.3. Public's Positioning of Presidential Candidates on Cultural Issues

Note: Figure entries are median scores for placement of presidential candidates and self-placement.

Source: American National Election Studies cumulative file and 2016 ANES. Only in-person interviews. Surveyed time points noted by line marker.

are Republicans. However, perceived Republican positions change very little over time, while Democratic candidates trend toward more liberal positions. Consequently, by 2016 the gap between the median citizen and Hillary Clinton was the widest in the entire series, while the gap to Donald Trump was about average for Republican candidates. Thus, citizens' relative proximity to the Democrats on this issue has widened over time.

The second panel of Figure 9.3 describes citizens' perceptions of the presidential candidates' position on government assistance toward African Americans.[29] This is not an ideal question because it combines both the cultural dimension in terms of minority rights, and the economic cleavage in terms of the redistributive aspect of government redistribution. However, this is the longest time series available.

The fundamental shift in party positions in the late 1950s–1960s produced a fairly wide gap between the two parties on racial matters.[30] People now consistently view the Democratic candidates as favoring greater government assistance to blacks, and even more so with the Obama and Hillary Clinton candidacies.[31] In most elections, however, the median citizen is fairly close to the Republican candidate's more conservative position except in 2016. Americans see Trump as the most conservative of any presidential candidate on this issue, and Clinton as nearly the most liberal. This is the widest partisan gap across this 44-year series, with the public positioning themselves close the midpoint of the scale.

Another potential cultural issue reflects the conservative position: support for defense spending.[32] This issue displays greater change among citizens and their party images than the other issues, in part because defense policy is more clearly driven by international events. This timeseries also brackets the transition from the Cold War era to the collapse of the Soviet Union and then the rise of international terrorist conflicts. The public leans more toward higher defense spending during the Reagan administration, which dips to a low point at the end of the Cold War in 1992, and then returns to a centrist position in recent elections. The familiar Liberal–Conservative alignment of the Democratic and Republican parties is also apparent, but it also ebbs and flows over time.

If we focus on the two domestic issues of the cultural cleavage, both the abortion issue and government aid for African Americans show a widening gap in perceived party positions between 1980 and 2016 (the longest time span for these questions). Americans also see themselves as closer to the Democrats in 1980, but closer to the Republicans in recent elections as Democrats moved leftward (except for Trump in 2016).

These six issues are not sufficient to confidently describe the details of party supply over this time span of several decades, since important issues are missing and the content of the issue agenda has changed over time.[33] Party positions on the new cultural issues of gay rights, transgender rights, Muslim immigrants, and other issues have not been examined in the same way even in recent surveys. Even the nature of the economic cleavage requires different questions than the ANES standards developed four decades ago. Still, several broad impressions come from these data.

Most obviously, the public sees a Liberal–Conservative alignment of the Democrats and Republicans on almost all issues at all time points.[34] This seems to be a constant for the public overall, appearing across different methods and issues. This also appears in a standard ANES question that asks which party is more conservative.[35]

The public's images of party polarization seem to follow a clear pattern. Americans see a widening gap between the political parties on most of these issues, summarized by overall Liberal–Conservative images (Figure 9.1). The public's perception of Democrats' cultural liberalism became more pronounced with Obama's election and the identity campaign of Hillary Clinton in 2016, just as perceptions of the Republicans on cultural issues became more conservative.[36]

The issues may be multiplying and their complexity might be increasing, but the clarity of party choice increases over time for the American public. And together these data imply that the broader trend observed in the Liberal–Conservative positions of the parties reflects increasing party polarization, especially on cultural issues.

Americans' Cleavage Positions Over Time

When Bill Clinton ran for office in 1992, his campaign's internal mantra was "It's the economy, stupid." When Hillary Clinton ran for office in 2016, her campaign's slogan was "Stronger Together" in an effort to produce a winning coalition of white progressives, ethnic/racial minorities, feminists, and the LGBTQ community. Do these two campaigns illustrate the changing preferences of the American public?

Despite the richness of the ANES, this is a difficult question to answer with the available survey data. Part of the limitation is the changing nature of political discourse; the issues relevant to the economic and cultural cleavages shift over time as a consequence of societal change. An appropriate measure of cultural positions in 1992 might be acceptance of gays in the military (which Bill Clinton avoided). By 2016, LBGTQ rights issues had expanded to marriage, adoption, and job protections (even in the military). Similarly, the introduction of NAFTA was a new economic development in 1992; by 2016, the unintended consequences of globalization and deindustrialization were apparent. Another limitation of the ANES is the uneven set of issues in each survey, and the recent failure to code open-ended questions that might provide richer evidence of citizen opinions.

To examine the electoral impact of the economic and cultural cleavages I pressed the ANES data beyond its normal bounds. I followed the model of Hanspeter Kriesi's European project and recent longitudinal studies in the United States.[37] I constructed indices of citizen positions on the economic and cultural cleavages from the relevant questions available at each election study from 1972 until 2016 (see Appendix G). For each election, I began with the 7-point issue scales analyzed in Figures 9.2 and 9.3, as well as any additional 7-point scales asked in each survey. Then I selectively added other issue questions that I believed might theoretically tap either cleavage. This was especially necessary for the cultural cleavage that was underrepresented in the surveys until recently. An interactive set of PCAs identified a clear economic and cultural dimension for each election, and this was done independently of subsequent analyses linking cleavages and voting choice. I used the PCA models to create scores for each respondent on both cleavages.

Appendix G presents the PCA results. There is a great diversity in the issues that define each cleavage over time. The basic economic issues from Figure 9.2 tend to load highly on the economic cleavage over time if they are included in a survey. More recent surveys have asked about the issue of national health insurance, which also loads highly on the economic component. In addition, the economic cleavage emerges as the first component of the PCA models in every election survey. This cleavage is well defined in the ANES.

The issues of the cultural cleavage are more varied. Early questions in the 1972 survey had been dropped by the 1976 survey. I also included foreign policy issues that might tap the nationalism aspect of cultural conservatism. However, the question on defense spending changes across election from an economic issue when people stress the spending aspect of the choice, to a cultural issue when they focus on the national defense aspect. And the standard ANES question on government support for African Americans tends to load on the economic cleavage. But in each year there are two or three questions in the pre-election survey that theoretically and empirically fit my expectations for the cultural cleavage.

A latent variable approach has advantages over a fixed set of questions because the world and the issue agenda are changing over time. And the set of available survey questions is highly varied over time. The salient cultural or economic issues in 1972 may be radically different from the salience issues in recent elections. The PCA methodology also allows the structure of each cleavage to vary, with issues changing their weight on a cleavage or even loading on different cleavages across surveys. Prior research shows that

Political Realignment

multiple issue indices provide a more robust assessment of citizen positions and thus stronger predictors of voting choice.[38]

In order to validate the cultural cleavage in particular, I sought an external validity test in the correlates of positions on this cleavage. The EES analyses and prior studies of the U.S. public identified age and education as predictable correlates of cultural positions. Younger Americans and the better educated should be more likely to hold liberal cultural positions.

Figure 9.4 tracks the correlation between year of birth and education level with liberal cultural positions. Both traits show significant positive relationships across all these elections, and no distinct trend for each set of correlations. The impact of education is generally stronger, but also more variable.[39] Younger people also tend to be moderately more liberal across years. More extensive and refined analyses could identify the precise influence of these traits and other factors in predicting cleavage positions. But these persisting correlations imply that the PCA scores on the cultural cleavage are capturing a common underlying concept over time.

Predicting Candidate Preferences

Since the classic *The American Voter* study, there has been an ongoing debate about the impact of issues on voting decisions.[40] The critical view holds that

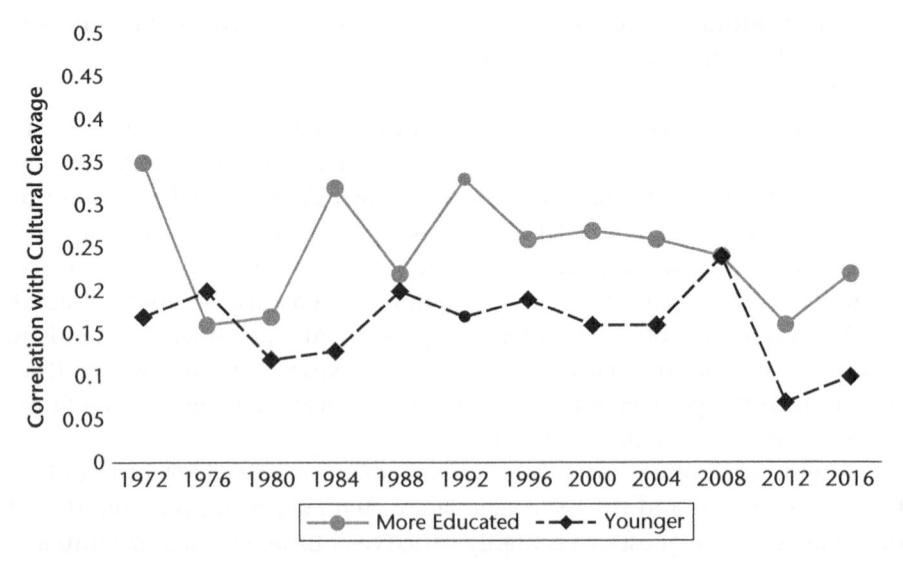

Figure 9.4. Education and Age Correlation with Cultural Cleavage

Note: Figure entries are Pearson's correlations of education level and age with the cultural cleavage index.

Source: American National Election Studies cumulative file and 2016 ANES. Only in-person interviews.

many citizens lack well-formed belief systems and a basic understanding of specific policy issues. The knowledgeable public is supposedly a small share of the electorate, and even their views are shaped by longer-term party identifications. The more positive view argues that most voters do have specific issue preferences that shape their voting behavior, even if this is complicated to measure.

However, this book focuses on how a set of issues forms a broader cleavage dimension, which addresses some of the critiques of issue voting. This places less weight on the specifics of any one issue, and asks about larger policy orientations. For example, a person might not be informed on current tax proposals before Congress, or the details of Medicare policy presented in the ANES (or the election survey may not ask about the issues of interest to the voter), but most people have a broad sense of the tradeoff between taxes and services relative to their own personal preferences. The same applies to orientations on cultural themes. Indeed, Stephen Ansolabehere and his colleagues argued that such broad multi-indicator methods are the most accurate way to tap public policy views and their voting impact.[41]

The other analytic decision is how to model party preferences. Research on American elections is typically simpler than European elections because there are only two main parties. But over a long period, there are recurring third-party challenges which can distort two-party trends. And a large percentage of Americans do not vote. Consequently, to simplify the modeling and focus on the broad political alignments (and not just voters), I analyzed preference differences between the thermometer ratings of the Democratic and Republican presidential candidates in each election.[42]

Figure 9.5 describes the correlations between citizen cleavage positions and Republican–Democratic candidate preferences from 1972 until 2016. Positions on the economic cleavage have a strong and relatively stable relationship with candidate preferences, which increases after the onset of the 2008 recession. The two strongest correlations are in 2008 and 2012.

Americans' cultural positions initially are almost unrelated to candidate preferences, and then steadily increase over time. The relationship peaked in 2004, almost matching the importance of the economic position as a correlate of Republican–Democratic candidate preferences. Cultural positions became less important in 2008 and 2012. Zingher and Flynn found a similar strengthening correlation for cultural positions in models predicting presidential vote and affect toward the parties from 1972 until 2012.[43] This may have reflected the dominance of economic issues following the Great Recession, especially by the social groups that are potentially most attuned to cultural conservatism. For example, Katherine Cramer's study of political resentment in rural Wisconsin found economic needs seemed to dominate cultural concerns in the 2008 election. These sentiments prompted many Wisconsinites to favor

Political Realignment

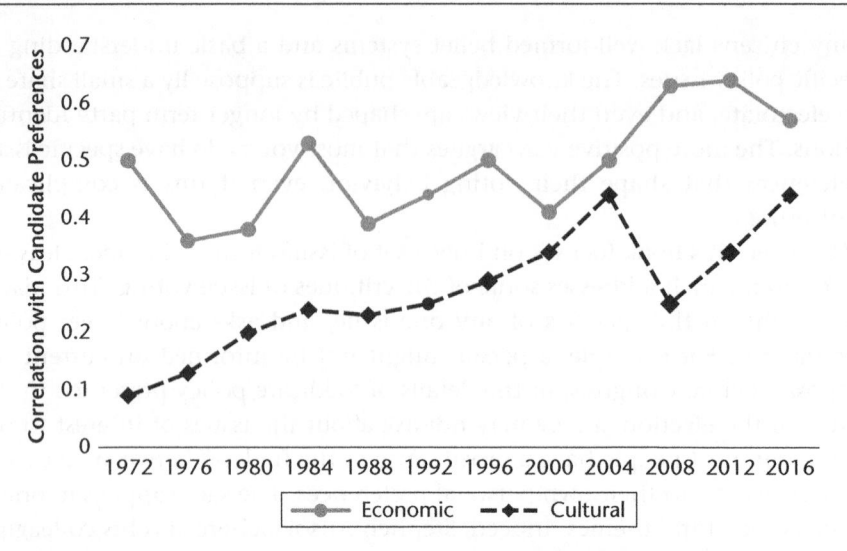

Figure 9.5. Economic and Cultural Correlates of Candidate Preferences

Note: Figure entries are Pearson's correlation between cleavage positions and the difference in thermometer scores between Republican and Democratic presidential candidates.

Source: American National Election Studies cumulative file and 2016 ANES. Only in-person interviews.

Obama's message of opportunity and change over Clinton's establishment message in the Democratic primary.[44] By 2016, cultural issues had rebounded to match its strongest relationship with candidate preferences (as discussed in the section "Making Candidate Choices").

One should discount the specific correlations for any single election because they are subject to sampling error, and the specific mix of issue questions in the survey can modestly affect results.[45] But this variation in measurement makes the results all the more impressive. Citizen positions on the broader economic cleavage have a strong and enduring relationship with candidate preferences. The electoral relevance of the cultural cleavage has increased over time, even as the content of the cultural cleavage has evolved over this time span. This could reflect the greater salience of cultural issues, an increased clarity in party positions (Figure 9.3), or a clearer sorting of cultural liberals and conservatives into the "right" political party. In short, the American patterns are consistent with the evidence from Europe.

A more complex latent variable model of ANES issues by Shaun Ratcliff and his colleagues comes to similar conclusions. They find a growing gap between Democratic and Republican party identifiers on both the economic and cultural cleavages.[46] The Pew Research Center finds a similar widening of the gap between Republican and Democratic partisans on both economic and cultural issues since 1994.[47] Since party identifications reflect a deeper commitment than voting choice, this signals an even more enduring impact of both cleavages for electoral behavior.

The "Historic" Election of 2016

After the 2016 election, I attended a post-election debriefing by consultants from the recent campaign, and all of the panelists expressed great surprise or even shock at the presidential outcome. A prominent Republican Party consultant said almost everyone in the pool of high-level Republican campaign activists had bet on Trump to lose (as had everyone in the pool of political scientists at UC Irvine). Of course, *The New York Times* and many other election forecasters were also wrong: So much for expertise.

The campaign and election were exceptional in many ways. Donald Trump's victory raised the specter of the far-right parties that had spread across Europe. The unusual tenor of the campaign rubbed nerves raw on both sides. Much of the policy attention focused on Trump's populist message and Clinton's liberal identity politics. The form of this culture clash was new in 2016, but it was also old in carrying forward past conflicts to this campaign. Much of the immediate research on the election seemed to focus on a single predictor of interest to the researcher: race, ethnicity, gender politics, an economic backlash, immigration issues, political distrust, and so on. These are all pieces of the puzzle, but not the full puzzle.

Thinking about political competition in terms of the economic and cultural cleavages subsumes most of these specific issues into a broader framework of political choices. The previous section described the impact of these two cleavages on citizen candidate preferences over time. But there is a complication in just focusing on the endpoint—the final voting decision in November 2016. The American electoral system is exceptional because only two viable parties compete in each election. So the diversity of party supply seen in most European party systems is lacking. Moreover, previous chapters demonstrate that the choices defined by the parties influence the correlates of voting choice. The greater the range of choices on a cleavage, the more people are likely to link their personal opinions to their party choices. When there are only two choices, all the various political issues are bundled up in two packages, so the voter's ability to choose is limited.

A second confounding factor in interpreting election results is the impact of party identifications on voting choices.[48] Elections are a continuation of an ongoing competition between the parties with new players. It's like the Dodgers–Giants baseball rivalry that continues season after season even with different stars and coaches on both sides—but the fans are constant supporters of their team. Elections in America are similar. Most people enter each election with a standing predisposition to support "their" party, and continue to support the same party (the same team) even when the players and issues change. Study after study shows that party identification is one of the most potent predictors of voting choices.

From 2000 to 2012, the degree of party loyalty is exceptional.[49] A full 97 percent of strong Democrats voted for their party across these elections, and 97 percent of strong Republicans did the same. It did not matter if the Democratic candidate was a white southerner with a long political resume, a liberal senator from New England, or a freshman senator from the Midwest who just happened to be black. The same pattern exists for Republican voters. The greatest swing in vote shares between elections occurs among those without party ties, especially if they are politically engaged.

The 2016 election seemed to challenge this conventional model of partisanship and voting. Hillary Clinton's campaign targeted women, Hispanics, and the LGBTQ community more explicitly than any Democratic candidate in the past. Donald Trump supposedly appealed to a different type of Republican voter and won three states from the Democrats' Midwestern blue wall. The rhetoric of the campaign also seemed to test traditional partisan loyalties. In almost every way, this was not a "normal" election. Yet despite the exceptional features of the 2016 election, voting tendencies were as clearly drawn as in the four previous elections. Lynn Vavreck gave a short, direct summary of the two political camps in 2016: "[People] will ask: What's the single best description of Trump supporters?" My answer often disappoints them. It's quite simple: They're Republicans. When they ask about Clinton supporters, the answer is similar: "They're Democrats."[50] Most partisans vote for their team, rather than the coach, which dulls the potential impact of other predictors of the vote. Current research shows that these identities have become more closely aligned with both the economic and cultural cleavage.[51]

Still, the interaction of political demands and political supply is important in describing the electoral outcome in 2016. In the United States, this generally occurs in the primaries where the candidates are selected. In 2016 the supply of candidates on the Republican side was exceptional in number and political views, more than would fit on a single television stage. The Democrats also offered a surprisingly close primary contest between Hillary Clinton and the upstart populist Democrat, Bernie Sanders.

One can map these candidates' cleavage positions through an innovative new voter advice application, *Societly.com*.[52] Societly describes itself as a nonpartisan platform defining how candidates, elected officials, and propositions align with citizens' views. A team of political scientists reviewed the candidates' official statements, information on their websites, and news coverage to locate each candidate on twenty central issues of the campaign. It made this information available through its website in partnership with

The American Experience

the *Washington Post* and other media. People marked their position on these twenty issues, and Societly calculated their agreement with each candidate across both party primaries.

Societly's information can locate candidates on the economic cleavage and cultural cleavage, similar to the spaces previously presented for European party systems.[53] Figure 9.6 shows a wide gap between the locations of the Democratic and Republican candidates in this two-dimensional space, with the exception of centrist Jim Webb. Herbert Kitschelt's 'left-libertarian' term might describe the main Democrat candidates. Bernie Sanders' progressive, populist campaign is the most liberal on both cleavages. Hillary Clinton offers a less progressive image in the primaries, although still located at a substantial distance away from the center of the political space.

More illuminating, perhaps, is the positioning of the Republican primary candidates. To varying degrees, the Republican candidates reflect some mix of conservative values on both cleavages. For example, Ben Carson, Marco Rubio, Rick Santorum, and Mike Huckabee are extremely conservative on

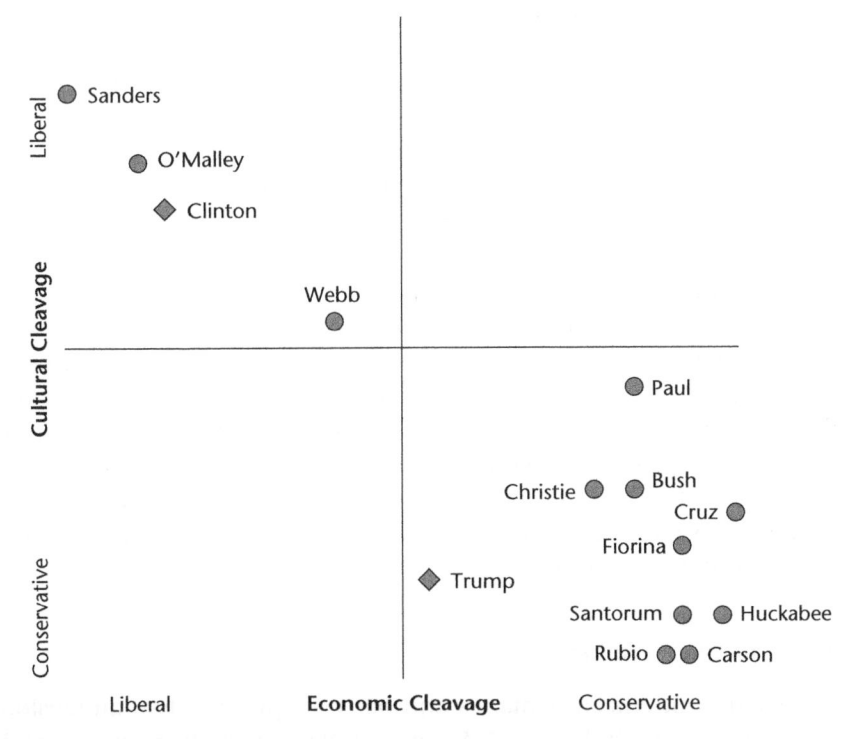

Figure 9.6. Candidate Supply in the 2016 Primaries

Note: The figure presents candidate positions on the economic cleavage and cultural cleavage based on the 20 issues coded by the project.

Source: Provided by researchers at Societly.com

both cleavages, while Rand Paul advocated strongly conservative positions on the economic cleavage but centrist positions on the cultural cleavage.

The most noticeable deviation from the Republican pack is Donald Trump. He expressed a culturally conservative position very near the most conservative Republican candidates, while advocating centrist economic policies. During the primaries, for example, Trump promised to protect social security, Medicare, and Medicaid, all the while railing about the advantages of the richest Americans. He promised to raise taxes on the richest Americans, including himself. He paired this economic message with toxic criticism of immigrants, Islam, gender rights, and LGBTQ rights. Trump reflects the mix of political positions that Theda Skocpol and Vanessa Williamson identified as epitomizing the Tea Party movement.[54] It was an appeal to cultural conservatives who were also concerned about social programs that protected their economic well-being: the sort of voters who swung the election to Trump in Michigan, Pennsylvania, and Wisconsin. Moreover, if we presume that the modal voter is located at the origin point in this figure, Trump is closer to the center than Hillary Clinton, Jeb Bush, Chris Christie, and nearly all the other candidates in the field.

The polarizing nature of the 2016 general election is largely a function of the two candidates that emerged from the primaries and the political choices they offered—rather than a new cleavage polarization by the electorate.[55] If the early forecasters were correct with an establishment Republican winning the nomination, or a more culturally moderate Democrat, we would not describe the 2016 elections as an example of cultural war. As pundits observed after the votes were counted, excluding the 77,000 voters in the upper Midwest, the political analysts would be proclaiming Clinton's nearly 3 million vote victory margin and the ascendancy of American liberalism.

Thus, the course of the election was largely decided in the primaries. Other data provided by Societly suggest that Clinton did not significantly moderate her positions in the general election, as often occurs in the transition from the primary to general election. In contrast, Trump's image moved slightly toward a more traditionally conservative position on the economic cleavage. Other surveys during the campaign matched these general candidate perceptions.[56]

Making Candidate Choices

The interaction of citizen demands and party supply in a two-dimensional space is difficult to study in a U.S. general election with only two major candidates. As Morris Fiorina has aptly concluded: "two sizes don't fit all."[57] But the relationship between diversity of party supply and choice should be apparent during the primaries.

The American Experience

During the 2016 primaries, the ANES ran a pilot study that provides evidence on the interaction of citizen demand and party supply.[58] The survey asked questions about the primary candidates and possible new political issue questions. I used these issue questions in a PCA to define the economic and cultural cleavages, and score citizens on these cleavages, much as was done for other elections (Appendix G). The survey also asked for thermometer ratings of three Democratic politicians (Obama, Clinton, and Sanders) and six Republicans (Bush, Carson, Cruz, Fiorina, Rubio, and Trump). This allows me to run "trial heats" of Clinton against six potential Republican opponents to see how the supply of candidates can potentially influence the correlates of vote choice. These trials are not predictive of the election because a lot of campaigning was still ahead in January of 2016, but this illustrates how citizens react to differences in the supply of choices.

Society's depiction of the political space during the primaries would suggest that people's positions on the economic cleavage would generally be a strong predictor of support for Democratic–Republican candidates, since nearly all Republicans offered economic programs that differed substantially from the Democrats. The one exception is Donald Trump, whose economic image should lessen the impact of economic cleavage voting. At the same time, cultural differences between Trump and the two leading Democrats would produce stronger effects for the cultural cleavage.

Table 9.1 tests these ideas with trial heats of Clinton and Sanders against each of the six Republican candidates in the survey. As expected, the economic cleavage is a strong predictor of all of Clinton's and Sanders' comparisons with Republicans. At the same time, the cultural cleavage also has a substantial, albeit weaker, correlation with candidate preferences.

More insightful are the variations from this general pattern. In the Clinton versus Trump comparison, the importance of the economic cleavage is weaker than for most of the other Republican contenders. Trump's mixed message on

Table 9.1. The Correlates of Candidate Preferences in the 2016 Primaries

Republican Candidate	Hillary Clinton Economic Cleavage	Hillary Clinton Cultural Cleavage	Bernie Sanders Economic Cleavage	Bernie Sanders Cultural Cleavage
Donald Trump	0.52	0.37	0.48	0.44
Jeb Bush	0.50	0.23	0.43	0.31
Ben Carson	0.60	0.27	0.57	0.34
Ted Cruz	0.63	0.29	0.60	0.37
Carly Fiorina	0.60	0.24	0.56	0.33
Marco Rubio	0.57	0.23	0.53	0.31

Note: Table entries are Pearson's r correlations.
Source: 2016 American National Election Studies Pilot Study.

Political Realignment

economic issues—stressing the need for jobs and economic growth at the same time as several social programs—narrowed the economic distance between him and Clinton. Simultaneously, his constant tweets and rally comments on cultural issues highlighted the distance between them. The result was a stronger impact of the cultural cleavage on the Clinton–Trump comparison than for any other Republican challenger. And even though we used different questions to measure both political cleavages in this pilot study, the strength of both correlations is about the same as in the general election.

Another interesting comparison involves Bernie Sanders' competition with Republicans. Sanders was more liberal than Clinton on both the economic and cultural cleavages. However, the economic cleavage has a slightly smaller relationship with Sanders–Republican comparisons than for Clinton. In addition, the cultural correlations are stronger for Sanders' comparisons to Republicans than for Clinton's.[59] This seems reasonable given the youth and progressive tone of the Sanders campaign, and his close ties to anti-establishment groups—even though Sanders was equally liberal on traditional economic issues.

A two-variable analysis is a relatively simple model of the public's voting decisions. Many other factors can affect the final voting choice including the characteristics of the candidates, government performance, and other issues beyond the economic and cultural cleavage.[60] However, since these two cleavages are statistically independent, their joint relationship with candidate preferences is quite powerful. Table 9.2 presents a multiple regression model based on the two cleavages; it generates a Multiple R of 0.64. This explanatory power is comparable to the venerable party identification measure ($R = 0.67$).

Table 9.2. Modeling Clinton vs. Trump Preferences

Predictors	Partisan Model b	Partisan Model β	Cleavages Model b	Cleavages Model β	Partisan and Cleavages b	Partisan and Cleavages β	Partisan and Cleavages (Only Voters) b	Partisan and Cleavages (Only Voters) β
Primary Election								
Party Identification	19.53	0.67	—	—	13.39	0.46	14.31	0.49
Economic Cleavage	—	—	31.92	0.52	17.68	0.29	18.69	0.31
Cultural Cleavage	—	—	22.50	0.37	15.30	0.26	15.13	0.24
Multiple R	0.67		0.64		0.75		0.79	
General Election								
Party Identification	21.19	0.75	—	—	13.72	0.49	15.07	0.53
Economic Cleavage	—	—	33.53	0.56	16.79	0.29	15.36	0.25
Cultural Cleavage	—	—	26.08	0.44	14.84	0.25	14.19	0.23
Multiple R	0.80		0.72		0.80		0.83	

Note: Table entries are regression coefficients from OLS models.
Source: 2016 American National Election Studies Pilot Survey for the primary; ANES time series for the general election.

If one includes party identification with the two cleavage indices, the third panel shows that the total explained variance increases slightly (R = 0.75) and the impact of each predictor moderates slightly. But this allocation of shared variance overlooks the logical assumptions that party identification can shape economic and cultural positions as well as voting choice. A two-step model of the primary electorate has party identification predicting candidate choice, and then cleavage positions predicting the residuals. This model shows a slightly weaker effect for the economic cleavage because it is more strongly related to partisanship and a slightly stronger effect for cultural positions.[61]

The lower half of Table 9.2 replicates the analyses for the ANES general election survey. Despite a narrowing of the political field, the intensity of the general election campaign, months of events and media exposes on both sides, and three debates, not much changed. The impact of partisanship is a bit stronger, and partisanship alone explains as much variance as the three-variable model. For example, strong Democrats rated Clinton 56 degrees more positively than Trump in the pilot survey, which widened to 68 degrees by the Fall. Trump's lead among strong Republicans increased from 53 degrees to 62 degrees.[62] With the coaches of each team selected, fans lined up behind their leader. In addition, the coefficients for the economic and cultural cleavages closely mirror the primary results.

While I have focused on broad patterns of partisan preferences among the entire public, only a bare majority actually turn out to vote in presidential elections. To ensure that the first three models are representative of the voting public, the fourth analyses in Table 9.2 include only voters (or likely voters in the primary survey).[63] Very little changes. The strength of party identification is marginally stronger, in part because partisans are the true fans who turn out to support their party in elections. The coefficients for the economic and cultural cleavage are marginally weaker. Overall, however, the political lines of division were apparent throughout 2016.[64]

Electoral Change in America

Many accounts of electoral change in the United States explain it in terms of unique aspects of the American political experience. For example, some experts suggest that the McGovern reforms of the Democratic Party led to the restructuring of electoral coalitions and a new political agenda. Or, the residual effects of the specific presidential candidates reshaped political alliances. The nation's unique religious history and the rise of the evangelical movement is another commonly cited reason. Desegregation and its consequences is a common explanation of shifting party alignments. And there are other American-centric explanations for the trends described here. But placed in the context of very similar patterns in European democracies, the first lesson of this chapter is the importance of the broader processes of social change that are affecting affluent democracies in Europe, North America, and beyond. The U.S. experience is not unique.

I see three other large lessons from this chapter's analyses. The first is that economic and cultural cleavages are both important bases of political competition in contemporary America. Issues related to the role of government in the economy and the level of social programs have been a continuing political cleavage for the past five decades and longer, even if the specific issues or salience of specific issues has changed. Thus, James Carville's advice, "It's the economy, stupid," is probably a good principle for most candidates of both parties.

The cultural cleavage has been evolving and strengthening since the first data point in 1972. Liberal culturalists expanded the political agenda to include new issues of gender rights, environmental protection, racial/ethnicity issues, LGBTQ rights. This generated a counter movement by cultural conservatives. The changing social composition of the United States also affected the salience of these issues. One sees this changing agenda in the list of questions included in the ANES core surveys. The first question on abortion was asked in the 1980 study; the first thermometer question about gay men and lesbians appeared in 1984 and for illegal immigrants in 1988. As political discourse drew attention to these issues, the relationship between cultural values and presidential preferences increased over time.

Some analysts have focused on a single aspect of the cultural cleavage, emphasizing the role of race, ethnicity, gender, or religion in affecting election outcomes. These are parts of the picture, but not the whole picture; only focusing on one part distorts our understanding of the election. A good illustration of the breadth of the contemporary cultural cleavage is the list of issues that load highly on the cultural dimension in 2016 (Appendix G). In the ANES pilot study, the issues were opinions toward immigrants, the death penalty, gays, and government treatment of African Americans. In the general election survey, the cultural questions were about transgender issues, abortion, defense spending, fighting ISIS, and gay rights.

This is not a cleavage singularly defined by racial or gender attitudes; it is a cleavage that is as much defined by reactions to social change, adherence to traditional values, and political resentment. Some cultural conservatives (and cultural liberals) hold extremist, intolerant, and even undemocratic views—and it would be naive and wrong to ignore this. But most Americans hold moderate positions on these two cleavages and the issues that comprise them.[65] Voting Republican does not mean a person is misogynist and racist, and voting Democrat does not mean one is an anarchist or immoral individualist. Real economic and social concerns motivate voters' choices. Conservatives who ignore the former are as myoptic as are liberals who ignore the latter. In the heat of partisan battle, some partisans forget that point in vilifying their opponents.

A second lesson is the diversity of the political choice on each cleavage and how this changes over time. Evidence from the ANES suggests that the parties and their presidential candidates have become more polarized over the past several decades.[66] The clearest evidence comes from the public's Liberal–Conservative perceptions of the parties (Figure 9.1). Since 1980, the Democratic presidential candidates have moved toward the liberal pole, increasing the Democratic–Republican gap by nearly a full point on the 7-point scale. The evidence on specific issues is mixed, but broadly illustrates this same pattern. Americans see Democrats as moving toward the liberal position on issues of the economic cleavage, and Republicans toward the conservative position. On the cultural cleavage, the evidence is even less complete. My general impression is that Democrats have more fully embraced cultural liberalism and expanded its meaning, as Republicans have endorsed cultural conservatism. These tendencies widen the gap between the parties and the electorate (and many of each party's former voters).

An imbalance in party positions may be the fate of parties with progressive goals, such as the Democrats. If the Democrats positioned themselves as equidistant from the median voter as the Republicans were on the conservative side, this would perpetuate the status quo. But since the goal of progressives is to change the status quo, they need to advocate more liberal views in their policy programs. Thus the Democrats face an inherent tension between winning elections and advocating their progressive goals. In sum, the supply of alternative party choices became clearer for the American public over time, which should increase the relevance of these cleavages for voting behavior.

Third, these trends reached a highpoint in the 2016 election. If a Democrat with a different political location and campaign rhetoric had been the candidate in 2016, the cultural cleavage might not have been so important. Hillary Clinton pursued a campaign highlighting identity politics and her cultural liberalism. If the Republicans had nominated an establishment candidate such as Mitt Romney or John McCain, culture-based voting would likely be weaker. Thus, those who see the 2016 election as an indicator of a regressive shift in the public mood in America are missing an important point.[67] *The public's cleavage positions didn't change in 2016 as much as the candidate choices did.*[68] The voters were presented with two choices that were more clearly aligned along the cultural cleavage so cultural issues gained in importance as a basis for vote choice. To vote for a candidate so distant from one's partisan position became difficult for many voters, even if they were disturbed by the tenor of the campaign and uncertain about the future. Few Republicans were willing to vote for Hillary Clinton because they objected to her policies and personal history, and few Democrats were willing to vote for the anti-establishment rhetoric of Donald Trump even if they shared some of his concerns. But just enough votes changed to produce the unexpected outcome.

Notes

1. Jonathan Allen and Aimie Parnes, *Shattered: Inside Hillary Clinton's Doomed Campaign*. New York: Crown, 2017.
2. Michael Tesler, Views about race mattered more in electing Trump than in electing Obama, *Washington Post Monkey Cage* (November 22, 2016); John Sides, Michael Tesler, and Lynn Vavreck, The 2016 U.S. election: How Trump lost and won, *Journal of Democracy* (2017) 28: 34–44; Michael Tesler, Economic anxiety isn't driving racial resentment. Racial resentment is driving economic anxiety, *Washington Post Monkey Cage* (August 22, 2016); Alan Abramowitz, Taking polarization to a new level: Racial resentment, negative partisanship and the triumph of Trump. Paper presented at the annual meetings of the American Political Science Association, 2017.
3. For example, Mel Robbins, Hillary Clinton lost because of sexism, *CNN* (May 3, 2017). http://www.cnn.com/2017/05/03/opinions/hillary-clinton-interview-sexism-robbins/index.html; Daniel Bush, The hidden sexism that could sway the election, *PBS News Hour*. http://www.pbs.org/newshour/features/hidden-sexism/.
4. Greg Sargent, Why did Trump win? New research by Democrats offers a worrisome answer, *Washington Post* (May 1, 2018).
5. Lyman Kellstedt et al., Religious voting blocs in the 1992 election, In John Green et al., eds., *Religion and Culture Wars*. Lanham, MD: Rowman & Littlefield, 1996, p. 286; also Warren Miller and J. Merrill Shanks, *The New American Voter*. Cambridge: Harvard University Press, 1996.
6. Larry Sabato, The perfect storm: The election of the century. In Larry Sabato, ed., *Overtime? The Election 2000 Thriller*. New York: Longman, 2002; Morris Fiorina, *Culture War?* New York: Longman, 2004; J. White, *The Values Divide; American Politics and Culture in Transition*. Chatham, NJ: Chatham House, 2002.
7. Andrew Hartman, *A War for the Soul of America: A History of the Culture Wars*. Chicago: University of Chicago Press, 2015; Stephen Prothero, *Why Liberals Win the Culture Wars (Even When They Lose Elections)*. New York: HarperOne, 2016; Jack Citrin and David Sears, *American Identity and the Politics of Multiculturalism*. Cambridge: Cambridge University Press, 2014, ch. 1.
8. Warren Miller and Teresa Levitin, *Leadership and Change: The New Politics and the American Electorate*. Cambridge, MA: Winthrop, 1976, p. 61. Also see Herbert Weisberg and Jerome, Dimensions of candidate evaluation. *American Political Science Review* (1970) 64: 1167–85.

9. Richard Scammon and Ben Wattenberg, *The Real Majority*. New York: Coward-McCann, 1968; also Kevin Phillips, *The Emerging Republican Majority*. New Rochelle, NY: Arlington House, 1969; William Jacoby, Is there a culture war? Conflicting value structures in American public opinion, *American Political Science Review* (2014) 108: 754–71.
10. Rick Perlstein, *Nixonland: The Rise of a President and the Fracturing of America*. New York: Scribner, 2008.
11. Thomas Frank, *What's the Matter with Kansas?* New York: Metropolitan Books, 2004. More recently, Frank has written on the Democratic Party's continuing focus on liberal cultural values and diminished concern for their traditional supporters: Thomas Frank, *Listen, Liberal: Or, What Ever Happened to the Party of the People?* New York: Metropolitan Books, 2016.
12. Katherine Cramer, *The Politics of Resentment: Rural Consciousness in Wisconsin and the Rise of Scott Walker*. Chicago: University of Chicago Press, 2016; Arlie Hochschild, *Strangers in Their Own Land*. New York: New Press, 2016; J. D. Vance, *Hillbilly Elegy*. New York: Harper, 2016; also see Justin Gest, *The New Minority: White Working Class Politics in an Age of Immigration and Inequality*. Oxford: Oxford University Press, 2016. Much earlier, the same basic observations were made in an influential article by Peter Hamill, The revolt of the white lower middle class, *New York Magazine* (April 14, 1969).
13. Stanley Feldman and Christopher Johnston, Understanding the determinants of ideology: Implications of structural complexity, *Political Psychology* (2014) 35: 337.
14. Shaun Ratcliff, Shawn Treier, Stanley Feldman, and Simon Jackman, The nature of ideological polarization in the American electorate. Paper presented at the annual meetings of the American Political Science Association, San Francisco, September 2017; Joshua Zingher and Michael Flynn, From on high: The effect of elite polarization on mass attitudes and behaviors, 1972–2012, *British Journal of Political Science* (2017) 48: 23–45; Paul Goren, *On Voter Competence*. Oxford: Oxford University Press, 2012.
15. John Jackson and John Green, The state of party convention delegates. In John Green and Daniel Coffey, eds., *The State of the Parties: The Changing Role of Contemporary American Parties*. New York: Rowman & Littlefield, 2010; Geoffrey Layman. Religion and party activists. A "perfect storm" of polarization or a recipe for pragmatism? In Alan Wolfe and Ira Katznelson, eds., *Religion and Democracy in the United States*. Princeton: Princeton University Press, 2010; Ryan Claassen, *Godless Democrats and Pious Republicans? Party Activists, Party Capture, and the "God Gap."* Cambridge: Cambridge University Press, 2015.
16. Pamela Johnston Conover and Stanley Feldman, The origins and meaning of Liberal/Conservative self-identifications, *American Journal of Political Science* (1981) 25: 617–45; Russell Dalton, David Farrell, and Ian McAllister, *Political Parties and Democratic Linkage*. Oxford: Oxford University Press, 2011, ch. 5.
17. For example, Morris Fiorina, *Unstable Majorities: Polarization, Party Sorting and Political Stalemate*. Stanford: Hoover Institution, 2017, ch. 3; Pew Research Center, *The Partisan Divide on Political Values Grows Even Wider* (October 5, 2017). http://

www.people-press.org/2017/10/05/the-partisan-divide-on-political-values-grows-even-wider/.
18. Royce Carroll, Jeffrey Lewis, James Lo, Nolan McCarty, Keith Poole, and Howard Rosenthal, *"Common Space" DW-NOMINATE Scores with Bootstrapped Standard Errors* (Joint House and Senate Scaling), February 6, 2013. Available from: https://legacy.voteview.com.
19. Russell Dalton and Ian McAllister, Random walk or planned excursion? Continuity and change in the Left–Right positions of political parties, *Comparative Political Studies* (2015) 48:759–87.
20. The ANES also asked about the location of the political parties on the various scales. I rely on presidential locations because the parties' questions were asked less frequently, and because the parties present different political stimuli across the U.S. regions. In general, parties are closer to the midpoint of the scale than the presidential candidates, but the trends are similar.
21. The most centrist Democratic candidate was Jimmy Carter in 1980, who lost, despite being much closer to the average citizen than Ronald Reagan. Carter's loss is widely attributed to a lack of public confidence in the competency of his administration, especially its handling of the U.S. Embassy hostage crisis in Iran.
22. Christopher Achen and Larry Bartels, *Democracy for Realists*. Princeton: Princeton University Press, 2016.
23. The standard question asked: Some people feel the government in Washington should see to it that every person has a job and a good standard of living. Suppose these people are at one end of a scale, at point 1. Others think the government should just let each person get ahead on their own. Suppose these people are at the other end, at point 7. And, of course, some other people have opinions somewhere in between, at points 2, 3, 4, 5, or 6. Where would you place YOURSELF on this scale, or haven't you thought much about this?
24. The standard question asked: "Some people think the government should provide fewer services even in areas such as health and education in order to reduce spending. Suppose these people are at one end of a scale, at point 1. Other people feel it is important for the government to provide many more services even if it means an increase in spending. Where would you place YOURSELF on this scale, or haven't you thought much about this?"
25. Stuart Soroka and Christopher Wlezien, *Degrees of Democracy*. Cambridge: Cambridge University Press.
26. The standard question asked: "There is much concern about the rapid rise in medical and hospital costs. Some people feel there should be a government insurance plan which would cover all medical and hospital expenses for everyone. Suppose these people are at one end of a scale, at point 1. Others feel that all medical expenses should be paid by individuals and through private insurance plans like Blue Cross or some other company paid plans. Where would you place YOURSELF on this scale, or haven't you thought much about this?"
27. The equal role for women question might tap the cultural cleavage, except that its wording yields highly skewed results. In most years, the public sees both parties as

more conservative than their own positions. Because it does not discriminate in measuring opinion or party positions, the question was last asked in 2008.
28. The standard question asked: "There has been some discussion about abortion during recent years. Which one of the opinions best agrees with your view? 1. By law, abortion should never be permitted, 2. By law, only in case of rape, incest, or woman's life in danger, 3. By law, for reasons other than rape, incest, or woman's life in danger if need established, By law, abortion as a matter of personal choice."
29. The standard question asked: "Some people feel that the government in Washington should make every possible effort to improve the social and economic position of blacks and other minority groups. Others feel that the government should not make any special efforts to help minorities because they should help themselves. Where would you place yourself on this scale or haven't you though much about this?" Beginning in 1988 the question refers exclusively to blacks.
30. Edward Carmines and James Stimson, *Issue Evolution*. Princeton: Princeton University Press, 1989.
31. Americans own political views became more conservative in 2008 and 2012, perhaps as a thermostatic reaction to the Obama administration. Michael Tesler, *Post-Racial or Most-Racial?: Race and Politics in the Obama Era*. Chicago: University of Chicago Press, 2016.
32. The standard question asked: "Some people believe that we should spend much less money for defense. Others feel that defense spending should be greatly increased. Where would you place yourself on this scale or haven't you thought much about this?"
33. An alternative methodology would have been to code the open-ended images of the good and bad points of the candidates and parties, but ANES essentially discontinued coding of these questions in 2008.
34. Another study uses a different methodology to compare party images from 1976 until 2008. They found that Americans perceived themselves as closer to the Republicans in nine of the twelve elections, even in Obama's victorious 2008 election. Paul Abramson, John Aldrich, and David Rohde, *Change and Continuity in the 2008 Elections*. Washington, DC: CQ Press, pp. 212–16.
35. The ANES Guide to Public Opinion and Electoral Behavior. http://www.electionstudies.org/nesguide/toptable/tab2b_5.htm.
36. From 1976 until 2016 the public perceived an increasing gap between the positions of the Democratic and Republican candidates. Regressing time on the size of the gap shows: Liberal–Conservative, $b=0.024$, $\beta=0.851$, $p<0.01$, $N=11$; Jobs, $b=0.035$, $\beta=0.761$, $p<0.01$, $N=11$; Services, $b=0.037$, $\beta=0.828$, $p<0.01$, $N=9$; Health, $b=0.042$, $\beta=0.974$, $p<0.01$, $N=6$; Blacks, $b=0.038$, $\beta=0.746$, $p<0.01$, $N=11$; Defense, $-b=-0.011$, $\beta=-0.215$, ns, $N=10$.
37. Hanspeter Kriesi et al., *West European Politics in the Age of Globalization*. Cambridge: Cambridge University Press, 2008; Simon Bornschier, *Cleavage Politics and the Populist Right*. Philadelphia: Temple University Press, 2010; Swen Hutter, Edgar Grande, and Hanspeter Kriesi, *Politicising Europe: Integration and Mass Politics*. Cambridge: Cambridge University Press, 2016. For similar dimensional analyses of ANES issues see Citrin and Sears, *American Identity and the Politics of*

Multiculturalism, ch. 8; D. Sunshine Hillygus and Todd Shields, *The Persuadable Voter*. Princeton: Princeton University Press, 2008; Zingher and Flynn, From on high: The effect of elite polarization on mass attitudes and behaviors; Goren, *On Voter Competence*.
38. Stephan Ansolabehere, Jonathan Rodden, and James Snyder, The strength of issues: Using multiple measures to gauge preference stability, ideological constraint, and issue voting, *American Political Science Review* (2008) 102: 215–32; Goren, *On Voter Competence*, ch. 4.
39. This may be a function of the different coding of education level across the various ANES surveys. I used the most detailed measure available in each year, rather than combining into a small number of standard categories.
40. Steven Weldon and Denver McNeney, The issues with issues. In *Oxford Research Encyclopedia on Politics*, 2018. http://politics.oxfordre.com/browse; Donald Kinder, Opinion and action in the realm of politics, *Handbook of Social Psychology*. Oxford: Oxford University Press, 2008.
41. Ansolabehere, Rodden, and Snyder, The strength of issues.
42. This is the difference between candidate scores on the feeling thermometer scale.
43. Zingher and Michael Flynn, From on high. They also found a small increase in the relationship for the economic cleavage over time, but this may reflect differences in our measurement methodologies.
44. Cramer, *The Politics of Resentment*.
45. I created indices for each election before correlating them with candidate preference. Then, I experimented by adding other relevant variables to see if this affected the results. For example, in recent surveys that lacked a question on LGBTQ rights (or gender) in the pre-election survey I added an item from the post-election survey. The range of differences from adding a single question was comparable to the sampling variation in the correlations.
46. Ratcliff, Treier, Feldman, and Jackman, The nature of ideological polarization in the American electorate.
47. Pew Research Center, *The Partisan Divide on Political Values Grows Even Wider*; also see Fiorina, *Unstable Majorities*, ch. 2.
48. Angus Campbell, Philip Converse, Warren Miller, and Donald Stokes, *The American Voter*. New York: Wiley, 1961.
49. Russell Dalton, The blinders of partisanship and the 2016 US election, *OUP blog* (January 9, 2017). https://blog.oup.com/2017/01/partisanship-voting-presidential-election/; Lynn Vavreck, The ways that the 2016 election was perfectly normal, *New York Times* (May 1, 2017).
50. Lynn Vavreck, A measure of identity: Are you wedded to your party? *New York Times* (January 31, 2017).
51. Fiorina, *Unstable Majorities*; Ratcliff, Treier, Feldman, and Jackman, The nature of ideological polarization in the American electorate; Pew, *The Partisan Divide on Political Values Grows Even Wider*.
52. http://www.societly.com (accessed October 19, 2017). The economic issues included topics such as taxes on investment income, government stimulus of the economy, provision of unemployment benefits, and Obamacare. The cultural

issues included items such as same-sex marriage, abortion, legalizing marijuana, immigration policy, punishing criminals, and fighting ISIS.
53. The project's academic director, Diego Garzia, generously provided these data.
54. Theda Skocpol and Vanessa Williamson, *The Tea Party and the Remaking of Republican Conservatism*. Oxford: Oxford University Press, 2012.
55. John Sides, Michael Tesler, and Lynn Vavreck, *Identity Crisis: The 2016 Presidential Campaign and the Battle for the Meaning of America*. Princeton: Princeton University Press, 2018, ch. 5.
56. However, surveys by YouGov show that after a year in office the public image of Trump's economic position had moved sharply to the right, as he attacked social programs and endorsed the Republic tax legislation. His cultural position barely changed from November 2016. Harry Enten, Voters used to see moderation in Trump: Not anymore (January 7, 2018). https://fivethirtyeight.com/features/voters-think-trump-has-moved-to-the-right/.
57. Fiorina, *Unstable Majorities*, p. 89.
58. The ANES 2016 Pilot Study was done in January of 2016 (http://www.electionstudies.org/). The study used the YouGov Internet panel. The analyses here utilize post-survey weighting to provide a more representative sample. I am cautious about using internet polls for multiple reasons, but this is the best available source at my disposal.
59. Treating Obama as a hypothetical choice in 2016 produced correlations closer to those for Sanders than for Clinton.
60. The potential impact of candidate traits was quite large in 2016 because of the popular images of some of the leading candidates. Sanders, for example, held a large affective lead over Clinton based on the feeling thermometers (Sanders 47.1 degrees, Clinton 41.6, Trump 40.0). However, both parties nominated the least-liked candidates in the modern era, even among their party identifiers, so the effects of candidate image cancelled out.
61. In this second step the economic cleavage coefficients are $b=11.89$, $\beta=0.26$; the cultural cleavage coefficients are $b=12.77$, $\beta=0.28$.
62. The largest swing was among pure independents, who favored Clinton by 14 degrees in the January and there was an essential tie by November.
63. I defined likely voter as those scored as a 75 percent or greater chance of voting in the general election.
64. This continuity argues that the results of the ANES pilot study are not produced by the data collection method or the set of specific issues offered in the pilot study, which almost all differ from the general election ANES. See Appendix G.
65. Fiorina, *Unstable Majorities*, especially chs. 10–11.
66. Keith Poole and Howard Rosenthal, *Ideology and Congress*. New York: Routledge, 2007.
67. They also sometimes overlook an even more basic point: most voters supported Clinton.
68. Sides, Tesler, and Vavreck, *Identity Crisis* demonstrate this by comparing Republican support for Trump in the 2016 primaries to Romney in 2012 or McCain in 2008.

Part III
Conclusion

10

Realignment and Beyond

In June 1963, U.S. President John F. Kennedy made his last state tour to several European capitals. In Bonn, he met with German Chancellor Konrad Adenauer, and then moved on to Berlin where he made his historic "Ich bin ein Berliner" speech. His next stop was a visit to his family's ancestral home in Ireland, where he gave an address to the Irish Parliament. The president then traveled to London to meet Prime Minister Harold Macmillan. His last stop was Rome, and a meeting with Italian political figures and Pope Paul IV. I begin with this *Back to the Future* story to remind us that in focusing on current political events it is easy to lose historical perspective. I think that if Kennedy and those European political leaders time traveled to today, they would experience future shock. Ireland was extremely traditional and religious in 1963.[1] Germany and Italy struggled with postwar economic recovery and the challenges of building democratic systems. British politics was still defined by class and the old political order. And Kennedy could never have imagined that Barack Obama would be the 44th president of the United States. The politics and issues of today would prompt them to look for signs of such historic changes that they had missed in the early 1960s.

Social modernization since the mid-1900s has been an overwhelmingly positive force for these societies and their citizens. This process dramatically improved the living standards of the average person, and produced a much more educated public with access to incredible information sources. These changes lessened many of the traditional economic hardships that had long been a source of political competition. The average European or American today lives longer and lives better than their post-World War II relatives. Economic needs and inequality still exist, but now in the context of affluent societies.

Modernization has also transformed the cultural bases of these societies. A recent study by Stephen Pinker provides an impressive inventory of how the human condition in affluent democracies has improved in fundamental ways.[2] The rights and status of women have improved dramatically, even if

Political Realignment

the journey is incomplete. Minority social and political groups now possess greater rights. Individual freedoms have dramatically expanded. People have more personal freedom in their life choices. Self-expressive values spread throughout these populations.[3] Social and political tolerance has generally increased, even if these norms seem strained in the current political climate. Modernization is how society makes progress in improving the human condition.

And yet, social modernization is also a disruptive force. Spreading affluence, increased education, and the development of an advanced industrial society transformed the economic base of these nations. Economic globalization improved average living standards in the West, but at the cost of deindustrialization and the marginalization of parts of society. The declining number of working-class employees and a rising new middle class redefined the occupational structure and the values of the average citizen. Inequality in income and wealth increased in parallel with economic growth. These trends reshaped the economic cleavage to address these changing circumstances, and these new economic divisions still impact political choices.

Equally important, modernization brought new cultural issues to the fore. Environmental quality has constrained economic growth, gender equality is more salient, citizens are increasingly concerned about their rights and their ability to influence decisions affecting their lives, and individual lifestyles are more varied. In reaction to these changes, a conservative counter-movement began stressing the perceived loss of traditional moral values, social relations, and a sense of nation.

This book has described this evolutionary tale in Western Europe and the United States. Social group alignments shifted in systematic ways to reflect this new constellation of political issues. The working class and elements of the new middle class shifted their positions on economic and cultural issues. Educational groups and generations also polarized on the cultural cleavage. Chapters 2–4 describe this realignment in the political demands of contemporary publics in terms of the economic and cultural cleavages that define the space for political competition.

Democratic party systems also responded to these changing social and political conditions. In the 1980–1990s, New Left and Green parties emerged to represent liberal cultural issues. More recently, new culturally conservative parties have formed to represent these views. The established parties were buffeted by these forces, adapting to changing political realities to ensure their continued parliamentary representation (or failing if they did not successfully adapt). This realigned party system now forms the basis of political competition in most of these affluent democracies. Chapters 5–8 described these changes in party supply.

Realignment and Beyond

Realignments, like many other phenomena, are easier to identify looking backward than looking forward. Political scientists initially could not determine how parties and voters would respond to these forces of social change, and there were reasons to doubt a new cleavage could generate a persisting realignment.[4] But the evidence presented here and in several recent studies is clear.[5] Democratic publics and party systems have undergone a realignment that reshaped the basis of political competition in most affluent democracies.

These developments have also introduced new political tensions into these systems as parties and governments confront a changing political reality and competing political demands. It seems that few of us feel we live in the best of times, especially when it comes to politics. Trust in government has declined in most affluent democracies, and many citizens feel their nation is on the wrong course.[6] Images of political parties are close to the bottom of the barrel. In 2017, California's former governor, Arnold Schwarzenegger, advocated several institutional reforms of U.S. politics with a video listing the things that Americans rated more positively than the U.S. Congress: hemorrhoids, Nickelback, traffic jams, cockroaches, root canals, colonoscopies, and even herpes.[7] It would be funny if it were not so true. And since then, the American public (and others) has probably become more cynical.

How is it that we live in the best of times, yet many of us feel it is the worst of times politically? And what are the consequences for public sentiments and electoral politics? This chapter reviews this book's evidence on the nature of political change among contemporary publics, and its implications for electoral politics and the democratic process.

Social Change and Political Cleavages

Modern societies have always been complex, but the complexity has increased. When Seymour Lipset and Stein Rokkan wrote about political cleavages in mid-twentieth century Europe, they identified four significant lines of political division.[8] Political cleavages comprise enduring differences in social interests and values that are expressed in a set of political issues. The issues might change over time as social conditions or political events change, but there is a continuity in the underlying social divisions. For Lipset and Rokkan, as well as others writing on political cleavages, there was also a social group basis for a cleavage, such as the labor movement, religion, or other parts of civil society.[9]

In most instances, the prominent political conflicts in a nation could be aligned along a single dimension. Typically this was an economic cleavage concerning the role of the state, social welfare provisions, and related issues. In other nations, such as France, Germany, and Italy, a secular/liberal economic

217

position competed against a religious/conservative economic position as the dominant line of cleavage. Regional and urban/rural differences existed, but were of lesser importance in most nations.

This study identified a fundamental change in the gradual expansion from a single dimension of political competition to a two-dimensional space defined in economic and cultural terms. The persistence of the economic cleavage reflects its importance in defining life chances and the conditions of life. This includes evolving issues on the role of the state, the protection of citizens from economic hardships, guaranteeing the vitality of the economy, the equality of opportunity, and similar issues. Governments of the left and the right vary in their positions on these issues, and public opinion shifts in response to current circumstances. An issue as basic as setting tax rates is subject to continual competition and negotiation. This study demonstrated the persistence of the underlying economic division over recent decades.

By its nature, modernization is a disruptive process that creates new economic conflicts with new winners and losers. Globalization and neo-liberal economic policies provide the most obvious example. Even if increased international trade provides a net benefit to a society, some may benefit more than others and some may lose.[10] The process of European unification also has winners and loser.[11] The disruptive effects of new technologies, such as has occurred in the internet age, can have similar outcomes. And, naturally but unfortunately, the winners are less concerned about the losers—which generates new economic policy differences or accentuates existing differences. These political issues involve self-interest as well as values such as acceptance of inequality, beliefs in a meritocracy, and other values.

Modernization also generates transformations in non-economic conditions that are bundled under the heading of cultural change. Environmentalism, for example, benefits the society overall but also creates economic or social costs for some. The progressive norms of social modernization come into conflict with the traditional norms of other citizens. Most affluent democracies are more socially and ethnically diverse than they were a generation ago. New tensions arise over the equality of opportunity versus the equality of outcomes.[12] Cultural cleavage issues involve both social norms and potential redistributive effects. Thus, the tension between modernization forces and traditionalism is a persistent theme in contemporary societies, which has become more apparent in recent years.

This study tracked the effects of this modernization process on electoral politics: first, through the changing issue demands of contemporary publics; second, through changes in the supply of political choices offered in party systems, and through the supply–demand relationship that has realigned party systems.

The Economic Cleavage

I briefly touch on the economic cleavage because political differences on the cleavage are a familiar part of society and politics because these issues are longstanding and easily interpreted in terms of the economic self-interest of contending groups. The less affluent and the working class are more positive toward government protections of social welfare and government involvement in the economy. The affluent and the middle class tend to lean toward more market-oriented government policies. These positions have not fundamentally changed over the time span of our study.[13]

Yet, I have described a modest change in citizen positions on the economic cleavage over time. As societies modernized and the working class share of the public decreased, the median voter shifted toward the growing middle class and their more conservative economic positions (Chapter 3). Economic change comes less from a shift in the position of class grouping than from the size of class groupings. This provides an opportunity and incentive for political elites to respond to the public's changing economic views. Geoffrey Evans and James Tilley utilized rich longitudinal data in Britain that tracks the broader cross-national patterns described here.[14]

The Cultural Cleavage

There is much more debate on the content and the meaning of the cultural cleavage so I give more attention to this topic.[15] For instance, some research emphasizes globalization as a driving force dividing winners and losers on cultural issues. Others attribute it to the tension between religious values versus secularism. Many liberal political analysts treat cultural conservatives as synonymous with racist, sexist, or homophobic views. Cultural conservatives, in contrast, label liberals as godless, socialist, snowflakes, or worse. Such labeling stifles discussion and lessens awareness of the nature of this cleavage.[16] The cultural cleavage has the potential to generate such passions because it represents alternative worldviews of who we are and what we value; to question these values is to question the identity and worth of those who believe them.

I see the wellspring of the current cultural cleavage as a tension produced by broad processes of social modernization, social changes that challenge the status quo, and resource redistribution embedded in social modernization. Specific issues flow from these forces, and attitudes toward social change are more than just one issue or another.

Some evidence of the breadth of the cultural cleavage comes from the diverse set of issues that define this cleavage in the various surveys used in this book. The clearest examples are the two U.S. surveys during the 2016 presidential election. The issues most related to the cultural cleavage cover a diverse range of topics: transgender policy, abortion policy, defense spending, sending troops to fight ISIS, providing services to same-sex couples, limiting immigration, the death penalty for murder, and the treatment of African Americans. There is even greater diversity if one compares the composition of the cultural cleavage across the various U.S. and European surveys used in this book.

If we view the cultural cleavage as a broad reaction to social modernization, this provides a different understanding of the cleavage and the forces influencing citizen opinions. Katherine Cramer and Arlie Hochschild describe one potential cause of cultural conservatism, which is seen in the demographic correlates of these opinions in Chapter 3.[17] The people they interviewed in rural America felt they were losing their place in line while trying to improve their lives and their families' lives; they felt the political establishment was unresponsive to their needs and values; and that resources were being given to less deserving individuals or groups. Noam Gidron and Peter Hall find similar evidence that those feeling "left-behind" by the modernization process in Europe look for expanded social recognition.[18] Self-interest differences across social groups reflect the same type of the social cleavages that Lipset and Rokkan described—groups competing for influence and policies favorable to their group.

Self-interest is only a partial explanation of positions on the cultural cleavage, however. The modernization/future shock literature implies that the process of social change itself evokes resistance along specific lines.[19] Research links the aversion to social change to core values and personality traits, such as an open/closed mind, risk aversion, openness to new experience, desires for predictability, or other apolitical traits.[20] That is, the cultural aspects of recent social modernization trends challenge communitarian values, concerns for stability and order, and respect for tradition that are often held by conservatives.[21] Some empirical evidence comes from research that separately predicts economic and social/cultural attitudes. For example, Stanley Feldman and Christopher Johnston demonstrated that abstract attitudes toward authority, egalitarianism, and the desire for cognitive simplicity are systematically related to economic and cultural attitudes.[22] Paul Goren and his colleagues have similarly shown that basic human values tapped by the Schwarz values battery are significantly related to policy preference indices.[23]

The most direct evidence comes from a recent study by Matt Grossman and Daniel Thaler. They developed a measure of aversion to social change and tested its influence on voting in the 2016 US elections. They make an important distinction: "our concept of attitudes toward social change is related to but distinguishable from racial resentment (which usually involves specific attitudes toward African Americans), authoritarianism (usually measured as parenting attitudes), and ethnocentrism (including attitudes toward Latinos and Muslim). Although related to conservative ideology and religiosity, it constitutes a separate set of ideas regarding the direction of society and its assumed high-paced shift from traditional values to more diverse ideas and groups."[24] Justin Gest and his colleagues have described this syndrome as "nostalgic deprivation," and demonstrated how a perceived loss in social status is correlated with support for far-right politics in the United States and Britain.[25]

In other words, the foundation of the cultural cleavage also arises from attitudes toward social change that can be traced to personality traits or core values, which are actuated by the specific social conditions in a nation. Some scholars interpret this reaction to social change through the prisms of race, gender, or some other identity-based framework,[26] but looking through prisms can also distort our vision. For most cultural conservatives, this is not a call for a return to a period of racial privilege, gender discrimination, or similar types of bias; although it would be a mistake to ignore that a minority still harbor these sentiments. Rather, it is that the balance between various desired norms has changed beyond their preference point. Many people can look back to the past and see things that they would prefer—such as the image of a simpler life, a greater sense of community, a more orderly society, or a less competitive society—even though they would rather live in the present. It might be described as nostalgic deprivation in the United States, or the appeal of Heimat in Germany, or similar traditional notions in other European countries. In simple terms, as society changes some people will want it to change even more rapidly, and other people will find change per se unsettling.

Social Modernization and the American Public

I explore the potential impact of attitudes toward modernization using a battery of questions in the American National Election Studies. These questions tap acceptance of social change, or what the ANES calls moral traditionalism. Since the 1980s the ANES has asked the following four questions:

- The world is always changing and we should adjust our view of moral behavior to those changes.
- The newer lifestyles are contributing to the breakdown of our society.
- We should be more tolerant of people who choose to live according to their own moral standards, even if they are very different from our own.
- This country would have many fewer problems if there were more emphasis on traditional family ties.

Political Realignment

Many Americans recognize these sentiments even if we don't agree; we hear them from relatives, co-workers, or neighbors who see their society changing and they are uncertain about their future or their children's future. Their personality may encourage these views even when things are not changing. Many European also share these sentiments when they worry about globalization, the transformation of contemporary society, their children's experiences, and the uncertainty of the future in a rapidly changing world. Moreover, embedded in these change questions is a concern about a specific direction of change: <u>away from the communitarian, moral and orderly patterns of the past toward the individualistic and universalist values encouraged by the modernization process.</u>

Figure 10.1 tracks public sentiment on an index combining these four social change questions.[27] Over this 28-year span, Americans become more supportive of social change with the highpoint in 2016. This should occur as a product of social modernization: rising education levels, increased living standards, the expansion of information through the mass media, more cosmopolitan lifestyles, and so on. Indeed, a similar liberal trend appears in public opinion toward race, gender equality, gay rights, political tolerance, self-expressive values, and other key elements of the cultural cleavage.[28] Moreover, this time series only begins in 1988 and therefore misses the presumably large changes starting in the 1960s and 1970s.

The easy assumption is that resistance to social change is concentrated among those social groups who benefitted in the stereotypical America of

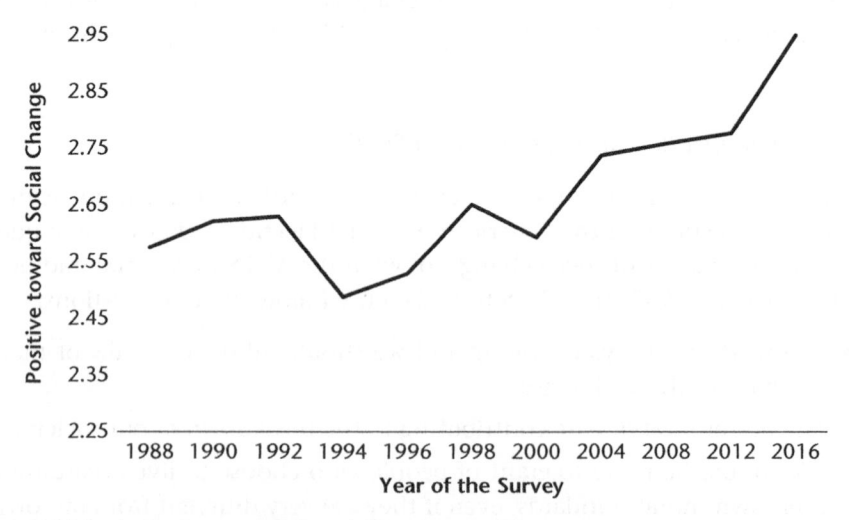

Figure 10.1. Attitudes toward Social Change over Time

Note: The vertical axis plots mean scores on the additive social change index; higher values are more supportive of social change.

Source: American National Election Study, cumulative file 1988–2012, 2016 face to face.

the 1950s. As E. J. Dionne, Norm Ornstein, and Thomas Mann have observed, "one person's reverence for tradition can be seen by another as a rationalization for prejudice and oppression," or as a reaction to changes in life opportunities.[29] Reality does not follow the negative stereotype because attitudes toward social change cut across the typical demographic markers. In the 2016 ANES, for example, gender differences are essentially nonexistent. Thirty-nine percent of men score in the top two quintiles supporting social change, as do 40 percent of women. Racial differences are also minor. Clear support for social change is expressed by 35 percent of African Americans, 39 percent of non-Hispanic whites, and 43 percent of Hispanics. Instead of these identity politics markers, the predictors of social change are factors such as age, education, and religiosity.[30] This implies that the survey questions are tapping attitudes toward modernization and rapid social change more than specific political controversies.[31]

The ultimate question is whether these attitudes are directly related to the issues defining the cultural cleavage. The solid line in Figure 10.2 presents the correlation between support for social change and liberal positions on the cultural cleavage. There is a very strong relationship in every survey since the series began in 1988.[32] This is all the more striking since each survey includes a different set of issues tapping the cultural cleavage, and the two indices are from different pre/post-election waves of the ANES. Moreover, the correlation

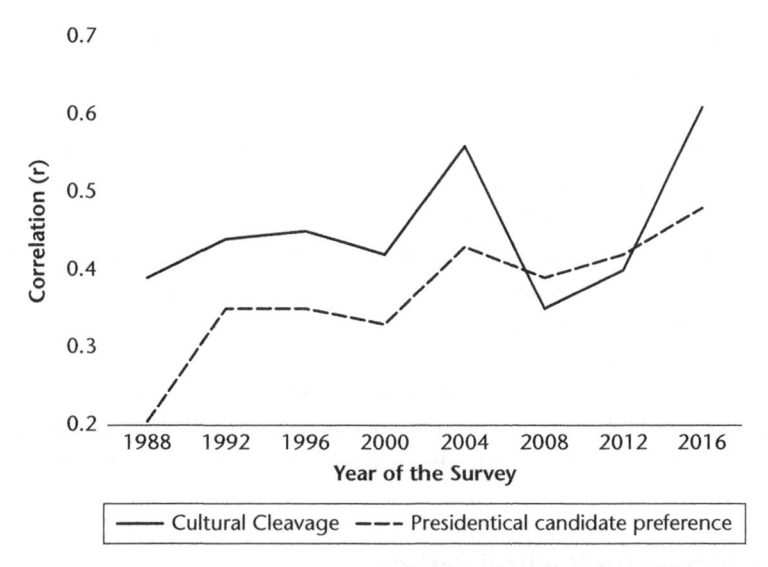

Figure 10.2. Attitudes toward Social Change, Cultural Cleavage Positions, and Vote

Note: The vertical axis plots the correlation of the social change index with positions on the cultural cleavage and presidential candidate preferences.

Source: American National Election Study, cumulative file 1988–2012, 2016 face to face.

between these two measures is strongest in the highly polarized 2016 election (r = 0.61).

The strength of the 2016 relationship is exceptional since test-retest statistics of many political attitudes often show lower correlations.[33] In part, the 2016 findings may be a reaction to the expansion of liberal cultural policies during the second term of the Obama administration; polarizing opinions among cultural liberals and conservatives.[34] The strong relationship is also likely a reaction to the two 2016 presidential candidates who articulated contrasting cultural appeals in their campaigns (Chapter 9). Indeed, reactions to social change have a growing relationship with presidential candidate preferences over time (the dashed line in the figure), which is further evidence of the growing political tensions over social change.

It may seem inconsistent that the impact of the cultural cleavage on candidate preferences strengthens over time, coterminous with increasing acceptance of social change. But the very process of liberal social change generates a conservative reaction. The goal of progressive politics is to change social and political standards, so the resolution of one issue leads to another challenge to the status quo and so forth. As liberal policies have expanded in the United States over the past several decades, this generates an evolving reaction from conservatives. This seems to be an inevitable byproduct of social modernization, which was not always recognized during the initial waves of social change.

Although the empirical evidence is drawn only from the United States, I expect the same patterns generally exist in other affluent democracies. As politicians pushed forward European unification, for example, the resistance to a mantra of "ever closer union" grew. At the rights revolution spreads to more sectors of society, cultural conservatives were more likely to resist. As non-European immigration increased, sensitivity to immigration also increased. Newton's Third Law applies to politics.

This evidence is not a justification or rationalization of those who hold liberal or conservative positions on the cultural cleavage. The very culturally liberal will vehemently disagree with the very culturally conservative because of their different worldviews. Centrists will see both poles as too extreme. The value of these analyses is in illustrating the broader source of these cleavage positions that go beyond the specific issues of debate. The democratic process provides a means to adjudicate such large value differences.

The Challenge for Political Parties

As societies change and citizens change, political parties as representative institutions should respond to these changes in the public's preferences.

One narrative describes a common pattern for many of the large social democratic/labour parties in Europe. The declining numbers of working-class voters created a problem for these parties if they wished to continue to win elections and promote their causes. In most cases, these parties broadened their political program to appeal to middle-class voters who were increasing in numbers, especially professionals, the well-educated, and members of the creative class.[35] These social groups are the main winners in social modernization. They are liberal on cultural issues, but often lean toward conservative socio-economic programs. Across the established democracies, many left-leaning political parties tried to align themselves with an economically liberal working class *and* a culturally liberal middle class. Parties that followed this strategy felt the strain of trying to address two constituencies with varied interests. As the cultural cleavage evolved and crystallized into a more distinct set of issues, this strain increased.

The PvdA is an exceptional example of a party that shifted its agenda toward postmaterial, liberal cultural positions after the collapse of the class and religious pillars in the Dutch system in the 1970s. The emergence of Green and New Left parties focusing on young, liberal middle-class voters—who might once have been members of the social democratic youth organizations—further encouraged the PvdA to adopt more culturally liberal positions while moderating its economic positions. The PvdA illustrates the consequences of riding two horses at once. Its vote share fell from 33.8 percent in 1977 to 5.7 percent in 2017. Neither constituency was well represented by the party.

The European Election Studies (EES) described how the mainstream leftist parties adjusted to the new two-dimensional political space by adopting policies oriented toward these new middle-class voters (Chapter 6).[36] The centrist shift on the economic cleavage and a liberal shift on the cultural cleavage were reinforced as the leadership of these parties became more middle-class and thus more attuned to these positions. Even in the 1979, Candidates to the European Parliament (CEP) study, clear liberal cultural positions (+ 0.50) were held by candidates from the German SPD, the French Socialists, British Labour, and the Dutch PvdA.

As the parties on the left changed, so too did the major parties on the right. Secularization decreased the social base for religious parties, as was evident in the several Catholic nations with Christian parties. Conservative parties did not become cultural liberals, but became less intensely conservative on many cultural matters. Following a contagion from the left, conservative parties enacted (or accepted) environmental legislation, greater protections for women's rights in society and the workplace, and other moderate cultural policies.

Political Realignment

At the same time, the major conservative parties in many nations actively pursued neo-liberal economic programs pushing them further to the right on the economic cleavage. This began with Thatcher's government in Britain, then Reagan's administration and the Kohl government in Germany. The process of European unification further expanded this economic trend throughout all of Europe—even when European citizens were less supportive. New conservative anti-tax parties, such as the Danish and Norwegian Progress parties, called for a further retrenchment of the European welfare state and a smaller government role in society.[37] In summary, the center point on the economic cleavage moved toward the right as the center point on the cultural cleavage moved toward the left (Chapter 6).

Such party moves might be an electorally sensible strategy in a Downsian one-dimensional space, where preferences and party strategies are constrained, and party preferences are presumably transitive. But political strategy is more complex in a two-dimensional space. If we assume a roughly normal distribution of the citizenry throughout the two-dimensional spaces constructed with the EES, the trends I have just described imply that gaps in party supply developed as parties adjusted their positions. The 1994 CEP showed limited party supply at the liberal end of the economic cleavage across Europe, as Socialist parties moved toward the center and communist parties faded with the collapse of the Soviet Union (Figure 6.2).

Another gap in party supply existed at the conservative pole of the cultural cleavage in the 1990s. The admittedly uneven empirical evidence suggests that the economic and social impact of modernization and globalization heightened liberal and conservative sensitivities to issues such as immigration, deindustrialization, gay rights, European integration, and other cultural issues. As noted earlier, there were signs of public ambivalence to the rapid pace of European integration pressed by political elites—but little partisan representation of these views.

Cas Mudde observed that this convergence created a void in which far-right parties developed:

> This convergence created a fertile breeding ground for populism, as many voters began to see political elites as indistinguishable from one another, regardless of their party affiliations. To many Europeans, mainstream elites of all parties also seemed to share an essential powerlessness, owing to two massive transfers of authority that took place in the second half of the twentieth century: from national governments to supranational entities such as the EU and the International Monetary Fund and from democratically elected officials to unelected ones such as central bankers and judges.[38]

Consequently, new culturally conservative parties entered many party systems or activists worked to transform existing parties. By the 2009 EES, a set of new far-right parties advocated extreme cultural positions (Figure 6.3), altering political discourse and public policy in Europe. Trump's election in 2016 reflects similar developments in the United States.

The role of government policy in creating the conditions for far-right parties is seen in the correlations between satisfaction with government and positions on the economic and cultural cleavages. Citizens and party elites who favor conservative economic policies are more trustful of government across Europe as a whole; they presumably see governments following these policies. Conversely, those who favor liberal cultural policies are more trustful of government than are cultural conservatives. This pattern likely varies with the partisan composition of the incumbent government and recent public policies, but it is a general pattern across established European democracies.

The end result of these processes is that the cultural cleavage now rivals the historic economic cleavage as a basis of electoral choice. In the 2009 and 2014 EESs, the cultural cleavage was generally a stronger predictor of party preferences when compared to the economic cleavage (Table 7.2). The cultural cleavage is also growing in importance in U.S. presidential elections (Table 9.1). This two-dimensional space now defines the major bases of political competition in these party systems. Clinton versus Trump, Macron versus Le Pen, Corbyn versus May, Danish Social Democrats versus the Danish People's Party—such seems to be the politics of our time.

Some people are aghast at the development of far-right parties because of their extremism. I share the concerns about the extremism of far-right party leaders, who make radical statements and feed anxieties in order to draw attention to their cause. To an extent, however, these parties are a response to a representation gap on cultural issues that are an inevitable part of the contemporary public policy debate (Chapter 8). Moreover, the EES shows that their voters are more moderate and diverse in their views. Party polarization on the cultural cleavage poses a challenge to democratic politics, but it is the type of challenge that democracy was designed to address.[39]

While this study has used the framework of the public's policy demands influencing the party system's supply of choices, I also want to acknowledge that this relationship runs in both directions. Parties are sensitive to changes in public opinion, but they also can shape the evolution of public opinion. Party leaders can focus public opinion on the issues they choose to discuss and avoid other issues. There is an asymmetry to this relationship, however. Voters can hold positions without a party to represent their views, but a party cannot win votes on a program when there is no citizen support. Ultimately, this is a symbiotic relationship between voters and political parties to find a shared set of political views.

In summary, most established democracies with proportional representation systems now include a diversity of parties to represent contrasting positions on the economic and cultural cleavages. Parties now populate the major choices in the two-dimensional space of political competition. These systems have a semblance of a demand–supply equilibrium because of this expansion in party choices.[40]

Looking Toward the Future

In most parliamentary democracies, the party systems of today bear only a partial resemblance to their structure several decades ago. There is increased volatility in election results, new parties emerge as some old parties disappear, seemingly at every election. Even if the party names remain the same, the content of party programs varies in fundamental ways. This book has described this evolutionary story. Unless there are unexpected changes (although there are always unexpected changes), this diversity in present-day political demands and party supply is likely to continue. Thus, what does this portend for the future of these democracies?

Some analysts claim that these patterns of electoral change are a sign of the failure of political parties.[41] The decline in turnout and the erosion of public trust and identification with political parties point in this direction. And there are many policy failures one could list, especially since the 2008 recession and ensuing financial crisis in Europe and the United States.

I am less pessimistic than some of my colleagues, however. The empirical findings on the evolution of the economic cleavage and the emergence of a clear cultural cleavage demonstrate that most party systems responded to changes in citizen demands. The stable (or sclerotic) system of party representation in past decades is less applicable in the more varied and dynamic contemporary party systems. This study also showed very high congruence between voters and their chosen party on both the economic and cultural cleavages, which may have increased between 1979 and 2009 (Chapter 8).

Political parties followed varied strategies in responding to the public's changing policy demands. Some tried to anticipate change and moved ahead of citizen demands. Other parties resisted change, and often lost votes and sometimes their political lives. However, the most distinctive aspect of the changing partisan landscape seems to come from new parties forming to represent new citizen demands on the cultural left—Green parties and New Left parties—and more recently far-left economic parties, and on the cultural right through far-right cultural parties. This realignment in party choices occurred in parallel with a realignment of the policy views of distinct social groups along the economic and cultural cleavages.

Several decades ago, I had doubts about whether a new party cleavage structure could endure.[42] The doubts reflected a concern that the new patterns of citizen demands were not embedded in institutionalized social groups as were the social cleavages described by Lipset and Rokkan. Labor union membership was decreasing, churches had more empty pews, and many of the social groups that focused on the cultural cleavage lacked comparable group-defined social networks that could inform and mobilize their political behavior. For example, there are no distinct clubs for postmaterialists or associations of millennials to politically engage these supporters of cultural liberalism. My colleagues and I had earlier stated that political divisions were becoming value-based cleavages with uncertain permanence because of the lack of an institutional group basis.

In electoral politics, three decades or more counts as permanence. The specific issues have often changed between elections, and the political actors have changed, but the economic and cultural cleavages have endured as a framework for political competition. Thus, issue-based cleavages and a realignment of party systems seem to be enduring consequences of this developmental process.[43] Class and educational groups have realigned across nations, social movements and other public groups provide cues on how others like yourself act politically, and social media are creating networks of like-minded people that can inform and mobilize their members.

Yet, issue-based cleavages should be more fluid than institutionalized group-based cleavages, such as workers voting for labor parties or Catholics voting for the Christian Democrats. This makes these alignments more susceptible to variations across elections as campaigns emphasize different issue agendas or political conditions change the emphasis on one cleavage or the other. It is noteworthy, however, that the cultural cleavage appears more stable and structured than the economic cleavage, perhaps because of its connection with basic human values.[44] Elements of continuing dealignment—weaker party attachments and a less deferential public—should contribute to this fluidity. This should produce a more dynamic process of party competition within the two-dimensional cleavage space.

While more choice is good for voters, it means more difficulty for parties in establishing an identity and appealing to voters. The relatively simple logic of appealing to the median voter in a one-dimensional political space allows parties to anticipate the vote gains/losses by moving right or left on the dimension.[45] Even these movements are constrained by existing parties to the left or right that limit the range of movement. The ranking of party preferences is also more clearly defined by distances on the dimension. However, campaign strategy becomes more complex, sometimes chaotic, in a two-dimensional space. There is often no dominant position in a two-dimensional space, and fewer constraints on the movement of parties because they can alter positions on either or both dimensions and the rank preference order can more easily be changed as a result.[46]

Without wading into the social choice literature, the implications are straightforward. Parties have to compete not only with the parties to their left and right, but also parties above/below them in the political space. A move in one direction creates multiple openings from competing parties.[47] I earlier cited an example from the German SPD, which struggled to fend off the culturally liberal Greens in one election by moving in their direction, and then lost its economic-oriented voters to the CDU/CSU. In the next election, the SPD tried to recapture these centrist voters, only to lose votes to the Greens. Expand this strategizing to the Dutch or other party systems with a dozen viable parties; a Voronoi diagram of the party space can approach the chaos predicted by social choice modeling. In such a space, what's a party to do? In the past, political parties had simpler campaign choices, and limited exposure to risk because of the constraints of a one-dimensional party system. The current framework of political competition creates greater challenges and risks for parties. Thus, I would expect more volatility in campaign programs, more volatility in voter choices, and more volatility in electoral outcomes around the structures of political competition described here.

The complexity of the electoral process can carry over to governing. When party competition was structured along a single dimension, a simple model of connected minimum winning connected coalitions (MWCC) was very likely in multiparty systems.[48] The largest party or median party that was typically the initial basis for coalition formation would look to its left or its right and select adjacent parties to form a majority. Now adjacent parties in a two-dimensional space might span different directions on one or both cleavages. Thus it appears that the MWCC model is confronting new challenges.

There are multiple examples of these tensions. The purple coalition of red and blue parties after the 1994 Dutch elections was a sign of things to come. The Belgian 2010 election was followed by 541 days of negotiations to create a new government; the 2017 Dutch election required 208 days to form the government. In Germany, the 1966 Grand Coalition was an exceptional development conditioned by external political and economic factors. Since 2005, eight of the following 12 years had a CDU/CSU-SPD government. Merkel's attempt at a very diverse CDU/CSU-FDP-Green coalition fell apart after the 2017 election, producing a long period of post-election negotiations and another grand coalition.

With extreme parties now competing and winning a significant share of the vote, this further complicates the coalition process. The German SPD rejects a national coalition with the Linke, the CDU/CSU rejects a coalition including the AfD. Excluding these parties severely restricts the available options. The 2017 Italian election produced a similar chasm between party blocs that had rejected coalition options before the election. This might be a transitory problem. When the Green parties first competed in elections they were also viewed as outside the range of legitimate coalition partners. But gradually these parties moderated, especially after sharing in a government.[49] So the treatment of economic and culturally extreme parties creates another governing challenge.

Perhaps the most basic challenge is how citizens react to this volatility, unpredictability, and the resulting public policies. Already, people are frustrated with governments and especially politicians and political parties. Part of this frustration comes from past unkept promises. One illustration is a quotation from a prominent political figure: "when I am [elected]...you will be forgotten no more."[50] Think for a moment about who might have uttered this catchy phrase before you flip back to the endnotes. It could be the pro-Brexit forces during the referendum, Marine Le Pen in the 2017 French presidential elections, or any number of conservative populist candidates in recent European elections, or Donald Trump.

The quotation is from Bill Clinton's acceptance speech at the 1992 Democratic Party convention. However, since the Democrats took office in 1992 (and then again in 2008), income inequality has increased, deindustrialization has continued, stalemate has replaced policy making, and Americans became even more critical of the government. More than two decades later, many of these same frustrations exist within the American public that had suffered through the Great Recession and watched Washington politicians respond to the needs of others. Thus, at his inauguration in January 2017 Donald Trump stated: "The forgotten men and women of our country will be forgotten no longer. Everyone is listening to you now." Sound familiar?

We now know more about these processes of electoral change than we did in the past. There is growing evidence that diversity of social and political interests is a defining characteristic of affluent democracies. A search for a single explanation of mass political behavior may be futile in a world where social interests are fragmented, people are more assertive, power is decentralized, and individual freedoms are given greater latitude. The diversity documented here may be the best forecast for the future, and this diversity constitutes a major departure from the structured partisan politics of the past.

Notes

1. On the 50th anniversary of the visit, the *Irish Times* wrote about the cultural contrast of 1963 to 2013. For example, "Catholicism was so powerful in 1963 that the Sunday before JFK's visit Primate of All Ireland John Charles McQuaid ordained 60 priests; 13,000 Irishwomen were nuns, the top profession for women ahead of teaching and nursing." Kate Holmquist, A visit that changed us forever,

1. *Irish Times* (June 19, 2013). https://www.irishtimes.com/news/a-visit-that-changed-us-forever-1.1433333.
2. Steven Pinker, *Enlightenment Now: The Case for Reason, Science, Humanism, and Progress*. New York: Viking, 2018.
3. Ronald Inglehart, *How People's Motivations are Changing And How this is Changing the World*. Cambridge: Cambridge University Press, 2017; Christian Welzel, *Freedom Rising: Human Empowerment and the Quest for Emancipation*. New York: Cambridge University Press, 2013; Russell Dalton, *The Good Citizen: How the Young are Reshaping American Politics*, 2nd ed. Washington, DC: CQ Press, 2015.
4. Russell Dalton, Scott Flanagan, and Paul Beck, eds., *Electoral Change in Advanced Industrial Democracies*. Princeton: Princeton University Press, 1984; Mark Franklin, Thomas Mackie, and Henry Valen, eds., *Electoral Change: Responses to Evolving Social and Attitudinal Structures in Western Countries*. Cambridge: Cambridge University Press, 1992.
5. Geoffrey Evans and James Tilley, *The New Politics of Class: The Political Exclusion of the British Working Class*. Oxford: Oxford University Press, 2017; Pablo Beramendi, Silja Häusermann, Herbert Kitschelt, and Hanspeter Kriesi, eds., *The Politics of Advanced Capitalism*. Cambridge: Cambridge University Press, 2015: Thomas Piketty, Brahmin left versus merchant right: Rising inequality and the change structure of political conflict. WID.world working paper series, 2018/7 (www.piketty.pse.ens.fr/conflict).
6. Christian Welzel and Russell Dalton, From allegiant to assertive citizens. In Russell Dalton and Christian Welzel, eds., *The Civic Culture Transformed: From Allegiant to Assertive Citizens*. Cambridge: Cambridge University Press, 2015; Klaus Armingeon and Kai Guthmann, Democracy in crisis: The declining support for national democracy in European countries, 2007–2011, *European Journal of Political Research* (2014) 53: 423–42; Carolien van Ham, Jacques Thomassen, Kees Aarts, and Rudy Andeweg, eds. *Myth and Reality of the Legitimacy Crisis*. Oxford: Oxford University Press, 2017.
7. This is part of his campaign for electoral reform: https://www.youtube.com/watch?v=Qfc3N0ZngXs.
8. Seymour Martin Lipset and Stein Rokkan, Cleavage structures, party systems, and voter alignments. In Seymour Martin Lipset and Stein Rokkan, eds., *Party Systems and Voter Alignments: Cross-national Perspectives*. New York: Free Press, 1967; also see, Richard Rose, ed. *Electoral Behavior: A Comparative Handbook*. New York: Free Press, 1974.
9. Kevin Deegan-Krause, New dimensions of political cleavage. In Russell Dalton and Hans-Dieter Klingemann, eds., *Oxford Handbook of Political Behavior*. Oxford: Oxford University Press, 2007; Oddbjørn Knutsen, *Social Structure, Value Orientations and Party Choice in Western Europe*. London: Palgrave, 2017.
10. Hanspeter Kriesi et al., *West European Politics in the Age of Globalization*. Cambridge: Cambridge University Press, 2008; Beramendi, Häusermann, Kitschelt, and Kriesi, eds., *The Politics of Advanced Capitalism*; Jack Vowles and George Xezonakis, eds. *Globalization and Domestic Politics: Parties, Elections, and Public Opinion*. Oxford: Oxford University Press, 2016.

11. Matthew Gabel, *Interests and Integration: Market Liberalization, Public Opinion, and European Union*. Ann Arbor, MI: University of Michigan Press, 1998.
12. David Broockman, Gregory Ferenstein, and Neil Malhotra, Wealthy elites' policy preferences and economic inequality: The case of technology entrepreneurs. Stanford Graduate School of Business, 2017.
13. Knutsen, *Social Structure, Value Orientations and Party Choice in Western Europe*.
14. Evans and Tilley, *The New Politics of Class*.
15. Kriesi et al., *West European Politics in the Age of Globalization*.
16. Peter Beinart, Republican is not a synonym for racist, *Atlantic* (December 2017); Morris Fiorina, *Unstable Majorities: Polarization, Party Sorting, and Political Stalemate*. Stanford: Hoover Institution, 2017, ch. 10–11.
17. Katherine Cramer, *The Politics of Resentment: Rural Consciousness in Wisconsin and the Rise of Scott Walker*. Chicago: University of Chicago Press, 2016; Arlie Hochschild, *Strangers in Their Own Land: Anger and Mourning on the American Right*. New York: New Press, 2016. Also see Jack Citrin and David Sears, *American Identity and the Politics of Multiculturalism*. New York: Cambridge University Press 2014.
18. Noam Gidron and Peter Hall, Populism as a problem of social integration. Paper presented at the annual meetings of the American Political Science Association, San Francisco, CA, September 2017.
19. Seymour Martin Lipset, The revolt against modernity. In Per Torsvik, ed., *Mobilization, Center-Periphery Structures and Nation-Building*. Bergen: Universitetsforlaget, 1981; Piero Ignazi, The silent counter-revolution, *European Journal of Political Research* (1992) 22: 3–14.
20. John Jost et al., Political conservatism as motivated social cognition, *Psychological Bulletin* (2003) 129: 339–75; Dana Carney et al., The secret lives of liberals and conservatives, *Political Psychology* (2008) 29: 807–40; Hulda Thorisdottier, Psychological needs underlying left–right political orientations, *Public Opinion Quarterly* (2007) 71: 175–203; Jeff Mondak, *Personality and the Foundation of Political Behavior*. New York: Cambridge University Press, 2010.
21. Jonathan Haidt, *The Righteous Mind: Why Good People Are Divided by Politics and Religion*. New York: Pantheon, 2012.
22. Jonathan Haidt, Jesse Graham, and Craig Joseph, Above and below Left–Right: Ideological narratives and moral foundations, *Psychological Inquiry* (2009) 20: 110–19; Stanley Feldman and Christopher Johnston, Understanding the determinants of political ideology, *Political Psychology* (2014) 35: 227–358.
23. Paul Goren et al., A unified theory of value-based reasoning and U.S. public opinion, *Political Behavior* (2016) 38: 977–97; also Paul Goren, *On Voter Competence*. New York: Oxford University Press, 2012.
24. Matt Grossmann and Daniel Thaler, Mass-elite divides in aversion to social change and support for Donald Trump. Paper presented at the 2017 annual meetings of the American Political Science Association, San Francisco, CA.
25. Justin Gest, Tyler Reny, and Jeremy Mayer, Roots of the radical right: Nostalgic Deprivation in the United States and Britain, *Comparative Political Studies* (2017). https://doi.org/10.1177/0010414017720705; Justin Gest, *The New Minority: White*

Working Class Politics in an Age of Immigration and Inequality. Oxford: Oxford University Press, 2016.
26. For example, see the reviews of Cramer's book in: Review symposium: The politics of resentment, *Perspectives on Politics* (2017) 5: 521–32. The cross-national breadth of the cultural cleavage also speaks to broader causal process. One can identify racial bias as a potentially important mobilizing factor in parts of the United States, but in liberal Sweden?
27. Two of the items were recoded so all have acceptance of change as the highest value. I added the four items together and then divided by four. The resulting index ranges from: 1) opposition to social change to 5) fully support for social change. In most years this index was asked in the post-election survey, while the measurement of the cultural cleavage and candidate preference come from the pre-election survey.
28. Pinker, *Enlightenment Now*, ch. 14; Inglehart, *How People's Motivations are Changing And How this is Changing the World*; Pew Research Center, *Political Typology Reveals Deep Fissures on the Right and Left: Topline* (October 24, 2017) http://www.people-press.org/2017/10/24/political-typology-reveals-deep-fissures-on-the-right-and-left/.
29. E. J. Dionne, Norman Ornstein and Thomas Mann, *One Nation after Trump*. New York: St. Martin's Press, 2017. They also noted that not every tradition or traditionalist is oppressive: "when those reacting to changes all around them say, 'I fear I will not be able to pass the world I grew up in to my children,' they are not displaying paranoia, and they are not necessarily being reactionary" (p. 218).
30. The Pearson r correlations are: −0.28 for age; 0.14 for education level, and −0.32 for frequency of church attendance.
31. Another sign of the centrality of these orientations is their stability over time. The modernization index shows a very strong correlation ($r = .64$) across the 1992–1996 ANES panel. By comparison, the liberal/conservative scale is slightly weaker ($r = .60$) even though it is a common political term and self-identity.
32. The dip in this correlation in the 2008 and 2012 elections mirror what was found in Chapter 9, as economic concerns dominated in these elections after the Great Recession (Figure 9.4). On the increasing relationship with Congressional vote see Jonathan Knuckey, A new front in the culture war? Moral traditionalism and voting behavior in U.S. House elections, *American Politics Research* (2005) 33: 645–71 Also see Paul Goren, *On Voter Competence*. Oxford: Oxford University Press, 2012.
33. Philip Converse and Greg Markus, Plus ça change . . . : The new CPS election study spanel. *American Political Science Review* (1979) 73: 32–49.
34. Pew Research Center, *The Partisan Divide on Political Values Grows Even Wider* (October 5, 2017). http://www.people-press.org/2017/10/05/the-partisan-divide-on-political-values-grows-even-wider; Fiorina, *Unstable Majorities*.
35. Case studies of Britain and France show these trends in greater detail: Evans and Tilley, *The New Politics of Class*; Simon Bornschier, *Cleavage Politics and the Populist Right. The New Cultural Conflict in Western Europe*. Philadelphia: Temple University Press, 2010; Piketty, Brahmin left versus merchant right: Rising inequality and the change structure of political conflict.

36. Oddbjørn Knutsen, *Class Voting in Western Europe: A Comparative Longitudinal Study*. Lanham: Lexington. 2006; Jane Gingrich, Silja Häusermann, The decline of the working-class vote, the reconfiguration of the welfare support coalition and consequences for the welfare state, *Journal of European Social Policy* (2015) 25: 50–75; Mark Bovens and Anchrit Wille, *Diploma Democracy*. Oxford: Oxford University Press, 2017.
37. Piero Ignazi, *Extreme Right Parties in Western Europe*. Oxford: Oxford University Press, 2003.
38. Cas Mudde, Europe's populist surge: A long time in the making, *Foreign Affairs* (November 2016) 95: 25–30.
39. Adam Przeworski, *Why Bother with Elections?* New York: Polity Press, 2018, ch. 1, 11; Fiorina, *Unstable Majorities*.
40. Herbert Kitschelt, Party families, *Oxford Research Encyclopedia on Politics*. http://politics.oxfordre.com/; Herbert Kitschelt and Philipp Rehm, Determinants of dimension dominance. In Philip Manow, Bruno Palier, and Hanna Schwanter, eds., *Worlds of Welfare Capitalism and Electoral Politics*. Oxford: Oxford University Press, 2017.
41. Peter Mair, *Ruling the Void: The Hollowing of Western Democracy*. London: Verso, 2013; Matthijs Bogaards, Lessons from Brexit and Trump: Populist is what happens when parties lose control, *Zeitschrift für Vergleichende Politische Wissenschaft* (2017) 11: 513–18.
42. Russell Dalton, Scott Flanagan, and Paul Beck, eds., Political forces and partisan change. In Russell Dalton, Scott Flanagan, and Paul Beck, eds., *Electoral Change in Advanced Industrial Democracies*. Princeton: Princeton University Press, 1984.
43. Herbert Kitschelt and Philipp Rehm, Party alignments. Change and continuity. In Pablo Beramendi, Silja Häusermann, Herbert Kitschelt, and Hanspeter Kriesi, eds., *The Politics of Advanced Capitalism*. Cambridge, MA: Cambridge University Press, 2015; Fiorina, *Unstable Majorities*.
44. For example, the general pattern is for the cultural cleavage to be more clearly structured in PCA models, to have higher explaining variance in predicting cleavages positions, and to be more closely tied to party choice with higher congruence levels between voters and parties. This may reflect the identity and value aspects of this cleavage which are less extensive for the economic cleavage. See Paul Goren et al., A unified theory of value-based reasoning and U.S. public opinion; Jost et al., Political conservatism as motivated social cognition.
45. Anthony Downs, *An Economic Theory of Democracy*. New York: Harper, 1957; James Adams, Causes and electoral consequences of party policy shifts in multiparty elections: Theoretical results and empirical evidence, *Annual Review of Political Science* (2012) 15: 401–19.
46. James Enelow and Melvin Hinich, *The Spatial Theory of Voting*. Cambridge: Cambridge University Press, 1984.
47. Richard McKelvey, Intransitivities in multidimensional voting models and some implications for agenda control, *Journal of Economic Theory* (1976) 12: 472–82; this has subsequently been extended to electoral choice.

48. Robert Axelrod, *Conflict of Interest*. Chicago: Markham, 1970; Abram De Swaan, *Coalition Theories and Cabinet Formations*. Amsterdam: Elsevier, 1973.
49. Ferdinand Müller-Rommel and Thomas Poguntke, eds., *Green Parties in National Governments*. London: Routledge, 2013.
50. William Clinton, Democratic Presidential Nomination Acceptance Speech, *Democratic National Convention*, 1992 (http://www.presidency.ucsb.edu/ws/?pid=25958).

APPENDIX A
Issue Questions from the European Election Studies

This appendix presents the questions that assess the opinions of European publics. I used Principal Components Analysis (PCA) of the issue questions to construct the economic and cultural cleavages. The Candidates for the European Parliament surveys in chapters 5 and 6 use comparable, but sometimes slightly different questions.

1979 European Election Study (Eurobarometer 11)

Q.159 We'd like to hear your views on some important political issues. Could you tell me whether you agree or disagree with each of the following proposals, and how strongly do you feel? 1. Agree strongly, 2. Agree, 3. Disagree, 4. Disagree strongly.

(A) Stronger public control should be exercised over the activities of multi-national corporations.

(B) Nuclear energy should be developed to meet future energy needs.

(C) Greater efforts should be made to reduce inequality of income.

(D) More severe penalties should be introduced for acts of terrorism.

(E) Public ownership of private industry should be expanded.

(F) Government should play a greater role in the management of the economy.

(G) Western Europe should make a stronger effort to provide adequate military defense.

(H) Women should be free to decide for themselves in matters concerning abortion.

(I) Employees should be given equal representation with shareholders <Germany: on the governing boards of large companies>.

(J) Economic aid to third world countries should be increased.

(K) Stronger measures should be taken to protect the environment against pollution.

(L) Stronger measures should be taken to protect the rights of individuals to express their own political views.

(M) Economic aid to the less developed regions of the European Community should be increased.

Appendix A

Q.221. In general, are you for or against efforts being made to unify Western Europe? <If for> are you very much for this, or only to some extent? <If against> are you only to some extent against, or very much.

2009 European Election Study

Now I will read out some statements to you. For each of the following statements, please tell me to what degree you agree or disagree with each statement. Do you 'strongly agree', 'agree', 'neither agree, nor disagree', 'disagree' or 'strongly disagree'?

Q56. Immigrants should be required to adapt to the customs of [Britain].

Q57. Private enterprise is the best way to solve [Britain's] economic problems.

Q58. Same-sex marriages should be prohibited by law.

Q59. Major public services and industries ought to be in state ownership.

Q60. Women should be free to decide on matters of abortion.

Q61. Politics should abstain from intervening in the economy.

Q62. People who break the law should be given much harsher sentences than they are these days.

Q63. Income and wealth should be redistributed towards ordinary people.

Q64. Schools must teach children to obey authority.

Q65. EU treaty changes should be decided by referendum.

Q66. A woman should be prepared to cut down on her paid work for the sake of her family.

Q67. Immigration to [Britain] should be decreased significantly.

Q80. Some say European unification should be pushed further. Others say it already has gone too far. What is your opinion? Please indicate your views using a scale from 0 to 10, where 0 means unification "has already gone too far" and 10 means it "should be pushed further." What number on this scale best describes your position?

2014 European Election Study

QPP17. Now I would like you to tell me your views on various issues. For each issue, we will present you with two opposite statements and we will ask your opinion about these two statements. We would like to ask you to position yourself on a scale from 0 to 10, where '0' means that you "fully agree with the statement at the top" and '10' means that you "fully agree with the statement at the bottom." Then if your views are somewhere in between, you can choose any number that describes your position best.

(1) State regulation and control of the market: 0, You are fully in favor of state intervention in the economy; 10, You are fully opposed to state intervention in the economy.

Appendix A

(2) Redistribution of wealth: 0, You are fully in favor of the redistribution of wealth from the rich to the poor in (OUR COUNTRY); 10, You are fully opposed to the redistribution of wealth from the rich to the poor in (OUR COUNTRY).

(3) Spending: 0, You are fully in favor of raising taxes to increase public services; 10, You are fully in favor of cutting public services to cut taxes.

(4) Same-sex marriage: 0, You are fully in favor of same-sex marriage; 10, You are fully opposed to same-sex marriage.

(5) Civil liberties: 0, You fully support privacy rights even if they hinder efforts to combat crime; 10, you are fully in favor of restricting privacy rights in order to combat crime.

(6) Immigration: 0, You are fully in favor of a restrictive policy on immigration; 10, You are fully opposed to a restrictive policy on immigration.

(7) EU Integration: 0, The EU should have more authority over the EU Member States' economic and budgetary policies; 10 (OUR COUNTRY) should retain full control over its economic and budgetary policies.

(8) Environment: 0, Environmental protection should always take priority even at the cost of economic growth; 10, Economic growth should always take priority even at the cost of environmental protection.

APPENDIX B
Citizen Issue Structures by Nation

Chapter 2 used Principal Components Analysis (PCA) to identify the issue content of the economic cleavage and cultural cleavage for the pooled set of EU15 member states in 2009 and 2014. This appendix compares these European-wide findings to the results in specific nations. The goal is to determine if the underlying patterns are broadly comparable across nations, making the pooled results reliable and valid.

I replicated the PCA methodology from Chapter 2 separately for each nation. As I have noted elsewhere, several of the national models show more variability in the number of components if the results are not constrained.[1] The cultural cleavage often separates from the three women's issues forming the second component in 2009; economic issues then load on a third component. When this occurred, I present the economic cleavage from the third component in the following analyses; these instances are denoted by "Econ3" in the table.

The highest loading issues in the 2009 PCAs are summarized in Chapter 4. Table B.1 gives the full results. Cultural issues form the first component, highlighting immigration and a mix of other cultural issues.[2] To an extent, there is some cross-national variation that may reflect the national salience of an issue. For instance, in most of Europe same-sex marriage is a significant component of the cultural cleavage, especially in several Southern European nations or in Sweden where legalization was under review in 2009; in the Netherlands, Belgium, and Denmark, the coefficients are substantially weaker. Attitudes toward the EU are part of the cultural cleavage in most nations, in some nations part of the economic cleavage, and neither cleavage in yet other nations. In overall terms, most nations agree that conservative cultural values involve immigration policies, harsher penalties for criminals, and teaching obedience in the schools.

The economic cleavage is defined by at least three of the four economic issues: reducing income and wealth inequality, state ownership of public services and industries, private enterprise solving societal problems, and political intervention in the economy. Yet in seven of the EU15 nations, the economic cleavage includes at least one cultural issue. A more balanced and larger set of economic issues might find the same consistency for the economic cleavage as is apparent for the cultural cleavage.

The value of the PCA model is that it uses all of this information to construct component scores for each survey respondent. The weight of each issue is a function of the strength of its relationship with the component, with large coefficients given disproportionate weight. Thus, the overall index should be a robust measure of the

Table B.1 Citizen Issue Structures by Nation, 2009

	Austria		Belgium		Denmark			Finland		France		Germany		Greece		Ireland	
Issues	Cult	Econ	Cult	Econ	Cult	Econ3		Cult	Econ	Cult	Econ	Cult	Econ	Cult	Econ	Cult	Econ3
Immigrants adapt to customs	.74	−.14	.73	−.07	.69	−.03		.67	.03	.69	.04	.69	.03	.61	.02	.29	.07
Private enterprise solve problems	.33	−.67	.33	.42	.61	−.33		.41	−.20	.34	−.46	.39	−.55	.54	−.29	.29	−.60
Prohibit same-sex marriages	.45	−.30	−.08	.70	.24	−.07		.42	.28	.49	−.25	.48	−.02	.63	−.23	.16	−.04
State owns public services industries	.16	.65	.04	.52	−.26	.54		−.02	.65	−.12	.56	.10	.67	.18	.57	−.27	.15
Women free to decide abortion	−.08	.19	.36	−.01	.07	−.02		.17	−.33	−.13	.42	.03	.16	−.17	.42	.02	.40
Politics should not intervene in economy	.29	−.29	.10	.64	.35	.27		.48	.04	.37	−.14	.39	−.36	.14	.07	.02	.47
Law breakers get harsher sentence	.64	−.04	.58	.20	.76	.036		.65	.15	.62	.02	.66	.12	.61	.06	.68	.11
Redistribute income and wealth	.21	.58	.43	.08	.11	.58		−.01	.58	.02	.56	.08	.65	.20	.50	.33	.49
Schools must teach obedience	.57	−.05	.70	.11	.62	.10		.62	.05	.59	−.08	.63	.01	.65	.02	.58	−.05
EU treaty changes by referendum	.59	.34	.54	.36	.10	.66		.23	.57	.32	.52	.23	.48	.14	.54	.58	−.05
Women should limit paid work	.57	−.08	.15	.69	.22	.12		.19	.44	.52	.09	.50	.09	.61	.26	.01	−.27
Immigration should be decreased	.80	−.07	.61	.15	.75	.03		.73	.24	.75	−.08	.68	.15	.64	.18	.52	.26
Attitude to European unification	.59	.05	.23	.01	.46	.31		.30	.54	.69	.04	.45	.09	−.27	.38	.14	.34
Explained variance	26.2	12.1	19.5	15.6	22.4	10.5		19.7	14.5	21.6	11.9	21.1	12.4	21.9	11.0	13.9	12.7

	Italy		Luxembourg		Netherlands			Portugal		Spain		Sweden		UK	
	Cult	Econ2	Cult	Econ	Cult	Econ3		Cult	Econ	Cult	Econ3	Cult	Econ	Cult	Econ
Immigrants adapt to customs	.65	−.03	.66	.14	.66	.19		.58	.27	.60	.08	.74	−.01	.69	.14
Private enterprise solve problems	.53	.20	.34	.06	.13	.02		.04	.79	.58	−.23	.29	−.56	.43	−.51
Prohibit same-sex marriages	.53	.45	.33	.09	.18	.03		.28	.05	.42	−.48	.58	.03	.43	.17
State owns public services industries	.00	.64	.05	.57	−.03	.39		.33	−.19	.12	.50	−.01	.66	−.05	.68
Women free to decide abortion	−.06	−.04	.15	.13	.18	.00		.17	−.31	−.20	.55	−.24	.03	−.04	−.12
Politics should not intervene econ	.11	.68	.17	.18	.16	−.52		.28	.16	.21	−.03	.20	.12	.29	.43
Law breakers get harsher sentence	.39	−.14	.44	.45	.72	.13		.47	.26	.55	.09	.62	.07	.65	.17
Redistribute income and wealth	.07	.39	−.09	.68	.18	.29		.36	−.17	.17	.60	.06	.69	.02	.72
Schools must teach obedience	.48	.14	.25	.44	.38	.63		.51	.21	.63	.11	.66	.03	.60	.07
EU treaty changes by referendum	.08	.21	.40	.38	.53	−.39		.54	−.10	.16	.34	.25	.57	.49	−.01
Women should limit paid work	.53	.17	.22	.42	.11	−.10		.49	−.08	.42	−.03	.45	.15	.31	−.05
Immigration should be decreased	.73	−.06	.68	.24	.68	.03		.68	−.11	.68	.03	.72	.01	.69	.10
Attitude to European unification	.44	−.20	.62	−.26	.59	−.27		.31	−.44	.21	−.36	.30	.38	.55	−.19
Explained variance	18.5	10.9	15.7	10.1	18.0	15.0		14.0	13.4	18.5	11.3	21.5	13.4	21.7	12.1

Note: Table entries are coefficients from Principal Component Analysis. Two extracted dimensions, Varimax rotation, pairwise deletion of missing data.
Source: European Election Study, 2009.

Table B.2 Citizen Issue Structures by Nation, 2014

Issues	Austria Econ	Austria Cult	Belgium Econ	Belgium Cult	Denmark Econ	Denmark Cult	Finland Econ	Finland Cult	France Econ	France Cult	Germany Econ	Germany Cult	Greece Cult	Greece Econ	Ireland Econ	Ireland Cult
State intervention in economy	.67	.17	.67	.10	.57	.32	.64	.08	.59	.07	.63	−.01	−.11	.30	.63	.03
Redistribution of wealth	.25	.42	.61	−.11	.64	.20	.73	−.04	.73	.06	.78	−.06	−.14	.71	.58	−.46
Raise taxes for social service	.66	.04	.26	.52	.69	.17	.70	−.04	.20	.59	.17	.37	.53	−.12	.43	.08
Same–sex marriage	.26	.58	.48	−.02	.45	−.11	.16	.57	.51	.29	.01	.70	.69	.11	.20	−.03
Privacy rights even if crime effects	−.32	.60	.04	.45	−.16	.64	.04	.47	.09	.55	.35	.32	.31	.34	.23	.50
Restrictive immigration policy	−.31	.09	.09	−.59	−.25	−.58	.03	−.66	−.31	−.50	.23	−.62	−.61	.15	.15	−.64
EU authority over economies	.65	.09	−.01	.68	.09	.63	−.18	.66	−.38	.64	.19	.54	.33	−.45	.08	.65
Economic growth vs. environment	−.09	.73	.57	.20	.63	−.07	.44	.46	.15	.57	.62	.28	.25	.65	.60	.31
Explained variance	20.3	18.2	18.2	16.6	23.7	16.6	21.2	21.4	18.1	21.6	20.3	18.6	17.8	17.4	17.4	17.4

Issues	Italy Cult	Italy Econ	Luxembourg Cult	Luxembourg Econ	Netherlands Econ	Netherlands Cult	Portugal Econ	Portugal Cult	Spain Cult	Spain Econ	Sweden Econ	Sweden Cult	UK Cult	UK Econ
State intervention in economy	.05	.68	−.07	.43	.72	−.06	.73	−.14	−.23	.58	.73	.11	−.23	.59
Redistribution of wealth	−.08	.68	.63	−.02	.72	.01	.46	−.03	.07	.73	.78	.11	.22	.52
Raise taxes for social service	.56	.03	.01	.69	.53	.28	.23	.15	.40	.17	.80	.03	−.15	.69
Same–sex marriage	.60	.14	.41	.30	.03	.35	.15	.70	.54	.20	.27	.57	.27	.41
Privacy rights even if crime effects	.31	.31	.56	.02	.20	.34	.33	.36	.66	−.03	.17	.55	.64	.04
Restrictive immigration policy	−.66	.35	−.58	−.01	−.08	−.72	.13	−.61	−.61	.04	−.21	−.68	−.64	−.01
EU authority over economies	.59	.25	.09	.70	.02	.77	−.03	.41	.30	−.06	−.27	.58	.69	.08
Economic growth vs. environment	.22	.55	.60	−.06	.49	.33	.65	.04	.33	.61	.62	.28	.28	.51
Explained variance	20.0	19.1	19.6	15.5	20.0	19.1	17.1	15.1	18.9	16.6	29.6	19.1	19.5	18.9

Note: Table entries are coefficients from Principal Component Analysis. Two extracted dimensions, Varimax rotation, pairwise deletion of missing data.
Source: European Election Study, 2014.

Appendix B

underlying cleavage positions and not overly dependent on any single issue. In short, small national variations are to be expected, but the question is whether the broad patterns are comparable cross-nationally.

To further validate the similarity of pooled and national level PCA results, I calculated individual scores from the pooled analyses of Table 2.2 and then compared them to the scores from the equivalent cleavage scores from the country-level PCAs. I matched the appropriate dimensions from the pooled and nation-specific PCAs. This method determines if the measurement of these two cleavages is basically similar across nations. For all EU15 nations, the two scores are correlated at 0.79 for the economic cleavage and 0.90 for the cultural cleavage. The economic cleavage is less robust, but only four items define this dimension. There is very little variation in these correlations across the subsets of the original six member states, the EU9 nations, or the EU15 nations.

I repeated these country-level analyses for the issue battery in the 2014 EES. The 2014 analyses are more complex because there are only eight issues in the battery. Three issues are distinctly economic: state intervention in the economy, redistribution of wealth, and taxes versus social services. Three are more clearly cultural: same-sex marriage, privacy rights versus crime, and immigration. The other two items have potentially mixed interpretation because they combine economic and cultural aspects: EU authority over economies and economic growth versus the environment. For example, in one nation environmental quality may emphasizes the cultural aspect of the issue; in another nation economic concerns may shift this issue to the economic cleavage.

Table B.2 shows some variation in the cleavage structure across nations. But the normal pattern is for at least two of the clear economic items loading highly on the economic cleavage, and at least two of the cultural issues loading on the cultural cleavage. The two ambivalent issues vary in which aspect of the issue is more salient in the national context—the economic or the cultural.

There is always a tension between the statistical consistency of issue components across nations and the conceptual equivalency of components represented by different mix of PCA coefficients.[3] Neither strategy can be fully accurate in describing public opinion. I have focused on conceptual equivalence based on all the available issue questions. The ultimate test of this strategy is the consistency of correlates of cleavage positions across nations and time.

Notes

1. Russell Dalton, Party representation across multiple issue dimensions, *Party Politics* (2017) 23: 609–22.
2. Because of its ambiguous meaning potentially bridging both cleavages, I do not consider the issue of referendums for EU treaty changes as part of this discussion.
3. Adam Przeworski and Henry Teune, Equivalence in cross-national research. *Public Opinion Quarterly* (1966) 30: 551–68.

APPENDIX C
Identifying Party Positions

This project relies on the self-statements of party elites—Candidates for the European Parliament (CEPs)—to identify party positions on a set of issues and thereby on the broad economic and cultural cleavages that structure political competition. One can make a strong claim that, as selected party representatives, CEPs' policy views represent the party's political positions. Indeed, many previous studies of political representation are based on elite self-placements.[1]

Elite positions, however, can yield imprecise or even biased estimates of party positions. For example, CEPs will differ from party candidates to the national parliament in various ways.[2] And as not all the CEPs were elected, some might have appeared on the ballot to address factional interests within a party. The sample size for many parties is worryingly small, and a rogue candidate, or a candidate in a bad mood on that day, can easily affect a party's scores. At a more basic level, what the candidates (or the party manifestos) say may not correspond to what the parties actually do.

Because of these concerns, I validated the party positions from the CEPs with other empirical evidence. One common method asks academic experts to position the parties along a Left–Right scale as well as on specific policy dimensions.[3] Such expert surveys summarize the totality of the parties' positions, including the content of recent campaigns and the policy activities of the parties. I use expert positioning of parties on a set of issues from the Chapel Hill Expert Surveys (CHES) in 2010 and 2014. This provides two measures to compare to the 2009 CEP party positions—and to determine if party positions changed by 2014.

The CHES data assessed party positions on over a dozen national political issues, and another battery on the EU (from which I selected a broad question to correspond to the broad EU question in the EES studies). In each nation, party experts placed the significant parties on each of these issue scales. Each party is a unit in our analysis.[4]

Table C.1 presents the Principal Components Analysis identifying the structure of these issue position. In both years, a two-component solution provides a good representation of the economic and cultural cleavage.[5] There is a clear structure with a high percentage of explained variance for the two-component solution.

The first component in both years taps party positions on cultural issues: homosexuality, expanded minority rights, multiculturalism, immigration policy, civil liberties vs. law and order, and religious principles in politics. For experts' images of parties, the cultural cleavage has a stronger race and ethnicity component than observed for the

Appendix C

Table C.1. Party Issue Positions from the Party Expert Surveys

	2010		2014	
Issues	Cultural	Economic	Cultural	Economic
Public services vs. reducing taxes	0.541	0.770	0.420	0.848
Deregulation of markets	0.360	0.878	0.262	0.919
Redistribution from the rich to the poor	0.489	0.805	0.461	0.846
State intervention in the economy	–	–	0.367	0.879
Civil liberties vs. law and order	0.894	0.320	0.883	0.375
Social lifestyle—homosexuality	0.932	0.147	0.911	0.146
Religious principles in politics	0.741	0.304	0.737	0.368
Immigration policy	0.897	0.328	0.909	0.256
Multiculturalism vs. assimilation for immigrants	0.912	0.264	0.906	0.187
Supports urban vs. rural interests	0.604	0.042	0.708	0.110
Supports environmental protection	0.790	0.424	0.735	0.403
Decentralization to regions/localities	0.222	0.050	0.185	0.110
International security vs peace keeping	−0.182	−0.869	−0.119	−0.841
More rights for ethnic minorities	0.915	0.232	0.893	0.259
Cosmopolitan rather than nationalist conceptions of society	–	–	0.913	0.025
Overall EU position	−0.536	0.668	−0.515	0.666
Eigenvalue	6.70	3.84	6.78	4.52
% Variance explained	47.9	27.4	45.2	30.1

Note: Table entries are coefficients from Principal Components Analyses with Varimax rotation and pairwise deletion of missing data.
Sources: Chapel Hill Expert Survey, 2010 and 2014. EU15 nations.

EES surveys of citizens and elites. This might be a function of the choice of issues included in the expert survey or more differentiation on this issue by political parties.

The second component in each year is a clear manifestation of the economic cleavage: deregulation of markets, state intervention in the economy, and the tradeoff between services and taxes. Experts also see party positions on the EU as strongly linked to this economic cleavage as well as linked to the cultural cleavage.

Comparing Party Positions Measures

For both CHES surveys, I computed cleavage indices as the scores from the PCA analyses.[6] This identifies experts' collective judgments of each party's position in the two-dimensional political space. I then compared these party expert scores to the party locations from the CEP study in 2009 (Table C.2). The right side of the table presents the intercorrelations among variables, and the left side is a PCA to summarize relationships.

The correlations between the three measures of cultural or economic cleavage positions—CEP and CHES 2010 and 2014—are all very highly correlated in the 0.80 to 0.97 range. At the same time, the cross-correlation between the two cleavages is minimal because of the methodology of the PCA. Also striking is the high continuity of the CHES measures over time. Experts in 2009 and 2014 gave virtually the same score to parties in both years, despite the tumult of Europe's financial and political conditions during this period.

245

Table C.2. Relationships between Party Cleavage Positions

Party Cleavage Positions	Principal Components		2009 CEP Economic	2009 CHES Economic	2014 CHES Economic	2009 CEP Cultural	2009 CHES Cultural
	Cultural	Economic					
2009 CEP Economic	0.164	0.905					
2009 CHES Economic	−0.054	0.975	0.811 0.000 (83)				
2014 CHES Economic	−0.015	0.968	0.793 0.000 (76)	0.955 0.000 (100)			
2009 CEP Cultural	0.918	0.027	−0.114 0.188 (134)	0.016 0.886 (83)	−0.063 0.590 (76)		
2009 CHES Cultural	0.973	0.040	0.204 0.064 (83)	0.026 0.792 (108)	−0.028 0.782 (100)	0.823 0.000 (83)	
2014 CHES Cultural	0.977	0.024	0.200 0.083 (76)	−0.011 0.911 (100)	−0.026 0.787 (112)	0.834 0.000 (76)	0.966 0.000 (100)

Note: The analyses on the left are from Principal Components Analysis with Varimax rotation and pairwise deletion of missing data. The analyses on the right are Pearsonr correlations, with significance level and the number of parties in parentheses.

Sources: Candidates for the European Parliament survey, 2009; Chapel Hill Expert Survey, 2010 and 2014. EU15 nations.

Appendix C

Our primary concern, however, is whether the cleavage positions of political parties as represented by the CEP issue positions correspond to the CHES measures. This provides a strong measure of the external validity of the CEP data because of the different methodology of both projects and the different issues used to define the economic and cultural cleavages.

The PCA on the left side of the figure, as well as the underlying correlations, show very high correlations between the two measurement methods, exceeding 0.90 coefficients for each cleavage. Given the inevitable imprecision in social science measurements, and the reliance on a small number of CEP candidates and CHES experts to position the parties, the consistency is very impressive.

These results give us confidence in using the CEP surveys to locate party positions. By corollary, this also implies that the time series of party locations might be expanded by using the CHES data and other expert sources to track party positions over time.

Notes

1. Warren Miller, Warren et al., *Policy Representation in Western Democracies*. Oxford: Oxford University Press, 1999; Jacques Thomassen and Hermann Schmitt, Policy representation, *European Journal of Political Research* (1997) 32: 165–84; Russell Dalton, Party representation across multiple issue dimensions, *Party Politics* (2017) 23: 609–22.
2. Richard Katz and Bernhard Wessels, eds., *The European Parliament, the National Parliaments, and European Integration*. Oxford: Oxford University Press, 1999.
3. Gary Marks, ed., Special symposium: Comparing measures of party positioning: Expert, manifesto, and survey data, *Electoral Studies* (2007): 1–234; Lisbet Hooghe et al., Reliability and validity of the 2002 and 2006 Chapel Hill expert surveys on party positioning, *European Journal of Political Research* (2010) 49: 687–703; Robert Rohrschneider and Stephen Whitefield, *The Strain of Representation: How Parties Represent Diverse Voters in Western and Eastern Europe*. Oxford: Oxford University Press, 2012; Ryan Bakker, Seth Jolly, and Jonathan Polk, Complexity in the European party space: Exploring dimensionality with experts, *European Union Politics* (2012) 13: 219–45.
4. The CHES study is directed by Gary Marks and Lisbet Hooghe, who generously make these data available at: http://www.unc.edu/~gwmarks/data_pp.php. The number of parties in the EU15 was 125 in 2010 and 137 in 2014.
5. The unconstrained 2010 solution had three components with Eigenvalues greater than 1.0. The third was the two regional variables (region and urban/rural).
6. I explored analyses using the Voter Advice Applications (VAAs) collected by the European University Institute. Diego Garzia and Stefan Marschall, eds., *Matching Voters with Parties and Candidates*. ECPR Press, Colchester, 2014. For a variety of methodological reasons, such as missing data and the set of issues in the VAAs, these issue questions did not produce clear cleavage dimensions. The best of these cleavage measures did load on the appropriate cleavage dimension in the PCA models, but with lower coefficients.

APPENDIX D

Party Cleavage Positions

This appendix presents the aggregate party scores on the economic and cultural cleavages constructed from the analyses of the Candidates for the European Parliaments studies in chapter 6. The candidate scores were aggregate for their party if (in most cases) at least three candidates provided issue responses and the party had at least 1.0 of the vote in the EP election.

Table D.1. Party Cleavage Scores in 1979
Cleavage scores are available from 44 parties in the 1979 CEP survey.

Nation: Party	Economic Cleavage	Cultural Cleavage
BE: BSP	0.77	0.34
BE: CVP	0.26	−0.75
BE: FDF	0.76	0.18
BE: PRLW	−0.44	−0.60
BE: PSB	0.75	0.22
BE: PSC	1.02	−0.76
BE: PVV	0.23	−1.10
DK: FP	−4.66	0.77
DK: KF	−0.81	−0.41
DK: SD	0.14	1.76
DK: V	−1.73	0.34
DK: Anti EC	−1.39	2.81
GE: CDU	−0.43	−0.80
GE: CSU	−0.87	−0.74
GE: FDP	−0.51	−0.12
GE: SPD	0.43	0.53
FR: PCF	−0.28	1.61
FR: PS	0.78	0.68
FR: PSU	0.23	2.12
FR: RPR	−1.41	−1.38
FR: UDF	−0.21	−0.51
FR: LO	−0.72	2.30
IRE: FF	−0.50	0.08
IRE: FG	−0.16	−0.07
IRE: Labour	0.97	1.13
IT: MSI-DN	0.50	−1.36
IT: DC	0.64	−1.09
IT: PCI	0.51	0.45
IT: PLI	−0.10	−0.57
IT: PR	0.64	0.89
IT: PRI	0.33	−0.67
IT: PSDI	0.60	−0.49
IT: PSI	0.71	0.25
IT: DP	0.48	1.53
LUX: PCS	−0.21	−0.69
LUX: PD	−0.88	−0.33
NL: CDA	−0.14	−0.35
NL: D66	0.20	0.52
NL: PvdA	0.53	1.02
NL: VVD	−0.62	−0.55
UK: CON	−1.37	−0.55
UK: Labour	0.18	1.10
UK: Liberals	0.59	−0.30
UK: SNP	0.10	0.21

Note: Positive scores denote liberal positions.
Source: Aggregated candidate scores from 1979 Candidates for the European Parliament study.

Appendix D

Table D.2. Party Cleavage Scores in 1994

Cleavage scores are available from 70 parties in the 1994 CEP survey.

Nation: Party	Economic Cleavage	Cultural Cleavage
B-SP (Fl)	0.72	0.81
B: ECOLO (Fr)	0.98	0.77
B: AGALEV	0.70	0.66
B: PSC (Fr)	0.31	−0.29
B: WOW (Fl)	−0.28	−0.49
B: PS (Fr)	0.83	1.24
B: VB (Fl)	−0.36	−1.40
B: VLD (Fl)	−1.38	0.79
B: CVPR (Fl)	−0.59	−0.57
B: FN (Fr)	0.20	−1.60
B: VU (Fl)	0.39	−0.62
DK: CPP	−0.69	−0.13
DK: Progress	−1.27	−0.60
DK: SF	1.04	0.82
DK: SDP	0.32	0.28
DK: RLP	−0.22	0.61
DK: Lib Party	−1.34	0.22
DK: KF	−1.17	−0.26
DK: June Mov.	0.88	1.14
DK: PMAE	0.63	0.43
FR: Verts	0.66	1.30
FR: ES	0.95	0.91
FR: UDF/RPR	−0.58	−0.29
FR: ER	0.55	0.54
FR: GE	0.43	0.42
FR: AP/MdC	0.42	0.44
FR: FN	0.13	−1.95
GE: Gruenen	0.25	1.57
GE: SPD	0.42	0.49
GE: PDS	0.99	1.01
GE: CDU	−0.80	−0.63
GE: CSU	−0.86	−0.43
BRD: FDP	−0.80	0.45
BRD: Rep	−0.56	−1.35
IRE: Greens	0.21	0.81
I: LN	−0.25	−0.40
I: FI	0.29	−0.63
I: AN	0.06	−0.70
I: PS	0.13	−0.47
I: RC	0.69	0.36
I: FDV	0.42	0.69
I: PSI-AD	0.71	0.14
I: PDS	0.31	0.40
I: PPI 72	0.48	−0.82
LUX: PSC/CSV	−0.58	−0.17
LUX: POSL/LSAP	0.57	0.19
LUX: PD/DP	−0.31	−0.03
LUX: GAP-GLEI	0.88	1.02
LUX: ADR	−0.01	−0.56
NL: CDA	−1.19	−0.05
NL: PvdA	0.29	0.34
NL: VVD	−1.49	0.14
NL: D66	−0.46	0.79
NL: KR	−1.10	−1.26
NL: CD	0.10	−1.10
NL: SP	0.98	−0.27
NL: GL	0.51	1.30
ES: PSOE	0.69	0.25
ES: PP	0.23	−0.59
ES: IU-IC	0.99	1.10
ES: CDC-Ciu	−0.12	−0.03
ES: Nat.Co	0.23	−0.24
POR: PSD	0.33	−0.85
POR: CDSP	0.76	−1.12
POR: MPdT	0.89	−0.50
GB: Greens	0.72	0.90
GB: Labour	0.91	0.59
GB: Lib Dem	0.31	0.62
GB: Conserv.	−0.99	−0.78
GB: SNP	0.72	0.30

Note: Positive scores denote liberal positions.

Source: Aggregated candidate scores from 1994 Candidates for the European Parliament study.

Appendix D

Table D.3. Party Cleavage Scores in 2009
Cleavage data are available from 88 parties in the 2009 CEP survey.

Nation: Party	Economic Cleavage	Cultural Cleavage
AU: GRUNE	0.35	1.06
AU: KPÖ	1.40	0.61
AU: SPÖ	0.68	0.43
AU: ÖVP	−1.53	−0.12
AU: BZÖ	0.01	−0.92
AU: FPÖ	0.55	−1.93
BE: (ECOLO)	0.08	0.89
BE: Groen!	0.30	0.96
BE: PS	−0.08	1.28
BEL SP.a	0.31	0.81
BE: Open VLD	−1.34	0.49
BE: MR	−0.87	−0.01
BE: CD&V	0.17	−0.01
BE: CDH	−0.62	−0.37
BE: VB	−0.01	−1.74
BEL N-VA	−0.18	−0.31
DK: SF	0.41	0.97
DK: SD	0.45	1.19
DK: RV	−0.48	1.28
DK: V	−0.34	0.36
DK: DF	−1.26	0.08
DK: F mod EU	0.94	0.11
FI: VIHR	−0.09	0.44
FI: VAS	0.93	0.171
FI: SDP	0.11	0.83
FI: KOK	−1.83	0.21
FI: KESK	−0.09	0.12
FI: PS	0.57	−1.26
FI: RKP	−0.87	0.35
FR: Libertas	0.55	−1.79
FR: EÉ	0.83	1.062
FR: Extrême gauche	1.39	1.12
FR: PS	0.55	0.74
FR: MoDem	0.03	0.16
FR: UMP	−0.69	−0.15
FR: NF	−0.03	−2.16
GE: B90/Grünen	−0.37	0.84
GE: SPD	0.11	0.93
GE: Linke	1.04	0.99
GE: FDP	−1.41	0.36
GE CDU/CSU	−1.33	0.04
GR: Ecol. Greens	0.19	0.60
GR: Radical Left	1.42	0.25
GR: PASOK	0.70	0.27
GR: ND	−0.37	−0.88
GR: POR	0.02	−0.71
IT: SEL	0.50	0.65
IT: LCeA	1.11	0.80
IT: PD	−0.22	0.28
IT: UDC/UdC	−0.24	−1.01
IT: PdL	−0.81	−1.03
IT: IdV	0.09	−0.04
IT: L'A	0.45	−1.18
LU: LSAP	0.15	1.25
LU: CSV	−0.61	0.24
LU: ADR	−0.16	−1.16
NE: Groen Links	0.26	1.17
NE: SP	1.30	0.08
NE: PvdA	−0.06	0.70
NE: D66	−0.68	0.58
NE: VVD	−1.56	0.30
NE: CDA	−0.95	0.24
NE: CU	−0.06	−0.84
NE: PVV	−0.61	−1.29
PT: Bloco de Esquerda	0.90	0.63
PT: CDU (PCP/PEV)	0.99	0.21
PT: PS	−0.05	0.72
PT: PSD	−0.79	−0.38
PT: CDS-PP	−0.53	−1.16
ES: UPyD	−0.15	−0.28
ES: PSOE	−0.10	0.51
ES: PP	−0.95	−0.28

Appendix D

Table D.3. Continued

SW: Piratpartiet	0.17	0.99
SW: Miljöpartiet	0.49	0.79
SW Vänsterpartiet	1.48	0.79
SW: SocD	0.17	1.01
SW: FP	−1.13	0.71
SW: KD	−1.02	0.30
SW: M	−1.58	0.54
SW: SwD	−0.05	−1.59
SW: C	−1.07	0.89

SW: Junilistan	0.52	−0.35
UK: Green Party	0.96	0.59
UK: Labour	−0.05	0.64
UK: LDP	−0.39	0.60
UK: Conservatives	−0.47	−0.84
UK: BNP	0.60	−1.80
UK: UKIP	−0.18	−1.48

Note: Positive scores denote liberal positions.

Source: Aggregated candidate scores from 2009 Candidates for the European Parliament study.

APPENDIX E
Party Cleavage Polarization Indices

This appendix provides a summary statistic of party system polarization along the economic and cultural cleavages for the 2009 and 2014 European Parliament (EP) elections. The index measures the spread of parties along both cleavages, similar to earlier measures of party polarization on the Left–Right scale.[1]

The Polarization Index (PI) uses each party's score on both cleavages as constructed from PCAs of the 2009 Candidates to the European Parliament (CEP) survey and the Chapel Hill Expert Survey (CHES) in 2010 and 2014. Each party is weighted by the vote share for the EP election. In some instances, I estimated party vote shares when parties ran in an electoral alliance, or when electoral returns were incomplete.

The formula for the Polarization Index is:

$$PI = \text{SQRT}\{\Sigma(\text{party vote share}_i) * ([\text{party L-R score}_i - \text{party system average L-R score}])^2\}$$

(i represents individual parties).

Party vote share is calculated as a percentage of parties represented in the each data source. Party system average cleavage score is weighted by the size of each party, that is, $\Sigma[(\text{party vote share}_i*\text{party L-R score}_i)/\Sigma(\text{party vote share}_i)]$, where the sum of available party vote share falls short of 100 percent. The PI is analogous to the weighted standard deviation of parties along each cleavage.

Table E.1 presents the party polarization scores for 2009 CEP surveys and the two CHES surveys. For the 2009 CEP and 2010 CHES, the correlation between polarization scores on the economic cleavage is r = 0.74 and r = 0.76 for the cultural cleavage. This consistency is to be expected because Appendix C shows very high correlations in the cleavage locations of parties across these two datasets.

However, there is a noticeable increase in the average polarization scores from the 2009 CEP to the 2010 CHES estimates. The average PI for both cleavages is approximately a point and a half higher for the CHES data for the twelve nations included in the 2009–14 time span. This occurs despite the fact that each PI estimate begins with standardized PCA scores on both cleavages.

I think this difference between CEP and CHES is largely a methodological artifact rather than a true change. For example, Figure E.1 plots the cultural cleavage positions for the parties included in both the 2009 CEP and 2010 CHES studies. There is a strong correlation between both measures (r = 0.85). At the same time, the CHES scores tend to be more polarized than the CEP measures. Of the ten parties where CEPs scored

Appendix E

Table E.1. Party Polarization Scores for Economic and Cultural Cleavage

| | Candidates for the European Parliament || Chapel Hill Expert Study ||||
| | 2009 || 2010 || 2014 ||
Nation	Economic Cleavage	Cultural Cleavage	Economic Cleavage	Cultural Cleavage	Economic Cleavage	Cultural Cleavage
Austria	9.2	8.2	8.1	8.1	6.5	10.9
Belgium	7.9	11.9	7.5	8.5	8.8	8.1
Denmark	6.2	4.2	7.9	8.1	9.6	9.4
Finland	8.7	5.4	8.1	9.0	8.6	10.3
France	7.2	8.9	7.2	9.1	8.1	10.5
Germany	7.5	4.6	7.9	6.3	6.5	8.0
Greece	5.4	5.1	10.1	9.5	9.8	11.2
Ireland	–	–	9.4	2.7	8.3	3.9
Italy	4.5	6.3	8.1	9.8	8.8	8.6
Luxembourg	–	–	–	–	3.2	5.3
Netherlands	7.0	4.3	9.9	10.7	10.2	10.6
Portugal	5.0	5.8	10.2	5.5	11.0	4.2
Spain	–	–	4.8	8.4	9.3	6.7
Sweden	8.9	5.1	10.7	5.6	10.3	9.5
UK	4.6	6.3	5.9	10.7	4.4	10.9
Average of 12	6.8	6.3	8.5	8.4	8.6	9.4

Note: Table entries are party polarization scores. The averages are based on the 12 nations in all in last three data points.
Sources: 2009 Candidates for the European Parliament study; Chapel Hills Expert Surveys for 2010 and 2014.

toward the conservative cultural pole, eight receive an even more conservative position in the CHES study. The reverse patterns apply for parties with culturally liberal CEPs.

Multiple factors seem to be at work. Some of the difference in polarization might arise because of the different set of issues used to construct cleavage scores in each study. The CEP estimates are also less precise because the representation of significant parties is incomplete.[2] If a large or ideologically distinct party did not participate in the CEP, or there were too few respondents to include them in the party analyses, this might distort the results. In general, the CHES coverage of the parties is more inclusive and should yield more reliable measures of the party systems' supply of choices.

The method of calculating party positions may be another source of the differences. The CEP PCA is based on individual candidates, which generates candidate scores that are then aggregated by the party. The CHES PCA analyzes the aggregate results from the party experts' scores for each party, rather than analysis using the individual experts. This difference in methodology might influence polarization scores. Whatever the source, party cleavage positions based on CHES scores have a larger standard deviation and wider range than cleavage scores based on the CEP study for an identical set of parties. The CHES standard deviations are larger for both the economic cleavage (0.97) and cultural cleavage (1.04) than found in the CEP results for the two cleavages (economic = 0.78, cultural = 0.83).

The other notable result from Table E.1 is the increase in cultural polarization between 2010 and 2014. In most nations, the polarization in parties' cultural positions increased.

Appendix E

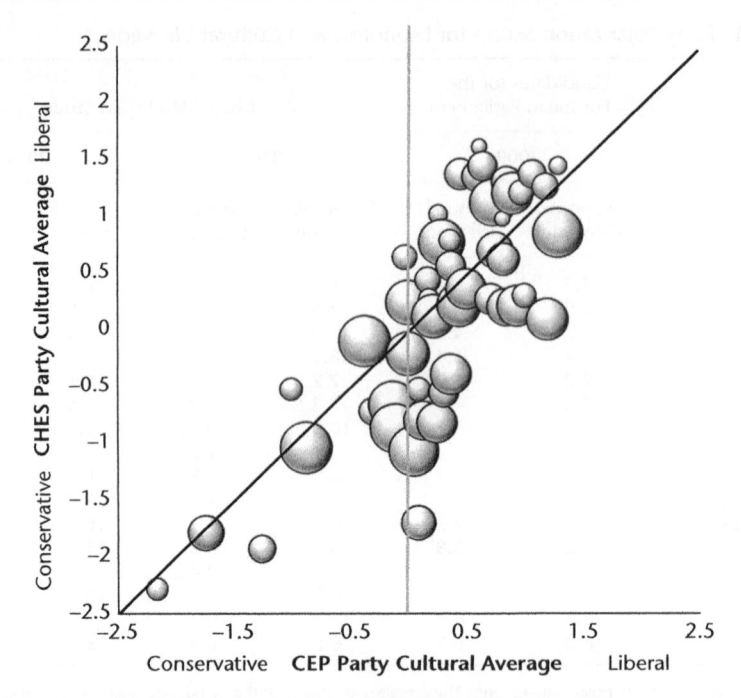

Figure E.1. Comparing Party Locations on the Cultural Cleavage

Note: Table entries are party scores on the cultural cleavage in both studies; the size of the bubbles reflects party vote share in 2009 European elections.

Source: 2009 Candidates for the European Parliament study; Chapel Hills Expert Surveys for 2010.

This was partly due to moderate parties moving in a more liberal direction, but more due to the emergence of new, clearly conservative cultural parties in several nations.

Consequently, comparison of the absolute value of the PI across projects may not be valid because of the equivalencies. Instead, any cross-time comparisons should focus on a single methodology, rather than merging CEP and CHES results.

Notes

1. Russell Dalton, The quantity and quality of party systems, *Comparative Political Studies* (2008) 41: 899–920.
2. Across the 13 nations in the 2009 and 2010 data, 85.3 percent of the total vote share is represented in the CEP data and 91.9 percent in the CHES data. The missing 6.6 percent in the CEP data increases the potential bias in these data.

APPENDIX F
The Complexity of Measurement

Chapter 8 utilized scores from separate citizen and elite PCA models to compare voter-party congruence. But this methodology raises questions in comparing citizens and party elites. Principal Components Analyses (PCA) provide an elegant way to deal with the variety of issues and question wordings to construct latent variables across surveys. The methodology uses the issue items to produce scores for the economic and cultural cleavages.

One important feature of the PCA scores, however, is that they are standardized. Consequently, one cannot compare absolute levels of citizen or elite opinions on the cleavage dimensions, only relative positions within a single PCA model. This restriction becomes more important in comparing citizen-party congruence. The separate standardized scores from the citizen survey and party elite survey both have a mean of zero and a standard deviation of one. Yet, there are reasons to expect that the distribution of positions is not the same in both samples. Research on the Left–Right scale shows that party elites tend to be more polarized than the electorate at large.[1] Analyses of additive issue scales based on the 2009 EES also demonstrate that citizens and elites differ in their distribution of issue opinions.[2]

There is no elegant statistical solution to this problem if we are comparing citizens and parties at different time points with different measurement of political cleavages. The 2009 EES provides a vehicle to study these potential measurement effects in more depth, which is the focus of this appendix.[3]

An alternative method combines citizens and party elites in the same PCA model to produce the two cleavage dimensions. As shown in Chapters 2 and 5, the structure of opinions is quite similar between citizens and party elites, so combining in a single PCA is warranted. Table F.1 presents this merged PCA analysis. These results are comparable to the separate citizen and elite samples for 2009. Immigration, stricter penalties against lawbreakers, women's issues, respect for authority, and, to a modest extent, EU attitudes define the cultural cleavage. Issues of income redistribution, state ownership of public services and industries, and opinions on private enterprise are the prime examples of the economic cleavage.

This PCA still produces standardized scores, but for the entire set of cases and not separately for citizens and CEPs. The much larger citizen sample reflects the basic values of a standardized score in its mean very close to zero and a standard deviation of essentially one. However, the CEPs deviate from this pattern. Elites are slightly more

Appendix F

Table F.1. Cleavage Dimensions for Citizens and Elites, 2009

Issues	Cultural	Economic
Immigrants adapt to country's customs	0.65	−0.06
Private enterprise solves economic problems	0.41	−0.52
Prohibit same-sex marriages	0.60	−0.05
State ownership of public services and industries	0.02	0.67
Women decide on matters of abortion	−0.25	0.24
Politics should not intervene in economy	0.35	−0.15
Harsher sentences for law breakers	0.68	0.06
Redistribute income and wealth	0.12	0.69
Schools teach children to obey authority	0.63	0.07
EU treaty changes by referendum	0.37	0.47
A woman should limit paid work for sake of her family	0.56	0.03
Immigration to should decrease significantly	0.76	0.05
Attitude to European unification	0.36	0.11
Eigenvalue	3.17	1.52
Explained variance	24.4	11.7

Note: The table presents coefficients from a Principal Axis Analysis with Varimax rotation and pairwise deletion of missing data.

Source: 2009 European Election Study and 2009 Candidates for the European Parliament Study merged file.

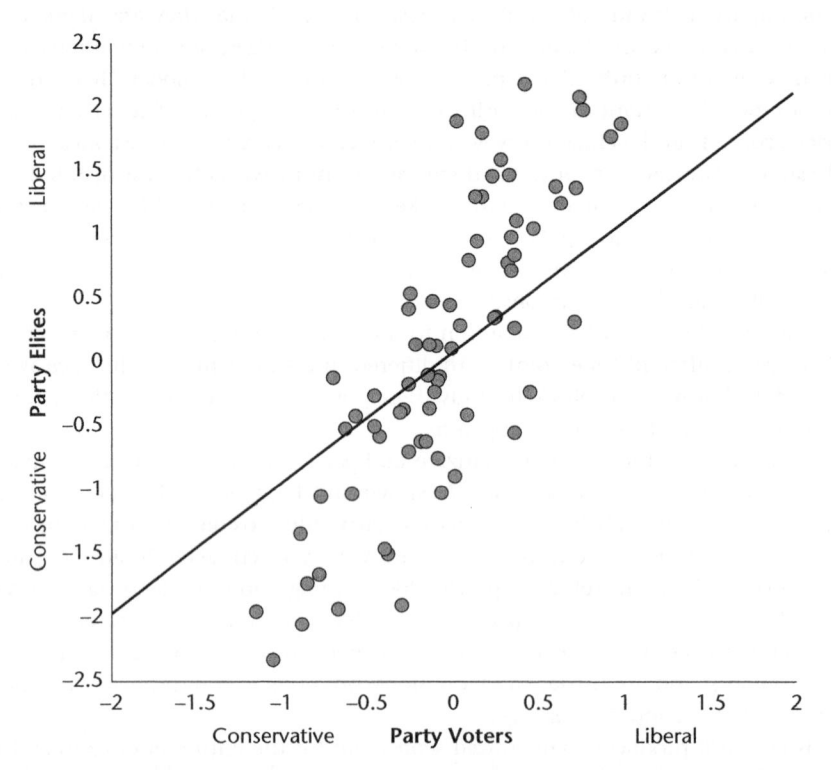

Figure F.1. Merged Comparison of Voters and Parties on the Economic Cleavage

Note: The figure presents mean scores for party voters and party elites on the economic cleavage.

Source: 2009 European Election Study and 2009 Candidates for the European Parliament Study merged file.

Appendix F

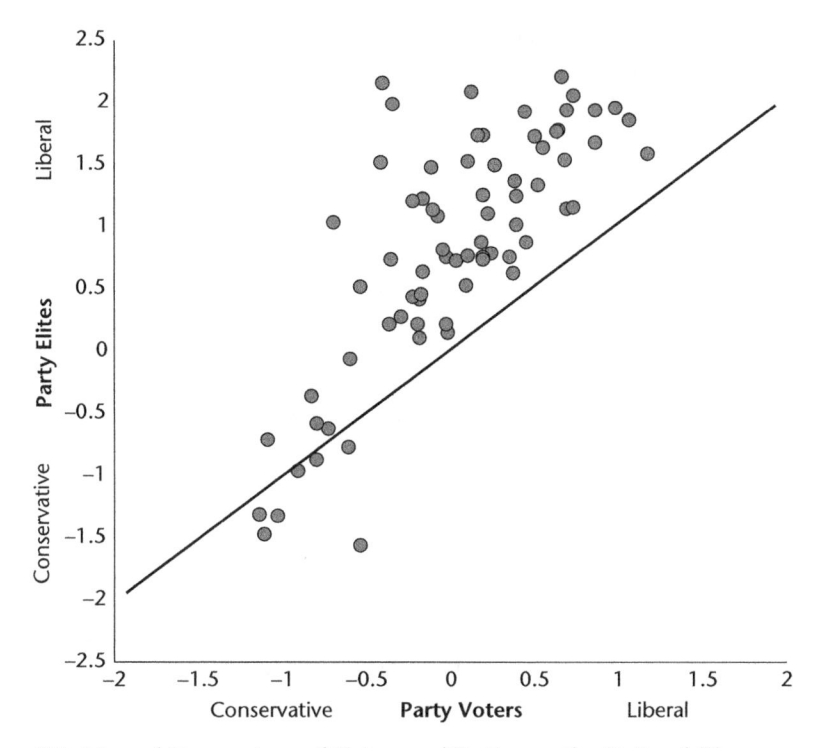

Figure F.2. Merged Comparison of Voters and Parties on the Cultural Cleavage
Note: The figure presents mean scores for party voters and party elites on the cultural cleavage.
Source: European Election Study and Candidates for the European Parliament Study merged file, 2009.

liberal on the economic cleavage (mean=.10) and much more liberal on the cultural dimension (mean=.59). This is consistent with the patterns shown in additive indices.[4] In addition, elites are more polarized on both the economic cleavage (st. deviation= 1.32) and the cultural cleavage (1.20).

I replicated several of the analyses in Chapter 8 with this alternative measure of voter and party elite positions in 2009, the only year when specific comparisons were feasible. The results are similar with either measurement method, but there are systematic differences. In terms of the economic cleavage, the greater variance of party elite positions means that conservative elites in Figures 8.1 tend to be even more conservative, and liberal elites tend to be even more liberal. For instance, in Figure 8.1 only a few parties were located beyond +/−1.50 on the economic cleavage because of the standardized scores on the elite-alone PCA. But when the PCA models include party elites with the general public, several parties approach +/−2.5 on this scale (Figure F.1). Thus, party voters who score −1.0 on the economic cleavage were represented by a party scoring about −1.75 on this cleavage in the original analyses; this increases to a −2.25 score on the alternative measure presented in this appendix.

An even more striking pattern occurs for the cultural cleavage. The variance of party positions is only a bit larger in the pooled analyses (Figure F.2). However, the vast

257

Appendix F

majority of parties from the center to the liberal pole are notably more liberal on cultural issues than their own voters. Cultural conservatives are closer to their own voter base, and only six parties have elites more conservative than their voters. The conservative parties may appear as more representative because the general liberal leanings of elites makes culturally liberal parties appear as less representative. This is different from the pattern presented in Chapter 8 (Figure 8.2).

The greater polarization of party elites means that the aggregate relationship between the average party voter and their respective party is even stronger using this alternative measure. The voter-party correlation on the economic cleavage rises from an R^2 of 0.57 to 0.66 on the economic cleavage, and from an R^2 of 0.55 to 0.61 on the cultural cleavage.

These comparisons imply that the pattern of parties "over-representing" their voters at the extremes of political cleavages is even greater than presented in Chapter 8. Thus, the absolute gap between voters and their parties may also be greater than first estimated. But both methodologies represent reasonable, but different, ways to think about citizen-party congruence.

Notes

1. Jacques Thomassen and Hermann Schmitt, Policy representation, *European Journal of Political Research* 32 (1997): 165–84; Russell Dalton, David Farrell, and Ian McAllister, *Political Parties and Democratic Linkage: How Parties Organize Democracy*. Oxford: Oxford University Press, 2011, ch. 5.
2. Russell Dalton, Party representation across multiple issue dimensions, *Party Politics* (2017) 23: 609–22.
3. The citizen and elite components of the 1979 EES asked slightly differently worded questions which limits such direct comparisons, and the sampling on the CEP survey also limits comparisons. The 2014 EES did not include an elite component.
4. Dalton, Party representation across multiple issue dimensions.

APPENDIX G
Construction of Economic and Cultural Indices in the United States

I constructed indices for the economic cleavage and cultural cleavage based on the issue questions available in each pre-election survey of the American National Election Studies. I began with the 7-point issue scales asked in each survey, and then iteratively considered other questions that theoretically might tap either cleavage. Supplementing questions was especially necessary for the cultural cleavage where there were fewer relevant 7-point scales. I used Principal Components Analyses to identify two clear cleavages and not just include all the issue questions asked in the survey. The final PCA results are listed in Table G.1, and component scores were calculated from these models.

Table G.1. Principal Components Analyses of US Cleavages

1972 Cleavage Dimensions

Issues	Economic Cleavage	Cultural Cleavage
Government guarantee jobs scale	0.732	−0.085
Government guarantee F.E.P.	0.702	0.084
School busing scale	0.689	0.197
Increase the tax rate	0.440	0.033
Legalize marijuana scale	0.234	0.715
Equal role for women scale	0.175	0.698
Changes for bigger Vietnam War	−0.239	0.618
Eigenvalue	1.84	1.43
Variance percent	26.2	20.4

1976 Cleavage Dimensions

Issues	Economic Cleavage	Cultural Cleavage
Government guarantee jobs scale	0.786	0.185
Government health insurance scale	0.786	−0.016
Protect rights of accused scale	−0.051	0.805
School busing scale	0.244	0.699
Aid to blacks/minorities scale	0.561	0.519
Eigenvalue	1.61	1.44
Variance percent	32.2	28.8

1980 Cleavage Dimensions

Issues	Economic Cleavage	Cultural Cleavage
Government services vs. spending scale	0.852	−0.087
Inflation vs. Unemployment scale	0.829	0.154
Defense spending scale	−0.098	0.804
Opinion on abortion	−0.130	−0.615
Eigenvalue	1.44	1.06
Variance explained	36.0	26.4

1984 Cleavage Dimensions

Issues	Economic Cleavage	Cultural Cleavage
Guaranteed job-income scale	0.769	−0.079
Government services vs. spending scale	−0.683	0.033
Assistance to blacks scale	0.625	0.194
Abortion policy	0.190	−0.737
Equal role for women scale	0.063	0.660
Defense spending scale	0.464	0.454
Relations with Russia scale	0.468	0.450
Eigenvalue	1.97	28.2
Variance explained	1.49	21.2

1988 Cleavage Dimensions

Issues	Economic Cleavage	Cultural Cleavage
Guaranteed job-income scale	0.778	−0.043
Assistance to blacks scale	0.673	0.095
Government health insurance scale	0.658	0.147
Government services vs. spending scale	−0.607	−0.094
Abortion policy	0.039	−0.714
Relations with Russia scale	0.191	0.615
Equal role for women scale	−0.028	0.671
Defense spending scale	0.287	0.467
Eigenvalue	1.98	2.48
Variance explained	1.60	2.00

1992 Cleavage Dimensions

Issues	Economic Cleavage	Cultural Cleavage
Government services vs. spending scale	−0.604	−0.036
Defense spending scale	0.290	0.436
Government health insurance scale	0.622	0.131
Guaranteed job-income scale	0.778	−0.015
Assistance to blacks scale	0.671	0.160
Abortion policy	0.083	−0.798
Urban unrest scale	0.549	0.267
Equal role for women scale	0.055	0.694
Eigenvalue	2.24	1.48
Variance explained	28.0	18.5

Table G.1. Continued

1996 Cleavage Dimensions

Issues	Economic Cleavage	Cultural Cleavage
Government services vs. spending scale	−0.629	−0.119
Defense spending scale	0.396	0.292
Government health insurance scale	0.672	0.156
Guaranteed job-income scale	0.843	0.032
Assistance to blacks scale	0.749	0.062
Abortion policy	−0.017	−0.756
Environment vs. jobs scale	0.194	0.565
Women's rights scale	0.093	0.768
Eigenvalue	2.32	29.0
Variance explained	1.61	20.1

2000 Cleavage Dimensions

Issues	Economic Cleavage	Cultural Cleavage
Government services vs. spending scale	−0.630	−0.057
Defense spending scale	0.335	0.322
Government/private health insurance scale	0.574	0.166
Guaranteed job-income scale	0.801	−0.015
Assistance to blacks scale	0.599	0.048
Abortion policy	−0.020	−0.670
Homosexuals in military	0.062	0.468
Environment vs. jobs scale	0.114	0.688
Equal role for women scale	0.064	0.691
Eigenvalue	1.86	20.7
Variance explained	1.76	19.5

2004 Cleavage Dimensions

Issues	Economic Cleavage	Cultural Cleavage
Government services vs. spending scale	−0.742	−0.102
Defense spending scale	0.324	0.421
Government/private health insurance scale	0.737	0.176
Guaranteed job-income scale	0.813	0.098
Assistance to blacks scale	0.633	0.185
Environment vs. jobs scale	0.321	0.445
Abortion policy	−0.074	−0.648
Equal role for women scale	0.117	0.547
Gay marriage	0.037	0.692
Eigenvalue	2.38	26.5
Variance explained	1.66	18.4

2008 Cleavage Dimensions

Issues	Economic Cleavage	Cultural Cleavage
Government services vs. spending scale	−0.677	−0.114
Government/private health insurance scale	0.700	0.224
Guaranteed job-income scale	0.825	0.019
Assistance to blacks scale	0.751	0.038
Environment vs. jobs scale	0.420	0.477
Defense spending scale	0.408	0.379
Equal role for women scale	−0.088	0.781
Job protection for gays	0.134	0.643
Eigenvalue	2.56	1.46
Variance explained	32.0	18.2

2012 Cleavage Dimensions

Issues	Economic Cleavage	Cultural Cleavage
Government services vs. spending scale	−0.713	−0.162
Defense spending scale	0.494	0.115
Government/private health insurance scale	0.715	0.265
Guaranteed job-income scale	0.794	−0.009
Assistance to blacks scale	0.718	0.131
Gays serve in military	0.032	0.739
Job protection for gays	0.163	0.722
Abortion policy	−0.139	−0.621
Citizenship for illegal immigrants	0.092	0.349
Eigenvalue		
Variance explained		

2016 Cleavage Dimensions ANES pre-election

Issues	Economic Cleavage	Cultural Cleavage
Government services vs. spending scale	−0.798	0.133
Government/private health insurance scale	0.741	−0.252
Guaranteed job-income scale	0.793	−0.196
Assistance to blacks scale	0.681	−0.334
Transgender policy	−0.189	0.766
Abortion policy	−0.193	0.661
Defense spending scale	0.273	−0.653
Send troops to fight ISIS	−0.093	0.652
Provide services to same-sex couples	−0.354	0.545
Eigenvalues	2.55	2.40
Variance explained	28.4	26.7

Table G.1. Continued

2016 Pretest Survey

Issues	Economic Cleavage	Cultural Cleavage
Government help people pay for health insurance	.854	.113
Government help with child care payments	.821	.142
Minimum wage	.756	−.008
Limit the number of legal immigrants	.204	.644
Favor the death penalty for convicted murderer	−.221	−.637
Owners can refuse wedding services to gays	.146	−.600
Federal government treats blacks better	.567	.455
Eigenvalue	2.41	1.42
Variance explained	34.4	20.3

Index

Abortion 30–1, 34, 35, 72, 73, 89, 90, 91, 94, 138, 189, 191, 204, 220
Adenauer, Konrad 215
AGALEV (Belgium) 34
Age 54, 66
  Cleavage 54, 58, 60, 64, 66, 79, 82, 93–4, 96, 194
Alternative for Germany (AfD) 120, 137, 173, 230
American National Election Studies (ANES) 16, 184–203, 221–4
Anonymous (Spain) 61
Austria 78

Back to the Future 14, 15, 215
Backlash 4, 5–6, 11, 27–8, 183, 189, 224
Bell, Daniel 27
Belgium 34, 230
Berlusconi, Silvio 120, 124
Blair, Tony 41, 87
Bornschier, Simon 6
Brexit 73, 153, 181
Buchanan, Patrick 182
Bush, George W. 183, 186, 187
Bush, Jeb 200, 201
Business owner 52, 53, 56, 60, 64, 66, 79, 83, 93, 95, 96

Cameron, David 73
Candidates to the European Parliament (CEPs) 16, 88, 91, 101, 109, 156
  Issue cleavages 88–92
  Social characteristics 92–7
Carmines, Edward 12
Carter, Jimmy 185
Catholic 40, 66, 73, 82, 83, 99, 100, 116, 225
Chapel Hill Expert Study (CHES) 114, 120, 139, 140, 142, 163
Christian Democratic parties 115, 167–8
Christian Democratic Union/Christian Social Union (CDU/CSU) 118, 125, 157, 160, 230
Christian Democrats (Italy) 115, 117, 118
Christian People's Party (Belgium) 115

Clinton, Bill 7, 13, 125, 187, 189, 192, 231
Clinton, Hillary 181, 182, 185, 186, 189, 191, 192, 197–203, 205, 206
Communist parties 119, 126, 134, 135, 167–8
Communist Party (France) 119, 164
Conservative Party (Britain) 114
Corbyn, Jeremy 153
Cramer, Katherine 195, 220
Cultural cleavage 1, 2, 3–4, 7–8, 29–30, 43–4, 65, 218, 219, 225, 226, 227
  Attitudinal correlates 60–3, 95, 97, 102
  Citizens dimension 33–9, 75–80, 101–2
  Elites dimension 89–92, 101–2
  National patterns 40–3, 98–101
  Party positions 12–13, 111–12, 114–16, 127
  Representation 157, 159, 160, 162, 164, 167–8, 173–4
  Social correlates of 51–9, 78–82, 92–7, 101–2
  United States 182–4, 189–92, 204–5
  Voting and 138–45, 146–7, 195–6, 202–3

Dealignment 229
Defense policy 34–5, 89, 109, 191, 193, 220
Democratic Party (U.S.) 181, 183, 184, 205
  Party position 166, 185–92, 199–200
Denmark 100, 109
Dionne, E.J. 223
Dodgers, L.A. 197

ECOLO (Belgium) 34
Economic cleavage 1, 3, 6–7, 43, 218, 219, 225, 226, 227
  Attitudinal correlates 60–3, 95, 97, 102
  Citizens dimension 32–9, 75–80
  Elites dimension 88–92
  National patterns 40–3, 98–101
  Party positions 12–13
  Social correlates of 51–9, 78–82, 92–7, 101–2
  Representation 13–14, 158, 160, 162, 164, 167, 173
  United States 187–9, 204–5
  Voting and 138–45, 146, 147, 195, 201–3

Index

Economic performance 62, 144, 145
Economic role of the state 3, 38, 43, 84, 88, 90, 229
Education 3, 92, 170, 172, 175, 194
  Citizen cleavages 52, 53–4, 55–6, 60, 64, 65, 74
  Elite cleavages 89, 92, 96, 102
Effective number of electoral parties (ENEP) 1, 113, 141, 147, 163, 164
Egalitarian system 82–3
Einstein, Albert 43
Employee representation 34, 88, 89
En Marche 10
Environmental issues 34, 36, 39
Environmental movement 5, 13, 36
European Election Studies (EES) 14–16, 32
European Parliament 3, 14, 32, 38, 88, 91, 101
European Union 16, 37, 39, 66, 72, 73
  Attitudes toward 34–5, 38, 39, 76, 89, 92
Evans, Geoffrey 7, 51, 55, 126, 219

Farage, Nigel 73
Farmers 11, 54, 56, 95, 96
Far-right parties 12–13, 91, 168
  Cultural cleavage 6, 7, 8, 10, 36, 122, 126, 134, 137, 143, 158, 167, 226–7
Feldman, Stanley 184, 220
Finland 79, 82
Flemish Bloc (Belgium) 117
Flemish Interest (Belgium) 158
Florida, Richard 51, 56
Flynn, Michael 195
Forza Italy (Italy) 124
France 30, 50
Free Democrats (FDP, Germany) 230
Freedom Party (Austria) 73, 120, 124, 159
Future Shock 5, 18–19, 215, 220

GAL/TAN dimension 3, 38, 43
Gay rights (*See* LGBTQ rights)
Gender 54, 83, 95, 96, 223
Gender equality 3, 5, 13, 34–6, 37, 54, 91, 225
Generations. *See* Age
Germany 8, 35, 40, 137, 221, 230–1
Gest, Justin 21
Gidron, Noam 220
Gilstrup, Mogens 109
Globalization 7, 8, 12, 28, 30, 36, 53, 62, 181, 192, 216, 218, 219, 226
Golder, Matthew 169
Goren, Paul 8, 28, 220
Government evaluations 143, 148, 217, 228
  Cleavages 61–2, 64, 79, 97, 124, 145, 227
Grande, Edgar 126
Great Recession 15–16, 62, 195, 231
Greece 79, 116
Greening of America 5

Green parties 5, 7, 13, 34, 112, 114, 116, 119, 122, 123, 126, 134, 167–8, 171, 225
Green party (Germany) 5, 13, 111, 120, 230
Grossman, Matt 220

Haider, Jörg 73
Hakhverdian, Armen 102
Hall, Peter 220
Häusermann, Silva 73, 78
Hellwig, Timothy 112
Hochschild, Arlie 220
Hofstadter, Richard 4
Human Development Index (HDI) 163, 164

Immigration 2, 7, 13, 16, 28, 30, 36, 50, 74, 109, 116, 197, 224, 226
  Attitudes toward 37, 38, 39, 43, 76, 90, 91, 160, 173, 220
Income 52
Income inequality 3, 12, 16, 36, 73, 216, 231
  Attitudes toward 31, 38, 76, 88, 90
Inglehart, Ronald 5, 7, 8, 11, 27, 63, 73
Ireland 215
Issue cleavages 11, 28–9, 43
  (*See also* cultural cleavage andeconomic cleavage)
Issue salience 145–7, 148, 170, 171
Iyengar, Sheena 148

Johnston, Christopher 184, 220
Junn, Jane 53

Kennedy, John F. 215
Kennedy, Robert 183
Kitschelt, Herbert 51, 56, 111, 112, 113, 116, 125, 199
Knowledge workers 3, 51, 53
Knutsen, Oddbjörn 31, 52, 54, 74
Kohl, Helmut 40, 226
Kriesi, Hanspeter 8, 44, 73, 78, 82, 193

Labour Party (Britain) 7–8, 87, 114, 120, 126, 142, 153, 160, 225
Labor Party, PvdA (Netherlands) 13, 114, 116, 137, 225
Left-libertarian 7, 43, 89, 112, 113, 116, 121, 125, 138, 145, 199
Left-Right 56, 58, 102, 121–2, 138, 157, 170, 172, 174
  Attitudes 63, 95, 97, 121–2, 138, 185
  Dimension 1, 7, 87, 110, 136, 147, 154, 155–6
  Party positions 121–2
  Representation 155
  U.S. parties 185–7
Le Pen, Jean Marie 73
Le Pen, Marine 50, 231
Lepper, Mark 148

266

Index

Levitin, Teresa 8, 182
LGBTQ rights 6, 29, 31, 37, 38, 42, 76, 91, 220
Liberal parties 167
Linke (Germany) 113, 119, 158, 173, 230
Linke (Luxembourg) 119
Lipset, Seymour Martin 4–5, 7, 9, 10–11, 28, 31, 35, 51, 66, 97, 121, 217, 220, 229
List Pim Fortuyn, LPF (Netherlands) 13, 20

Maastricht Treaty 7, 116
Macmillan, Harold 215
Mann, Thomas 223
Manual workers 52, 53, 56, 60, 64, 66, 79, 82, 83, 95, 126, 216, 219
Mattila, Mikko 165
McCarthy, Gene 183
McGovern, George 183, 185, 187, 203
Meguid, Bonnie 164
Merkel, Angela 230
Miller, Warren 8, 182
Minimum Winning Connected Coalition (MWCC) 230
Mowlam, Marjorie 87
Mudde, Cas 226
Multinationals 32, 35, 36, 88
Muslims 13, 109, 192

National Front (Belgium) 117, 118
National Front (France) 5, 6, 73, 117, 118, 164
Netherlands 12, 102, 117, 133, 143, 230
New Politics and the American Electorate 182
New Left parties 8, 10, 111–14, 122–3, 125, 143, 184, 216, 225, 228
  See also Green parties
New Social Movements (NSM) 5, 7, 8, 27, 29, 34, 36, 38, 65, 67
Newton, Isaac 27, 183, 224
Nie, Norman 53
Nixon, Richard 183, 186
Norris, Pippa 73
Nuclear power 11

Obama, Barrack 7, 183, 185, 187, 191, 192, 196, 201, 215, 224
Occupation groups 2–3, 51, 52, 53, 114, 216
  Citizen cleavages 17, 55–7, 60, 64, 65–6, 74, 79, 82
  Elite cleavages 93–4, 95, 96, 102, 144
Occupy Wall Street 61, 62
Ornstein, Norm 223

Party for Freedom, PVV (Netherlands) 120, 132, 137, 159
Party identification 133, 170, 172, 175, 195–6, 197–8, 202–3, 228
Party space 110–13, 125–7, 224–8
  1979 114–16

1994 116–18
2009 118–20
2014 120
Predicting party positions 121–4
U.S. 184–92, 198–200
Party supply 2, 11, 13, 17, 18, 87, 102, 110–13, 115, 120, 122, 125–7
  Voting 134–7, 140–1, 143, 147, 182, 183–4, 226–8
  Representation 174–5
  U.S. 182, 183–4, 185, 191–2, 198–200, 201, 205
Party volatility 1, 109, 127, 147, 228, 230–1
Patrikios, Stratos 53
People's Party, CDS (Portugal) 118
People's Party for Freedom and Democracy, VVD (Netherlands) 133
Perlstein, Rick 183
Pew Research Center 196
Pinker, Steven 215
Pitkin, Hanna 169
Podemos (Spain) 120
Polarization 141–3, 163, 164, 165–6, 192, 205
Pope Paul IV 215
Popular Party (Italy) 118
Popular Party (Spain) 120
Postmaterial values 5, 11, 12, 27, 38, 43, 54, 225
Principal Components Analysis (PCA) 31, 35
  Citizen cleavages 32–4, 36–9, 193–4
  Elite cleavages 88–92
Professionals 3, 51, 52, 53, 56, 60, 64, 65, 93, 95, 96, 97, 225
Progress Party (Denmark) 6, 109
Protestant 40, 82, 83, 99, 100
Putnam, Robert 101

Race/ethnicity 4, 18, 116, 181, 193, 198, 203, 220–1, 223
Rally for the Republic, RPR (France) 114
Ratcliff, Shaun 196
Raunio, Tapio 165
Reagan, Ronald 183, 185, 186, 191, 226
Realignment 2, 217, 228, 229
  Partisan change 96, 97, 102, 120, 125, 147, 181, 185, 217, 229
  Social group change 56, 60, 64, 65, 228
Reich, Charles 5
Religiosity 73
  Citizen cleavages 53, 58, 60, 64, 73, 79, 83–4
  Elite cleavages 94–5, 102
Religious parties 5, 115, 116, 117, 118, 122, 133, 134, 225
Representation 154–6, 173–5
  Correlates of 162–8, 170–3
  Cultural cleavage 158–9, 160, 162, 164, 167–8, 173–4

267

Index

Representation (*cont.*)
  Economic cleavage 158, 160, 162, 164, 167, 173
  Measurement 156–7, 160–1, 169
  Micro-level 169–73, 175
Republican Party (U.S.) 10, 181, 183, 184, 205
  Party positions 166, 185–92, 199–200
Repuklikaner (Germany) 117, 118
Rokkan, Stein 7, 9, 10–11, 28, 31, 35, 51, 66, 97, 121, 217, 220, 229
Romney, Mitt 186, 205
Rural/urban 9, 28, 54, 97, 183, 195, 220

Sanders, Bernie 198, 199, 201–2
Scammon, Richard 183
Schakel, Wouter 102
Schröder, Gerhard 125
Schwarzenegger, Arnold 217
Skocpol, Theda 200
Social class. *See* Occupation Groups, Education
Social cleavages 9, 10–11, 28, 67, 220, 228–9
Social Democratic parties 111–12, 116, 120, 134, 167, 225
Social Democrats (Denmark) 114, 227
Social Democrats, SPD (Germany) 12, 29, 111, 114, 120, 126, 225, 230
Social Democrats (Sweden) 142
Social modernization 1–10, 27, 54, 64–5, 73, 97, 116, 134, 183, 210, 215–16, 220–1, 224
Social modernization index 222–3
  Cultural cleavage 223–4
  Measurement 221–2
Socialist Party (Belgium) 116
Socialist Party (France) 116, 225
Societly.com 198–9, 200, 201
Soviet Union collapse 90, 116, 187, 191, 226
Spain 61, 79
Stehlik-Barry, Kenneth 53
Stimson, James 12
Stokes, Donald 148, 168
Stramski, Jacek 169

Syriza (Greece) 61, 120

Tea Party 5, 61, 183, 200
Tesler, Michael 181
Thaler, Daniel 220
Thatcher, Margaret 40, 116, 226
Thomas, Frank 6
Thomassen, Jacques 155–6
Tilley, James 7, 51, 55, 126, 219
Toffler, Alvin 18–19
Transgender issue 189, 192, 204, 220
Trump, Donald 10, 181, 183, 186–7, 191, 197–8, 201–3, 206, 227, 231

UK Independence Party (Britain) 5, 61, 73, 120, 159
Unions 3, 7, 9, 11, 13, 87, 112
  Members 52, 87, 229
Union for a Popular Movement (France) 164
United Kingdom 7–8, 40, 55, 56, 87, 92, 126, 153, 213, 219, 221, 226
United States 4, 7, 8, 16, 18, 28–9, 50, 54, 181–206, 215, 221–4, 231

Vance, J.D. 50
Vavreck, Lynn 198

Walker, Scott 183
Wallace, George 5, 183
Watson, Tom 153
Wattenberg, Ben 183
Webb, Jim 199
Wilders, Gert 133
Williamson, Vanessa 200
Wisconsin 183, 195
Women's rights. *See* Gender equality

XA (Greece) 120
Xezonakis, Georgios 53

Zingher, Joshua 195